DAVID BERGELSON'S STRANGE NEW WORLD

JEWS IN EASTERN EUROPE

Jeffrey Veidlinger
Mikhail Krutikov
Geneviève Zubrzycki
Editors

DAVID BERGELSON'S STRANGE NEW WORLD

Untimeliness and Futurity

Harriet Murav

INDIANA UNIVERSITY PRESS

This book is a publication of

Indiana University Press
Office of Scholarly Publishing
Herman B Wells Library 350
1320 East 10th Street
Bloomington, Indiana 47405 USA

iupress.indiana.edu

Manufactured in the United States of America

Cataloging information is available from the Library of Congress.

ISBN 978-0-253-03690-2 (hdbk.)
ISBN 978-0-253-03691-9 (pbk.)
ISBN 978-0-253-03692-6 (web PDF)

1 2 3 4 5   24 23 22 21 20 19

For Sam, David, Penelope, and Sissela

CONTENTS

ACKNOWLEDGMENTS

COLLEAGUES AND GRADUATE STUDENTS IN SLAVIC, HISTORY, JEWISH Studies, REEEC, and Comparative Literature at the University of Illinois at Urbana-Champaign provided a warm but also intellectually challenging environment for the exchange of ideas, and I have benefitted from their company. I am grateful to the Center for Advanced Study for awarding me a semester of teaching leave, and to the Research Board for funding research travel to Moscow and New York. The Slavic Reference Service, headed by Joe Lenkart, not only answered numerous questions, opening doors for new approaches, but also acquired new materials for me in lightning-quick time. Nadja Berkovitch and LeiAnna Hamel provided invaluable research assistance. I was privileged to be an external faculty fellow at the Stanford Humanities Center in 2012–2013, which made many delightful and productive conversations possible, including those with Mark Antliff and Patricia Leighten, Grisha Freidin, Monika Greenleaf, Gabriella Safran, and Zachary Baker. Dr. Marina Bergelson Raskina gave generously of her time to speak with me about her grandfather and provided wise insights about his art. Dr. Arkady Zel'tser kindly shared Yad Vashem's extensive archival holdings, which revealed new perspectives on Bergelson in his later years. Martin Kavka helped me better understand what I was trying to say about Bergelson and Gershom Scholem. The experience of translating Bergelson together with Sasha Senderovich, with the mentoring of Susan Bernofsky, made possible by a Yiddish Book Center Translation Fellowship, brought me closer to Bergelson. Gennady Estraikh and Misha Krutikov heard many parts of this study in various conference settings, and I am very grateful for their enthusiastic and helpful interest along the way. I also feel privileged to be part of the new series "Jews in Eastern Europe" and thank the editors for including me.

Bruce Rosenstock and I happened to be working on vitalism at the same time, and strangely, or perhaps appropriately for a book on time and memory, I can't remember who started talking about Henri Bergson first—probably Bruce. I owe him more than I can say for his extraordinary erudition, stunning clarity of thought, and endless patience with my repeated "Does this make sense?" "What if I said . . . ?"

Part of chapter 8 and the introductory material to part 3 were previously published in *David Bergelson: From Modernism to Socialist Realism*, edited by Joseph Sherman and Gennady Estraikh (Legenda, 2007), *Children and Yiddish Literature: From Early Modernity to Post-Modernity*, edited by Gennady Estraikh, Kerstin Hoge, and Mikhail Krutikov (Legenda, 2016), and *Three Cities of Yiddish: St. Petersburg, Warsaw, and Moscow*, edited by Gennady Estraikh and Mikhail Krutikov (Legenda, 2017). I am grateful to the publisher for permission to reprint them. A section of chapter 9 originally appeared in *Music from a Speeding Train: Jewish Literature in Post-Revolutionary Russia* (2011) and is reprinted with the permission of Stanford University Press. An earlier version of the conclusion was published in *East European Jewish Affairs* in 2018, and I thank the editors and publisher for permission to use some of the same material.

NOTE ON TRANSLITERATION AND TRANSLATION

IN TRANSLITERATING RUSSIAN, I HAVE FOLLOWED THE LIBRARY of Congress System, except for words and names commonly appearing in English. For Yiddish, I followed the YIVO guidelines, with the same exception. The transliteration of Hebrew words that have entered Yiddish reflects their pronunciation in Yiddish, and not modern Hebrew.

DAVID BERGELSON'S STRANGE NEW WORLD

INTRODUCTION

"There are in our lives moments of eternity. My life is an example.
It consists only of such moments."

David Bergelson, Letter to Yosl Kiper, 1924.[1]

WHILE WILLIAM BLAKE WISHED TO EXPERIENCE "ETERNITY IN an hour," the Yiddish author David Bergelson needed only a moment to expand time beyond all limits. Not given to direct autobiographical statements, Bergelson chose to characterize his life in terms of temporality—significantly, the radical contraction and dilation of the time of his life. Bergelson was forty years old when he wrote about his moments that were eternities. He was residing temporarily in Berlin, having left Moscow in 1921. Born in Okhrimovo, a shtetl in Kiev province in the Pale of Settlement in 1884, Bergelson had begun writing in Kiev, traveling to Odessa, Vilnius, and Warsaw as a young man. He lived through World War I and the Russian revolution and civil war. Lacking formal secular schooling, he had read the Russian and European classics, as well as the Yiddish and Hebrew works of the most important authors of his time. He had risen from obscurity to the top of his profession, having transformed himself from an unknown (who had to pay for the publication of his first literary work) into an acknowledged master of Yiddish prose. Bergelson would remain in Berlin for another nine years, until Hitler came to power. He lived in Copenhagen in 1933 before returning to the Soviet Union in 1934, and he spent almost another twenty years writing and publishing in Yiddish before his execution in 1952.

"Yiddish" and "shtetl" may suggest to some readers a self-enclosed community of pious Jews, celebrating their rituals in an unchanging annual cycle. In Bergelson's world, however, time is out of joint. Anachronism, belatedness, and untimeliness, both joyful and tragic, unfold as an emotional, sensory, and existential condition in the world his fiction creates and the world in which he lived. For Bergelson, Yiddish is the vehicle for untimeliness and futurity, the realm of memory and the "strange new world" created by the Russian revolution.[2]

Bergelson used Yiddish to draw attention to the materiality of language and to experiment with the acoustic properties of words and the graphical features of writing. He explored what the literary theorist Viktor Shklovsky called the "tactile perception" of literature by using rhythm, repetition, and sound play. Bergelson introduced Hebrew, Russian, French, Latin, and German into his Yiddish texts. He remarked that his language was strange because he was, so to speak, translating into Yiddish conversations that the younger generation of Jews would have had in Russian.[3] In addition to the device of translation, he used deafness, stuttering, blindness, and other disabilities as artistic devices that impede the transmission of meaning and thus heighten readers' attention to the sensory qualities of his language and the strangeness of the world that it describes. I take the title of this book from Bergelson's 1929 novel *Judgment* (*Mides-hadin*), in which the Russian revolution gives rise to a "strange new world." The "strange new world" begins for Bergelson before the revolution, and it is not only strange, but also rich with possibility.

In this study of Bergelson, I focus on time, and in addition to analyzing time as the central theme of Bergelson's writing, I place Bergelson in his time, a period of overwhelming cataclysmic events and enormous innovation, discovery, and creativity.[4] The scientific, technological, and artistic innovation; social transformation; political upheaval; and violence of this period seemed to its observers to break time apart. Osip Mandelshtam remarked, "The concept of a unit of time has began to falter and it is no accident that contemporary mathematics has advanced the principle of relativity."[5] Shklovsky similarly observed that every day "social reality . . . is multi-temporal."[6] Mandelshtam, Shklovsky, and Bergelson shared a common milieu whose multiple temporalities coexisted and collided: subjective, emotional time, the mechanized production schedule of the factory, the natural cycle of the seasons, the annual round of Jewish religious holidays (observed and observed in the breach), end-time of the collapse of empires, the new time of revolution, and the forward-looking linear time of building socialism.

The ticking of the clock measuring out one identical moment and the next—neutral, quantifiable time—rarely appears in Bergelson's fiction. Time has peaks and valleys of emotion; indeed, emotion is often expressed in terms of time, so that anxiety or frustration is described as the feeling of being late, even though the action in question is not late: the emotion is mapped onto the time sense in a temporal and emotional synesthesia. Fixed units of time extend past their boundaries, as in the author's characterization of his life as moments of eternity. In his fiction, instances of heightened emotional intensity seem to repeat other, similar episodes. Déjà-vu, the momentary loss and return of the world, the uncanny feeling that I have already experienced a particular moment, accompanies Bergelson's descriptions of both love and loss. His writing not only reflects the variegated fullness of time but also creates it as an effect of reading. The elastic temporality of Bergelson's fiction thus presents a literary parallel with the new temporal theories of his epoch. The great modern theorists of time, memory, and the past, all contemporaries of the Yiddish author— Henri Bergson, Sigmund Freud, and Walter Benjamin—and the Marxist-Leninist theorization of a new future—inform Bergelson's work and provide the conceptual point of departure for my readings of his essays, novels, short stories, and plays.

In Bergelson, untimeliness can be accompanied by the feeling that nothing can ever happen again. Bergelson's heroine Mirl Hurvits in *The End of Everything* (*Nokh alemen*) feels that someone else lived the "springtime of her life." Bergelson's characters find themselves between the times, in the aftermath of a past that they cannot know, and in the post–World War II fiction, the aftermath of monumental destruction. Yiddish uses a single word to convey the painful aftereffect of the past: *nokhveyenish*, which translates as "the state of pain that comes after something" (comparable to Freud's *Nachträglichkeit*). The feeling of having arrived at the scene of action too late—after everything has already happened, the sense of an impassible gulf separating now and the past—undergirds the modern and the modernist perspective.[7] The term "belatedness" captures this sensibility.

A few examples from the critical literature illustrate the centrality of belatedness for the twentieth-century timescape. Freudian temporality grants more weight to the past than the present. As Miriam Hansen puts it, "The Freudian theory of repression relies on the assumption that everything truly significant has already happened in the past."[8] Psychoanalysis, in addition to being a theory of subjectivity and sexuality, is also a theory about time, in which belatedness plays a key role, as Laplanche and others have shown.[9] In *Cinema II: The Time Image*, Gilles Deleuze describes Italian film director Michelangelo Antonioni's method as "drawing all the consequences from a decisive past experience," and he goes on to quote Antonioni's reflection on the temporality of his films: "When everything has been said, when the main scene seems over, this is what comes afterward."[10] For Deleuze, the time of the aftermath begins with the end of World

War II. Giorgio Agamben similarly characterizes the present, contemporary moment in terms of "the untimeliness, the anachronism that permits us to grasp our time in the form of a 'too soon' that is also a 'too late'; of an 'already' that is also a 'not yet.'"[11] Pierre Nora, writing in the mid-1960s, describes his own moment as the "sense that everything is over and done with."[12] It is striking that even though most twentieth-century observers locate the time of the aftermath after World War II, Bergelson's masterful reflection on belatedness, *The End of Everything*, was first published in 1913, before World War I, in the same period that Proust published *Swann's Way* and Joyce, *Dubliners*.[13] The argument that Yiddish became a modern literary language belatedly, after other European languages, or that Yiddish modernism is belated with respect to other modernisms, is not my concern.[14] On the contrary, the chapters that follow explore the conditions and causes of Bergelson's precocious belatedness as well as the literary structures that produce it as an effect of reading.[15]

Delay, lag, and untimeliness can result in repetition, and in the physical clumsiness of bodies stumbling through the actions of daily life, unable to gauge time and space, their gestures prolonged and inefficient. Out of sync, utterances and actions stutter—a number of Bergelson's protagonists have hearing and speech impairments. But untimeliness can also reveal another rhythm, a different tempo, the pause before something new emerges, the accompaniment to great joy, the joy of love and creativity. Mourning one's belatedness is only one side of the modernity/modernism story in general and for Bergelson in particular. Although his work depicts the decline of a way of life, and even its deliberate destruction, Bergelson, without flinching from the confrontation with disaster, sounds another note, resonant with joy, redemption, and celebration. The term for this in Yiddish is *yontevdikayt*, the state or condition of festivity.[16] Writing in 1929, the Yiddish critic Nakhmen Mayzel used the term to characterize Bergelson's literary work as a whole, and especially to underscore the sense of joy in Bergelson's creativity. Note the date. Mayzel was writing about joy on the eve of World War II, after World War I, and after the Russian revolution and civil war, which destroyed thousands and thousands of lives, and in the civilian population, Jewish lives in particular.

Joy is usually missing from the critical portrait of Bergelson's life, but it belongs there nonetheless. Bergelson was the youngest of nine children. Like other Jewish boys of this time, he attended heder, Jewish elementary school. The Bible and commentaries were taught by rote memorization, matching Hebrew with Yiddish, word for word. He also was introduced to secular knowledge by a tutor his father employed. Again, like other Jewish boys of the time, Bergelson educated himself by reading—in Hebrew and Russian translation—Henry Thomas Buckle, Herbert Spencer, Baruch Spinoza, Dmitrii Pisarev, Vissarion Belinsky, Anton Chekhov, Leo Tolstoy, and Fyodor Dostoevsky, among others. This was in addition to the new literary canon of the time in both Hebrew and Yiddish, and histories of the Jews, by Heinrich Graetz and Josephus, for example. I base this selected bookshelf on the reading of the child hero Penek, from Bergelson's two-volume autobiographical novel, *At the Dnieper*, discussed in chapter 8.

By the time Bergelson turned fourteen, both his parents had died, and his older brothers and sisters took him in, using his inheritance for his room and board.[17] On the one hand, loss and sorrow, but on the other hand, the young Bergelson had a bit more freedom to do as he pleased. In 1903 he lived at his brother Yakov Bergelson's house in Kiev, where David spent his time writing, reading, playing his violin, talking, boating on the Dnieper—in other words, having fun. Most accounts of Bergelson neglect this point, except those written by people who knew him at the time. Nakhmen Mayzel was Bergelson's friend in the early 1900s in Kiev, and Mayzel underscores the overall pleasant and warm atmosphere surrounding Bergelson as a young man. Among Bergelson's other friends in Kiev were the Hebrew poet Uri Gnessin, and Fishl Schneersohn, from the Hasidic Lubavitcher dynasty, who was interested in psychoanalysis and would go on to write scholarly work intertwining these two threads, Hasidism and psychoanalysis.[18] The philosopher Lev Shestov was part of the wider circle of Bergelson's acquaintances at this time. Bergelson lacked a secular education, but his friends were his university.

The emotion of joy, and especially the artist's joy in the creative act, is itself a new beginning in Yiddish literature at the turn of the twentieth century. Bergelson's literary work and Bergelson's literary persona are distinct from the often-repeated formulation of "laughter through tears," associated with the fictitious world of Sholem Aleichem's Tevye the Dairyman, but also found in Sholem Abramovitsh's Mendele the Book Peddler—a verbose, folksy narrator who shares the difficult lot of the impoverished, oppressed Jewish people. Bergelson rejected Sholem Aleichem's verbosity and the orientation toward the spoken language of the people as unsuitable for his artistic vision.[19] In contrast, Bergelson's art emphasizes instead the individual personality of the artist, his moods, his emotions, and his changing sensibilities—expressed in compressed, elliptical prose and terse dialogue. In a letter to his friend, the critic Shmuel Niger, from around 1911–1912, Bergelson said that everything he had written thus far had given him "joy" (*hanoe*). The pleasure he received from his own creativity stemmed in part from his awareness that he had prepared for himself his own "drill and saw"—in other words, his own unique toolkit by which he could craft his work.[20]

Jewish Time

The Yiddish term *yontevdikayt* consists of the Hebrew world for holiday and the Germanic ending for a condition or state, corresponding to the English suffix "-ness," hence "the state of festivity," or, holiday-ness. While it is typical to speak of Jewish time as cyclical, the picture is more complex. Jewish time is not merely a matter of memory as opposed to history—or, to expand Yerushalmi's formulation, a habit of mind that absorbs ongoing historical events into an unchanging biblical template.[21] Jewish time is not only cyclical; it is also linear, because Jewish holidays (like the consciousness of individual, perceiving human beings in Henri Bergson) both remember and anticipate: holidays remember the creation of the world, lament sinfulness and destruction, and also anticipate redemption. How redemption takes place—or rather, when, whether by extending or ending historical time—is a matter of debate, but waiting and delay are key to Jewish redemption. The Messiah has not yet come. Jewish time is thus also time that is becoming, as in the phrase "the world to come." As Sylvie Anne Goldberg writes, there is a "plurality of time in Judaism."[22] Regardless of his departure from daily Jewish religious observance, Bergelson evokes the changing modalities of Jewish time, drawing upon belatedness and delay, but also returning again and again in his fiction to the concept of festivity, and the alteration between festivity and mere workaday time.

Bergelson published his first story in 1909. Emerging from a Jewish milieu at the beginning of the twentieth century to confront secular modernity, Bergelson had at his disposal a vast reservoir of images and stories from Jewish liturgy, the Hebrew Bible, and classical rabbinic literature—the past preserved in textual form. In addition, he drew from the Jewish calendar of celebrations and remembrances and the entire set of bodily dispositions, gestures, and tonalities of voice characteristic of these marked times. Writing about the Jewish Autonomous Region of Birobidzhan, for example, Bergelson evokes the emotions associated with Yom Kippur, the Jewish "Day of Atonement," to describe the anxiety of a Jewish official whose work did not satisfy the quotas set by Moscow. In a 1946 novel, one of the characters speaks about Jewish gestures as "relics from an old, outdated world," but it is precisely the embodied connection to this world that enables the protagonists to continue living. Bergelson embeds the Jewish textual and corporeal archive into the dislocations and estrangement characteristic of his modernist style, not so much discarding the past as transforming it.

Bergelson's stories and novels describe forms of life that have withered and gone under, and yet they are imbued with the intoxication of love; from out of the ruins, Mayzel says, comes the birth of something new. Mayzel's "festivity" (*yontevdikayt*) thus fused a Jewish religious concept with the temporal sensibility of modernism, which emphasized newness, a radical break with the past, and a joyous departure from the mournfulness of the fin de siècle.

Modernism

Bergelson's life span of 1884 to 1952 roughly coincides with the emergence and ascendancy of modernism as an aesthetic form, although the historical period of modernity began centuries earlier. I have already suggested belatedness as a key feature of modernism and modernity, but a broader discussion is necessary.[23] Although my focus is the aesthetics of modernism and not the condition of modernity, this barely limits the problem of definition. Victor Erlich puts the problem well when he says, "One can easily despair of finding a common denominator for W. B. Yeats and Vladimir Mayakovsky, for Velimir Khlebnikov and Wallace Stevens, for Virginia Woolf and Bertold Brecht."[24] Add Bergelson to the mix, and the difficulties increase, for a number of reasons. Discussions of modernism rarely include Yiddish authors, the very mention of which evokes an old world, "the old country," and "tradition." Chana Kronfeld points out that although Yiddish and Hebrew literary movements in the interwar period embraced multiple forms of modernism, producing nineteen literary journals in interwar Berlin alone, for example, these movements are relegated to the margins of scholarly attention.[25] Bergelson not only authored Yiddish modernist texts; he actively promoted new forms of Yiddish expression in multiple media in his work for the Kiev Kultur-Lige; in Berlin, he edited a lavish Yiddish and Hebrew literary and art journal, called *Milgroym* (Pomegranate), whose first issue, for example, featured discussions and images of Cubism, Rembrandt, and short fiction and poetry by Bergelson and other Yiddish writers.

Adding the Yiddish author Bergelson to the discussion of modernism is difficult also because he was drawn to opposing tendencies within it. He resembles Woolf and Proust, because of their common emphasis on memory, but also can be compared to the Russian Futurists and Mayakovsky, because of their experimentation with language and attraction to socialism. David Bergelson's modernism includes an intensified relation between the body and things, nature, and the built environment, a focus on movement and gesture, a shift away from semantics to the acoustical qualities of words, subjective time, the experience of the aftermath, an emphasis on memory and the recuperation of the past, and also metamorphosis: the rapid, joyous transformation of one thing into another.

Impressionism

Avraham Novershtern and other prominent scholars and critics of Bergelson, going back to his contemporaries, have used the term "impressionism" to characterize Bergelson's style. The parallel between the "static" plot and the "slow rhythm of its sentences and hypnotic repetition of words and phrases" make Bergelson's debut work "At the Depot" (*Arum vokzal*) "the first significant manifestation of impressionism in Yiddish prose," according to Novershtern.[26] The Yiddish critic Maks Erik (1898–1937) wrote that the fundamental features of Yiddish impressionism, in its "autumnal ripeness," were to be found in Bergelson.[27] Nakhmen Mayzel argued to the contrary, that the longstanding view that Bergelson was an impressionist was incorrect; Bergelson was instead a "neo-realist."[28] The very first critic to characterize Bergelson as an impressionist was Shmuel Niger, whose 1909 article about "At the Depot" also suggested that in addition to impressionism, symbolism might also be appropriate.[29]

What literary impressionism means, however, is difficult to say, since it covers a range of stylistic features and philosophies, including phenomenology, the representation of fleeting visual effects, "a theory of imagination," and a "mood of isolation."[30] Mood, imagination, and visual effects are certainly important to Bergelson, and I discuss the significance of mood (in Yiddish, *shtimung*) and Bergelson's engagement with this concept in chapter 1. If impressionism is a good way to describe Bergelson's style, it is only good for the earliest period of his work, because as most critics agree, Bergelson's writing changed in Berlin.

Henri Bergson

To avoid terminological overload and to make a larger point about Bergelson and his milieu, however, I don't use "impressionism" or other literary

labels, except modernism, an admittedly capacious term. Rather than offer a list of literary terms, beginning with impressionism and ending with
socialist realism, I prefer to define the basic building blocks of Bergelson's
art, tracking how they persist but also change and develop in interaction
with his context. And rather than attempt a common denominator that encompasses the multiple varieties of modernism, including impressionism, I
suggest a common source. Henri Bergson is the point of departure for many
experimental art and literary movements in the early twentieth century. Indeed, as one recent volume puts it, to understand Bergson is to understand
modernism.[31] Bergson's work made possible a new emphasis on dynamism
and change, the body, and the entire sensorium, on the one hand, and on
the other, a focus on memory, the preservation of the past, individual freedom and creativity, and an altered relation to time and space. Artists, intellectuals, and philosophers across a wide spectrum of styles, media, ideologies, and politics developed these concepts after their own lights.

To see how Bergson is the catalyst for seemingly opposed strands of
modernist artistic practice requires an approach that adds greater depth to
the picture of Bergson the philosopher of intuition, the anti-rationalist, or
the near-mystic—although this dimension of his work is also important.
It means seeing Bergson the philosopher who put human consciousness
on a continuum with inanimate matter. Vitalism is generally understood
to be a reaction against the forces of modernity, which, broadly speaking,
encompasses the rise of scientific rationalism, the homogenization of space
and time, globalization, capitalism, urbanization, industrialization, and
mechanization. Bergson, in this reading, sought to renew, restore, and re-
cuperate temporal flow, along with an organic, holistic view of the human
being whose nonrational, intuitive powers could be recovered in order to
spark new creativity and a truly living mode of life. While intuition and
creativity were critical to Bergson's thought, he did not argue that modernity or science had destroyed some prior organic mode of life. There is no
originary Eden of the human being in tune with life, or a romanticization
of some former authentic existence. The Yiddish writer Bergelson similarly
did not represent the shtetl or Yiddish as an object of nostalgia or lost authenticity. Modernity's displacements, possibilities, joy, and mobility were
the oxygen he breathed. Far from rejecting science, the French philosopher
Bergson's theorizations of memory and perception were based on the science of his time, and even beyond his time.[32] Even though he was opposed
to a technologized approach to the human being *tout court*, the application

of mechanical laws to life, Bergson was not opposed to technological development, seeing in it evidence of continuous human evolution.

A broader explication of Bergson sets the stage for my discussion of the modernist context, the Yiddish author Bergelson, and the theoreticians—Shklovsky and Benjamin—who received and transformed the French philosopher. According to Bergson, both matter and memory are images.[33] I am the moving center of images surrounded by the aggregate of images that constitutes matter. What we perceive as having fixed and final form in the surrounding material world is the consequence of the pragmatic necessity of responding to the world; what we discern to be the contours of a particular object is rather "the plan of an eventual action that is sent back to our eyes, as though by a mirror."[34] The return gaze of objects receives considerable play both in Benjamin and the Yiddish author Bergelson, appearing in his first published work, "At the Depot," the subject of chapter 1.

Cubism and other modernist visual art stresses movement and dynamism; Cubist images insert movement and temporality into the pictorial plane, thereby also requiring the formerly fixed artist and spectator to move. Bergson's theorization of perception as embryonic movement—the sketch of what I am about to do—conditioned by the body and its affective states, is the ground of possibility for much of this work. Mark Antliff has shown that Cubists and other modernist visual artists read and interpreted Bergson for their own purposes.[35] Charlotte Douglas, James Curtis, Hilary Finke, and Gerald Janecek, among others, have established Bergson's importance for visual and literary Futurism in Russia.[36] Discontinuous, percussive, or machine-like forms of visual and verbal art may seem to oppose Bergsonian notions of organic flow, but Bergson's theories of intuition and knowledge that go beyond scientific abstraction were crucial to the development of the theory and practice of Futurism, both in Russia and elsewhere.

Perception is nascent action; however, according to Bergson, even the performance of the most mundane and habitual actions involves memory, because the blueprint of the action—which is nothing other than the way that I perceive the world—refers back to other, similar previous actions, from which the brain selects the memory best suited to the immediate need. Modernist artists demanded that history, the academy, and the canon be destroyed, as in the Russian Cubo-Futurist "Slap in the Face of Public Taste" that called for "Pushkin, Dostoevsky, etc. etc." to be thrown "overboard from the Ship of Modernity."[37] Their own past and memory, however, served as a source for their creativity. The Yiddish author Bergelson also made use of his own memory and specifically Jewish forms of memory and commemoration.

In *Creative Evolution* Bergson elaborates how action cuts memory short, therefore suggesting the opposite: how memory could be expanded. The greater the time between the sensation and the motor response, the greater the opportunity for the mind to imagine and thus create alternative responses: "Representation is stopped up by action; if the accomplishment of the act is arrested or thwarted by an obstacle, consciousness may appear."[38] Memory is central to imagination, and inaction nurtures memory. Inaction opens a gap for the possibility of a representation or consciousness of a less well-defined memory not fitting the immanent future, from the more remote past, and potentially the most remote past—the entirety of the past. The past is real; it is preserved in memory, and it leaves its traces on the present. The more memory I can bring to bear on a given instant, the more freedom I exert and the more I escape from the law of necessity. While Bergson and Freud similarly theorize an opposition between consciousness and memory, unlike Freud, the unknown past in Bergson is not the source of our compulsion to repeat. As I will show in the chapters that follow, Bergelson's inactive heroes experience a strangely expansive form of memory—Bergsonian memory—when they remember the memories of previous generations. The hyperexpansive memory of the Yiddish author's characters makes the past come alive in the most unlikely settings and at the most unlikely moments.

Bergson builds from his discussion of the material universe and the mind to the broader question of biology. In *Creative Evolution,* as in his earlier works, he argues that time means continual change: "The more we study the nature of time, the more we shall comprehend that duration means invention, the creation of forms, the continual elaboration of the absolutely new."[39]

The life urge is to push ahead to an ever new and unforeseen future. Change, for Bergson, cannot be reduced to the rearrangement of what has already been given. Matter is characterized by extension, but it is not identical with space, because the "vibrations" that are typical of matter also possess a slight degree of "duration." The French philosopher writes, "The role of life is to insert some *indetermination* into matter."[40] In the Yiddish author Bergelson's fiction, a flicker or a breeze signals the opening of indeterminacy and the beginning of expansive, imaginative memory that goes beyond mere habitual perception.

For Bergson, life is mobility itself, but the differential forms that are the particular manifestations of life—the various species of organisms—continually lag behind. Thus delay and belatedness, the modern and modernist sensibility par excellence, are integral to Bergson's theory of life. Life is "always going ahead and they [the species] want to 'mark time,'" to defer change.[41] Automatism and repetition, however, are necessary to life. Without automatic, habitual response, I would not survive the exigencies of a single day; without the suspension of habitual action, I would never do anything new. The range of possibility extends from mere habitual action to artistic creativity to the unknown and unknowable future of humanity in interaction with the nonhuman and the inanimate. To read Bergson without recognizing his own dialectic between repetition and change oversimplifies the interdependence of the vital and the not-vital. David Bergelson's second novel, *Descent* (*Opgang*), reveals the consciousness of characters caught between repetition and the world of the dead, on the one side, and the living world of change and possibility, on the other.

Bergson's theorization for the necessity of slowed action and inaction as a means by which the unknown past can rise to consciousness was an important point of departure for modernist artists in the early years of the twentieth century. Although the zeitgeist of speed, as Tim Harte puts it, was central to various modernisms, they also shared another dimension: the opposite of speed. Bergson's emphasis on inaction finds its way into modernist artwork in the form of slow motion and delay—in literature, slow or weak plots and the withholding of action. Marcel Duchamp famously called his artwork "delays." Instead of heightened velocity, modernists like Duchamp, Bergelson, and others made slowed motion and impeded perception the hallmark of their aesthetics; in literature this goal was served by means of a difficult, self-referential style. Modernist aesthetics, as Ryan Bishop and John Phillips write, "had the tendency to slow down the reading and perceptual processes of its addressees."[42] Delay and inaction are the defining features of David Bergelson's characters, as well as a decentered narrative, which fuses the moods and emotional timbre of the characters with the barest traces of exposition, making it difficult to distinguish one character from another, and generally slowing the plot to the point of near-immobility.

To return to the problem I raised earlier, let us contemplate the seemingly incongruous picture of Virginia Woolf, the Futurists, Bergson, and the Yiddish author Bergelson all sitting at the same kitchen table (whose existence is subject to doubt). As Mark Antliff has shown, the Italian Futurist Gino Severini explicitly linked Bergsonian theories to his own form of artistic production. In a manifesto of 1913, he explained the genesis of his use of blue and yellow elements in a particular painting in his memory of a girl dancing, and he cited Bergson as the rationale: "To perceive, is after all, nothing more than to remember."[43] When Marinetti visited Russia in 1914 and talked about the necessity for an "intuitive" apprehension of the world, his Russian listeners, the Futurist literary and visual artists Nikolai Kul'bin, Benedikt Livshits, and others, were quick to recognize his dependence on Bergson.[44] Even though modernist artists touted quick time and acceleration, slow time and memory were as much a part of the experience of creating modernist artworks as they were receiving them.

Both Woolf and Bergelson depict a process in which images arise through memory, even though in Bergelson creative memory is not the particular possession of artists, who tend to appear in a negative light. In the third and final part of *To the Lighthouse*, Lily Briscoe solves the problem of the painting she is trying to finish by remembering the dead Mrs. Ramsay. The protagonist of David Bergelson's 1909 novella, "At the Depot" (*Arum vokzal*), bewildered by the new economics of the grain trade, and unsuccessful at making a profit, tries to understand his own position. He does so by remembering his past: To apprehend is to remember.

To be sure, the modernists sitting at my imaginary kitchen table did not share every view. Whereas Marinetti celebrated war and violence, Woolf and Bergelson were sensitive to the pain of history. In the middle section of *To the Lighthouse*, Mrs. Ramsay, her son Andrew, and her daughter Prue die (Andrew at war, Prue in childbirth). The glasses in the cupboard cry out in pain. In *Judgment* (*Mides-hadin*), Bergelson's ambivalent embrace of the new Bolshevik order, the branches of the trees groan; in his fiction generally, objects and buildings respond to human beings when other human beings do not. I do not read either Bergelson or Woolf indulging in a kind of sentimental poetics of personification, but rather as embedding human life in an environment in which humans are not the only actors. Both authors introduce life into matter, and also introduce things and larger forces of the material universe into life. Claire Colebrook finds a "blank and inhuman materiality" in Woolf's "Bergsonian modernism"; the resistance of things to human imagination and ordering is a prominent feature also of Bergelson's modernism.[45] Bergelson was fascinated by technology, imagining in various works a mutual interpenetration of humans and their devices. I explore

Bergelson's imagination of the object/machine/body connection through-out this study and in chapter 4 in particular.

Bergson cannot account for all manifestations of modernism. Con-structivism emphasized "the construction of a future," the rapid transform-ation of the human body, consciousness, and society by means of science, technology, and art that celebrated the mechanical and the abstract.[46] Il'ia Erenburg, the Russian-language fiction author, journalist, and critic, who, like Bergelson, lived in Berlin in the 1920s, proclaimed, "The new spirit of the age is the spirit of construction."[47] Erenburg, contemptuously dismis-sive of Bergson, observed that World War I brought a greater rapproche-ment between human beings and "the miracle of our age, the machine."[48] The crosscurrents and connections between technological innovation and artistic experimentation have been broadly discussed in the scholarly lit-erature on modernism; their importance for Yiddish, less so.[49] New forms of technology, including the train, the telegraph, the camera, and the auto-mobile, make their appearance in Bergelson's work. These innovations change perception by speeding up and slowing down the passage of time. The train and the camera make new forms of seeing possible, and Bergelson, like other artists of his epoch, was deeply interested in these possibilities.

Shklovsky and Benjamin, who also serve as interlocutors in my read-ings of the Yiddish author Bergelson, develop Bergson's concepts in differ-ent ways, Shklovsky with a greater emphasis on aesthetics. Mere recogni-tion, or, as Bergson puts it in his essay on laughter, merely reading the labels of things—diminishes experience. Any object that has claims to be art, ac-cording to Shklovsky, "has been intentionally removed from the domain of automatized perception." The device of defamiliarization prolongs the spectator's experience of the artwork.[50] Benjamin's critique of the notion of historical progress inveighs against the notion of "empty, homogeneous time," the premise for which comes from Bergson's attack on the scientif-ic, abstract form of knowledge that quantifies time, making it more like space.[51] Both Shklovsky and Benjamin emphasize, for different purposes, the importance of impeding and stopping automatic perception and action. For Benjamin, the cessation of action has messianic potential. In chapters 5 and 6, I discuss the convergence of Benjamin's concepts of aura and the "suddenly emergent image" and Bergelson's interwar fiction.

There are, of course, different Bergsons for every era, and the interpret-ation I gave earlier does not address Bergson's appeal in the fin de siècle. Here the opposition to science and abstraction is important. Bergelson's popularity stemmed from his emphasis on a unifying life force (the *élan vital*), his insistence on freedom and creativity, his proposition of an alternative form of knowledge—intuition, a nonanalytic, sympathetic apprehension of the self in the world—and his view of art, which, in its approximation of intuition, and especially its suggestive use of rhythm and melody, transcends the limitations of philosophy.[52] Bergson's lectures and writings were extraordinarily popular in Europe and America; his ideas about perception and memory were central to William James's "stream of thought." James, following Bergson, argued that consciousness could not be parceled out into discrete bits, but that it proceeds rather by the intermixing of one state with another.[53] Bergson was crucially important for Russian thought, literature, and visual art in the first part of the twentieth century, and especially in the turn against positivist thought and science that had dominated since the end of the nineteenth century.[54] Bergson's *Creative Evolution,* first published in France in 1907, was translated into Russian in 1909, before its translation into German and English.[55] Scholars have established his influence on Russian literary authors, theorists, and philosophers, including Mandelshtam, Andrei Bely, Shklovsky, Nikolai Lossky, Semen Frank, and Lev Shestov.[56]

My study explores Bergson's significance for Yiddish, and thus introduces a whole network of convergences and parallels previously overlooked. In positing a set of encounters between Bergelson and Bergson and other figures, I rely on Dan Miron's concept of "contiguity." In *From Continuity to Contiguity: Toward a New Jewish Literary Thinking,* Miron rejects traditional models of literary influence, arguing instead for a more open-ended model of parallel and overlapping thought among a range of writers in a free-floating zone of contact.[57] Henri Bergson was widely discussed in Yiddish print culture. His *Introduction to Metaphysics* and his book on laughter were translated into Yiddish; discussions of and excerpts from these and other works appeared in the Yiddish press in New York, Warsaw, and Vilnius.[58] Among them was the *Jewish World* (*Di yidishe velt*), a journal whose literary and cultural section David Bergelson edited. In 1913 the *Jewish World* carried several articles on Bergson, including one on *Creative Evolution* and one on his essay on laughter.[59] The opening chapter of Bergson's *Two Sources of Morality and Religion* appeared in the Polish Yiddish journal *Globus* in 1932, the same year that the book was published in French, under the title *The Individual and Society* (*Yekhid un gezelshaft*).[60] When Bergson, a Jew whose father's family was from Poland, won the Nobel Prize for literature in 1927, the Yiddish press took notice.[61] Although it is not my purpose to examine Bergson's writings from the perspective of Judaism—I do not discuss Bergson as a Jewish philosopher—he can be understood from this perspective. The historian Hans Kohn, for example, sees Bergson's emphasis on time as a facet of the Jewish mind, which "lives more in time than in space," and whose god is a god of history, unlike the Greek gods of nature.[62]

Networks

Although nothing remains of Bergelson's Berlin archive, a few bits and pieces from his life and work can indicate more concretely the overlapping networks that bring him into a zone of contact with Bergson, Benjamin, and Shklovsky. Shklovsky's *Sentimental Journey*, published in Russian in Berlin in 1923, ends as follows: "Now I live among emigrants and am myself becoming a shadow among shadows" (Ia seichas zhivu sredi emigrantov i sam obrashchaius' v ten' sredi tenei).[63] The last line of Bergelson's "Tsvishn emigrantn" ("Among Refugees"), written while the author was living in Berlin and first published in Kiev in 1927, reads, "I'm an emigrant . . . among emigrants . . . I don't want to be one anymore" (Ikh bin an emigrant . . . tsvishn emigrantn . . . ikh vil es mer nisht [ellipsis in the original]).[64] The speaker in Bergelson's story is not the first-person narrator or Bergelson himself, but what he says reflects Shklovsky's text, and the similarity reflects the larger experience that both authors shared, the sense of dislocation in the same urban setting at the same moment full of echoes and aftermaths—of World War I, the Russian revolution, and the civil war—which enters into their common articulation of the experience of diaspora.[65] During his time in Berlin, Bergelson frequented the Romanisches Café, where Benjamin was also a frequent customer.[66] Both Bergelson and Benjamin traveled from Berlin to Moscow in 1926, Bergelson from August to September, and Benjamin a few months later, from December 1926 to January 1927. Benjamin attended a performance of the Moscow State Yiddish Theater, which left little impression on him. The Moscow State Yiddish Theater would perform a theatrical version of Bergelson's "The Deaf Man" in 1930. In his *Moscow Diary*, Benjamin represents Moscow as trapped in a time warp, in which all meetings are missed and the city's inhabitants and visitors are perpetually in a state of frustrated waiting. For Bergelson, in contrast, the giant clock that hovers invisibly over Moscow's horizon makes everyone younger (presumably because it is racing so quickly to the future). In the same period, 1926–27, the Yiddish author Bergelson and the French philosopher Bergson both reacted to the extraordinary affair of Shlomo

Schwartzbard (1886–1938), who had confessed to assassinating Symon Pet-liura in Paris in May 1926. Petliura was the former head of the Ukrainian government during 1918–19. The Jewish community considered Petliura re-sponsible for the slaughter of Jews during the Russian Civil War. The French jury acquitted Schwartzbard in 1927. Henri Bergson and many other figures of world renown, including Albert Einstein, were listed as defense witnesses. Bergelson's "Among Refugees" (*"Tsvishn emigrantn"*) tells the story of a self-styled "Jewish terrorist" who plans on assassinating a well-known Ukrainian leader considered responsible for thousands of Jewish deaths.[67]

My point is not that Bergelson was personally acquainted with Berg-son, Benjamin, Shklovsky, or Freud, or that it matters whether he was or not—but rather, regardless of the fact that Bergelson wrote in Yiddish, Shk-lovsky in Russian, Benjamin and Freud in German, and Bergson in French, despite the difference in their life trajectories (and there are similarities here as well), they overlapped in time, space, and in the realm of thought, ideas, and expression. Bergelson was "contiguous" with these theorists, and others, including the German Jewish philosophers Gershom Scholem and Martin Buber, whom I discuss in chapter 6. Drawing attention to these points of contact and interaction helps pull Bergelson, and Yiddish, out from the wings of world literature and onto center stage, where he belongs. In 1925 the Yiddish critic Max Erik anticipated that the time would come when Bergelson "would occupy a place in world literature."[68]

Creating a network of contacts is one way of establishing contiguity; another is tracing the similarities and parallels between Bergelson's experi-mental techniques and themes and those of artists of his time who worked in other media. I use visual art and artists in particular, because of the cen-trality of the theme of visual art in Bergelson's oeuvre—his stories feature painters and sculptors—and because Bergelson was the coeditor of an art journal in the early twenties in Berlin. Photography is another key thread in Bergelson's writing: from his first published work to his post–World War II novel *Aleksander Barash*, photographs exert an unusual force over their viewers. I discuss the intensified relation between human beings, photo-graphic images, and afterimages throughout this study.

Bergson's emphasis on the withdrawal from action and "the will to dream" resonates with the specific qualities of Bergelson's literary work. His characters sleep, dream, daydream, and wander aimlessly. Their failure to act has been interpreted as the expression of the author's despair over the stagnation and decline of the shtetl and the existential emptiness of the people who lived in it.[69] Reading Bergelson's texts solely as the reflection of the grim political and socioeconomic reality of his time, however, obscures what is new, innovative, and joyful in his writing, including his explorations of time, memory, and consciousness. Bergelson's fictions are durations: expanded moments of time in which the past mingles with the ongoing present. Reading his narratives about "untimely" human beings living behind and ahead of their time—inattentive to the ongoing world, to progress, to new forms of mobility in every sense of the word—together with the French philosopher's theories of the creative potential of inaction suggests alternatives to the conclusion that Bergelson was interested only in decline, stagnation, and the end. Using Bergson as an interlocutor for Bergelson leads to an alternative interpretation that emphasizes the possibility of transformation.

This is not to say that Bergson's philosophy is without blind spots. His ideas about the life force and memory were used to defend fascism and antisemitism.[70] His notion of freedom and positing of the individual as a "zone of indeterminacy" neglect the constraints imposed by overpowering historical and social forces.[71] For David Bergelson, those forces were the Russian revolution and civil war, Stalinism, the Terror, and Nazism. Bergson's notion of flowing, ever-changing time is sharply opposed to the Marxist-Leninist scientific demarcation of the stages of history In the 1930s, Marxist critics labeled Bergson a mystic and an idealist.[72] These arguments and critiques notwithstanding, Bergelson returns to Bergsonian ideas in his later writing, introducing modifications along the way. For example, he proposes delayed judgment for the perpetrators of anti-Jewish violence during the Russian Civil War (the subject of chapter 6). He depicts a form of embodied memory in his autobiographical novel *At the Dnieper* (*Baym Dnyepr*), which I discuss in chapter 8. In his unfinished novel *Aleksander Barash*, examined in chapter 9, Jewish memory is the source of healing in the aftermath of the Nazi genocide.

Attending to the alternative world of memory in Bergelson makes possible more nuanced interpretations of his literary works, especially those written after 1926, when Bergelson publicly stated his support of the Soviet Union. Most discussions of Bergelson end in the mid-twenties, with a condemnation of Bergelson's shift toward the Soviet Union and especially an interpretation of his 1929 *Judgment* as an unequivocal endorsement of Bolshevik terror. As one authoritative Yiddish-language literary encyclopedia put it, in *Judgment*, Bergelson "openly declares his recognition of the dictatorship of the proletariat."[73]

Its scenes of memory, however, suggest otherwise. Yuzi Spivak, imprisoned for anti-Bolshevik activities, sits in his cell in a strange, dreamy state and reexperiences his own past as a child during the New Year's holiday; he inhales the fragrance of watermelon; the gleam of the white tablecloth on the family's holiday table sparkles in his eyes. He, along with other Bergelson protagonists, experiences not only his own past but also the past of the generations before him, thus entering a zone of memory that transcends the limits of the single individual. The reanimation of generations of the past casts an altogether different and far less favorable light on the gray, cold Bolshevik present. In other works of the same period, Bergelson expressed ambivalence about the Russian revolution by describing it as either the "greatest sin" or the "greatest blessing," its outcome unclear. Bergelson describes post-1917 as "a strange new world," but this language also serves as an emblem for the world created by his writing as a whole.

Bergelson left Berlin in 1933, when Hitler came to power, and resettled permanently in the Soviet Union in 1934. Many admirers of Bergelson condemned him for this decision, the rationale for which may not have been fully clear to the author himself. Factors included a desire for both physical and financial security, the need for a Yiddish-language reading audience, a certain measure of ambition, and socialism, which in Bergelson's case was something resembling a vague attraction and not a deeply held ideology.

Socialist Realist and Modernist

The unintended consequence of the overly ideological approach is that few scholars read late Bergelson, or they do so only to condemn him. Scholars in the West largely find Bergelson after 1926 too Soviet; Cold War cultural politics, which dictated that there was no Jewish culture in Soviet Russia, played a role in this assessment. On the other side, the Soviets ultimately sentenced Bergelson to death for being too "nationalist"—that is, Jewish. Interpretations based on ideology as a litmus test are inevitably short-sighted. I argued against this position in *Music from a Speeding Train* and expand my argument here. I devote chapters 7, 8, and 9 to Bergelson's writings after 1926. My question is not what Bergelson believed but rather how he reinvented his modernist aesthetic to meet the new demands of socialist realism. In 1934 "the truthful, historically concrete representation of reality in its revolutionary development" became an official doctrine.[74] Even though socialist realism rejects the difficult style of modernism, to accept a straightforward opposition between the two overly simplifies the question.

Boris Groys argues that for one variant of modernism in particular, the avant-garde, there is a clear continuity, because both the avant-garde and socialist realism embody a will to power.[75] I explore the relation between Bergelson's modernist and socialist realist work not so much in terms of a shared project of the construction of a new reality—although he made a number of proclamations along these lines—but more in terms of their shared temporality.

Most scholars of socialist realism agree that its temporality departs from the flux of chronological, historical, human time to enter a changeless realm of myth or "petrified utopia."[76] Petre Petrov adds an important new twist to this characterization: the perfect future had already arrived in the present and needed only to be revealed by socialist realist writers and authors, who had fallen behind the accomplishment of the people. Socialist realism does not look ahead but rather "looks backwards to a pre-existing state of being."[77] The artist's work confirms the truth of what socialism has already accomplished. I explore the relation between socialist realist temporality and Bergelson's poetics of belatedness, tracing how Bergelson modified his characteristic time lag, "afterwardsness," and slow time, and what he accomplished artistically by working with the new aesthetic norms of the 1930s.

During World War II, Bergelson, like other prominent Jewish writers in the Soviet Union, joined the Jewish Anti-Fascist Committee and wrote articles and short stories for its newspaper *Eynikayt* (Unity). My focus is not so much on Bergelson's literature of mobilization and propaganda as on his postwar fiction and especially work that takes the perspective of "after"— that is, after the overwhelming catastrophe and monumental destruction of the Nazi genocide. Bergelson had already worked out his own unique poetics of belatedness before World War I, and his fiction about World War II expands the temporality of "afterwardsness" into literary works that serve as acts of testimony and witnessing. In his last play, *Prince Reuveni*, written in the mid-1940s, Bergelson reflected on the meaning of Nazism by contemplating the murderous modernizing projects of several centuries earlier: the beginning of global exploration and the Spanish expulsion of the Jews. *Prince Reuveni* is not a lament; rather it is a vision of radical hope.

Some may wonder why I do not discuss Bergelson's work as a whole in terms of trauma, since it easily lends itself to this interpretative lens. It would be a fairly straightforward process to read Bergelson symptomatically. In other words, the motifs of opacity and repetition in his early fiction and the theme of belatedness in his civil war and World War II work could be read as signs of trauma. The opacity of the past and the compulsion to repeat it are the key elements of Cathy Caruth's argument about trauma, which she derives from Freud's *Beyond the Pleasure Principle*. Trauma for Caruth is fundamentally "unclaimed experience," however, note that for Bergson, in contrast, the unclaimed experience of memory allows for creative improvisation with life. We already possess a great number of studies of literature and trauma, which has become something of a universal key that unlocks all doors. Caruth proposes an all-embracing network in which "we are implicated in each other's traumas."[78] The phrase "the presence of the past" both in her work and elsewhere functions as a shorthand signaling the haunting aftereffect of catastrophic loss. I am interested in broadening the discussion beyond this kind of interpretation, for several reasons.[79] One is that Bergelson throughout seeks to recover the relation between the human being and life, and reading him symptomatically would obscure this important dimension of his work. It would also obscure the joy and humor of his writing and the joy he took in his own creative process. Bergson, whose ideas about art and intuition focused on music, rhythm, and nonsequential time, can help shed light on the meaning of futurity in Bergelson's writing as a whole.

In our own epoch, scholars and creative artists are returning to Bergson for new insights about time and the relation between the mind, the body, and the surrounding world. *A Strange New World* adds to the growing discussion about the texture of time, its evocation in art, and its potentiality from the perspective of the early twentieth century. My emphasis on futurity and renewal can also help balance the humanities today, which are dominated by a sense of futility. Many theorists see the past only as the source of the traumatic wound that we are compelled to repeat in the present. In contrast, Bergelson, like the French philosopher Bergson, did not lose faith in life and the human capacity for creativity beyond the technology of death.

Structure of the Book

A Strange New World is organized chronologically and thematically into four parts, each of which has its own introduction. Part 1, "Postscripts and Departures," explores the themes of time, memory, and the past in work Bergelson wrote before World War I. Chapter 1 examines "At the Depot," largely neglected in the critical literature. Everything and everyone at the train station is slowed down, petrified, congealed (*farglivert*), but Bergelson inserts the emotions of sadness and longing into a space that is otherwise moribund. Surprisingly, inanimate objects and technologies provide emotional responses lacking in human protagonists. I contextualize the author's emphasis on mood and atmosphere (*shtimung*) in light of broader discussions of this concept at the time and in conjunction with Bergson's theory of time's flow.

In *The End of Everything* (*Nokh alemen*), the subject of chapter 2, Bergelson temporalizes emotion, translating a range of feelings into the sense of being too late. The personal or existential problem of the heroine's belatedness with respect to her own life resonates with the broader political, social world: to Mirl Hurvits, new professions and new ideologies are merely a way of passing time; the new opportunities lack substance and meaning. Mirl's tragedy is that in attempting to solve the puzzle of her own belatedness, she is led to her own undoing.

I analyze the problem of repetition and the dead weight of the past in chapter 3, devoted to *Descent* (*Opgang*). The relation between Khaym-Moyshe and his dead friend Meylekh takes center stage in the novel and in my discussion. *Descent* ultimately buries the dead, disposes of metaphysics, and embraces experience. Art itself offers the possibility of transformation. The strangeness of Bergelson's use of forms of address is a key part of the argument. Hope, no matter how fleeting, appears at the very end of the novel, when two characters who previously referred to themselves in the third person tentatively address each other directly.

Part 2, "Bodies, Things, and Machines," revisits the early works as well as key stories from the Berlin period, tracing the often botched encounters between individuals and the surrounding world, as well as the new emphasis on the possibilities created by machines that absorb human qualities.

Chapter 4 explores sensory motor failure—the glitch—in *Descent*, "In a Backwoods Town" ("*In a fargrebter shtot*"), "The Deaf Man" ("*Der toyber*"), and "The Hole Through Which Life Slips" ("*Der lokh, durkh velkhn eyner hot farloyrn*"). I frame my discussion in the broader context of debates around the relation between human beings and machines in Bergelson's era and in particular Russian futurism and its reflection in the Yiddish press.

I examine the link between belatedness and desire in chapter 5, which turns to a series of stories Bergelson wrote while in Berlin. Looking, seeing, being seen, the recurrence of images from the past, and the loss of sight emerge as central themes in these works. No direct apprehension of the lover and the beloved is possible, however. The impediment and the obstacle are the vehicle and stimulus for desire. The catastrophes of World War I and the Russian Civil War interpose a particular mechanism for desire, in which the unexpected appearance of the past plays a significant role.

Part 3, "A Strange New World," interprets Bergelson's representation of the Russian revolution and civil war as time out of joint. Chapter 6 shows that the experiential and existential meaning of waiting, delay, and deferral undergoes significant transformation in "At Night" ("*Bay nakht*"), "Old Age" ("*Altvarg*"), "Among Refugees," "Two Murderers," and other stories from the mid-1920s, including "Birth" ("*Geburt*"), which has not been discussed in the critical literature. Bergelson takes his inquiry about impeded action and slowed motion from the realm of experience and extends it to the realm of law, judgment (*din*), and justice. Instead of a delayed encounter between two characters, what gets postponed is the execution of judgment, both human and divine. By framing Bergelson's literary representations of the delay of judgment in the context of the interwar German Jewish intellectual world, in particular the writings of Scholem and Buber, I explore previously neglected confluences of thought.

Chapter 7 turns to *Judgment* and other civil war work. Bergelson's depiction of the strange new world created by the Russian revolution does not abandon the multiple and subjective temporalities of his earlier work in favor of a single united teleology. The artistic experimentation with rhythm and the appearance of a new collective subject does not mean that Bergelson embraces the end of time and total utopian transformation.

Part 4, "Time Cannot Be Mistaken," traces Bergelson's work after his return to the Soviet Union in 1934. In chapter 8, I interpret Bergelson's major Birobidzhan novel in light of the belated temporality of socialist realism and also offer a reading of Bergelson's own rich exploration of his memory and Jewish memory culture in his two-volume autobiographical novel, *At the Dnieper (Baym Dnyepr)*, published in the late thirties and early forties. The early Soviet emphasis on the genre of the historical novel provides the context for my discussion.

Chapter 9 addresses Bergelson's work for *Eynikayt* (the newspaper of the Jewish Anti-Fascist Committee) in addition to his postwar fiction and the extraordinary play *Prince Reuveni (Prints Ruveni)*. Some of this material, in particular the unfinished novel *Aleksander Barash*, has never been discussed in the critical literature. Bergelson's Reuveni addresses time itself, asking whether it will bring renewal to the Jews. *Prince Reuveni* thus engages the problem central to Bergelson's work and to my project: untimeliness and futurity.

Notes

1. YIVO, RG 1017, Folder D. Bergelson, "Letters." I have not been able to confirm who Kiper was; Bergelson's letter mentions that Kiper was living in Cleveland. Motl Kiper was the head of the Jewish Section of the Ukrainian Communist Party. See Gennady Estraikh, *In Harness: Yiddish Writers' Romance with Communism*, Judaic Traditions in Literature, Music, and Art (Syracuse, NY: Syracuse University Press, 2005), 122–23.

2. I take this language from David Bergelson, *Judgment*, trans. Harriet Murav and Sasha Senderovich, Northwestern World Classics (Evanston, IL: Northwestern University Press, 2017), 82.

3. David Bergelson, "Materyaln tsu D. Bergelsons bio-bibliografye," *Visnshaft un revolutsye* 1–2 (1934): 73.

4. For other book-length studies of Bergelson, see Yekhezkel Dobrushin, *Dovid Bergelson* (Moscow: Der emes, 1947); Avraham Novershtern, "Aspektim mivniyim ba-prozah shel David Bergelson me-reshitah 'ad 'Mides ha-din'" (PhD diss., Hebrew University, 1981); Susan Slotnick, "The Novel Form in the Works of David Bergelson" (PhD diss., Columbia University, 1978).

5. Osip Mandelshtem, *The Complete Critical Prose and Letters* (Ann Arbor, MI: Ardis, 1979), 117.

6. Ellipsis added. See Viktor Shklovsky, *Energy of Delusion: A Book on Plot* (Champaign, IL: Dalkey Archive Press, 2007), 3.

7. A discussion can be found in Victor Erlich, *Modernism and Revolution: Russian Literature in Transition* (Cambridge, MA: Harvard University Press, 1994), 2–6.

8. Miriam Hansen, "Benjamin, Cinema and Experience," *New German Critique*, no. 40 (1987): 197.

9. See Jean Laplanche, *Essays on Otherness* (Florence, KY: Routledge, 1999), 234–59.

10. Cited in Gilles Deleuze, *Cinema 2: The Time Image* (Minneapolis: University of Minnesota Press, 1989), 7.

11. Giorgio Agamben, *What Is an Apparatus?* (Stanford, CA: Stanford University Press, 2009), 47.

12. Cited by Jean-Phillipe Mathy, *Melancholy Politics: Loss, Mourning, and Memory in Late Modern France* (University Park, PA: Penn State Press, 2011), 145.

13. In the realm of literary aesthetics alone, Harold Bloom detected a sense of belatedness in the Romantic poets of the early nineteenth century, who suffered from the "anxiety of influence." Harold Bloom, *The Anxiety of Influence: A Theory of Poetry*, 2nd ed. (New York: Oxford University Press, 1997).

14. For a study of Yiddish and other "peripheral modernisms" that does take up this question, see Marc Caplan, *How Strange the Change: Language, Temporality, and Narrative Fiction in Peripheral Modernisms* (Stanford, CA: Stanford University Press, 2011).

15. Irving Howe and Eliezer Greenberg note that Bergelson himself "is a latecomer in relation to the traditional Jewish past while too much of an outsider in relation to the revolutionary future. Irving Howe and Eliezer Greenberg, *Ashes Out of Hope: Fiction by Soviet-Yiddish Writers* (New York: Schocken Books, 1977), 24.

16. I take this term from the Yiddish critic Nakhmen Mayzel. See Nakhmen Mayzel, "Yontevdikayt," *Literarishe bleter*, no. 37 (1929): 217–20. A similar discussion can be found in Nakhmen Mayzel, *Onhoybn: David Bergelson* (Kibuts Alonim: Bet Nahman Maizel, 1977), 11–20.

17. For Bergelson's biography, I rely on Joseph Sherman, "David Bergelson (1884–1952): A Biography," in *David Bergelson: From Modernism to Socialist Realism*, ed. Joseph Sherman and Gennady Estraikh (Oxford: Legenda, 2007), 7–78.

18. Nakhmen Mayzel, *Forgeyer un mittsaytler* (New York: YKUF, 1946), 326–28.

19. See Bergelson, "Materyaln tsu D. Bergelsons bio-bibliografye," 70; Sherman, "David Bergelson (1884–1952): A Biography," 9.

20. David Bergelson, "Letter to S. Niger" (Vilnius, n.d.), RG 360, Shmuel Niger, Box 7, Folder 9e, YIVO.

21. Yosef Hayim Yerushalmi, *Zakhor: Jewish History and Jewish Memory* (New York: Schocken Books, 1989).

22. See Sylvie Anne Goldberg, *Clepsydra: Essay on the Plurality of Time in Judaism*, trans. Benjamin Ivry (Stanford, CA: Stanford University Press, 2016), 70–78, 141–42.

23. Out of the vast ocean of literature about modernism and modernity, I have found the following particularly helpful: Raymond Williams, *Politics of Modernism* (New York: Verso, 2007); Maria Todorova, "The Trap of Backwardness: Modernity, Temporality, and the Study of Eastern European Nationalism," *Slavic Review* 64, no. 1 (2005): 140–64; and Maria Todorova, "Modernism," in *Modernism: The Creation of Nation-States*, ed. A. Ersoy and M. Gorny (Budapest: Central European Press, 2010), 4–22. A summarizing discussion of the modernity/modernism relation can be found in David Harvey, *The Condition of Postmodernity: An Enquiry into the Origins of Cultural Change* (Cambridge, MA: Blackwell, 1989), 10–38. For a literary analysis of Russian modernisms, see Victor Erlich, *Modernism and Revolution: Russian Literature in Transition*; Julia Vaingurt, *Wonderlands of the Avant-Garde* (Evanston, IL: Northwestern University Press, 2013); Tim Harte, *Fast Forward: The Aesthetics and Ideology of Speed in Russian Avant-Garde Culture, 1910–1930* (Madison: University of Wisconsin Press, 2009).

24. Erlich, *Modernism and Revolution*, 2.

25. Chana Kronfeld, *On the Margins of Modernism: Decentering Literary Dynamics*, Contraversions (Berkeley: University of California Press, 1996), 13. A discussion of Yiddish and modernity can be found in Mikhail Krutikov, *Yiddish Fiction and the Crisis of Modernity, 1905–1914* (Stanford, CA: Stanford University Press, 2001). For an anthology of essays discussing Yiddish modernist work in multiple media, see Seth Wolitz, *Yiddish Modernism: Studies in Twentieth Century Eastern European Jewish Culture* (Bloomington, IN: Slavica, 2014). Comparisons of Hebrew and Yiddish modernism can be found in Shachar Pinsker, *Literary Passports: The Making of Modernist Hebrew Fiction in Europe* (Stanford, CA: Stanford University Press, 2011); Allison Schachter, *Diasporic Modernisms: Hebrew and Yiddish Literature in the Twentieth Century* (New York: Oxford University Press, 2012); Dan Miron, *From Continuity to Contiguity: Toward a New Jewish Literary Thinking* (Stanford, CA: Stanford University Press, 2010).

26. Avraham Novershtern, "Bergelson, Dovid," trans. Marc Caplan, YIVO Encyclopedia of Jews in Eastern Europe, accessed July 25, 2017, http://yivoencyclopedia.org/article.aspx /Bergelson_Dovid.

27. Maks Erik, "Dovid Bergelson," *Yidishe kultur* June–July (1964): 41.

28. Nakhmen Mayzel, "Dovid Bergelson," *Literarishe bleter* 42 (October 19, 1934): 678.

29. The article was reprinted in the special 1934 issue of *Literarishe bleter* entirely devoted to Bergelson. See Shmuel Niger, "A nayer," *Literarishe bleter*, no. 42 (October 19, 1934): 684.

30. I take this description from Jesse Matz, *Literary Impressionism and Modernist Aesthetics* (Cambridge, UK: Cambridge University Press, 2001), 15.

31. Paul Ardoin, S. E. Gontarski, and Laci Mattison, *Understanding Bergson, Understanding Modernism* (New York: Bloomsbury Academic, 2013). I am grateful to Mark Antliff for sharing the text before it was published. Some other works that discuss Bergson and modernism are Stephen Kern, *The Culture of Time and Space 1880–1918* (Cambridge, MA: Harvard University Press, 1983); and Sanja Bahun, *Modernism and Melancholia: Writing as Countermourning* (Oxford: Oxford University Press, 2013).

32. In 1932, Bergson wrote with a sense of wonder about the powers that science would unleash when it would "liberate the force which is enclosed, or rather, condensed, in the slightest particle of ponderable matter." See Henri Bergson, *The Two Sources of Morality and Religion* (Garden City, NY: Doubleday, 1954), 312.

33. The discussions of Bergson that I have relied on include Gilles Deleuze, *Bergsonism* (New York: Zone Books, 1991); Keith Ansell Pearson, "Introduction," in *Mind Energy*, ed. Keith Ansell and Michael Kolkman Pearson (New York: Palgrave, 2007), xi–xli; Suzanne Guerlac, *Thinking in Time: An Introduction to Henri Bergson* (Ithaca, NY: Cornell University Press, 2006).

34. Henri Bergson, *Creative Evolution*, trans. Arthur Mitchell (New York: H. Holt, 1911), 11.

35. See Mark Antliff, *Inventing Bergson: Cultural Politics and the Parisian Avant-Garde* (Princeton, NJ: Princeton University Press, 1993); Mark Antliff, "Bergson and Cubism: A Reassessment," *Art Journal* 47, no. 4 (1988): 341–49.

36. Charlotte Douglas, "Suprematism: The Sensible Dimension," *Russian Review* 34, no. 3 (1975): 266–81; Gerald Janecek, *Zaum: The Transrational Poetry of Russian Futurism* (San Diego, CA: San Diego State University Press, 1996).

37. The "Slap" was signed by David Burliuk, Aleksey Kruchenykh, Mayakovsky, and Khlebnikov. See Anna Lawton, *Russian Futurism through Its Manifestoes, 1912–1928*, trans. Anna Lawton and Hebert Eagle (Ithaca, NY: Cornell University Press, 1988), 51–52.

38. Henri Bergson, *Creative Evolution* (Lanham, MD: University Press of America, 1984), 144.

39. Ibid., 11.

40. Ibid., 126.

41. Ibid., 128.

42. Ryan Bishop and John Philips, "The Slow and the Blind," *Culture and Organization* 10, no. 1 (2004): 62.

43. I take this from Mark Antliff, "Cubism, Futurism, Anarchism: The Aestheticism of the 'Action d'Art' Group, 1906–1920," *Oxford Art Journal* 21, no. 2 (1998): 115–16.

44. Benedikt Lifshits, *Polutoraglazyi strelets* (Leningrad: Sovetskii pisatel', 1989), 153.

45. Claire Colebrook, "The Joys of Atavism," in *Understanding Bergson, Understanding Modernism*, ed. Paul Ardoin, S. E. Gontarski, and Laci Mattison (New York: Bloomsbury, 2013), 293.

46. Williams, *Politics of Modernism*, 53.

47. Il'ia Erenburg, *A vse-taki ona vertitsia* (Berlin: Gelikan, 1922), 55.

48. Ibid., 57.

49. For more on this topic generally, see Vaingurt, and for a broader study, see Anson Rabinbach, *The Human Motor: Energy, Fatigue, and the Origins of Modernity* (New York: Basic Books, 1990).

50. Viktor Shklovsky, *Theory of Prose* (Normal, IL: Dalkey Archive Press, 1990), 12.

51. Benjamin discusses empty, homogeneous time in his "Theses on the Philosophy of History." See Walter Benjamin, *Illuminations* (New York: Schocken Books, 1969), 260–61.

52. See Henri Bergson, *An Introduction to Metaphysics: The Creative Mind* (Totowa, NJ: Littlefield, Adams, 1965), 135.

53. See Shiv K. Kumar, *Bergson and the Stream of Consciousness Novel* (New York: New York University Press, 1963), 14–15.

54. For a discussion of this point in relation to modernist Czech artists, see Thomas Ort, *Art and Life in Modernist Prague: Karel Capek and His Generation, 1911–1938* (New York: Palgrave Macmillan, 2013), 63–65.

55. Frances Nethercott, *Filosofsksaia vstrecha: Bergson v Rossii (1907–1917)* (Moscow: Modest Kolerov, 2008), 158.

56. For a discussion, see James Curtis, "Bergson and Russian Formalism," *Comparative Literature* 28, no. 2 (1976): 109–21; Hilary L. Fink, *Bergson and Russian Modernism, 1900–1930*, Studies in Russian Literature and Theory (Evanston, IL: Northwestern University Press, 1999); Nethercott, *Filosofsksaia vstrecha: Bergson v Rossii (1907–1917)*.

57. See Miron 2010, 305–09.

58. See, for example, Sh. Rudnyanski, "Anri Bergson vegn estetik," *Di yidishe velt* 8 (1913): 82–88; Henri Bergson, "Dos geheymnis fun shafn," *Di literarishe velt* 1, no. 12 (1913): 3–4; Avraham Gliksman, "V. Natanson, Shpinoza un Bergson," *Bikher-velt* 3, no. 1–2 (1924): 38–40; Khaim Zhitlovski, "Anri Bergson: Araynfir in der metafizik," *Bikher velt* 3, no. 1–2 (1924): 14–17; Meylekh Ravitsh, "Di filosofye fun lakhn," *Naye folkstsaytung* 3, no. 261 (1928): 6.

59. See Rudnyanski, "Anri Bergson vegn estetik"; Bergson, "Dos geheymnis fun shafn."

60. Henri Bergson, "Yekhid un gezelshaft," *Globus* 2, no. 6 (1932): 49–60.

61. Yeshaye Klinov, "Tsi hot Bergson, 'der zun funem Varshever soykher,' fardint dem Nobel-Prayz?" *Haynt* 272, no. 21 (November 21, 1928): 4.

62. Hans Kohn, "The Essence of Judaism," *American Scholar* 3, no. 2 (Spring 1934): 166.

63. For the English, see Shklovsky, *A Sentimental Journey: Memoirs, 1917–1922* (Normal, IL: Dalkey Archive Press, 2004), 276; for the Russian, see Shklovsky, *Eshshe nichego ne konchilos'* (Moscow: Vagrius, 2002), 266.

64. The Yiddish is cited from Bergelson, *Geklibene verk*, 8 vols, vol. 5 (Vilnius: B. Kletskin, 1930), 199; and the English from Bergelson and Neugroschel, *The Shadows of Berlin* (San Francisco, CA: City Lights), 43. I have modified the English translation.

65. Galin Tihanov emphasizes the importance of the war on the formulation of Shklovsky's notion of defamiliarization in Tihanov, "The Poetics of Estrangement: The Case of the Early Shklovsky," *Poetics Today* 26, no. 4 (2005): 666–696.

66. See Shachar Pinsker, "The Literary Cafes of Berlin as Urban Spaces of Jewish Modernism," accessed September 29, 2016, http://quod.lib.umich.edu/cgi/p/pod/dod-idx/literary-cafes-of -berlin-as-urban-spaces-of-jewish-modernism.pdf?c=fia;idno=11879367.2008.011.

67. For a substantive historical introduction and document collection, see David Engel, *The Assasination of Symon Petliura and the Trial of Scholem Schwartzbard 1926–1927: A Selection of Documents* (Gottingen: Vandenhoeck and Ruprecht, 2016). A broad-based discussion of the trial and responses to it from the perspective of law and literature, including Bergelson's story, can be found in Anna Schur, "Shades of Justice: The Trial of Sholom Schwartzbard and Dovid Bergelson's 'Among Refugees,'" *Law and Literature* 19, no. 15 (2007): 15–43.

68. Maks Erik, "David Bergelson," *Literarishe bleter* 53 (May 8, 1925): 3. For a discussion of Yiddish and world literature, see Saul Zarrit, "The World Awaits Your Yiddish Word: Jacob Glatstein and the Problem of World Literature," *Studies in American Jewish Literature* 34, no. 2 (2015): 175–203.

69. An example of this approach can be found in Ruth Wisse's introduction to the English translation of Bergelson's first published work, "At the Depot" (*"Arum vokzal"*). See Schur, "Shades of Justice," 15–43.

70. The concrete case of Georges Sorel is discussed in Mark Antliff, "'The Jew as Anti-Artist: Georges Sorel, Anti-Semitism, and the Aesthetics of Class Consciousness," *Oxford Art Journal* 20, no. 1 (January 1, 1997): 50–67.

71. Benjamin writes, "Bergson rejects any historical determination of memory." Benjamin, *Illuminations*, 157. For a critique of Bergson's concept of freedom, see Donna Jones, "The Eleatic Bergson: Review of *Thinking in Time: An Introduction to Henri Bergson* by Suzanne Geuerlac," *Diacritics* 37, no. 1 (Spring 2007): 21–31.

72. See Fink, *Bergson and Russian Modernism*, 101–11.

73. See Shmuel Niger and Jacob Shatzsky, *Leksikon fun der nayer yidisher literatur*, vol. 1 (New York: Congress for Jewish Culture, 1956), 380.

74. For a discussion of Stalin's revolution on the cultural front, see Galin Tihanov and Katerina Clark, "Literary Criticism and the Transformations of the Literary Field during the Cultural Revolution, 1928–1932," in *A History of Russian Literary Theory and Criticism*, ed. Tihanov, Galin and Evgeny Dobrenko (Pittsburgh, PA: University of Pittsburgh Press, 2011), 43–63.

75. Boris Groys, *The Total Art of Stalinism: Avant-Garde, Aesthetic Dictatorship, and Beyond*, trans. Charles Rougle (Princeton, NJ: Princeton University Press, 1992), 14–74. The major studies of socialist realism include Katerina Clark, *The Soviet Novel: History as Ritual*; Régine Robin, *Socialist Realism: An Impossible Aesthetic* (Stanford, CA: Stanford University Press, 1992); E. I. Dobrenko, *Metafora vlasti: Literatura Stalinskoi epokhi v istoricheskom osveshchenii* (Munich: Verlag Otto Sagner, 1993); Vladimir Papernyi, *Kul'tura dva* (Moscow: Novoe literaturnoe obozrenie, 2006); Lilya Kaganovsky, *How the Soviet Man Was Unmade: Cultural Fantasy and Male Subjectivity Under Stalin* (Pittsburgh, PA: University of Pittsburgh Press, 2008). For a concise overview of various trends in the study of socialist realism, see Stephen Lovell, "Politekonomiia sotsrealizma, Der Gorki-Park: Freizeitkultur Im Stalinismus 1928–1941, and: Sovetskaia prazdnichnaia kul'tura v provintsii: Prostranstvo, simvoly, istoricheskie mify (1917–1927)," *Kritika: Explorations in Russian and Eurasian History* 10, no. 1 (Winter 2009): 205–15.

76. See Clark, *The Soviet Novel*, 145–46; 172–76; Yampolsky, "In the Shadow of Monuments: Notes on Iconoclasm and Time"; Dobrenko, "Socialism as Will and Representation, or What Legacy Are We Rejecting?" For a discussion of Stalin's revolution on the cultural front, see Tihanov and Clark, "Literary Criticism and the Transformations of the Literary Field During the Cultural Revolution, 1928–1932."

77. Petre Petrov, *Automatic for the Masses: The Death of the Author and the Birth of Socialist Realism* (Toronto: University of Toronto Press, 2015), 152.

78. Cathy Caruth, *Unclaimed Experience: Trauma, Narrative, and History* (Baltimore, MD: Johns Hopkins University Press, 1996), 24.

79. Andreas Huyssen describes the "problematic privileging of the traumatic dimension of life" in Andreas Huyssen, *Present Pasts: Urban Palimpsests and the Politics of Memory* (Stanford, CA: Stanford University Press, 2003), 8.

PART 1

POSTSCRIPTS AND DEPARTURES

Introduction

"Postscripts and Departures" discusses Bergelson's early fiction, written between 1909 and World War I. Two very short stories published in the same period, "Two Roads" ("*Tsvey vegn*," 1910) and "The Last Rosh Hashanah" ("*Der letster Rosheshone*,"1911, suggest the larger themes of the longer and better-known fiction.[1] "Two Roads" explores the transformation of space into story. Instead of the conventional narrative in which the hero journeys through a space, in this work the narrative emerges out of the space. Bergelson is experimenting with the temporalization of space or the saturation of space with emotion. This structure is important to "At the Depot" and Bergelson's second novel, *Descent*. "The Last Rosh Hashanah" creates the experience of being left behind that is central to much of his early writing, especially "At the Depot" and *The End of Everything*.

"Two Roads" is the more innovative of the pair, because it lacks both plot and characters; more a lyrical prose poem than a short story, its subject matter is the quality of movement itself, suggested primarily by changing sound patterns. Each of the roads has its own mood, which transforms into scraps of narrative; for example, the road used by merchants produces a miniature story about an old merchant who is ready to die; this story emerges from the description of the road and then just as quickly fades away, like the larger narrative of which it is a part. The narrow road leads down to a valley, a wood, a village, and a brick factory and then on to a paved highway. The sound made by the wagon wheels creates an echo, "a pure, naïve, childlike echo" that traverses the surrounding fields and ends in the "barely perceptible" rustling of trees in the nearby wood.[2] In the summer, everything turns green except the paved road, which retains its leaden color and "ordinary" appearance. Bergelson describes space using qualities pertaining to time: the word translated as "ordinary" is *vokhedik*, which can also be translated as "workaday," or having to do with the work week as opposed to the Sabbath or a holiday.

A couple from the city "may turn up" to spend a month in this place of green fields and valleys; the Yiddish original *megulgl vern* for "may turn up" also means to turn or be transformed into, to be reincarnated as. Bergelson accentuates the latter meaning of reincarnation by hinting that this unnamed couple might stay in this place and with "slow, mythically huge steps . . . reach the distant end of the horizon in just a few paces."[3] The mythic proportions of their gait suggest the giants in Genesis 6:4: "There were giants on the earth then." The motif of reincarnation and metamorphosis will figure importantly in Bergelson's subsequent works.

To come to the place of the "two roads" is to be transported to a different time, ancient and mythical, when fallen angels bore children with humans. But the sadness of the place overtakes the couple, and the story ends in silence: they cannot say a word to each other. With this the meditation called "Two Roads" comes to its conclusion. The couple—unnamed and about whom readers know nothing—are precisely not of interest as actual human beings; the narrative weight lies instead in the transformation they undergo in the particular space marked out by the two roads. The couple is as important or unimportant as the roads, fields, hills, and woods and the stories these spaces become; there is something abstract and schematic about these two figures. They are an element in and not actors determining the overall "atmosphere," or *shtimung*. This concept has wide-ranging resonance in Bergelson's milieu.

While "Two Roads" does not take place in a recognizable historical or Jewish context, emphasizing instead abstraction and transcendent legend and myth, "The Last Rosh Hashanah" explicitly refers to larger trends in Jewish history and the Jewish lifeworld at the turn of the twentieth century, including migration, Zionism, and anti-Jewish violence. Unlike "Two Roads," human actors play an important role. "Mistifke" ("Trashville") is a shtetl in the process of being abandoned. Family after family leaves for America, driven in part by opportunity and in part by pogroms. Bergelson does not focus on the outward journey, however, but on those who remain behind. For one of the townspeople, the experience of a pogrom left him with a peculiar "inheritance." When he boards up the windows of his house before leaving for America, he hammers away at the planks of wood with ferocity, cursing them as if they were "pogromists," before realizing his delusion. The intensified relation with inanimate objects takes a disturbing turn in the aftermath of violence. Bergelson returns to this motif through-out his work, especially in fiction written after the Nazi genocide, discussed in part 4.

In "The Last Rosh Hashanah," the remnant of the shtetl's population is overwhelmed by loneliness and a sense of abandonment—these are the dominant emotions of Bergelson's protagonist in "At the Depot." They and the place they continue to inhabit feel orphaned and "ownerless." Construction on a new house to replace one destroyed in a fire comes to a halt. The four foundation posts extrude "foolishly" from the abandoned building site without a master or owner to take care that the work will continue. The original Yiddish uses the Hebrew term *hefker*, which can also signify "up for grabs" or "free."[4] To put it another way, the spaces and people described in "The Last Rosh Hashanah" inhabit the position of the modern and modernist subjects who joyously proclaim their emancipation from the past and their separation from the community. In later work, to be discussed in part 3, Bergelson probes the meaning of this condition, both the experience of utter freedom and the aesthetic possibilities it creates. In this early story, in contrast, the sort of freedom that severs all connections does not make anyone happy. It is not only that the town is very nearly abandoned; the loss of Jewish population means that the necessary quota of Jewish men required for prayer can no longer be fulfilled, and thus those who remain in the shtetl have been edged out of the Jewish calendar of prescribed celebrations and observances. An entire structure of time is lost to them. As its title indicates, the earlier story focuses on one holiday in particular, the Jewish New Year. It is Rosh Hashanah, the "day of remembrance," and yet the inhabitants of the shtetl cannot properly celebrate Rosh Hashanah. Those who remain in the shtetl are out of sync with the shtetl calendar and thus thrust out of Jewish memory culture. Without the capacity to remember the past, possibilities for the future grow dim: the day of remembrance also marks the new year.

The temporalization of space—making space alive and mobile, infused with emotion and subjectivity—is the key innovation of Bergelson's first published work, "At the Depot." He will revisit this technique in the 1920s and particularly in narratives of the Russian Civil War, when the ordinary, daily life experience of time and space radically changes. In his first novel, *The End of Everything*, Bergelson's heroine experiences the loss of the temporal pattern of holiday/weekday time and consequently the loss of the past. Mirl Hurvits, as I will show, experiences the condition of belatedness, the defining feature of modernity. But abandonment, loss, and obsolescence do not tell the whole story. In his second novel, *Descent*, Bergelson introduces the temporality of new beginnings and transformation, coming back to the motif of *gilgul* (metamorphosis) that he touches on in "Two Roads."

Notes

1. "Tsvey vegn" was originally published in *Idisher almanakh* in 1910; I use the edition David Bergelson, "Tsvey vegn," in *Verk: Naye farbeserte oysgabe*, vol. 3 (Berlin: Vostok, 1922), 97–100. For the English translation, see David Bergelson, "Two Roads," in *No Star Too Beautiful: An Anthology of Yiddish Stories from 1832 to the Present*, ed. and trans. Joachim Neugroschel (New York: W. W. Norton, 2002), 417–18. "Der letster Rosheshone" was originally published in *Vuhin* in 1911 and later in David Bergelson, "Der letster Rosheshone," in *Verk: Naye farbeserte oysgabe*, vol. 4 (Berlin: Vostok, 1923), 21–38 and also in Geklibene verk, vol. 1 (Vilnius: B. Kletskin, 1929). There is no English translation.

2. Bergelson, "Two Roads," 417.

3. Ibid., 418.

4. David Bergelson, "Der letster rosheshone," in *Geklibene verk*, vol. 1 (Vilnius: B. Kletskin, 1929), 166.

1

CONGEALED TIME

The train station was tall, red, and two-storied. It had stood there for years, petrified (*fargliverter*) and dead, and to everything surrounding it, the station seemed to be an enchanted sentry, over whom someone had once cast a spell—that it would sleep forever in a melancholy slumber. The unknown, silent, and spiteful magician who had cast the spell was dead; his bones long ago had darkened in the damp earth. The station nonetheless was not freed from its sleep . . . Because the village and the whole area kept silent, the old petrified (*fargliverter*) station also kept silent, even though it looked into the depths of the blue distance with a hidden longing, as if it were the heart of the matter and one day a mighty, proud helper would arise from there, rumbling, rushing, its power expanding into every sleeping corner to restore to life all that had languished for years. But the distance was quiet and melancholy, disgusted by the sleep around it, and it too fell asleep [ellipsis added].[1]

THIS PASSAGE COMES FROM THE OPENING OF DAVID Bergelson's 1909 "At the Depot" ("*Arum vokzal*"), his first published work. It presents a startling contrast to most depictions of the train in the same time period. In the late 1890s, the Lumière brothers shocked the world with their moving images, including their film of a train arriving at a station, which terrified and entranced audiences.[2] By the turn of the twentieth century, the image of the train in Russian and Yiddish literature was associated with modernity and technological progress in both a positive and a negative sense, signaling rapid change, ease of access to goods, people, and services, and the dissolution of class and national boundaries, but also the risks of travel, transience, impermanence, disruption, and neurosis.[3] As the opening of "At the Depot" reveals, Bergelson uses the train, the symbol of mobility, commerce, and modernity, to indicate stasis and immobility.[4]

Far from signaling the new twentieth century, Bergelson's train station is enmeshed in some ancient, mysterious conflict. As in "Two Roads," space is infused with time that stretches back before human history. The great hulking station, however, no matter how moribund, is still alive, and it yearns and hopes for a messianic redeemer. All is not lost, appearances to the contrary. In a few words, Bergelson indicates the theme that will occupy him for the entirety of his career, from "At the Depot" to *Prince Reuveni* (*Prints Ruveni*), his play from the 1940s about the sixteenth-century false messiah: the possibility of salvation that may or may not be realized. From Bergelson's perspective, and, I dare say, a Jewish perspective, its failure to materialize does not mean catastrophe, but rather, the possibility of more time, the opportunity for some other change that might occur. Salvation is always deferred. As I will show in this chapter in particular and in part 1 generally, the possibility of redemption does not depend on working, striving, or acting but rather the opposite. Repetition, inaction, and slowed action provide the conditions for something new to emerge. The deferral of redemption, the deferral of experience, and the deferral of the punchline— are all of a piece in Bergelson's fiction and his world.

The description of the train station, significantly, paints a picture of what did *not* happen: the resurrection that could have taken place did not. The nonevent creates a fork in time in which there are two possibilities, one of which is realized and the other not, but the second possibility is not thereby eliminated. It remains in virtual form. To be "at the depot" is to inhabit a particular space and time in which the normal laws of physics do not apply, because motion ceases. Bergelson emphasizes throughout the novella that the train station is completely cut off from the surrounding world. Time stops. Expectation flows indistinguishably into disappointment, but no one in particular feels these emotions; they appear instead as features of the landscape. It is not *in* the distance or *from* the distance that help could come, it is rather the distance itself that is "the heart of the matter" ("*der iker*"). "Distance" is an abstraction, but Bergelson loads abstraction with emotion as part of the process of creating "atmosphere" (*shtimung*), to be discussed in greater detail below. In qualifying space in this way and assigning emotion to objects and aspects of the natural world, Bergelson transforms the world he depicts. He overcomes the separation between thought, feeling, and the surrounding world of other people and objects, both making it difficult to tell who is speaking, or feeling a particular emotion, and also making every dimension of the narrative poetic and musical.

The mutual interpenetration of human beings and things in Bergelson is distinct from the more traditional poetic device of personification, a one-way street, a projection from human emotion to the surrounding world. In this work, the projection goes the other way round. The space of the depot is "intensive," so that individual objects and people are nearly indistinguishable from what surrounds them.[5] Reading "At the Depot" thus requires a shift in perspective. Action and movement—to the extent that they are found in this narrative—are born out of the space, not the characters, in the same way that miniature narratives emerge from the roads in the story "Two Roads." What Bergelson creates approximates something like a supra-individual consciousness.

The negligible plot of "At the Depot": Beynish Rubinshteyn, an unsuccessful grain broker, is preoccupied by memories of his dead wife and neglectful of his second, sickly wife, whose complexion is greenish. He makes a series of bad deals, loses hundreds of rubles as a consequence, and flirts with another man's wife. Mocked and baited by his fellow traders, he assaults one of them and spends a few weeks in jail. At the end, he embarks on another deal and resumes contact with his second wife. He writes her a letter in stilted Hebrew phrases, informing her of his arrival for the Sabbath. The final line of the novella returns to the opening passage: "On the hilltop that remained just behind them, the station dozed with fixed (*farglivert*) half-open eyes staring into the deep unknown distance."[6] The interval of action, as limited as it was, is over, and everything returns to its prior state. Yet here in the backwater, the small shtetl, the nearly defunct train station, a remarkable metamorphosis is taking place.

This chapter focuses on inaction, impeded action, and slowed action as the central theme and key narrative device of "At the Depot." The term that best captures this condition of slowed activity is *farglivert*, rendered in the passage I quoted earlier as "petrified," but which can also be translated as "congealed," "stiffened," "gelid," and "frozen." Bergelson also uses the term to suggest an emotional state. To congeal is to transform a liquid into a solid; motion is suspended. The obverse can happen as well: the gel can be unset. In the passage from "At the Depot," virtual redemption takes the form of a substance that expands in space, as if a solid had become a liquid. Bergelson's literary art transforms the petrified space and time of the depot and other dead and frozen places.

In "At the Depot" Bergelson reveals the potentiality of renewal through the reanimation of materiality. The emotionality of the surrounding inanimate world contains the potential for answerability. Something—not someone—is listening to Beynish Rubinshteyn, the protagonist of "At the Depot." Something new can happen here.

Shtimung

Other Yiddish writers before Bergelson had characterized Jewish life in the shtetl in terms similar to those of "At the Depot." Marital misery, cutthroat competition, violence, poverty, ignorance, financial failure, and boredom appear in works by I. L. Peretz, Sholem Abramovitsh, Sholem Aleichem, and others. Bergelson, however, uses the backdrop of the shtetl's economic and cultural decline to explore a new way of writing, in which time, perception, memory, and emotion come to the fore, fusing with time and space. Bergelson's earliest critics were keenly sensitive to this dimension of his art. A. Vayter, for example, writing in 1909, noted the "mystical character" of the train station and described the "unexpected joy" that "At the Depot" created in him.[7] Shmuel Niger put it well when he wrote that it is not the station so much as what is *around* it, the "air" (*luft*); not the individuals but the shadows they leave behind; not their conversations but the hidden source of these conversation.[8] The "air" is prior to the characters.

In 1910 Bergelson used the term *shtimung*, which can be translated as "air," "atmosphere," or "mood," to explain that it was not difficult for him to work on several pieces at once: "The first thing that gets born is the *shtimung* of the story with the main character (the latter is almost always unclear), and they affect me so deeply that it is simply impossible to stand it. Such a strange longing appears together with the *shtimung* for each unique detail of that world, which the main character bears and which is in the *shtimung*. My entire purpose is to convey this *shtimung* bound together with the life and the events that take place around it, and (if it is possible to say this) in it."[9]

The word *shtimung* in Yiddish relates to mood, temper, and emotionality, and additionally to melody, tone, rhythm, tempo, and atmosphere.[10] Bergelson also used the Russian term *nastroenie* for the Yiddish *shtimung*; the Russian has most of the same meanings.[11] There is clearly an overlap between Bergelson's use of the term and the German *Stimmung*, which was the object of intense aesthetic debate in the first half of the twentieth century, although its use predates that period.[12]

The Yiddish literary world beyond Bergelson made ample use of the concept. In a Yiddish language review of Martin Buber's German translation of the tales of the Hasidic R. Nakhmen of Bratslav, Avraham Koralnik used the term to characterize Jewish life generally; Jewish culture, according to Koralnik, is "the culture of shtimungen" (here, spirituality).[13] For the

Yiddish poetic movement known as Introspectivism, *shtimung* was also a key term. In the 1920s, the Yiddish Introspectivists proclaimed that poetry's task was the expression of each poet's individual *shtimung*, which reflected the chaos and unpredictability of modern life, the separation that obtained among individuals, and the labyrinthine disunity of the poet's psyche.[14] Bergelson's prose has much in common with Introspectivist poetry.

From Bergelson's entangled description of *shtimung*, one thing is clear: there is nothing neutral or impartial in his narratives. There is no objective outer world. Another way to put this is to say that space is not homogeneous or empty in Bergelson; there are no abstract categories that are the same for everyone. There is only the world refracted through the consciousness of a particular individual. Everything in a Bergelson story is filled with and animated by *someone's* mood. In the 1920s, the Yiddish critic Max Erik noted the overlay of *shtimung* and narrative space: "Bergelson's surrounding world is his own mood [*shtimung*]" ("Bergelson's svive—dos iz zayn eygene shtimung").[15] In the early twenty-first century, Hans Gumbrecht argued that "reading for the *Stimmung* makes us sensitive to modes in which texts as meaning realities and material realities quite literally surround the reader, both physically and literally."[16] Texts have meanings, which can be decoded, but they also work on the emotions, sensibilities, and sensations in an immediate way. To read for the first without the second is to impoverish the encounter with the text and with the world.

Modernists sought to accentuate the sensory qualities of their art, to pull the body into aesthetics. Sound is an important method to achieve this goal. In "At the Depot" and indeed in Bergelson's subsequent work, sound and rhythm are important. Readers hear what inanimate objects and nature say; the narrative is filled with ambient sound. Bergelson's train speaks aloud the fate of the brokers at the station; its rhythmic echo sounds out the words: "pointless . . . pointless . . . an all for nothing, all for nothing" (umzist . . . umzist . . . un farfaln . . . alts farfaln).[17] Later in the work, the twilight, the wind, the hammering of the blacksmith, the sound of train as it passes the station, and the leaves that fall from the trees all tell the story of something that has ended, passed, and cannot return. The sound of the repeated phrase "geendikt, geendikt" ("it has ended, ended") also suggests the rhythmic echo of a passing train. Inserting musicality into the text and attributing emotion to things creates the *shtimung* in which the entire work is immersed. Emphasizing the aural and not the semantic features of words adds to the effect. For Bergson, rhythm increases the receptivity of the viewer or listener, because it lulls us into a state of sympathy with the artist. Here again, the body plays a key role in the reception of the artwork.

The mood of "At the Depot" is *troyer*, which can be translated as "grief," "sorrow," "melancholy," "sadness," and "mourning." Niger wrote that frustration and "nail biting" also play a key role.[18] At the end of the day, the brokers leave the depot and return home:

> There they calmly and deliberately settled into tea drinking, smiling at their families, hugging and kissing the children, chatting—all in order to drive away the sadness that was on the other side of the lit windows, but the sadness managed nonetheless to reach the station to spread its melancholy influence there. Together with the regular railroad ties and tall telegraph poles it rose higher and higher, climbing above the earth until it reached the farthest edge of the horizon, where it got stuck.[19]

The image of the railway and telegraph conjures what Wolfgang Schivelbusch calls the "machine ensemble" of the railway journey, the aggregated, interlocking system of transportation and communication that changed the nineteenth-century landscape.[20] Bergelson realizes emotion as a physical force in the world by giving it location and dimension. The grain brokers do not feel this sorrow; instead the emotion feels them; it is not in them, but *they are in it*. I resort to this strange formulation in order to highlight the significance of Bergelson's innovation. Being "at the depot" means living in a state of suspended animation. From this stasis arises a single, all-consuming feeling that permeates everything in the work. The wind, the moon, the darkness of night, the world of nature, the buildings and objects created by human beings, and the thoughts, imaginings, and memories of the protagonist—all are awash in unfulfilled longing (*benkshaft*) and sorrow ("troyer").[21] The mood, or atmosphere, of the work as a whole solidifies into some sort of physical, material thing. The human emotion—which belongs to everyone and no one, a ghost from the past or future—appears as an appendage disturbing the symmetry of the machine ensemble of the railroad and the telegraph. Sadness intrudes into the grid, interfering with the regular predictability of communication and travel in this space. The human emotion, transformed into something resembling particulate matter, pushes at and distorts technology's grid.

It is illuminating to compare Bergelson's use of "*der troyer*" and Marc Chagall and David Hofshteyn's collaborative project, the poem cycle *Troyer* (here the term is best translated as "grief").[22] Hofshteyn knew Bergelson and was a member of the "Kiev group" of writers that also included Bergelson. It is highly likely that he had read "At the Depot" by the time he began working on his own *Troyer.*[23] The point, however, is not whether Bergelson influenced Hofshteyn. The point is rather that the two works can be seen as "contiguous" with one another: A comparison of the Bergelson passage and the Hofshteyn/Chagall work reveals fascinating similarities in the configuration of text, image, graphics, and pictorial and narrative space. As Seth Wolitz has shown, the book uses all these elements to produce "the greatest possible" emotional response in the viewer. *Troyer*, published by the Kiev Kultur-Lige in 1922, was a response to the pogroms that had taken place a few years earlier, during the height of the Russian Civil War. The poem cycle polemically asks how the victims should be mourned, refusing all traditional practices, and concludes that the sheer scale of the poet's *troyer* (grief) is his only comfort. On the book cover, the Hebrew letters spelling out *troyer* are in red, and they descend diagonally across the pictorial space from right to left, cutting through the two-headed human figure depicting Hofshteyn and Chagall. The last letter of *troyer*, *resh*, is pictured as a ram's horn, the shofar, which is blown as a call to prayer and a warning to the Jewish people. It is used on the Jewish New Year, the "Day of Remembrance," when God remembers every act of every creature and Jews remind God of his covenant with them. In their famous manifesto of 1912, "A Slap in the Face of Public Taste," Russian futurist visual and literary artists proclaimed themselves the only "face of time" and the vehicle through which the "horn of time" blew (Tol'ko my—litso nashego vremeni/ Rog vremeni trubit nami v slovesnom iskusstve). In contrast, Chagall and Hofshteyn reinterpret the "horn of time" as the shofar, as an instrument for the expression of their towering grief and a reproach to God, who forgot his covenant. A shtetl scene, consisting of a house and a human figure with a horse and cart, is depicted on the shofar/*resh*. The shtetl is both the frame for and a composite element of the graphical and semantic scene of mourning. Reading the word and viewing it as a pictorial motif take place simultaneously, blurring the distinction between figure and ground. *Troyer* as both mourning and sadness saturates the entire pictorial plane and the blood-soaked landscape of Ukraine to which the graphical image and the poem cycle refer.[24]

In contrast to Hofshteyn's poem cycle, Bergelson's *troyer* in "At the Depot" has no single discernible cause. Bergelson's depiction of the atmosphere at the train station is not intended as a sociologically accurate portrait of the general mood of the Jewish or the larger population of the time, or an expression of the author's own grief.[25] There is nothing in the novella that links the cloud of sorrow at the horizon with the early part of the twentieth century specifically, although there were events that could have prompted a sense of despair, including the Kishinev pogrom of 1903, and as Nakhmen Mayzel argues, the failed Russian revolution of 1905.[26] In other work written in the early years of the twentieth century, Bergelson more closely links the mood of his characters to the historical events of their time. "The Last Rosh Hashanah," discussed in the introduction to part 1, is an example.

In "At the Depot," however, even though Bergelson hints at the larger forces of history, it is not events per se that motivate him but rather the overall quality of the time, its tonality and weight, which history helps to shape and color. He uses his narrative art to transform space, things, people, and nature into vectors of emotion-laden time. Even though the general quality of time in "At the Depot" is mournful and the train station "petrified," the play of transformation as a particular feature of the space of the train station and its narration continues unabated. In the opening, a blind man wants to tell his story, but no one listens, and the words become the tapping of his cane on the platform and the gestures he makes, "sign language." The church bells pick up the thread of the narrative, explaining to the surrounding fields what happened; the sound of banging on a window tells the night what is taking place. On his way to borrow money on a bitterly cold day, Beynish is being driven in a sleigh; the driver turns to face him, but instead of hearing coherent speech, Beynish sees "disjointed words" beginning to emerge from the driver's open mouth that freeze on their way to Beynish and then disappear. Hearing is transformed into seeing, as words (a form of breath) transform into particulate matter that then melts.[27] Houses, train cars, and human beings emerge out of the darkness only to be swallowed up in it again. All of nature and the built environment participate in this seemingly infinite process. Describing the transformation from one medium to another in a kind of literary metamorphosis is key to Bergelson's art, his imaginative depiction of "creative evolution."

Belatedness

The economic life of the traders at the station marks a departure from the typical economic activity in the shtetl, because it depends on a nascent stock market.[28] The new way of making money, however, is already obsolete and soon to be swept aside, but the traders fail to notice their own belatedness. Beynish comes the closest to this realization, while his cronies behave as if nothing has changed. The inhabitants of the depot remain on the platform to watch the trains as they go by. Bergelson dramatizes belatedness by calling upon the familiar sensation of being thrust backward as you watch an adjacent vehicle go forward. Being left behind has its own unique rhythm, which plays out in Bergelson's early work in general, and in "At the Depot" in particular. The protagonist Beynish Rubinshteyn looks at the passengers in the train as it passes the platform and recalls that he too once had money.

In "At the Depot" it is not only the passing train but also the circumstances of their own lives that have left the characters behind. Most of them share the condition of having once been or having once had someone or something of value. The future of the past they once lived has ended, or it has continued but without them. The protagonist Beynish Rubinshteyn once had a pretty and intelligent wife, but she died. Nothing remains of her except Beynish's memory of her, and the memory of how, after she died, he tore her photograph to bits and then, four months later, married again, for the sake of the dowry provided by the second wife. At the train station, Beynish feels "strangely left behind and forgotten" (*modne ibergeblibn un fargesn*).[29] Pinye Lisak once had money. Itsik-Borukh once lived in the big city and once was a revolutionary. Itsik-Borukh now spends every evening lying in bed and staring at the ceiling.

It is significant that an earlier Hebrew-language version of "At the Depot" adds a political edge to the problem of being left behind. The story, titled "Emptiness," describes a deserted, dull train station, much like the one in the 1909 work. On their way to a meeting, a group of Zionists stop to refresh themselves at the station. They create noise and commotion at the depot, but when they leave, it returns to its former empty state. Missing the train and being left behind here translate into an ideological challenge. Zionism does not take root in Bergelson's shtetls.

The condition of having been left behind is one of the richest and most important temporal states in Bergelson's corpus as a whole. It most often appears in the setting of a train station. Mirele, the heroine of *The End of Everything* (*Nokh alemen*), the subject of chapter 3, has the habit of standing at the rails as the passenger trains rush by, "[leaving] behind in the surrounding silence of the fields the mournful echo of many unhappy talks begun but not concluded."[30] In "Station Burgers" ("Stantsye kotlety"), a train carrying Jews is forced to delay its departure so that the stationmaster can sell the hapless passengers his wife's food. In "Left at a Burning Shtetl" ("Hinter a brenendikn shtetl"), set during the Civil War, refugees fleeing anti-Jewish violence watch helplessly as the Bolshevik armored train pulls away, leaving them behind. Bergelson's use of this trope is not unique. In Chekhov's *The Seagull*, Trigorn says, "I seem to see life and learning vanishing into the distance, while I lag more and more behind, like the village boy who missed the train."[31] The theme of waiting for and missing the train as a theme also appears in Yiddish and Russian poetry of the early decades of the twentieth century; Perets Markish is an example from Yiddish.[32] Bergelson's use of this temporal image, however, is distinct, not only because it is relentless, but also because in his work, remaining behind and falling back have creative potential. Regardless of subsequent statements he made about progress, literary and otherwise, Bergelson's perspective as an artist remained with those left behind.

Inaction

Inaction, delayed action, and belatedness—remaining on the platform, so to speak—create the conditions for new forms of action and for new forms of interacting the world. The depot, both the place Bergelson represents and the story that he tells, is devoid of meaningful action. The grain dealers do the same thing over and over again, and Beynish Rubinshteyn barely acts at all; instead, he remembers. The same can be said for other early Bergelson works, whether they take place in the shtetl, for example, *Descent*, and "In a Backwoods Town," or in the city as well, as for example in *The End of Everything*.

Bergelson's narratives *depict* consciousness in a state of delay and also *create* delay as an effect of reading. "At the Depot" provides examples of both. As I have already discussed, Bergson describes the appearance of images as the result of a gap between perception and action. The spatial metaphor is significant; Bergson speaks of the obstacle that thwarts action as opening up a "void," an empty space. When Bergelson describes the process by which images appear to Beynish Rubinshteyn, he also invokes the spatial metaphor of a void.

It is evening and the work of the day is complete; the other traders are going home. A policeman slams the station door shut as he goes: "The door banged shut behind him, resounding loudly, not as in a building with rooms and corridors, but like a big, empty barrel."[33] Characteristically for Bergelson, the aftereffect both suggests the vast empty space of the deserted train station and initiates the series of images that Beynish sees. Space, which would normally be *seen* as empty or full, is transformed here into something whose qualities are *heard*. This is one of several instances when sound takes precedence over vision. It is part of the ongoing critique of vision that was taking place in the arts generally at the beginning of the twentieth century.[34]

Alone, feeling "left behind," and unable to leave the big empty barrel of the train station (because he doesn't have the fare for a carriage), Beynish cannot move, but he can imagine and remember, and the open space of the depot becomes full of images: "He could see as vividly as if he were actually there, the shtetl hidden by the horizon."[35] The shtetl, as Leah Garrett points out, the typical market town of Jewish habitation, has no place in "At the Depot." It has disappeared, having been replaced by the train station. The train station also disappears, replaced by the image of the shtetl in Beynish's memory. The empty station serves as the catalyst to his internal dreamscape. Beynish follows the long, narrow street of the shtetl where the herd is being driven, he sees women sitting in the doorways of their houses, waiting for their husbands, and finally he comes to his own house, which has a padlock on the door. "Were he now to arrive, he would try the lock, peer through the closed window into the empty house, and then set out to look for his wife."[36] The motif of empty space appears in this scene, which combines the memory of the past and the imagination of the future. The protagonist arrives and will always too late to meet his wife, who will have already gone. Bergelson uses temporality to describe Beynish's relation to his wife: His failure to arrive in time to see her stands in for his failure generally with regard to her.

Beynish's memory takes him even further back in time to the shtetl of his birth, to the house where he was born and the study house where he spent much of his childhood. Bergelson describes the succession of memories further back in time in terms of a greater distance in space: "and far, far from the other side of the horizon lies another shtetl."[37] Beynish recalls that his father is still a figure of respect in the community because of the wealth that once belonged to *his* father-in-law.

The succession of memories ends in Beynish's return to the place he never left, the "empty train depot," thinking about his "empty, empty" house. The word "empty" (*pust*) serves as a visual and acoustic motif, first introducing the image of the station as an "empty barrel." In the Yiddish original the words for "empty" and "barrel" are alliterative ("eyn . . . puste pas"); the same key term "empty" then marks his wife's house ("in the empty house," "in der puster shtub"), and finally rounds off the figurative journey by uniting the empty station ("at the empty station," "baym pustn vokzal") and the image of his wife's "empty, empty" house ("pust, pust"). The repetition of the word unites the disparate elements of time and place into a rhythmic whole. Making the train station null and void allows for the image of the shtetl to appear to Beynish.

The peculiarities of the protagonist's psychological state, his lack of success as a grain broker, and his physical immobility make him particularly susceptible to his memories, which occupy his attention more than his business dealings, as Mikhail Krutikov shows.[38] Instead of looking ahead to the next deal, Beynish looks back to the details of his own particular life, back to the lives of previous generations. But the qualities that make for a successful trader result in an impoverished perception of the surrounding world, reduced to the absolute minimum of information necessary for the performance of actions. Good businessmen end up merely "reading labels" instead of experiencing the fullness of the surrounding world.[39] This is the major point of Sh. Rudyanski's article about Bergson, "Bergson vegn estetik" (Bergson on aesthetics), which appeared in *Di Yidishe velt* (The Jewish World) in 1913, when Bergelson was editor.

Delay as Narrative Device

Bergson's ideas were profoundly significant for the Russian Formalists, particularly Viktor Shklovsky. In "Art as Device," Shklovsky argued that the purpose of art was to impede the mere recognition of the objects depicted, thereby making perception slow and "laborious." He showed how estrangement and other devices, such as "retardation" (slowing down) of the plot, achieved this end. The emphasis on perception as opposed to mere recognition echoes Bergson, who affirmed that art "dilates our perception."[40]

The use of delay as a feature of narrative is not, of course, new to the early twentieth century. *The Odyssey* is premised on Odysseus's delay in returning to Ithaca. The examples that Shklovsky gives in "Art as Device" are drawn from the Psalms and *War and Peace*. What makes Shklovsky's intervention on the function of delay in narrative specific to the early twentieth century is his linkage of this device to the crisis of perception in his time. Perception had become automatic, and therefore the specific texture of the world was lost. Without delay and estrangement, Shklovsky argues, we merely recognize objects; we fail to perceive them. Shklovsky, Bergson, and Bergelson shared the impetus to restore a fuller engagement with the world from which habit and routinized behavior remove us. For Shklovsky, technological and narrative devices fundamentally change the human subject who uses and is used by them. The de-centering of the human author, both in the literal and the figurative sense, is a key offshoot of the concept of "art as device."

One of the devices that makes Bergelson difficult is the absence of a single omniscient narrator. Avoiding omniscient narration allows Bergelson to distribute the narrative expository function among the characters in the fictitious world the text creates. Both sound and vision can be impeded or distorted so as to make the objects perceived unrecognizable. It is not only the blind, deaf, and mute characters who function as vectors of delay in Bergelson's works but also characters who encounter purely contingent and ordinary obstacles and whose mediating role changes and shifts accordingly. The impeded and altered perceptive capacities of Bergelson's characters thus impede and change the perception of his readers. The world is thereby made strange.

Nineteenth-century realist fiction made use of the go-between and the eavesdropper to create a similar effect. The difference for Bergelson and for other modernist writers is the focus on the process of perception itself. The resulting delay mimes Bergson's model of the time lag between the sensory stimulus and the motor response that allows for recollection to appear. Disability in Bergelson, including deafness, blindness, and muteness—both permanent and temporary—serves as a narrative device to impede the process of reading.

In "At the Depot" Beynish Rubinshteyn often spends his evenings with the silent Itsik. On one occasion, he stays for the night. Itsik rents a room from a peasant who leaves his home every night to go to work. Beynish drifts off to sleep but is suddenly awakened by the sound of someone banging on the window in the other part of the house. Then he hears the sounds of the door being opened and someone entering. This is Avromtshik, a wealthy merchant, come to sleep with the peasant's pretty wife. How Bergelson recounts this episode is important. He indicates unclear sounds that have to be interpreted for us by the protagonist, who first listens to these sounds and then receives an explanation about them from someone else. Itsik functions here as Beynish's hearing device.

In a subsequent episode, Avromtshik marries his new wife and installs her in a nearby house. Again Beynish provides narrative exposition. As in the previous example, the author imposes an obstacle that delays and distorts what Beynish sees and hears and thereby also changes what readers know. The multiple layers of mediation interposed between Bergelson's readers and the events and people he describes constitute a key feature of his narrative style, or what can be termed the interlocking gears of his narrative technology. This technology ensures that we will never hear or see all there is to hear and see; we will never even come close—an app that makes it harder instead of easier to find information. The seemingly endless deferral is both maddening and enticing. Bergelson tantalizes his readers with the promise of a final definitive meaning, of some kind of reconciliation, and we almost arrive at the point of disclosure, but the moment passes, and it turns out that we missed it. Bergelson thus connects the reader's experience to the experience of his characters.

Beynish goes to Avromtshik's house, which is at first dark but then "suddenly illuminated"; at the end, it becomes dark again. It is as if Beynish (and we along with him) have gone to the cinema, where the hall is first dark, then light, then dark again when the film ends. The heroine stands in her bedroom with a lit candle in her hand; in the manner of a surrealist film, "the twin beds, bookcases, and night tables silently and angrily stare back at her."[41] She leans forward to inspect the hostile furniture more closely, but "something" frightens her and she "jumps back," dropping the candle, which goes out. The action in the scene is pantomimed, the heroine's sudden terror conveyed in her exaggerated gestures. Beynish considers a typical melodramatic scenario, imagining that a villain might be lurking in her bedroom, but also considers another alternative: the sight of the twin beds, the reality of the marriage and its consummation are scary enough for her, according to Beynish. Beynish sees what he wants to see: in this case, that marriage to Avromtshik is repulsive.

The second visit to Avromtshik's house is similar. It begins with Beynish "looking in through the window."[42] Bergelson delays his explanation of what Beynish sees, drawing out the moment with a series of questions and answers:

> What was he, Beynish Rubenshteyn, a teacher, thinking?
> "She" was there.
> "What did they say at the station that her name was? Klare, Klare."[43]

When Beynish asks and answers his own question about Avromtshik's wife's name, readers learn for the first time that her name is Klare.

As the episode continues, the object of Beynish's gaze comes more clearly into focus. Readers learn Klare's position in the room ("She was sitting at a table with her face turned toward the window and she was star-ing at something"). Then the narrative camera, so to speak, moves in for a close-up on Klare's face, which in the next shot fills up the screen entirely: "Her earnest dark-complexioned face was so familiar and so very near." Beynish thinks that he already knows Klare: "Her eyes, with their earnest and clever expression, and her entire body, slender and supple—he had seen them always, from before, from childhood on, brrr."[44] A return to the past in some form is the characteristic trait of the protagonist's heightened emo-tion, whether joyful or mournful; nothing important happens just once or only in the moment. To perceive is to remember This holds true equally for the French philosopher Bergson and the Yiddish author Bergelson, who used this motif throughout his writing career. In this scene from "At the Depot," the sound "brrr" indicates shivering from the cold and from desire. Beynish finally knocks on the door and speaks with Klare, initiating a ser-ies of meetings with her. By the end of the novella, she confesses that she married for the wrong reasons.

Beynish and Klare, and the passengers on the train and the station people on the platform, look at each other. Schivelbusch argues that the invention of the train, like the cinema, created a crisis in perception, simi-lar to what Benjamin describes in his essay "The Work of Art in the Age of Mechanical Reproduction." The panoramic view made possible by the train created a superficial familiarity with the changing landscape not premised on a genuine knowledge of any particular setting. Seeing and being seen was a longstanding phenomenon of the theater, but the train generated a new form of fleeting spectacle.

In "At the Depot" Bergelson emphasizes the extent to which the sta-tion people and the passengers are cut off from one another: "They did not know where the passengers had come from or what their destination was, what they [the passengers] did for a living, and what they thought about."[45] Because of their mutual ignorance of each other and the brevity of their encounter, the station people can try to impress the travelers with the sophistication of their appearance. The two processes of withholding and revealing operate in relation to one another; sometimes the faces of the pas-sengers are visible to the station people and sometimes not, and one dimen-sion brings the other into prominence. In one episode, a passenger train arrives at the station, but no one gets off or boards, and there is not even an exchange of glances, because the train is filthy and smoke-covered; the complete opacity and lack of activity create the impression that "each coach held a corpse whose disconsolate relatives were escorting it to some distant burial."[46] Again, Bergelson is not hinting at mass death (or even the figurative death of the shtetl) so much as intensifying the phenomenon of the strange on/off perception created by the train. The experience of perception in these train station scenes is similar to Beynish's off-and-on view of Klare through the window. She is illuminated by her candle, but it suddenly goes out. The train similarly produces a fleeting, flickering spectacle staged between the travelers and the station people. Beynish at Klare's window and the train passengers and the station people exchange looks through a medium that changes how and what they see. Christa Blümlinger argues for a "technical affinity between cinema and the railway" because of the way they both "organize the gaze."[47] Bergelson uses the motif of flickering to show how human actors may free themselves from these organizing matrices. Fluttering, flickering light signals the work of imagination.

The Return Gaze

In the episodes I have just described, the sensory and narrative functions of "looking" and "hearing" assume the affect of the character performing them and take on a life of their own, infused with pleasure, desire, and other emotions. Bergelson uses the figure of the witness/spectator/voyeur/ eavesdropper to introduce delay into the narration and to draw attention to the functions of seeing and hearing as phenomena changed by new technologies and thus heightening the reader's experience of perception. The figure of the voyeur/eavesdropper is the mediator of the general principle of delay and hesitation that Bergson defines as characteristic of consciousness itself. This figure is not always masculine, as will become clear from my discussion of *The End of Everything* (*Nokh alemen*) and other works in which the protagonists are women.

Men look at women, but they also experience the sensation of being looked at. In the scene where Beynish is left alone at the depot, the departing policeman is tempted to say a few words to him, but anticipating the disapproval of the "authorities," he decides to keep silent. Bergelson uses the image of multiple eyes and switches the point of view to a point above his human actor to suggest the sensation of their omnipresence. It seems as if the policeman "were being observed from the station and its tall swaying trees by the thousand piercing eyes of his superiors."[48] Spending the night in Itsik's room, Beynish watches the peasant leave for his work as a night watchman; in Ruth Wisse's translation, "the lantern bobbed under his [the peasant's] arm like a gigantic fiery eye, now fading, now disappearing from view, but never extinguished."[49] The Yiddish original attributes more agency to the "gigantic eye." A more literal translation reads, "One could see long after how the lantern under the arm of the departing peasant quivered, bobbed and sparkled, like a great red, fiery eye, which could go somewhere, hide itself, but could never be extinguished."[50] Playing with the image of the eye of God, Bergelson diffuses the all-knowing and menacing gaze of the omniscient narrator into the surrounding world of inanimate objects. The eye of the lantern resonates with the red light in Itsik's room, associated with the arousing bare arms of the peasant's pretty wife and Beynish's yearnings for his dead wife. As in the train spectacle and the scenes in which Beynish looks through windows, the experience of perception flickers and fades.

The Photograph

Beynish remembers his dead first wife by remembering the "lovely" photograph she had given him as an engagement gift. Remembering a photograph and not the person pictured nests one memory in another. The conventional photographic portrait affirms that the person pictured was present where and when the photograph was taken. The photograph is a direct indexical trace of its sitter; as Thierry de Duve puts it, the "direct causal link . . . is light and its proportionate physical action on silver bromide."[51] That moment, however, no matter its length, cannot return. In order for the image to be processed and for the photograph to become a photograph, the prolongation of the sitter's presence must be broken. The photograph must necessarily follow on the absence of the sitter; it is always in the temporal relation of the aftermath. Marilyn Hirsch says that every photograph has a "retrospective irony" because photography reveals the simultaneous attempt to touch the past and the awareness that this is impossible. Photography already includes an element of belatedness and has an association with death.[52] Indeed, in the early twentieth century, sitting for a photograph meant utter immobility for a prolonged period. Bergelson alludes to this phenomenon in "Joseph Shur," his novella about a young man from the shtetl who comes to the city with what turns out to be the false hope that a marriage is being made for him. He is no match for the sophisticated city Jews, who are conversant with the world of art in Europe and Russia.

Bergelson began the work in 1913 but did not publish it until 1919. Joseph Shur attends a party at the home of a rich relative of the young woman to whom he thinks he will be engaged. He sees a group of six or seven people sitting in deep-slung chairs, "petrified and distracted from fatigue, as if they were being photographed."[53] Here technology disrupts and deadens attentiveness and responsiveness.

In "At the Depot," in contrast, Bergelson resurrects the sitter and the photograph from death. Technology, in this instance, enlivens. As I have already mentioned, when he decided to marry again, Beynish tore up the photograph of his dead wife and hid the pieces in a table. In Itsik's room, he remembers what happened when his second wife found the scraps. She

> picked them up and studied them. Her eye looked up gently and without reproach from one of the scraps. "Whose picture is this?"[54]

In Wisse's translation, it is unclear whose eye looks up gently and without reproach: the first or the second wife. The Yiddish original, however, makes it clear that it is from one of the scraps of the photograph that the eye of the first wife gazes back at Beynish:

> hot zey oyfgehoybn un zey batrakht, af eyn shtikl iz geven nor eyn oyg, vos hot gekukt ruik un on shum forvurf. "Fun vemens bild is dos?"[55]

A more literal translation reads,

> [She] picked them up and studied them. On one piece there was only one eye, which looked up gently, without reproof. "From whose picture is this?"

The second translation better serves to emphasize the grotesque elements in the scene, in particular the violence done to the photograph that resulted in the fragmentation of the human face. This moment in the text is another instance of the penetration of matter by memory; this photograph is a work of art in the age of mechanical reproduction that has not lost its aura, not in the sense of artisanal authenticity, but rather in the sense of the return gaze of an object.[56]

In Beynish's memory, the one-eyed scrap from his wife's photograph uncannily returns his gaze. The photograph bears the traces of the two sets of hands that first tore it to pieces and then reassembled it. It is not only the singularity and haptic qualities of the work here that constitute its aura. The aura of this photographic collage is the return gaze that provokes the combination of dread and relief in its viewer, Beynish. Beynish's own violence looks back at him, the violence he committed against the memory of his wife, both by destroying her photograph and by replacing her so quickly for the sake of the second dowry. And yet the unspoken forgiveness of the glance from the single eye mitigates the violence that was committed against it and the past to which it belongs. This may be nothing more than Beynish's own wish, of course. The Cubist image of Beynish's first wife as a gentle Cyclops nonetheless softens the isolation and self-loathing that the protagonist experiences. Photographs are often understood as bits of frozen time, but Bergelson's photograph makes time flow again.

At the same time that Bergelson published "At the Depot," the Russian Futurist painters David and Vladimir Burliuk (who were brothers) produced works focusing on the image of a single eye. David Burliuk signed the futurist manifesto "A Slap in the Face of Public Taste" that I mentioned earlier; he and his brother both participated in the experimental book of the same title.[57] Vladimir Burliuk's *Eyes* (*Glaza*), dated 1909–10, pictures multiple single eyes as if through a kaleidoscope. David Burliuk's painting *Time* (*Vremia*), dated 1910, shows a one-eyed woman at the center of a multi-perspectival urban backdrop. A railway track penetrates what would have been her left eye, and the railway ties and telegraph poles that would have appeared in the front plane of the picture are thrown into the air, the train cars floating above them.

Time is an example of what Burliuk called "displaced construction." Rhythmic dynamism and the deliberate dislocation of any stable point of view characterize the Burliuks' images. The motif of the single eye indicates the crisis in perception broadly attested in the early twentieth century.[58] In the case of David Burliuk, its use is overdetermined: Burliuk himself had lost an eye in a childhood accident. Bergelson had already published his novella by the time these images were produced. During the period 1910–11 when the author traveled back and forth between Kiev and Odessa, there were major exhibitions of the newest trends in Western European and Russian painting, which included the work of the Burliuks, Kandinsky, Nikolai Kulbin, and others.[59] The crisis in perception was also a tenet of the emerging Cubo-Futurist visual art of the time.

While there is no specific evidence that Bergelson viewed these exhibits, in "Joseph Shur," which Bergelson worked on during this period, there are specific references to paintings, Jewish painters, a woman sculptor who studies in Berne and St. Petersburg, and their reception in the press. At the very least, it is reasonable to conclude that Bergelson was aware of the stir that trends in visual art were creating. In "At the Depot" the spectral illusion of the single eye that looks up from the photograph completes the series of images of single eyes dispersed throughout the narrative. In the opening pages, an old, decrepit beggar sits at the station, left behind by his children, who have immigrated to America. He is blind in one eye and would like to tell someone about his poverty and loneliness, but there is no one to listen to him. Along with this image, the thousands of eyes of the authorities, the judging eye of the peasant's lantern, and the gentle gaze of Beynish's dead wife's single eye make the problem of perception and optics an explicit theme of his text. A range of contradictory emotions, including fear, pleasure, judgment, and forgiveness, change the experience of seeing.

Synesthesia and Metamorphosis

The reason that the surrounding world looks back at the human beings who are part of it stems from the emphasis on mood and atmosphere—*shtimung*. The human *shtimung* infuses the surrounding world; everything is permeated by consciousness. To put this in Bergsonian terms, memory penetrates matter, creating new possibilities for life itself.

Bergelson's use of metamorphosis heightens the sense of the potential animation of inanimate objects in the surrounding world. In "At the Depot" he describes the raised voices—carried from a distance—of two merchants quarreling. The abuse that one merchant shouts at the other provokes this response:

> The long row of lamps bore silent witness to the curse. In each of them the little flames bobbed and nodded slowly like so many tiny human heads, just as if that unknown individual out in the dark were to testify and they would respond to him: "We heard, we heard."[60]

The resemblance between the quivering little flames and the shape of human heads provokes the imaginary courtroom scene. As in the scene of the passenger train and the train station people, and Beynish and Klare at the window, the beginning and cessation of a visual experience—the very process of flickering—signifies the beginning of an act of imagination that is transformative. The visual impression of the quivering lantern flames becomes a sound impression, the sound of their voices speaking. The perception of a set of visual qualities registers by means of the perception of another set of qualities. Bergelson's use of synesthesia corresponds to Bergson's point about the intermingling of different qualities in time rather than the juxtaposition of distinct entities in space. The greater the intensity of the experience, the more different sense organs respond to it and the more varied my experience of it. For Bergelson, it's not merely a question of the phenomena of experience; it is also the relation between human beings and the world. The transformation of the lantern flames into little human heads that acknowledge and answer the human cry amounts to an uncongealing of the surrounding world, a form of resurrection. The lantern flames that have "heard" the human cry of anger suggests the possibility of reconciliation that is otherwise unavailable. The "help" that the frozen train depot seeks but does not find can be glimpsed in this passage.

"At the Depot" infuses the inorganic matter of the train depot with the longing and desire—the *shtimung*—of the human beings who inhabit the "frozen" and "dead" spaces of the unhappy present. Art, both visual and verbal, restores the flow within and between the surrounding world and the human being, revealing the rhythm of things as it uses rhythm to communicate directly with viewers and readers. Bergelson does not pit the machine ensemble of the modern landscape against the human being but rather links the two together more closely. The train and other inanimate objects have more pity on Beynish than his fellow merchants. Bergelson's protagonist, in his very failure as a grain broker, his delay in making the right deal at the right time, reexperiences the past in memories that overtake him in solitude, when the train depot seems to him to be a vast empty space. His distracted gaze, bad for business but good for a peculiar receptivity to the surrounding world, makes the uncanny return glance of objects possible.

Reawakening perception is not limited to enhancing our aesthetic appreciation of objects in the world, by intensifying sight, hearing, or touch, or, as Shklovsky puts it, making the stone "stony" again. Perception also additionally involves a form of attention that has ethical implications, since it creates a relation between the perceiver and the perceived. The late nineteenth-century Austrian art historian Alois Riegl defined *Stimmung* as the unifying ambience of a given painting, which goes beyond its frame to draw in the beholder. The painting engages the viewer in an emotional relationship; the artwork "looks" at the beholder. As Margaret Olin aptly puts it, "Art does not depict a relationship, but *performs* it with the beholder."[61] In his discussion of the Dutch landscape artist Jacob von Ruisdael, Riegl stresses both the activity of the beholder and the activity of the objects depicted in the work. In one painting, houses "gaze *at* the beholder"; in another, the sky peering through the trees "looks at the beholder with hundreds of eyes."[62] Riegl's 1902 discussion of Dutch portraiture also places great stress on the participation of the beholder, who has to "complete" the action that the painting only suggests; the "participatory attention or compassion" of the viewer was Rembrandt's overarching goal.[63] Riegl's work on Dutch landscape and portraiture suggests the ethical underpinning of the aesthetic encounter, later developed by both Buber and Bakhtin.[64] Both theorists emphasize the relationship between subjects as constitutive of subjectivity. The demand for an answer from the other is a central concern for Bergelson, not only in work that explicitly raise the question of justice in a legal setting, but also in work in which the relations between human beings are paramount, as I will show in the next chapter.

The question of judgment and justice, and the fundamental outline of answering the other and answering for the other, emerges in "At the Depot." Legal language about taking testimony appears in the hallucinatory scene in which the depot's lanterns take on the form of little human heads that say, to no one in particular, "We have heard, we have heard." They are answering the half-blind man who wants to tell the story of his suffering, to whom no one listens, and they are also answering all those, like Beynish and Klare, who share the very human desire to be heard. Legal language also appears in the "judgment" (*mishpet*) against Beynish, who receives a two-week jail sentence for assaulting another merchant.

In "At the Depot," inaction makes enhanced perception possible. Heightened perception is not limited to seeing, and when sight is involved, it is not the all-knowing gaze of power. Seeing takes place within a framework of reciprocity. The *shtimung* of the work suggests both a state of immobility and the possibility for renewal. Congealed time can start moving again. The penetration of human qualities into objects in the world intensifies the relation between the self and the world: the photograph of Beynish's dead wife looks back at him, the bobbing heads of the lantern flames listen to him. The relation between technological devices and the human being is not a rigid barrier but rather a porous membrane, through which the qualities of things, human beings, and the surrounding world intermingle with one another.

In *The End of Everything*, Bergelson takes his inquiry about time and perception in a new artistic direction. Like Beynish Rubinshteyn, Mirl Hurvits is unwilling to act, but she sees and hears what others do not. In this novel, there is less metamorphosis and more belatedness. Mirl arrives too late for the main action of her own life. Instead of mere inaction, the failure to do, she actively undoes what has already been completed. She desperately searches the past to find the cause of her unhappiness, but she is too late. Her life unfolds in a particular time zone that permeates every dimension of her experience. The best term for this time zone is the aftereffect.

Notes

1. David Bergelson, "Arum vokzal," in *Geklibene verk*, vol. 1 (Vilnius: B. Kletskin, 1929), 7. This is my translation. For an English translation of the entire work, see Ruth Wisse, "At the Depot," in *A Shtetl and Other Yiddish Novellas* (New York: Behrman House, 1973), 81–139. I will refer to the Yiddish original when the translation is mine and in all other cases to Wisse.

2. For a discussion, see Mary Ann Doane, *The Emergence of Cinematic Time: Modernity, Contingency, the Archive* (Cambridge, MA: Harvard University Press, 2002), 177.

3. In Dostoevsky's *Idiot*, Lebedev interprets the new network of railways as signs of the coming apocalypse; Tolstoy's Anna Karenina is killed by a train, and his Pozdnyshev is doomed to remain on the train forever, confessing his murder of his wife to the passengers. For studies of the image of the train in Chekhov see Stephen Baehr, "The Locomotive and the Giant: Power in Chekhov's 'Anna on the Neck,'" *Slavic and East European Journal* 39, no. 1 (1995), 29–37; and Stephen Baehr, "The Machine in Chekhov's Garden: Progress and Pastoral in the Cherry Orchard," *Slavic and East European Journal* 43, no. 1 (1999), 99–121. For the positive and negative image of train travel in works by Abramovitsh, Sholem Aleichem, and Bergelson, see Leah Garrett, *Journeys Beyond the Pale: Yiddish Travel Writing in the Modern World* (Madison: University of Wisconsin Press, 2003), 90–122. Another discussion of train imagery is in Joseph Sherman, "Bergelson and Chekhov: Convergences and Departures," in *The Yiddish Presence in European Literature: Inspiration and Interaction*, ed. Joseph Sherman and Ritchie Robertson (London: Legenda, 2005), 117–33.

4. As Leah Garrett shows. For her discussion of "At the Depot" in the context of Yiddish travel literature and the train, see Garrett, *Journeys Beyond the Pale: Yiddish Travel Writing in the Modern World*, 91–120.

5. Deleuze characterizes expressionism as "the subordination of the extensive to intensity." See Gilles Deleuze, *Cinema 1: The Movement Image* (London: The Athlone Press, 1986), 52.

6. Shmuel Niger, "Briv fun Dovid Bergelson," *Zamlbikher* 8 (1952), 91.

7. A. Vayter (Ayzik-Mayer Devenishki), Bergelson's first critic, noted the "mystical character" of the train station. See A. Vayter, "David Bergelsons 'Arum vokzal,'" in *Oysgeklibene shriftn*, ed. Shmuel Razshanski (Buenos Aires: Literatur-gezelshaft baym Yivo in Argentine, 1971), 293.

8. The article originally appeared in the Yiddish journal *Der fraynd* in 1909. I used Shmuel Niger, "A nayer," *Literarishe bleter* 42 (October 19, 1934), 683–85.

9. Sh. Niger, "Briv fun Dovid Bergelson," *Zamlbikher* 8 (1952), 91. For another translation of this passage and discussion of its meaning, see Daniela Mantovan, "Language and Style in Nokh Alemen (1913): Bergelson's Debt to Flaubert," in *David Bergelson: From Modernism to Socialist Realism*, ed. Joseph Sherman and Gennady Estraikh (Oxford: Legenda, 2007), 88–112.

10. See Nahum Stuchkoff, *Der oytser fun der yidisher shprakh* (New York: YIVO Institute for Jewish Research, 1991), 252, 544.

11. See Letter to Sh. Niger, 1919, RG 360, Shmuel Niger, Box 7, Folder 9e, YIVO Archive.

12. Leo Spitzer's 1944 study of the German *Stimmung* traces the history of the term to Classical and Christian concepts of "world harmony." The end of the eighteenth century, according to Spitzer, marked the end of the "blossoming life of *Stimmung* under the weight of the modern mechanistic spirit." Leo Spitzer, "Classical and Christian Ideas of World Harmony: Prolegomena to an Interpretation of the Word 'Stimmung' (Part II)," *Traditio* 3 (1945), 316.

13. Avraham Koralnik, "R. Nakhmen's mayses," *Dos yidishe folk* 1, no. 30 (1906), 1–4.

14. Yankev Glatshteyn, A. Leyeles, and N. Minkov, "In zikh," in *In zikh: A zamlung introspektive lider*, ed. M. Apranel (New York: M. N. Mayzel, 1920), 5–27.

15. Maks Erik, *Konstruktsiye-Shtudyen* (Warsaw: Farlag arbeter-kheym, 1924), 39.

16. Hans Ulrich Gumbrecht, "Reading for the Stimmung? About the Ontology of Literature Today," *Boundary 2* 35, no. 3 (2008): 213–21. For a fuller discussion, see Hans Ulrich Gumbrecht, *Atmosphere, Mood, Stimmung: On a Hidden Potential of Literature* (Stanford, CA: Stanford University Press, 2012).

17. Bergelson, "Arum vokzal," 9.

18. Niger argues for aggravation, nail-biting, as the dominant *shtimung* of the work. See Niger, "A nayer."

19. Zey hobn zikh dortn ruik getrunken tey, pamelekh geshmeykhlt tsu di shtub-mentshn, gehaltn a kind af di hent, dertsu getsmoket, geredt, kidey dem troyer fun yener zayt baloykhtenem fentser tsu fartraybn, hot zikh der troyer fun dortn tsum vokzal farklibn un do farshpreyt zayn moyre-shkhoyredike shlite. Tsuzamen mit der glaykher relsn-shnur un hoykhe slupes fun telegraf hot er zikh alts hekher un hekher af der erd gedrapet un tsuzamen mit zey shtekn geblibn inem vaytn ek himl, vos in horizont. Bergelson, "Arum vokzal," 31.

20. Wolfgang Schivelbusch, *The Railway Journey: Trains and Travel in the 19th Century* (New York: Urizen, 1979), 24.

21. Bergelson, "Arum vokzal," 81.

22. For an English translation, see David Hofshteyn, "Grief," in *From Revolution to Repression: Soviet Yiddish Writing 1917–1952*, ed. Joseph Sherman (Nottingham, UK: Five Leaves Publications, 2012), 66–90.

23. For a discussion of the Kiev Yiddish literary scene in the late nineteenth and early twentieth centuries, see Gennady Estraikh, "From Yehupets Jargonists to Kiev Modernists: The Rise of a Yiddish Literary Centre, 1880s–1914," *East European Jewish Affairs* 30, no. 1 (2000): 17–38.

24. For a discussion of Chagall's use of Yiddish text in his images, including other illustrations to Hofshteyn's poem cycle, see Gennady Estraikh, "From Yehupets Jargonists to Kiev Modernists: The Rise of a Yiddish Literary Centre, 1880s–1914," *East European Jewish Affairs* 30, no. 1 (2000): 17–38. An in-depth analysis of Chagall's graphics for the Hofshteyn cycle can be found in Seth Wolitz, "Chagall's Last Soviet Performance: The Graphics for Troyer, 1922," *Jewish Art* 21–22 (1995–1996), 95–115.

25. For a study that analyzes the mood of St. Petersburg at the turn of the century in these terms, see Mark Steinberg, *Petersburg Fin de Siècle* (New Haven, CT: Yale University Press, 2011).

26. For emotions as a source of revolutionary Jewish activity, see Inna Shtakser, *The Making of Jewish Revolutionaries in the Pale of Settlement* (Hampshire, UK: Palgrave Macmillan, 2014), 101–30. A recent and important discussion of Kishiniev can be found in Steven J. Zipperstein, *Pogrom: Kishinev and the Tilt of History* (New York: Liveright, 2018).

27. Bergelson, "Arum vokzal," 54.

28. For a discussion, see Yekhezkel Dobrushin, *Dovid Bergelson* (Moscow: Der Emes, 1947), 25–27.

29. Bergelson, "Arum vokzal," 20.

30. David Bergelson, *The End of Everything*, trans. Joseph Sherman, New Yiddish Library (New Haven, CT: Yale University Press, 2009), 36. For the Yiddish, see David Bergelson, *Nokh alemen*, vol. 2 (Vilnius: B. Kletskin, 1929), 58.

31. Anton Chekhov, *Five Plays*, trans. Ronald Hingley (New York: Oxford University Press, 1977), 90. For another comparison of Chekhov and Bergelson that emphasizes their common depiction of a collapsing way of life, see Sherman, "Bergelson and Chekhov: Convergences and Departures" (ibid). Sherman also stresses Bergelson's artistic innovation.

32. For a discussion of Markish's "Azoy in a vinterik vistn vokzal" in the context of Hebrew and Yiddish modernist movements, including expressionism, see Jordan Finkin, "Constellating Hebrew and Yiddish Avant-Gardes," *Journal of Modern Jewish Studies* 8, no. 1 (2009): 1–22.

33. Wisse, "At the Depot," 93. The Yiddish: "Nokh im hot a shtark klap geton di tir, glaykh vi der vokzal volt nisht bashtanen fun khadorim un koridorn, nor fun eyn groys un pust pas." Bergelson, "Arum vokzal," 20.

34. As Martin Jay argues, Bergson's attack on the notion of spatialized time was key to this critique. Martin Jay, *Downcast Eyes: The Denigration of Vision in Twentieth-Century French Thought* (Berkeley: University of California Press, 1993), 186–203.

35. Wisse, "At the Depot," 94. I have slightly modified the translation.

36. Wisse, "At the Depot," 94.

37. Bergelson, "Arum vokzal," 21.

38. Mikhail Krutikov, *Yiddish Fiction and the Crisis of Modernity, 1905–1914* (Stanford, CA: Stanford University Press, 2001), 41.

39. Martin Jay, *Downcast Eyes: The Denigration of Vision in Twentieth-Century French Thought* (Berkeley: University of California Press, 1993), 186–206.

40. Viktor Shklovsky, *Theory of Prose* (Normal, IL: Dalkey Archive Press, 1990), 6. Henri Bergson, *An Introduction to Metaphysics: The Creative Mind* (Totowa, NJ: Littlefield, Adams, 1965), 157.

41. Bergelson, "Arum vokzal," 41.

42. Bergelson, "Arum vokzal," 44.

43. Bergelson, "Arum vokzal," 44. Wisse's translation shortens the passage by omitting the question and answer, thus speeding up the narrative.

44. Bergelson, "Arum vokzal," 45.

45. Bergelson, "Arum vokzal," 8.

46. Wisse, "At the Depot," 121.

47. Christa Blümlinger, "Lumière, the Train and the Avant-Garde," in *The Cinema of Attractions Reloaded*, ed. Wanda Strauven (Amsterdam: Amsterdam University Press, 2006), 245.

48. Wisse, "At the Depot," 94. The Yiddish: "fun dem gantsn leydikn plats un hoykhe shoklendike boymer voltn af im aroysgekukt toyznter ofene oygn fun zayn natshalstvo." Bergelson, "Arum vokzal," 20.

49. Wisse, "At the Depot," 97.

50. In Yiddish: "M'hot nokh lang gezen vi baym avekgeyendikn tsitert der lamtern unter orem, beygt zikh un finklt, vi a groys royt un fayeridik oyg, vos kon ergets avekgeyn, zikh ergets bahaltn, ober keynmol nisht oysgeloshn vern." Bergelson, "Arum vokzal," 24.

51. Thierry de Duve, "Time Exposure and Snapshot: The Photograph as Paradox," *October* 5 (Summer 1978): 114.

52. Miriam Hansen, for example, speaks of the "photograph's constitutive relation to death." Miriam Bratu Hansen, "Benjamin's Aura," *Critical Inquiry*, Winter 2008: 341.

53. The Yiddish reads, "Farshteynert un fartrakht, glaykh zey fotografirn zikh." See David Bergelson, "Yoysef Shur," in *Geklibene verk*, vol. 3 (Vilnius: B. Kletskin, 1929), 117–18. The English translation omits the reference to photography. See Irving Howe and Eliezer Greenberg, *Ashes Out of Hope: Fiction by Soviet-Yiddish Writers* (New York: Schocken Books, 1977), 67.

54. Wisse, "At the Depot," 97.

55. Bergelson, "Arum vokzal," 26.

56. Benjamin's famous essay of 1936 laments the decline of aura, understood as consisting of its uniqueness, but Miriam Hansen shows that the term in Benjamin is far more complex than this definition would allow; the history of aura "runs from early romanticism through Henri Bergson," and throughout this trajectory, the "ability to return the gaze is already dormant in, if not constitutive of, the object." See Hansen, "Benjamin's Aura," 341.

57. David Burliuk studied in Germany, where he exhibited with the Blue Rider group; he lived and worked in Japan, and he spent over forty years in the United States. For a brief discussion of his literary work, see Sergei Gollerbakh, "David Burliuk i futurizm glazami nashego vremeni," *Novyi zhurnal* 256 (2009): 194–201.

58. For a discussion, see Jonathan Crary, *Suspensions of Perception: Attention, Spectacle, and Modern Culture* (Cambridge, MA: MIT Press, 1999), 281–359.

59. For an overview of these exhibits, see John E. Bowlt, *Russian Art of the Avant-Garde: Theory and Criticism, 1902–1934* (New York: Viking Press, 1976), 17–19.

60. Wisse, "At the Depot," 105. I have modified the translation. I wish to thank Zachary Baker for his help with this difficult passage. The Yiddish reads, "A lange shure fun angetsundene lampternes zenen geven shvaygndike eydes fun der klole. In yedern fun zey hot pamelekh getsitern der klayner flam, zikh genoygt un geshoklt, vi klayne mentshlekhe kep, glaykh vi yener umbavuster, vos iz in der finster, volt bay zey goyve eydes zayn un zey voltn im entfern: 'Gehert, gehert.'" See Bergelson, "Arum vokzal," 39.

61. Margaret Olin, *Forms of Representation in Alois Riegl's Theory of Art* (University Park: Pennsylvania State University Press, 1992), 168.

62. Alois Riegl and Christopher Heuer, "Jacob van Ruisdael, *Translation* 4, no. 2 (2012): 158.

63. Alois Riegl and Benjamin Binstock, "Excerpts from 'The Dutch Group Portrait,'" *October* 74 (1995): 18.

64. In 1896 Buber matriculated for two semesters at the Vienna Franz-Joseph University and took art history with Riegl. See Gerhard Wehr, *Martin Buber: Leben-Werk-Wirkung* (Munich: Random House, 2010), 45. Olin discusses Buber in Olin, *Forms of Representation in Alois Riegl's Theory of Art*, 167; for Bakhtin, see xviii–xix. For a comparison of Buber and Bakhtin, see Nina Perlina, "Mikhail Bakhtin and Martin Buber: Problems of Dialogic Imagination," *Studies in Twentieth Century Literature* 9 (1984): 13–28.

2

THE AFTEREFFECT

A stranger lives my life,
My love is a fantasy of love,
Dreaming, I wander outside life and love
I am only a reflection reflecting my abyss.

Es lebt in mayn lebn a lebn a fremder,
Es libt in mayn libe a libender troym,
Ikh kholem bloyz lebn, ikh kholem bloyz libe
Ikh bin nor an apbild, vos s'shpiglt mayn thoym.

Yekhezkel Dobrushin, *Farnakhtn* (1911–1914)[1]

THE EPIGRAPH FOR THIS CHAPTER COMES FROM A collection of poetry by Yekhezkel Dobrushin (1883–1953) titled *Dusk* (*Farnakhtn*), published in the early years of the twentieth century. Dobrushin would go on to a career as a Soviet Yiddish critic and literary consultant for the Moscow State Yiddish Theater. A year before his arrest in 1948, Dobrushin's book-length study of Bergelson (in Yiddish) was published in Moscow. Bergelson championed the young Dobrushin's work, praising it as full of thought and "feeling" (*shtimung*). Dobrushin had emerged from a shtetl environment to be educated in Europe, and according to Bergelson, his time abroad moderated and developed his poetic sensibilities. In letters written from 1910 to 1912 to his friend the critic Shmuel Niger, Bergelson explained that for both the heroine of his new novel— *The End of Everything*—and for the Jewish intelligentsia generally, "the time was twilight"; "this is often my feeling," he went on to say.[2] Dobrushin's poetry expressed this mood. My life is only the shadow of another life; my life is not real life and it is not mine; I have been thrust out of my own existence.

It is a commonplace to define modernity as the denaturing and alienation of the human being under the conditions of urbanization, capitalism, and industrialized labor. Bergson's theories of intuition and creative evolution arose in part as a response against these social and economic forces. The atrophy of experience, the crisis of perception, and the condition of shock constitute the modern experience, according to Walter Benjamin, writing in the interwar period.[3] Bergelson reaches similar conclusions, making the loss of experience the central theme and organizing principle of his first novel, *The End of Everything* (*Nokh alemen*). It has been called the first modern Yiddish novel. Yet few of the modern conditions associated with the loss of experience can be found in the small shtetl and the "provincial capital" (Kiev) where the novel is set: capitalism has yet to arrive; there is no mass-scale industrialization; science with its rational abstractions is not yet ascendant; and while certain urban mores have an impact on the heroine, who has an adulterous affair, urban shock as a whole is lacking. Everything in the novel nonetheless suggests the aftermath of some unknown and overwhelming loss. The spatial metaphors of dispossession and exile in Dobrushin's poem appear in Bergelson's novel in temporal terms: the heroine's life is her afterlife. This particular temporal quality is the sense in which I understand *The End of Everything* to be both a novel about modernity and a modernist novel.

In *A Singular Modernity*, Frederic Jameson refers to the revolutionary year 1913, which alludes to both political and artistic events, including the revolution in Mexico, the beginning of revolution in Ireland, the massive strike in St. Petersburg, the publication of the first volume of Proust's *In Search of Time Past*, and the performance of the first futurist opera, *Victory Over the Sun*.[4] 1913 was also the year that Bergelson published *The End of Everything*. There is no reference to political revolution in the novel, and although the text plays with the sounds of words, there are other Bergelson works that use futurist techniques to a far greater extent, which I discuss in chapter 5. Finally, unlike Proust, the chief protagonist of *The End of Everything* does not remember the past. Yet this novel is artistically significant—and, I would add, revolutionary—because of its relentless insistence on the experience of what comes after the end of everything.

As I showed in chapter 1, the mood of "At the Depot" lends a particular quality to its ambient space. *Troyer*, sadness, infuses the railroad ties and the telegraph poles as they meet on the horizon. When in *The End of Everything* Bergelson returns to the same space he had used in "At the Depot," the telegraph poles and railway ties where passenger trains go by, it is "stories" that infuse the landscape with sorrow and, importantly, their lingering aftereffect. Bergelson describes the passage of trains through the space and the way they "left behind in the surrounding silence of the fields the mournful echo of many unhappy tales begun but not concluded."[5] The stories have no ending because their actors are the passengers in the train, which is in motion, departing before the endings of the stories can happen or be told. Readers of this work, like the characters standing at the platform while the train passes, are left with the strands of these stories trailing after the train. Readers and characters thus experience the palpable qualities of time as aftermath.

Bergelson's first novel set the pattern he would use for his entire corpus of work. It opens in medias res: the engagement in a small shtetl that has "dragged on for four long years" finally ends. Already in the first sentence a period of time expands beyond its usual and accepted boundaries. The waiting period of betrothal that usually elapses fairly quickly has gone on too long and does not result in a marriage. Mirl Hurvits sends back the financial agreement, the *tnoyem*. At the end of part I, her former fiancé, Velvl Burnes, asks, quoting the novel's title, "Did this mean that the betrothal was really over, that this was the end of everything?"[6] In this instance the phrase "*nokh alemen*," the end of everything, is used as a noun; later, it will function as an adverb, suggesting that events in the world of this novel have the temporal quality of "after the end."

The Temporalization of Emotion

Bergelson's short story "Impoverished" ("*Yordim*"), written between 1909 and 1910, provides a transition between "At the Depot" and *The End of Everything*.[7] Like "At the Depot," the story uses the train to indicate mobility and change, from the perspective of those who remain behind. Like "At the Depot," the temporal effect of "afterwardsness" permeates the text. A man, who was once rich and important, now blind, spends his days lying in bed; his two unmarried daughters live with him. His successful son Shmuel has long ago moved away and sends money to support the family. When the younger daughter, Tsvie, finds life unbearable, she embarks on a frenzy of housecleaning, which culminates in days of loud weeping and cursing: "God in heaven, we're rotting here before we're even in our shrouds."[8] On one occasion, Shmuel sends a letter suggesting that he has found a match for the younger sister, but it comes to nothing. Then he sends a telegram requesting that the family meet him at the train station. They think the match is on again. The sisters bake cookies to give their brother and, dressing with care, set off for the station with their father.

They arrive very early and (ironically) have to wait hours for their brother's express train. He only has time to greet them quickly between the second and third bells. Here, as in "At the Depot," the rushing train leaves the shtetl dwellers behind: the moment of reunion and the promise of joy for which they have been long waiting passes so quickly that it is as if it never took place; the sisters return home having forgotten to give Shmuel the cookies. In a parody of the biblical story of Isaac on his deathbed, the blind father stretches out his hand to grasp his son's, but Shmuel leaves so abruptly that the father's fingers remain quivering in the air even after the express train's departure. The quickened pace of the express train and the slowed time of the shtetl jar against one another. The family sees an extended, beautiful sunset on their way home, one reminiscent of the sunset in Givon. In the Bible, Joshua commands the sun not to set in Givon, so that Israel has daylight by which to destroy its enemies. God, people, and nature act in concert. In "Impoverished," in contrast, the unnaturally long sunset only confirms the sisters' desolation: their peculiar time zone is so dilated that nothing can happen in it; they are utterly out of sync with the rest of the world. Bergelson will use the image of the slow sunset again in *The End of Everything*, *Descent*, and *Judgment*.

In "Impoverished" and other works of this period, Bergelson is, to be sure, tracking the economic decline of the shtetl. He is not suggesting, however, that there once was a time when it thrived and that his readers ought to return to the good times of the past. While "Impoverished" has none of the expressionist motifs of "At the Depot," no fiery eyes or photographs that stare back at the spectator, nonetheless it is not a mimetic, realist rendering of the shtetl in 1909. In the small scale of the short story "Impoverished," Bergelson introduces a technique that will be the centerpiece of *The End of Everything* and other works. Bergelson uses expressions of time to signal the emotions of disappointment and frustration; one or another character is described as "as if late for the Sabbath" or "late for a wedding." The failure to experience joy and renewal is couched in terms of mistiming. As Wolitz puts it, "Chronological time transmogrifies into psychological time."[9] I call this the temporalization of emotion, an approach that I take from Jean Laplanche, who wrote about the "temporalization of the human being."[10] In this chapter I introduce, in addition to

Henri Bergson's notion of the openness of the past, other temporal models emerging in the same period. For Freud the past is important but opaque, and instead of providing new possibilities, as in Bergson, it rather tends to constrain the future. Laplanche aptly argues that Freud's work offers a theory of time, namely "afterwardsness" (in German, *Nachträglichkeit*).[11] Psychoanalysis, in addition to being a theory of subjectivity and sexuality, is also a theory about time, and one in which belatedness plays a key role, as Laplanche and others have argued.[12] Bergelson, like his contemporaries Bergson and Freud, was also interested in time, and in *The End of Everything* he proposes his own version of "afterwardsness."

Endings and belatedness imply a relation between different moments of time. An event's timeliness or untimeliness is always relative to something else. When actors find themselves perpetually late, it suggests that whatever interlocking grid that kept them abreast of one another's clocks and calendars has come undone. When Mirl visits the midwife Shats, who talks about her friend the Hebrew poet Herts, the room is so quiet that it seems to be "very late" (*shtark shpet*), as if time had sped up in the midwife's room separately from its normal passage elsewhere. Yet time has not sped up there but rather slowed down to the point where "you could hear the dying fall of the carefully considered words."[13] The description draws attention to the arc of the articulation, utterance, and then fading away of the sounds of the words, almost as if the listeners were moving away from the source of the sound, in a Doppler effect. In the midwife's room, however, everything and everyone is absolutely still. Bergelson's emphasis on the dying fall of the sounds of the words resonates with Bergson's notion of duration, as in the previous example of the trailing threads of the train stories.

It is important that Bergelson did not title his first novel with a reference to its heroine, Mirl Hurvits, or to the setting of the story. Indeed another character in the novel, the Hebrew poet Herts, suggests an alternative title when he calls Mirl "a small-shtetl tragedy."[14] Instead of a reference to a particular place, however, Bergelson refers instead to time and to endings; *nokh alemen*, "the end of everything," can also be rendered as "when everything ended" (the Russian translation of the title is *Kogda vse konchilos'*), and in addition, "after the end of everything."[15] As the examples above show, Bergelson is thinking about delay and deferral in relation to the makeup of the individual taken separately and in relation to broader issues of modernity, history, Jewish literature, and the Jewish people. The personal or existential problem of the heroine's belatedness with respect to her own life resonates with the political, historical, and theological problem of the belatedness of the Jews. The Jewish press and Bergelson himself, in his correspondence and fiction, were preoccupied with the "new Jew." The need to define the new Jew meant that already existing Jews were old and obsolete. In a letter from 1912, for example, Bergelson characterized his historical moment as "a time when the new Jew is being born."[16]

The conflicting elements of arrival, birth, twilight, and belatedness coexist in one temporal fabric. These elements will reappear and recombine in new ways throughout Bergelson's writing. In *The End of Everything*, as in "At the Depot," the train and the *shtimung* are mobilized in service of these larger concerns. Unlike "At the Depot" and in a major departure from Yiddish literature up to this point, the figure who embodies the pull forward toward some undefined future life and the fall back to the obsolete but powerful patterns of the past is a woman: Mirl Hurvits.

Mirl Hurvits, the twenty-one-year-old only daughter of Gedalye and Gitl Hurvits, ends her four-year-long engagement to Velvl Burnes, a successful businessman and factory owner. She takes up wandering around the shtetl with the lame student Lipkis, without any intention of a serious relationship with him. She had previously been in love with Nosn Heller, who lives in the city and plans to publish a penny newspaper. Shats the midwife, who lives in a room on the outskirts of town, tells her about the Hebrew poet Herts, with whom Shats had previously been in love. Mirl's father, Gedalye, a scholarly man without a head for financial affairs, is on the verge of bankruptcy when Mirl, in order to save him, agrees to a new engagement to Shmul Zaydenovski, a man from a nouveau-riche family. Herts appears in the shtetl, and Mirl falls in love with him. After nearly canceling her second engagement, Mirl goes through with the marriage to Shmul, having decided that she can be married "for a while." On the verge of getting a divorce, Mirl learns that she is pregnant. She has an abortion and moves out of her husband's house, returning to her shtetl only after her father has died and her mother has left. At the novel's conclusion, Mirl departs, but whether it is to journey to another town or to commit suicide is left unclear. Her unfinished story thus becomes one of the half-completed train stories whose echoes we hear in the opening of the novel. The end circles back to the beginning.

Calendars, Clocks, and Seasons

Because calendars, clocks, seasons, and cycles play a key role, a few words about time references and the use of Jewish time in particular in *The End of Everything* are in order.[17] The novel begins in the Jewish month of Elul, which takes place in the fall; during this month, the Jewish New Year takes place, as well as Yom Kippur, the day of repentance. The busy harvest and threshing time of the agricultural cycle, occurring in the same fall season, is a welcome distraction for the jilted Velvl Burnes. The life cycle events of birth, marriage, and death unfold according to the Jewish tradition of the era. Gitl observes the seven-day mourning period after Gedalye dies, but Mirl does not. The period of betrothal, as I have already shown, is prolonged, as is the time when parents might expect their children to marry. In the opening of the novel, Velvl Burnes's mother wonders whether she will live to see her son married. Mirl, cut off from the regularly occurring cycles of the Jewish calendar, is also remarkably unaware of the meaning of the delay in her monthly cycle. It is her mother-in-law who informs her that she is pregnant.

The novel's temporal references include some that can be found in any work of fiction of the time. The train and telegraph impose their own schedule; for example, a character only has an hour and a quarter left before the train leaves; someone travels eighteen hours on the train; at the end of the novel, Mirl desperately waits for a telegram from Herts. She reads a book about women in different historical epochs; another character, Montshik, reads Julius Leppert's history of culture in a Hebrew translation. Bergelson's heroine also talks about the need for "new people" to be born, an allusion to Nikolai Chernyshevsky's *What Is to Be Done: Stories of the New People*, published in the early 1860s. *The End of Everything*, like all works of fiction, calls upon the naturally occurring alterations of night and day and of the seasons of the year. Bergelson, however, dilates the regular cycle; for example, "The dark beginning of the Elul day approaching silently and sadly from the northeast corner of the sky, slowly but steadily drawing closer, mutely drove away the final moments of the pale, lingering night."[18] In Yiddish the night is *farshpetikter*; it is late, having overextended its stay, each of its moments resisting departure.

Bergelson also takes note of the alternation between the weekday and the Sabbath and the succession of Jewish and non-Jewish holidays. In the embedded story by the Hebrew poet Herts, forgetting to keep track of the distinction between the Sabbath and the weekday indicates utter disorientation. When the normal order is disrupted, Bergelson uses the Jewish calendar to indicate the disturbance. Mirl and her husband's part of the house receives a fresh coat of paint, which requires the furniture to be moved, and it ends up in her room: "Everything here resembled a bizarre pre-Passover eve that had fallen in the middle of the month of Elul."[19] Passover takes place in the spring and Elul in the fall. Bergelson refers to the daily cycle of Jewish prayer, specifically mentioning the afternoon and evening prayers, the late-night "third watch," and the second portion of the Sabbath and holiday liturgy, the *musef* service, which he alliteratively characterizes as having its own "tired mood" (*mide musef shtimung*).[20] Although Mirl does not participate in the observances mandated by the religious calendar, she expresses emotion using its terms. She articulates her fear that her entire life will be joyless by saying that "her life dragged by in such a workaday fashion . . . It had been workaday right up to this midwinter Christian holiday and it would go on and on being workaday."[21]

The "midwinter Christian holiday" is Christmas, a time of redemption, which Mirl, as a Jew, does not celebrate or experience, but Jewish holidays have fallen out of her calendar as well. The key term in the passage is *vokhedik*, which I have translated as "workaday." It is repeated three times. Mirl worries that her life will be *vokhedik*, composed only of weekdays and without festive Sabbaths and holidays. The regular alteration of workdays and holidays is the fundamental temporal feature of Jewish religious life; the clothes that are worn, the foods that are eaten, the behaviors and affects that are prescribed and proscribed all depend on this calendar. The distinction between the week (*vokh*) on the one side and the Sabbath and holidays on the other is critical to Mirl's reflection on the course of her life up to now and her perspectives for the future. This is a temporalization of emotion in a specifically Jewish key.

Bergelson refers to this fundamental temporal structure throughout the novel, using it in miniature narratives whose sole function is to express a particular mood or combination of emotions. For example, Mirl is on the way to a party at the home of a wealthy Jewish businessman. She encounters the sight of the Jew's refinery against the backdrop of the surrounding houses, whose inhabitants are less wealthy and satisfied than the refinery owner. This is how Bergelson describes the mood the scene provokes:

> And the surrounding houses with their alien appearance awakened a very particular kind of disquiet, the mournful Friday evening disquiet of a Jew who'd been delayed in returning home in time to welcome the Sabbath, who in the sanctified twilight was still lugging himself and his wagon through the deep mud on the country roads, hauling himself onward slowly and calling to mind:

There in the brightly lit synagogue in the shtetl, Jews were already swaying in prayer, swaying together in unison as they full-throatedly followed the
cantor's lead:
Give thanks unto the Lord for He is good, for His mercy endureth forever. . . .
[ellipsis in original].[22]

As in "Two Roads," space transforms into time. The unfamiliar setting is
disturbing to Mirl, but instead of naming her emotions of disappointment,
frustration, regret, and resentment, Bergelson creates a scrap of narrative
about some unnamed and unknown Jew alone in the mud on a Friday
evening, when everyone else is already dressed in Sabbath finery and in
the synagogue singing praise to God for his mercy that endures forever.
God is eternal, but human beings are in time, and they can be late, and the
emotion of being late for the Sabbath—missing their chance for access to
this once-a-week bit of eternity—is the best way to describe what it feels
like to be poor next to a rich man and what it feels like to be Mirl, who
never experiences the Sabbath or holidays but only the week. The only kind
of time on her calendar is empty and homogeneous. The late-for-Sabbath
mood that Bergelson describes is alien to Mirl.

Bergelson will come back to the distinction between the weekday and
the Sabbath and holiday in later works, even including his two-volume
autobiographical novel, *Baym Dnyepr* (*At the Dnieper*), published in the
Soviet Union, where references to Jewish observance were usually couched
in a negative light. He frames his own process of literary creativity and
the suspension of that process in terms of the alteration between holiday
and weekday time. In exploring the existential significance of this temporal pattern, Bergelson is participating in a larger discussion taking place
at the time. Jewish philosophers of the first part of the twentieth century,
including Matvei Kagan, Martin Buber, and Franz Rosenzweig, used the
alternation of weekday work and Sabbath and holiday celebration in their
arguments about the Jewish view of the meaningfulness of human history.[23] Kagan (1889–1937) contrasted the model of the final, perfect condition
of some future messianic era with the notion of continual ongoing work
in history, in the here and now, and stressed the sanctity of work. There is
no festival (rest, redemption, Sabbath) without work.[24] Rosenzweig attributed great value to the holidays of both Christianity and Judaism because
of their capacity to link the present time with future redemption.[25] Buber
emphasized the interpenetration of redemption and daily life as central to
Hasidism. In an unpublished lecture given in 1901, he described holidays as
forming a "community of celebration" during which the celebrants feel a

unity with all things. The festive calendar provides a "jubilant rhythm" that replaces mere convention.[26]

Bergelson, in contrast to Rosenzweig and Buber, did not write philosophical treatises. His prose fiction is his way of thinking about the issues of time and renewal that so preoccupied Jewish and non-Jewish writers in the early years of the twentieth century, the "renewal of the relation to reality," as Buber puts it. Bergelson's heroine expresses her despair by describing her own calendar as one in which there will be no festive time but only workday drudgery. When she gets married, it feels like any other ordinary day; she might slip out and buy something at the pharmacy. It is not only the new opportunities for work that fail to inspire Mirl; it is also the new opportunities for pleasure; she experiences desire but does not derive pleasure from it. As the narrator archly remarks, the young women in the provincial capital where Mirl moves long to betray their husbands but do not know how. Their desire for desire is thwarted. To live a life deprived of holidays is to merely be alive. The loss of the religious calendar is the loss of joy, not necessarily because of the loss of God, but rather because of the loss of hope and the loss of the temporal ordering that religion provides, the celebrations and remembrances that it creates. The "atrophy of experience," according to Benjamin, results from the loss of history and memory as well as the routinization of the body under capitalist, industrialized labor. Removed from urban shock and mechanized labor, Mirl's "small shtetl" loss of holiday time nonetheless dramatizes a central experience of modernity.

Endings

The overpowering emphasis in *The End of Everything* on the "sense of an ending," to borrow Frank Kermode's term, is undeniable. The historical and cultural phenomena of the turn of the twentieth century that Kermode sees as contributing to the "sense of an ending" among Western European writers are relevant to Bergelson's time and place. These include new discoveries in science and technology that made uncertainty a new principle inherent in nature and raised the question of the death of the universe due to entropy.[27] The theories that Freud propounded from the 1890s through the first part of the twentieth century ended the notion of a unified, stable subject that progresses in linear time. Max Nordau's *Degeneration*, to which Bergelson explicitly refers in *The End of Everything* and other works, spells out the decline of the human organism. Mirl explains that her father's ancient family had for so long intermarried among its own members that "it was degenerating with age," with the result that "she was fit for nothing."[28]

Jewish writers reflecting on the Jewish community also emphasized the theme of decline and endings in their work. Shloyme Zanvil Rapaport, better known by his pen name S. An-sky, launched his ethnographic salvage journeys to the Pale of Settlement in 1912 (while Bergelson was writing *The End of Everything*) convinced that the artifacts and folklore of the Jewish people would soon be lost to social and political change. Several decades later, in the early 1930s, when he had just returned to the Soviet Union, Bergelson said that his early work, including *The End of Everything*, described the end of the shtetl. There is, however, an obvious rationale for this Marxist and sociological explanation for his literary work. The author said what his Soviet listeners wanted to hear: namely that the shtetl, whose former inhabitants the new regime had "productivized," was already obsolete and in decline in the early years of the twentieth century.

The philosopher Lev Shestov (1866–1938) is an important voice in the discourse of crisis and endings in the early 1900s through the 1920s.[29] Shestov, who was Jewish (his original name was Shvartsman), was the son of a wealthy manufacturer in Kiev. During his early years in that city, Bergelson met Shestov through their common friend Elkhonon Kalmonson.[30] In a series of works written before World War I, Shestov argued that philosophy had come to the end of its rope, so to speak; it had reached the point of utter groundlessness. The *Apotheosis of Groundlessness* was the title of a collection of aphorisms Shestov published in 1905. According to Shestov, neither metaphysics nor positive science could claim access to the truth. Technological advances and notions of progress were also targets of his criticism. Shestov particularly emphasized that the principle of cause and effect had seen its day. For Shestov, at least in his early period, there were no certainties, no God, no scientific causality, and no rationality—only chance and the "void." Bergelson's heroine Mirl Hurvits proceeds as if her life and her unhappiness could be reduced to a chain of cause-and-effect sequences. Her efforts to improve her life, as I will show, are based on this assumption, which turns out to be false. Immediate prior events, such as her marriage, cause her to be unhappy, but more important are the delayed aftereffects of indeterminate events in the more remote past. The search for immediate and determinate causes is futile.

Bergelson particularly admired Chekhov, and while I do not argue for a direct influence on the Yiddish author, there are parallels and confluences to be noted.[31] In the opening of *The Seagull* (*Chaika*, 1896) Masha says she wears black because she is "in mourning" for her life (*eto traur po moei zhizni*); Mirl expresses a similar sentiment when she says that "someone else lived out the springtime" of her life.[32] The narrator compares her to a "mourner" (*shive-zitserin*). Natasha, the arriviste young wife in *Three Sisters*, takes over the Protopopov house and plans to cut down the trees; by the end of Bergelson's novel, the house in which Mirl was born is empty and boarded up, her father is dead, and her mother is gone; a group of tailors' apprentices carouse outside and break the windowpanes.

The loss of the native home, a motif in both *Three Sisters* and *The End of Everything*, speaks to the deterioration of the economic system that sustained domestic life, as well as to a more diffused collapse of the old patterns of life. These changes emerge in Chekhov's *Three Sisters* (1901) and other late works: the values of the intelligentsia, including the emphasis on education, good taste, decorum, and service, no longer carry the same weight they once did. The traditions of the past are shattered, like the precious clock that used to belong to the Protopopov mother. Andrei did not become a professor, his sister Irina forgets her Italian, the doctor forgets his medicine, and Natasha abuses the family's old nurse. The play opens on the anniversary of the father's death (from the Jewish perspective, an occasion known as the *yortsayt*) and ends with the death of Baron Tuzenbach, the substitute for the husband whom Irina "would have loved."

The parallels between Chekhov and Bergelson emerge particularly clearly through the mediation of Shestov. Chekhov, according to Shestov, created his works from the perspective of the "void," as the title of his 1905 essay on Chekhov, "Creation from the Void" ("*Tvorchestvo iz nichego*"), reveals. To put it another way, there are no general principles, ideals, or ideas that could guide human life.[33] A similar problem haunts Bergelson's heroine in *The End of Everything*: she searches for but does not find "the main thing" (*der iker*). To be sure, Dostoevsky had already descried the loss of a general guiding idea in *The Brothers Karamazov*, which was first published serially in 1878. Dostoevsky's own "sense of an ending" was precocious. Given the history of catastrophe, and especially, Jewish catastrophe in the twentieth century, so was Bergelson's.

Troyer

In "At the Depot," *troyer*, sadness, is part of the landscape. In *The End of Everything* it is also a fundamental element of the heroine's personality. It is chronic. *Troyer* is a nearly constant feature of Mirl's face, as for example in the line "With sorrow in her blue eyes, she stared for a morosely long time into the corner."[34] Her *shtimung* (mood) is characteristically "desolate" (*umetike*).[35] Mirl and Shats read from the Book of Job and find comfort in so doing, because Job's grief is greater than their own. The object of their mourning remains undefined. In contrast to Job, they suffer no palpable injury or loss.

Mirl's sadness changes her perception of time: Bergelson describes her mood by means of an unusual dilation of time. She senses the present, the moment of now, as stretched beyond its normal limits. On one occasion when she feels especially hopeless, burdened, and dull, "this day seemed to be taking place not in the present but five or six years earlier."[36] The line is difficult to parse. It could mean that there had been no other kind of day but this one for the past five or six years, or it could be that Mirl was suffering from a false memory that linked the present and the past. Alternatively, it could mean that the day seemed to have begun five or six years ago, that it seemed exceptionally long. "Now" oozes out into the distant past. The time sequence in which "after" follows directly on "before" is disturbed.

Mirl's former fiancé Velvl experiences the return of the betrothal agreement as the "end of everything." Mirl experiences this sense of an ending in a more diffuse way when she returns to her father's house after having spent some time living in Shats's room. She enters the house and goes from room to room, as she used to:

> As in times gone by, the gloom of twilight held sway, intensified and was transmuted into haze. But in times gone by there had been people here and now there were none . . . No one stopped her, no one was made happier by her arrival. Something, it seemed, was too late here, had already ended [ellipsis added].[37]

Here is the reference to twilight that Bergelson singles out as the defining mood of the Jewish intelligentsia of the time. The last line of the passage presents difficulties in both Yiddish and English, since the expressions of time "too late" and "already ended" are strangely used to describe not an action but rather some unspecified thing: something was "too late" and has "already ended." The title phrase, *nokh alemen*, is in the last line of the Yiddish, translated here as "already ended." Bergelson is heightening the qualitative, emotional experience of time.

Bergelson uses the device of Mirl's mistimed arrival to suggest a broader temporal problem. Gitl's absence from the house is only temporary; she has gone to sell her jewelry to her rich uncle. She will return, and the next time Mirl enters the house, presumably there will be someone to greet her, someone who will be gladdened by her arrival. What has ended in this house (or what is shortly going to end) is the entire way of life that Gedalye and Gitl embody, and thus what remains is belated and afterward. Mirl experiences this hazy and diffuse sense of an ending, ironically, when it is springtime.

In chapter 1, I argued that the sorrow "at the depot" (both the place and the narrative) should be seen not as a prophecy of doom but instead as a way of reanimating something whose motion has become suspended. The protagonist's inactivity made him more susceptible to seeing what others could not. Beynish sought and found, if only fleetingly, an answer from the surrounding world. The measure of reconciliation that he experiences relieves the isolation and dread that is part of the depot itself. Beynish contemplates returning to a previous profession rather than continuing as a trader at a train station: he wonders if he can earn enough money as a Hebrew tutor. Notwithstanding his animosity toward his second wife, he considers the shtetl of his childhood as "beloved" and precious.

In *The End of Everything*, however, Bergelson emphasizes the rupture between the past and the present, the sense that it is too late and that it (whatever it is) is over. This much seems obvious from his description of the mood at Mirl's father's nearly empty house in the passage I quoted above, where "something, it seemed, was too late here, had already ended." Beynish Rubinshteyn extracts some kind of response to his misery; Mirl, in contrast, gets no answer. She looks out at the landscape and asks Lipkis, "Can you hear the way the world keeps silent?"[38] It is not the paradox of "hearing" the world's silence that makes this line difficult. The difficulty lies in formulating the question whose answer is the world's silence: in response to what is the world refusing to speak?

Deleuze's notion of the time image can help shed light both on the time problem in the Hurvits house and the impulse behind Mirl's question. Using Bergson, Deleuze argues that cinema in the second part of the twentieth century no longer emphasizes action but rather depicts time itself in visual form. Characters in these films do not act; instead, they bear witness. Deleuze's reliance on Bergson for his own theory of cinema is not free from controversy and criticism, because Bergson himself referred to the cinematic frame as the antithesis of flowing time. While it may appear farfetched to use Deleuze to explicate early twentieth-century Yiddish prose, and even though he pinpoints the transition from movement images to time images in the era immediately following World War II, the time image and the movement image are not so much historical phenomena as different responses to history. Instead of movement, time images introduce "purely optical or sound perception of a divested present, which no longer conveys links with a disconnected past."[39] Bergelson captured this sense of withdrawal and belatedness as early as 1909. Figures like Beynish, Mirl Hurvits, and Khaym-Moyshe (from *Descent*) cannot act in the world in which they find themselves. But their failure makes them better witnesses to the lingering past and the empty present. Another way to say this is that they are better witnesses to the experience of the end of everything.

In an essay written in 1914, Nakhmen Mayzel says that in *The End of Everything*, Bergelson describes the "consequences" and "[painful] aftereffect" (*nokhveyenish*) of events that took place earlier; the most important of these do not appear in the book directly but rather take the form of "clues" or "allusions" (*remozim*).[40] Mayzel's insight points to the limited knowledge that readers have about the causes of the "aftereffect" that dominates *The End of Everything*. Bergelson's heroine shares the epistemological problem. Incapable of understanding her own malaise, she mistakenly thinks Herts knows more than she does and says so explicitly: "Herts, it still seems to me that you know much more than I do."[41] She seeks knowledge, imagining that "somewhere there were still a few such individuals who knew *something* but they kept their knowledge secret."[42] Mirl places Herts in the same position her father would place a rabbi; she seeks to believe in him as her father would the legendary thirty-six hidden righteous men on whom the world depends. Bergelson makes this point explicitly in a letter that I will discuss below. In Mirl's quest Bergelson translates a religious idiom into secular terms. Her search for meaning, however, cannot be satisfied by new scientific knowledge, new professions, or new political ideologies, because none of these things provide a ground, basis, or source of action for her. These new forms of life and belief don't speak to her. The answer to the question I raised earlier, about the paradox of the world's refusal to speak, its silence in response to the crisis no one knows about, is simple: in the aftermath of the end of everything, there is nothing to say. That is why the world keeps silent.

Deprived of what she believes is hidden knowledge, Mirl attempts to revisit her own past. Unlike Beynish Rubinshteyn in "At the Depot," who embraces inaction and remembers his past, Mirl has no interiority and no memory. As a consequence, the only way for her to revisit the past is to undo or attempt to undo what she has previously done, as if she could unravel the causes of her despair or regain an earlier time without the knowledge or experience that has since accumulated. Unhappy with her engagement to Velvl Burnes, she sends back the *tnoyem*, the engagement contract. Agreeing to marry Shmul Zaydenovski, she tells herself that it will be a marriage in name only and only a temporary marriage. On the verge of securing a divorce, she discovers her pregnancy and gets an abortion. She moves out of her husband's house in the city and returns to her shtetl, and at the end of the novel she removes herself altogether from the scene, although we do not know whether this is by suicide or departure to another location. Each of her subsequent acts revisits the immediate past; each is an attempt to restore the past as it was. There is something almost clinical and detached in these efforts, as if the consequences would not touch her; Mirl does not realize that in undoing her own actions, she is also undoing herself. The step-by-step effort is a failure, however, because the premise of immediate causes and effects is faulty. To put this in other words, Mirl fails to understand the particular qualities of the time that she inhabits and that is in her. Who she is and what happened to her in the immediate past have little connection. The "law of sequence" that Shestov says is the idol of nineteenth-century thought has collapsed, but she is the only one in her immediate milieu to experience the breakdown. Everyone else around her pursues either the same course of life and pattern of behavior or some new form, both of which she already feels to be groundless.

Mirl realizes the problem at the very end of the novel. The lame student Lipkis, who has had an operation to heal his foot, returns to the shtetl after his old companion Mirl has already left. It seems hardly necessary to point out that he is too late. Lipkis discovers a letter that she wrote but never sent: "The thought that someone else has lived through my springtime grows more and more obvious to me from day to day: even before I was born, someone else had lived out my springtime."[43]

It is not merely that a single emotion appears in the form of an expression of the seasons of the year; it is that the entire meaning of her life is expressed as a temporal loss; a certain period of time corresponding to "spring" has been denied her, and this was decreed or took place before she was born, adding to the weight of *nokhveyenish*, the painful aftereffect. This passage corresponds closely to the Dobrushin poem I quoted in the opening of the chapter: "A stranger lives my life." The important difference is that Bergelson expresses his character's alienation in terms of time, so that the emphasis is not on a loss of authenticity or self-determination but rather on the belated aftereffect of something that happened much earlier.

To be deprived of springtime is to lose the possibility of renewal. A striking example of this loss can be found in Mirl's experience of the Passover season (Passover is the spring holiday celebrating the exodus from Egypt). Passover requires a thorough cleaning of the house to remove all traces of leavened food products. Mirl lies in her bedroom listening to the sounds of the preparations, including her father's recitation of the Hebrew benediction over the ritual search for leavened food. The narrator emphasizes her distance from these proceedings by defamiliarizing them, as in the phrase "the stove was heated for some reason."[44] The stove is being heated in order to burn the remains of the forbidden food—as Mirl and Bergelson's readers know full well. The description of the Passover preparations continues.

> the stove was being heated for some reason, and across the silent house its inner little cast-iron door could be heard thumping as it was sucked rapidly backward and forward over the flame:
> —Pakh-pakh-pakh . . . pakh-pakh-pakh . . . [ellipsis in original][45]

For Yiddish speakers, the name of the Passover holiday is Peysekh, which the narrator mentions immediately before the passage I have quoted. The sequence "Peysekh . . . pakh . . . pakh . . . pakh" suggests a comparison between the two terms "Peysekh" and "pakh." The meaningless sound "pakh" absorbs Passover (Peysekh) into itself.

Roman Jakobson's description of poetic language sheds light on Bergelson's technique in this passage. Poetic language, according to Jakobson, privileges "equivalence" over "sequence": "any sequence of semantic units strives to build an equation."[46] Bergelson's prose is poetic in Jakobson's sense.[47] The link between "Peysekh" and "pakh" in the passage above is an example of Jakobson's principle of equivalence. The relationships of sound created by the semantic units in the sequence are more important than the story they tell, even though the pattern of sound is not isolated from the meaning of the line; again, in the passage above, the sound play suggests the loss of the emotional value and weight of the holiday for the heroine. Jakobson's stress on the "equational principle," as distinct from "sequence," has implications for my argument about the loss of festive time in this novel. When the principle of equivalence dominates sequence, the motion of time stops and the possibility of change—let alone renewal—is suspended. Each subsequent moment is like the previous one. Passover is merely "pakh"; there is no festive time.

The springtime renewal that would have been Mirl's has been taken away; someone else used it up, as it were, and what is more, this usurpation of the "good" time of her life happened in the past, before her life even began. It is not a matter of a chain of causes and effects, each of whose links could be undone. It is a matter of the "aftereffect," as Mayzel writes.

The Power of the Past: Bergson and Freud

Thus far I have read Bergelson together with the French philosopher Bergson to highlight the ways that Bergelson's writing called upon notions of potential, possibility, and harmony between the individual and the world. *The End of Everything* does not open out to futurity but is instead preoccupied with the past. It calls for a different interlocutor. The philosopher Vladimir Jankélévitch describes Bergsonian duration as "a continuous springtime," but as I have shown, in this novel it is precisely springtime that is missing for the heroine.[48] The temporality of aftereffects challenges Bergson's notion of the fluidity of past and present. Bergson uses the metaphor of a musical composition, in which the notes of the melody melt into one another, to describe the seamless intermingling of the past and the present. As Jankélévitch puts it, for Bergson, freedom is "the expression of a personality [that] does not introduce a revolutionary discontinuity in our personal biography but rather emanates from the past like a perfume."[49] For Bergson, the possibility of creative evolution depends on continuity; there is no "before" in contrast to which there could be an "after," no radical break in the continuity and flow of time.

In contrast, *The End of Everything* depends precisely on rupture, on the felt reality of a particular life as an "aftereffect" (*nokhveyenish*) of something that has happened before. Freud's theory of repression, his notion of the relation between the unconscious and perception, and his discussion of the compulsion to repeat offer a model of temporal discontinuity that can be useful in interpreting both this novel and other, similar works by Bergelson. A brief comparison of Freud and Bergson will reveal the differences that are important for my discussion and will also introduce "afterwardsness." Although I am not arguing that Bergelson knew Freud's work or vice versa, I note that Freud came to his major ideas about the significance and yet fundamental unknowability of our past as early as 1900. Both Bergelson and Freud, each along very different pathways, as I will explain, come to an understanding of the significance of belatedness and delay before the first world war and the rupture in time that it created. I will rely on the discussion of several theorists to explain "afterwardsness," a concept that encompasses delay, deferral, and belatedness.

For both Freud and the French philosopher Bergson, the past is preserved. Paul Ricoeur calls them "the two advocates of the unforgettable."[50] The past is preserved in the unconscious. Keith Ansell Pearson notes that Bergson's *Matter and Memory* was published in 1896, four years before *The Interpretation of Dreams*. In *The Interpretation of Dreams*, Freud proposed that "memory and consciousness are mutually exclusive"; in "Note on the Mystic Writing Pad," he modified this to say that "consciousness arises instead of the memory-trace."[51] For Bergson, the unconscious is the "whole of the past"; for Freud, it is the past that has been repressed.[52] Consciousness, for Bergson, is attention to life, and as such, it only uses a tiny fraction of memory for the execution of actions. The ever-growing remainder of the past is preserved and endures as a source of virtual or future actions. It is this kind of expansive, non-episodic, or "pure" memory that Mirl Hurvits lacks.

Both Bergson and Freud characterize repetition as a loss of vitality. Bergson distinguishes inorganic matter from memory on this basis: life is choice, freedom, whereas materiality is sheer repetition. The acoustical correlative of this in the Yiddish author Bergelson's novel is the "pakh-pakh-pakh" of the oven's internal door as it is being heated, without "Peysekh"; that is, without the holiday celebrating freedom and renewal. Bergson defines the comic as the mechanical encrusted over the living, linking repetition to that which opposes life: "The attitude, gesture, and movements of the body are laughable in exact proportion as that body reminds us of a mere machine."[53] The loss of flexibility or suppleness that Bergson attributes to the body, Freud attributes to the psyche. It "mechanically" repeats the earlier injury.

Laplanche and Derrida both see "afterwardsness" (although Derrida does not use the term) as central to Freud's entire project, beginning with his work on hysteria and running through *Beyond the Pleasure Principle* and beyond it to later works. Derrida cites *Moses and Monotheism* (1937) as an example of Freud's application of his notion of deferral and latency "over large historical intervals."[54] Freud's theories of sexuality and repression are well known, but what is important for my purposes is the distinctive temporality of delayed effects, a process by which more recent events change the meaning of chronologically remoter events. The future can change the past.

Building on Freud, Laplanche develops his concept of "afterwardsness"—his suggested English term for the German *Nachträglichkeit*. Laplanche argues for two dimensions of afterwardsness: the deferred action and the after-the-fact understanding. There is both retrogression and deferral. Freud's theory of dreams, like his work on hysteria, posits a wish that has been repressed but reappears, translated and transformed by various processes (in dreams, condensation, and displacement) into symptoms and the visual representations of dreaming. Both Freud's and Bergson's notions of the unconscious involve creativity—Freud describes the work of dreaming as if it were poetry. The repetition of earlier repressed wishes and feelings in both hysteria and dreaming is artfully disguised. Bergson attributes creative futurity to the past that is preserved in memory, because memory preserves potential, or virtual possibilities. Neither Freud nor Bergson sees a chain of cause and effect. But in contrast to Bergson, for Freud time has lost its flow. It stops and starts. Freud is careful to point out that even though the mental processes of the unconscious are timeless, time "changes them and can be applied to them."[55] Bergson's metaphor of melody, in which the notes of the tune melt into one another, cannot apply, because the interval between the notes is too great.

One could say that time as flow and time as rupture are two sides of the same coin, two different perspectives on the same thing. An event only becomes *the* event when there is a subject who names it as such, when a subject creates a narrative in which this event is particularly laden with consequence. Mirl searches for this event, which she calls *der iker* ("the main thing"), but cannot find it. In the absence of a subject and a narrative, the "main event" remains as one of a series of moments not particularly marked with significance. After the end of everything, any moment will do and no moment is *the* moment. From the perspective of psychoanalysis, *the* event is repressed or in other ways denied. For Freud, the organizing significance of a single event in the plot of someone's life is hidden under the guise of a symptom, a dream, or a slip of the tongue.

The temporality of afterwardsness is key to *The End of Everything*. As the passages that I quoted earlier show, a whole array of negative emotions, including boredom, loneliness, isolation, alienation, disappointment, frustration, and a generalized sadness, are couched in terms of afterwardsness.

It is too late; everything has ended. There is, however, no originating event in respect of which "arriving on time" would solve the problem. To be in the world of "the end of everything," the world of aftermaths and afterwardsness, is to be always and already too late. This is the essence of Bergelson's modernist and modern poetics. He returns to it again and again, particularly in work written in the aftermath of disaster.

A distinction, however, should be made between the author and the person. Regardless of his statement about the frequency of his "twilight mood," during the period when he composed the novel, Bergelson's letters do not project a mood of despair and sorrow. He instead uses language about with birth and describes his own literary fecundity. He refers to the journal the *Jewish World* (*Di yidishe velt*) as a "beloved child" and talks about the array of characters and "millions of images" among which he finds himself.[56] It is therefore all the more striking that Bergelson should have written a letter specifically comparing the writing of *The End of Everything* (*Nokh alemen*) to the experience of losing children. I quote at length from an undated and unpublished letter to Niger:

> About *Nokh alemen*:
> I knew a woman all of whose five grown sons died at the same time. The old woman saw this and beat herself on the head with both hands.
> Writing this book I was this old woman. The only difference is that I experience the greatest blows not externally, but deep inside myself. Perhaps this is why Mirl's tragedy is also deep inside the book, in *Nokh alemen*.
> If I were the kind of person who thought that screaming would make a difference, the book would run out into the street and it would scream:
> —Listen, you people! A terrible thing is happening. For whole generations intellectual content has been sufficient for men, and for women, patient waiting, in order for them to live out all their years like R. Gedalye and Gitl. I am showing you a person for whom patience and intellectual content have been lost.
> I keep thinking that Mirl is a transitional point not only from the old type of woman to the new, but also to a certain extent, from the old Jew to the new. She is a person who does not go where everyone else does, but off to the side, and the time is twilight and she [Mirl] is an orphan alone in the whole world.
> What can the surrounding world give her? It is not hers.[57]

This letter has not been discussed in the existing scholarship on Bergelson. The author divides Jewish life into a feminine and masculine realm. For women like Mirl's mother, the steadfast observance of Jewish practice within the home, and for men like Mirl's father, the study of Jewish texts were meaningful forms of life. Both women and men patiently waited for exile to end and for the messiah to come in a deferred future. Mirl, however, cannot live the way her parents did. Bergelson uses the same phrase "transitional point" to characterize Mirl in the novel; the Hebrew poet Herts calls her a "transitional point in human development."[58]

The woman whose grown sons died at once is likely a variant on the martyrdom of the mother and her seven sons in 2 Maccabees. The key line in the Revised Standard Version of the Bible is remarkably close to the opening of Bergelson's letter: "though she saw her seven sons perish within a single day" (2 Maccabees 7:20). The story is not historical, but it is connected to the history of the Maccabean revolt against Antiochus Epiphanes in the second century before the Common Era. In the familiar Hanukkah story, the Maccabees regained control over the temple and succeeded in establishing their own kingdom. Another rebel group, the Assideans or Assidaioi (Graetz calls them the "pious Chasidim"), more radical than the Maccabees, believed that their martyrdom would bring the end of time and the messianic era. In 2 Maccabees, the seven sons refuse Antiochus's demands that they violate Jewish law, and they are tortured and killed. The mother says that God, and not she, is responsible for the birth of her sons and that God will restore their life, "giving life and breath back to them," signaling that the messianic era was about to approach. In a letter from 1910, Bergelson wrote that he was planning a novel about Greek and Roman times, and although nothing came of the project, it is safe to assume that he was familiar with 1 and 2 Maccabees and that he had read Graetz.[59] In the letter cited above, Bergelson remembers, so to speak, the apocryphal story, disguising it as personal experience.

The Maccabean revolt and the conflict between the Maccabees and the Assidaioi hold more than mere historical interest for Bergelson. The underlying issue of assimilation and the extent to which assimilation would bring political rights and independence for Jews was a deeply contested question in the first part of the twentieth century. In letters from 1912 through the first world war, the author also talks about the necessity to part with Russian Jewish literature "once and for all." Some of these letters were written in Russian, because of the tsarist ban on correspondence and publication in Yiddish. Bergelson talks about the necessity for a battle against the "idiots" in the circles associated with such publications as the *Jewish Week* (*Evreiskaia nedelia*), a weekly Russian Jewish journal that began publication in 1915. He singles out the Russian Jewish writers David Aizman (1869–1922) and Andrei Sobol (1888–1926) for particular contempt because they proclaimed their interest in Yiddish while "living in an alien culture and speaking to their children in an alien language."[60] The lethal threat to Jewish life and creativity stemmed from linguistic assimilation. Bergelson fought against it his entire life; during his secret trial in 1952, he talks about the "protracted agony" of the loss of Yiddish.

There is more to say about the extraordinary letter written some forty years earlier. Writing *The End of Everything* inflicted a terrible sense of loss. The process of literary creation, typically likened to giving birth, is compared to the experience of seeing one's own children die. I give birth to you and nurture you—my literary offspring—and in so doing I destroy you and I am destroyed. Recall that in *The End of Everything*, Bergelson's heroine aborts her pregnancy. Giving birth to and suffering the death of beloved children takes place at the same time. Bergelson's allegory of literary birth as the death of all one's children, with its hidden reference to the Maccabean revolt, suggests that in his novel he was portraying massive, overwhelming destruction that could not be described directly, let alone remedied, and yet was necessary and inevitable. Bergelson's Mirl Hurvits is the aftereffect of this destruction, the consequence of the endless deferral of redemption. Bergelson is not an emotional writer, and the suffering he describes in creating Mirl's story is therefore all the more extraordinary. Benjamin characterized the "shock experience" at the center of Baudelaire's "creative process."[61] Bergelson places another kind of shock experience at the center of his composition of *The End of Everything*.

Ghost Stories

Early in the novel, the midwife Shats recites from memory Herts's story about a dead town. In the embedded story, the first-person narrator comes to a place in which the houses are filled with dead bodies and stones that the people meant to throw at their enemies but did not. The sole remaining survivor is a tall woman in a black dress, who clutches a waxen doll to her breast, naming it as a "veiled mistake" (*farshleyerter toes*).[62] She reprimands the narrator for his tardiness:

> —You have come so late, she murmured to me with quiet indifference.—We have been waiting for you so long here, and now look: they are all dead.[63]

The townspeople and their would-be messiah miss each other, the former dying too soon, and the latter arriving too late. The wanderer decides nonetheless to remain at the gates of the dead town, as its guardian.[64] Bergelson's allegory of failed salvation as the belated messiah is a reframing of a well-known story in the Talmud. The messiah sits at the gates of Rome, disguised as a leper. He is distinct from all the other beggars: while they unwrap and rewrap their sores all at once, he unwraps and rebandages each sore separately, so that he will not be delayed should the moment arrive when the Jewish people are ready for him. Bergelson's messiah, on the contrary, misses his chance to save his people.

The "mood" (*shtimung*) and "spirit" (*gayst*) of the story work on Mirl, who cannot move from her place after hearing the midwife recite it. Later in the novel, at her own engagement party, dressed in a new gray silk dress and wearing a tightly laced corset, Mirl feels that all the fuss is not for her but for some other Mirl, while she, the true Mirl, observes everything taking place around her. She feels foolish and uncomfortable "decked out and dolled up" (*vi epes a geshleyerte lyalke*).[65] The image calls to mind Herts's story: the "doll" (*lyalke*) that the madwoman clutches to her breast, which she calls a "veiled mistake" (*farshleyerte toes*).

Mirl belongs both to the frame and to the embedded story about the dead town; she is both figure and ground, the doll clutched to the woman's breast and the woman, part of the audience of this story's narration, the center of attention at her engagement party, and the observer looking in all at once. Herts's story has an impact on her because she is its heroine; she is the survivor of the dead town. She both haunts others as a ghost and is herself haunted by the dead past. In the same letter I quoted earlier, Bergelson goes on to link Mirl and her father:

> Between R. Gedalye's belief that the sinful world is sustained by the thirty-six righteous men, and Mirl's belief that somewhere in the world there are people who know "something" and keep it a secret—hang thin invisible threads. With these invisible threads of legacy woven around her Mirl wandered off into the distance of the world of chaos.[66]

The people who know "something" and the thirty-six righteous men are similar. Mirl's problem is not that she is cut off from the past; it is rather that she is bound to it and thereby to her father with these "invisible threads." She is bound, by means of a strange psychic umbilical cord, to a past that is dead, and she cannot sever herself from it. In this light, the image of the threads woven around her suggests a shroud. Mirl, encased in an invisible shroud, belongs to the world of the dead even though she is still alive.

Bergelson uses a similar image of death in life in the first lines of "Impoverished," which I discussed in the opening of this chapter. Like a ghost, Bergelson's heroine haunts the world of the living; her endless rambling walks around the shtetl emphasize her disquiet and her search.

Laplanche writes that analysis means severing the threads that bind the subject to the lost object. Here, however, there is no cutting off the past. Bergelson's friend and close associate Shmuel Niger published a lengthy review of *Nokh alemen* (*The End of Everything*) in 1913. I already quoted from his review earlier, in referring to *nokhveyenish*. Niger's evocative description of the strong bond between Mirl, her father, and the past is also worth quoting: "And like the ruin of an old castle or from an old temple her father's house remains standing after his death. The emptiness from this ruin penetrates Mirl's heart, an emptiness that is full of phantoms from old times that whisper quietly and beckon her somewhere, allowing her no rest."[67]

In Niger's rendering, Bergelson's novel—full of ruins, ghosts, and secrets—belongs to the gothic tradition. Mirl carries the "ruin" of the old temple within her; she bears the legacy of a past that is already destroyed. Niger's review and Bergelson's letter (to Niger) are of a piece: Mirl, a ghost who haunts the living, is at the same time haunted by the "phantoms" of the past, the loss that began before she was born. Mirl's experience of doubling (the second "fiery" Mirl that looks at her from the horizon), her belief that her own life does not belong to her but rather to someone else, and the abstracted way that she looks at her own body—all are part of the haunting that Niger describes. In a terrible way, Mirl, who aborts her pregnancy, is the consummate heir of Gedalye's destroyed world. She cannot reproduce what no longer exists. She does not come home when her father dies, and he, dying, says that if only he had an heir, he would go to the next world as if to a dance.

Mirl comes to the realization that her parents cannot help her but can only be "witnesses" to her blighted life. They can look upon her tragedy and, in so doing, serve as "witnesses" to it, but of course there is no court before which they or she can testify. There is nothing to adjudicate. In "At the Depot," in contrast, the ghostly apparition of the tiny human heads in the train station lanterns function as members of a court who affirm that they have listened to the witness. Their flickering glow provides something of a response to the cry of suffering.

The legacy of the past cannot bear fruit in the present generation in the form in which it previously existed. The present is inhabited by the nouveau-riche Burnesses and Zaydenovskys and the new type of young men and women who take university courses and enter the professions. Mirl is asked by one of these new professionals, the pharmacist's assistant, "why she didn't prepare herself for some public examinations and so equip herself for some kind of cultivated profession."[68] For Bergelson's heroine, the new social and economic opportunities are merely a way of passing the time, comparable to chewing on sunflower seeds or reading books. As in "At the Depot," the story that *The End of Everything* tells does not embrace the progress of its time, instead challenging the value of upward mobility. The temporality of the aftereffect in Bergelson's first novel closely resembles the Freudian temporality of afterwardsness, because the heroine experiences the aftereffect of an overwhelming loss that is constitutive of her existence. She loses the past, and this loss began before she was born. She can no more live the life of her mother, Gitl, than she can live the life of the new type of young, educated Jewish professional.

I have argued thus far that time is out of joint in *The End of Everything*. Nature and human clocks and calendars fail to keep pace with one another, as do public time and inner time. The Jewish calendar has no meaning for Mirl, who does not even mourn her father's death. However, there are two moments in the narrative in which Mirl's actions correspond to the events celebrated in the Jewish calendar. When she returns to her parents' house to find her mother gone and her father gravely ill, she decides to save him from ruin by accepting the marriage offer proposed by Shmul Zaydenovski. Her action coincides with Purim, when Esther's intervention saves the Jewish people from death. Gitl returns home the same evening, and as a pious woman, she has the scroll of Esther read aloud; the Hebrew words for "In those days while Mordechai sat in the king's gate" appear in the Yiddish text. Whether Mirl's effort is successful or not, the episode shows that the template of sacred Jewish history has a certain resonance in *The End of Everything*.

Its echo resounds more loudly, and in a tragic key, in the novel's ending. Mirl has returned to her shtetl after her father has died and her mother has left. Her parents' house is empty, its windows boarded up. Bergelson inserts the novel's title into his description of Mirl's former home:

> The room was filled with silence, and the desolation that follows when everything has ended clung to the walls and ceiling, calling again to mind that Reb Gedalye was now dead and that Gitele had now no single place on earth.[69]

The Yiddish:

> In kheyder iz geven shtil, un a pustkeyt fun nokh alemen hot zikh geklapt tsu di vent un tsum balkon un dermont, az R. Gedalye is shoyn toyt, un az Gitele hot shoyn in ergets keyn ort nisht.[70]

A very awkward rendering of the first line would read, "It was quiet in the room, and the desolation emanating from the end of everything clung"— or, to push more on the substantive, weighty qualities of time, "the desolation of afterwardsness clung." As in "At the Depot," where sorrow became a palpable presence in the landscape, temporalized emotion transforms into something approaching matter. The French philosopher Bergson argued against the spatialization of time; that is, its transformation into atomistic, countable units. To imagine time as qualitative, the Yiddish author gives it properties that typically belong to matter. Paradoxically, "emptiness"—the literal meaning of *pustkeyt*, which corresponds to Mirl's and Gitl's psychological state and which also corresponds to the time in which they find themselves—is sticky. Emotion-laden time changes the material universe.

Mirl, living with the rabbi's wife, sends word to Herts, asking him to visit her, and learns that he will arrive on the nineteenth of the present secular month. Mirl wants to know what this corresponds to in the Jewish calendar. For the first time in the novel, the cycle of Jewish observances and celebrations has meaning to her. It turns out that the nineteenth corresponds to the ninth of Av, the commemoration of the destruction of the two Temples. In traditional observance, various restrictions are kept during the days leading up to the ninth of Av, and the day itself is a fast day. The prescribed mood for this period is one of mourning. As Bergelson writes, "The melancholy of the approaching 9 days lay heavy on the shtetl."[71] The destruction and abandonment of her parents' home resonates with the destruction of the Temples. For the first time, Mirl's mood, the Jewish calendar, and the mood of the shtetl overlap. For the first and last time, her emotions are timely. Her personal tragedy is in sync with the time of Jewish national disaster.

Notes

1. Yekhezkel Dobrushin, *Farnakhtn* (Kiev: Y. Shenfeld, 1917), 51.

2. Bergelson repeats the same term in two different instances: "dos iz dos beynhash-moshesdik gefil funem itstiken yidishn intelligent" and "un di tsayt iz beynhashmoshes." Undated letters in YIVO, RG 360, Shmuel Niger, Box 7, Folder 9e.

3. For example, he describes the atrophy of experience in his essay on Baudelaire; see Walter Benjamin, *Illuminations* (New York: Schocken Books, 1969), 180.

4. Frederic Jameson, *A Singular Modernity: Essay on the Ontology of the Present* (London: Verso, 2012), 195. For the libretto of the opera and discussions of it, see Rosamund Bartlett and Sarah Dadswell, eds., *Victory Over the Sun: The World's First Futurist Opera* (Devon, UK: University of Exeter Press, 2012).

5. David Bergelson, *The End of Everything*, trans. Joseph Sherman, New Yiddish Library (New Haven, CT: Yale University Press, 2009), 36. The Yiddish reads: "un lozn iber in der arumiker feld-shtilkayt a troyerikn viderkol, fun fil angehoybene un nisht farendikte umglikhlekhe mayses." David Bergelson, *Nokh alemen*, vol. 2 (Vilnius: B. Kletskin, 1929), 49.

6. Bergelson, *The End of Everything*, 20. Unless otherwise noted, I use this English translation throughout. The Yiddish: "iz shoyn, heyst es, an ek tsu di tnoyem? . . . iz shoyn, heyst es, nokh alemen?" Bergelson, *Nokh alemen*, 2:29.

7. The title could also be translated as "Down and Out." I am using the Yiddish version found in David Bergelson, "Yordim," in *Verk*, vol. 2 (Berlin: Vostok, 1922), 151–65. Seth Wolitz describes the story as a "wonderful distillate" of *The End of Everything*. Seth Wolitz, "Bergelson's Yordim and I. B. Singer's," *Prooftexts* 2, no. 3 (1982): 314.

8. David Bergelson, *The Stories of David Bergelson* (Syracuse, NY: Syracuse University Press, 1996), 14. In Yiddish, "Reboyne-sheloylem . . . me'foylt dokh do in shtub on takhrikhim" Bergelson, "Yordim," 151.

9. Wolitz, "Bergelson's Yordim and I. B. Singer's," 315.

10. Jean Laplanche, *Essays on Otherness* (Florence, KY: Routledge, 1999), 238.

11. See "Time and the Other" in Laplanche, *Essays on Otherness*, 234–59.

12. See for example Cathy Caruth, *Unclaimed Experience: Trauma, Narrative, and History* (Baltimore, MD: Johns Hopkins University Press, 1996).

13. Bergelson, *The End of Everything*, 44. The Yiddish "hert zikh nokh vi s'shtarbn pamelekh op di batrakhte verter," Bergelson, *Nokh alemen*, 2:60.

14. "klaynshtetldike tragedye," Bergelson, *Nokh alemen*, 2:149.

15. See David Bergelson, *Kogda vse konchilos'* (Berlin: Grani, 1923). I am grateful to Mikhail Krutikov for directing me to this translation. The 1941 Soviet translation of the novel uses the title *Mirele*.

16. Shmuel Niger, "Briv fun Dovid Bergelson," *Zamlbikher* 8 (1952): 96.

17. I have found Tony Tanner's discussion of the organization and derangement of natural, social, and religiously ordered patterns in novels of adultery very helpful. See Tony Tanner, *Adultery in the Novel: Contract and Transgression* (Baltimore, MD: Johns Hopkins Press, 1979), 16–17.

18. Bergelson, *The End of Everything*, 21.

19. Bergelson, *The End of Everything*, 173. I have modified the translation.

20. Bergelson, *The End of Everything*, 128.

21. Bergelson, *The End of Everything*, 61. I have modified the translation, substituting "workaday" for Sherman's "banal."

22. Bergelson, *The End of Everything*, 69. The Yiddish: "Un aza troyerike, fraytog-farnakhtike zorg hobn shoyn di arumike hayzer mit zeyer fremdn blik dervekt, a zorg fun a farshpetiktn erev-shabesdikn yidn, vos shlept zikh nokh mit zayn fur in dem gehayliktn binhashomoshes iber der tifer blote, vos af de feldvegn, shlept zikh pamelekh un gedenkt: Dortn inem shtark baloykhtenem beys-hamidresh, vos in zayn shtetl, shoklen zikh shoyn shabesdikn shemerirndike yidn, shoklen zikh ale tsuzamen un zingen nokh dem hozn: 'Hodu l'shem ki to-v, ki leolam khas—d—o—o.'" Bergelson, *Nokh alemen*, 2:91.

23. For a discussion of Kagan, see Roman Katsman, "Matvei Kagan: Judaism and the European Cultural Crisis," *Journal of Jewish Thought and Philosophy* 21 (2013): 73–103. I am grateful to Roman Katsman for sharing his work with me. For a discussion of Rosenzweig contextualized in a broad discussion of Stanley Cavell and Hannah Arendt, see Bruce

Rosenstock, *Philosophy and the Jewish Question: Mendelssohn, Rosenzweig, and Beyond* (New York: Fordham University Press, 2009), 276–308.

24. I am paraphrasing from Katsman, "Matvei Kagan: Judaism and the European Cultural Crisis," 93.

25. David Bergelson, *Kogda vse konchilos'* (Berlin: Grani, 1923).

26. Paul Mendes-Flohr, *From Mysticism to Dialogue: Martin Buber's Transformation of German Social Thought* (Detroit, MI: Wayne State University Press, 1989), 77.

27. For a discussion, see Anson Rabinbach, *The Human Motor: Energy, Fatigue, and the Origins of Modernity* (New York: Basic Books, 1990), 32–33.

28. Bergelson, *The End of Everything*, 51. The Yiddish: "aponim fun altkayt degenderirt." Bergelson, *Nokh alemen*, 2:69.

29. For a recent studies of Shestov, see Michael Finkenthal, *Lev Shestov: Existential Philosopher and Religious Thinker* (New York: Peter Lang, 2010); Boris Groys, *Introduction to Antiphilosophy* (New York: Verso, 2012), 33–49. Groys argues that a single definitive event helped to shape Shestov's philosophy.

30. See Joseph Sherman, "David Bergelson (1884–1952): A Biography," in *David Bergelson: From Modernism to Socialist Realism*, ed. Joseph Sherman and Gennady Estraikh (Oxford: Legenda, 2007), 7–78; and Nakhmen Mayzel, *Forgeyer un mittsaytler* (New York: YKUF, 1946), 327.

31. For accounts of Bergelson's interest in Chekhov, see Joseph Sherman and Gennady Estraikh, *David Bergelson: From Modernism to Socialist Realism* (Oxford: Legenda, 2007), 8, 10, 84.

32. Anton Chekhov, *Five Plays*, trans. Ronald Hingley (New York: Oxford University Press, 1977), 67. For the Russian, see A. P. Chekhov, *Dramy i komedii* (Berlin: I. P. Ladyzhnikov, 1920), 98.

33. Lev Shestov, "Tvorchestvo iz nichego," Biblioteka "VEKHI," 2000, http://www.vehi.net /shestov/chehov.html. For a discussion of Shestov on Chekhov, see Olga Tabachnikova, ed., *Anton Chekhov Through the Eyes of Russian Thinkers: Vasilii Rozanov, Dmitrii Merezhkovskii and Lev Shestov* (Cambridge, UK: Cambridge University Press, 2012), 167–246, https://www .cambridge.org/core/books/anton-chekhov-through-the-eyes-of-russian-thinkers/3CD49882F72 AF93EB78270DE8B5BC6CB.

34. Bergelson, *The End of Everything*, 31.

35. Bergelson, *The End of Everything*, 37.

36. Bergelson, *The End of Everything*, 173. The Yiddish: "der hayntiker tog kumt far nisht itst, nor mit finf, zeks yor tsurik." Bergelson, *Nokh alemen*, 2:217.

37. Bergelson, *The End of Everything*, 92–93. In Yiddish: "Vi amol, hershn itst do di khoyshekhdike beynashmoshes, shtarkt zikh un geyen iber in nepl. Nor a mol zenen do geven mentshn, un itst iz do keyner nishto . . . Zi, Mirlen, bamerkt do keyner nisht. Keyner shtelt zi nisht op un vert mit ir kumen nisht freylekher. Epes iz do shoyn, dukht zikh, shpet un nokh alemen." Bergelson, *Nokh alemen*, 2:119.

38. Bergelson, *The End of Everything*, 40. In Yiddish: "Ir hert, vi di velt shvaygt?" Bergelson, *Nokh alemen*, 2:40.

39. Gilles Deleuze, *Cinema 2: The Time Image* (Minneapolis: University of Minnesota Press, 1989), 56.

40. Nakhmen Mayzel, *Noente un vayter* (Warsaw: Kultur-Lige, 1924), 138.

41. Bergelson, *The End of Everything*, 257.

42. The Yiddish: "ergets-vu zenen nokh faran azelkhe eyntsike, vos veysn 'epes' un haltn 'es' besod." Bergelson, *Nokh alemen*, 2:319.

43. Bergelson, *The End of Everything*, 264. In Yiddish: "Emetser hot im far mir ibergelebt, ot dem friling, un mir vert dos shoyn fun tog tsu tog klerer: nokh eyder ikh bin geboyrn gevorn, hot emets mayn friling ibergelebt." Bergelson, *Nokh alemen*, 2:329.

44. Bergelson, *The End of Everything*, 122. The Yiddish: "hot zikh tsulib epes geheytst in der hrube." Bergelson, *Nokh alemen*, 2:152–53.

45. Bergelson, *The End of Everything*, 122. The Yiddish: "Un gehert hot zikh aher, vi s'klapt dortn dos inveynikste tshugenene tirl, rirt zikh ibern flam, un tsit zikh geshvint ahin un tsurik: pakh-pakh-pakh . . . pakh-pakh-pakh . . . pakh-pakh-pakh . . ." [ellipsis in original]. Bergelson, *Nokh alemen*, 2:153.

46. Roman Jakobson, *Language in Literature* (Cambridge, MA: Harvard University Press, 1987), 85.

47. For an in-depth analysis of sound patterns in relation to meaning, which also includes a discussion of prose, see Benjamin Hrushovsky, "The Meaning of Sound Patterns in Poetry: An Interactive Theory," *Poetics Today* 2.1 (1980). I am grateful to Bruce Rosenstock for alerting my attention to this article.

48. Vladimir Jankélévitch, "Bergson and Judaism," in *Bergson, Politics, and Religion*, ed. Alexandre Lefebvre and Melanie White (Durham, NC: Duke University Press, 2012), 232.

49. Jankélévitch, "Bergson and Judaism," 229. I am grateful to Mark Antliff for directing me to this essay.

50. Paul Ricoeur, *Memory, History, Forgetting* (Chicago, IL: University of Chicago Press, 2004), 445.

51. Sigmund Freud, *The Interpretation of Dreams* (New York: Avon Books, 1965), 578n1.

52. Ricoeur, *Memory, History, Forgetting*, 445.

53. Henri Bergson, *Laughter; An Essay on the Meaning of the Comic* (New York: Macmillan, 1911), 29.

54. Jacques Derrida, *Writing and Difference* (Chicago, IL: University of Chicago Press, 1978), 203.

55. Sigmund Freud, *Beyond the Pleasure Principle* (New York: W. W. Norton, 1961), 22.

56. From an undated letter in YIVO, RG 360, Shmuel Niger, Box 7, Folder 9e.

57. Letter to Shumel Niger, undated. YIVO, RG 360, Shmuel Niger, Box 7, Folder 9e. Buber used the same term *inhalt* (in German) to say that no matter what the content of a particular individual's life was, the structure always included duality and therefore it was necessary to strive for unity. Martin Buber, *On Judaism* (New York: Schocken Books, 1967), 25. The essay in which this term appears, "Judaism and Mankind," was translated into Yiddish. Martin Buber, "Di yehudes un di menshhayt," *Di yidishe velt*, no. 2 (1913): 91–101.

58. Bergelson, *The End of Everything*, 135.

59. Letter to Shmuel Niger, July 18, 1910. YIVO, RG 360, Shmuel Niger Box 7, Folder 9e. A Hebrew translation of Graetz's *History of the Jews* had been published before 1900.

60. Undated letter to Niger from Crimea. YIVO, RG 360, Shmuel Niger Box 7, Folder 9e.

61. Benjamin, *Illuminations*, 163.

62. Bergelson, *Nokh alemen*, 2:62.

63. Bergelson, *The End of Everything*, 46. The Yiddish: "Azoi shpet bistu gekumen, hot zi tsu mir shtil un glaykhgiltik gezogt, m'hot do af dir azoy lang gevart, un itst kuk: zey zenen shoyn ale toyt." Bergelson, *Nokh alemen*, 2:62.

64. As Mikhail Krutikov has observed, the embedded narrative alludes to Y. L. Peretz's "Dead Town."

65. I cannot agree with Sherman's translation of "vi epes a geshleyerte lyalke" (132) as "like some sort of chrysalis in a cocoon" (Bergelson, *The End of Everything*, 104). This translation masks the link between Mirl at her engagement party and the earlier figure of the survivor, both of whom share the motif of the doll.

66. Letter to Shumel Niger, undated. YIVO, RG 360, Shmuel Niger, Box 7, Folder 9e. I am grateful to Zachary Baker for reading this letter with me.

67. Sh Niger, "Briv vegn der nayer yidisher literatur," *Di yidishe velt*, no. 9 (1913): 58–59.

68. Bergelson, *The End of Everything*, 51.

69. Bergelson, *The End of Everything*, 240.

70. Bergelson, *Nokh alemen*, 2:300.

71. Bergelson, *The End of Everything*, 254.

3

TAKING LEAVE

Every now and then I feel that I am breaking through a wall.
(David Bergelson, Letter to Shumel Niger.)

IN THE PECULIAR TIME ZONE OF *THE END* of *Everything* life feels like a remnant of someone else's existence. Belatedness and a painful sense of "afterwardsness" overwhelm the heroine. Delay and belatedness also mark the writing and publication history of *Descent* (*Opgang*), Bergelson's second novel. Bergelson began *Descent* in 1913. He did not submit it for publication until 1919, and it was first published in his journal *Our Own* (*Eygns*) in 1920. *Descent* explores the presence of the past by estranging it, making it mysterious and difficult; it thus resembles a sequel that is missing its first part. It can be compared also to detective fiction. Meylekh has mysteriously died before the novel begins, and his friend Khaym-Moyshe arrives on the scene to figure out what happened to him—but unlike a conventional detective, he cannot solve the mystery. Even though the gap left by Meylekh's death remains, nevertheless, Bergelson's second novel, unlike his first, offers a glimmer of potential. Some kind of future is possible.

In order to put the puzzle pieces together, it is helpful to use the distinction between the fabula, the story as it happened in time, and the siuzhet, the way the story gets narrated. The story in chronological order goes as follows. Meylekh and Khaym-Moyshe were close friends in a big city. Meylekh became involved in anti-tsarist political activity, was exiled to Siberia, and finally settled in the shtetl Rakitne. He opened a pharmacy, became involved with several young women, and died a few years later. He poisoned himself over the course of a week. Readers must stitch together this story from the various versions that other characters provide. *Descent* opens with Meylekh's funeral and zigzags back and forth from his prior life to the funeral and from the funeral forward. There is, however, no unified narrative of Meylekh's past. There is no single account of Meylekh, who was many things to many people: lover to Etl Kadis, Khave Poyzner, and Khanke Lyuber; son to his disappointed mother and would-be son to Yitskhok-Ber; friend and alter-ego to Khaym-Moyshe. Everyone lives in the shadow of Meylekh's death.

The novel features lengthy conversations between Khaym-Moyshe and the dead Meylekh: in these exchanges, the past, in the form of the dead man's thoughts and words, comes alive and seems real, more alive and real than the world of the living. In a Russian-language letter to Shmuel Niger from 1916, Bergelson commented that he was proud of this aspect of his novel and considered it an innovation in Yiddish prose; he praised his own accomplishment of having depicted the union of two lives, Khaym-Moyshe's and Meylekh's, and also said that the "mood" (*nastroenie*) of the novel was unique. It was difficult for him to talk about the work, Bergelson wrote, because he "loved it too much." His novel, he continued, was "an attempt, an experiment . . . which had come alive." And furthermore, the work showed that Yiddish literature was alive and "lived deeply within itself."[1] These remarks indicate Bergelson's optimism about the future of Yiddish literature and about his own contribution to its rebirth after World War I.

The comments Bergelson made about *Descent* in 1919 contrast sharply with his characterization of the novel in 1934, after his return to the Soviet Union. In 1934 Bergelson said, "In previous works I had shown the death of the shtetl and the end of the bourgeoisie . . . now I showed the death of the intelligentsia, which no longer had anyone to talk to . . . Khaym-Moyshe speaks only to a dead person, to Meylekh."[2]

In 1919 Bergelson said he had made something come alive; in 1934 he spoke only of death. In 1919 it was a new kind of writing that had quickened to life; in 1934 it was an entire way of life that had died. As far as *Descent* is concerned, the 1919 remarks about his own writing are more accurate than those of 1934. It is true that Khaym-Moyshe remembers his own childhood and his late father, visits the place where his father's house stood, and meets and talks with people who knew him when he was younger; nonetheless, the novel is not primarily dedicated to remembrance of things past. More than a mere memory, Meylekh haunts his friend Khaym-Moyshe, who not only speaks with his dead friend but also repeats his actions. As I will show, the most significant "departure" (the alternative translation for the title word *opgang*) in this novel is not the economic decline of the shtetl—which in fact in this work grows in size and prosperity—but rather the fact that Khaym-Moyshe stops imitating and talking to the dead Meylekh and begins addressing someone else, someone who is alive. In the midst of haunted time and spectrality, in an ongoing frenzy of repetition, moments of promise and futurity emerge.

Contexts: The Compulsion to Repeat

Contextualizing Bergelson in the broader framework of early twentieth-century thought helps shed light on his approach to the past and the possibilities for the future. During the time that Bergelson was postponing the completion of *Descent* and other works, Henri Bergson and Sigmund Freud took up the question of repetition, exhaustion, and decline. For Bergson, sheer repetition is characteristic of matter and not life, which produces continual novelty. In *Creative Evolution* (1907) Bergson wrote that automatism dogs the perpetual self-creation of life and in certain settings provides the basis for laughter (*Laughter: An Essay on the Meaning of the Comic*, 1911). Freud's approach to the problem of repetition emerges in *Beyond the Pleasure Principle,* first published in 1920. Using the traumatic war neuroses as a point of departure, Freud argues that life seeks to shield itself from novelty of any kind, and he proposes that the compulsion to repeat is an aspect of instinctual life.

During World War I, Bergson used his two opposing concepts—self-creating life versus repetitive materiality—to characterize French and German society respectively. I am less interested in his politics than in the way he transformed his own ideas to offer a diagnosis of these two tendencies in social life.[3] Noting the ever-increasing addition of new technological devices available in his time, Bergson observed that while each new artificial organ augmented the size of the human body, the soul did not follow suit, resulting in the creation of a "soulless void." Some societies responded to this new problem by increasing liberty and therefore diversity, while others filled the void with more materiality, so that instead of creating a more diverse harmony among their members, they transformed persons into things, creating a greater uniformity: "the uniformity of things."[4] The image of the "mechanical encrusted on the living" may provoke laughter, but the transformation of human life into a mechanism is death-dealing.

Bergson attributed the tendency toward mechanical repetition to Prussia, as opposed to France. Freud, in contrast, concluded that it was characteristic of all life. *Beyond the Pleasure Principle* is familiar to most readers for its theory of trauma. Indeed, the work begins with the "traumatic war neuroses" and the evidence they present of the compulsion to repeat. The dreams of patients suffering from these neuroses return them to the situation that caused their suffering in the first place. They repeat certain dimensions of the event without remembering it. Freud also finds examples of the compulsion to repeat in the play of children: the "fort/da" game reveals how the young child masters his mother's occasional departures by repeating them. In his essay Freud explores the broadest possible implications of his theory about repetition, extending the compulsion to repeat to life in general. The regeneration of limbs and human embryology are further examples of the fundamental organic urge to repeat. The human embryo recapitulates all the forms from which it arises, instead of proceeding quickly by the shortest path to its final shape.[5] In direct contrast to Bergson, Freud finds that if left to its own devices, the "elementary living entity" never would have changed; instead, it would have repeated the same "course of life."[6] External and not internal forces led to the change in forms; that is, to evolution. The "goal of life," Freud argues, is to return to the prior state of things, and that state is "inorganic matter." The goal of life is death.[7]

Bergson, in contrast, finds that life constantly wants to go ahead and change, but the particular manifestations of life want to remain the same; as he puts it, they want to "mark time"—to put off change.[8] Bergson argues that in the course of the war, the drive to differentiate—the force of life, in other words—came to a standstill in Prussia, which replaced it with the drive for uniformity, manifesting not "creative evolution" but rather devolution. To reiterate, while the war directly influenced Bergson's and Freud's thinking about the fundamental nature of organic life generally, the difference is that Freud concluded that the urge to repeat—to return to the previous inanimate state, and hence to death—is characteristic of all life.[9] Bergson, in contrast, still contemplated the possibilities for creative futurity.

It is against this backdrop that I turn to Bergelson's novel *Descent*. Bergelson, like the French philosopher Bergson, is similarly poised between repetition and renewal. As I have argued earlier, my point is not to show that Bergson and Freud influenced the Yiddish author; the publication dates of Freud's essay and Bergelson's fiction (both 1920) make that impossible. Bergson's writing on the war was available earlier, but I have no evidence that the Yiddish writer was familiar with the French philosopher's work on this subject. The point is not influence, however, but rather the common framework of the World War I and the interrelated questions of time, memory, and the past that all three writers shared. Even though *Descent* lacks direct mention of the war, the motif of young deaths, including Meylekh's own premature death, resounds throughout the work, suggesting a connection to the massive death toll of the war. Bergelson would explicitly refer to World War I in his Berlin-era fiction, which I discuss in part 2. The themes of repetition and the devolution of life into a more uniform and materialized condition are nonetheless key to this novel: these are the central themes discussed by Bergson and Freud in response to the war. Suicide and the death drive—the drive to repeat—are at the novel's core. Begun in 1913 but not finished until 1919, *Descent* was a way for Bergelson to respond to the war, albeit indirectly and not explicitly.

In *The End of Everything*, Bergelson had already raised the question about the sources of renewal needed to "remake" (*ibermakhn*) life. Art has a role to play, but the figure of the artist in *The End of Everything* and other works is negative. Bergelson disparages the isolated artist, who is cut off from the daily life of other people. Herts, the Hebrew poet in *The End of Everything*, writes at night, when everyone else is sleeping. In *Descent* moments of transformation arise from a physical and synesthetic response to music; responsiveness to music and nature is not limited to the single figure of the artist but rather is dispersed among several characters and thereby part of the novel's fabric as a whole. Bergelson thus returns to the notion of *shtimung* and the related concept of interaction with the surrounding world. Expansive time and what might be called "memories of the future" also have a significant role. Instead of mere repetition, and thus in opposition to Freud, the sudden strange familiarity of what is unexpected may open a different future. In a work concluded after World War I, and in the broad context of devolution, collapse, and destruction, Bergelson finds a way to introduce the possibility of transformation and renewal. I examine three such possibilities in this chapter: the motifs of expansive time, music, and dialogic human interaction.

The Trace

In *Descent* Bergelson takes pains to emphasize that fundamental unknowability of another's life. The French philosopher Bergson has an interesting argument about knowledge of the other and self-knowledge, which he discusses in "Introduction to Metaphysics," first published in 1903. It was translated into Russian in 1914 and was broadly discussed in the Russian press, including articles that appeared before its translation.[10] The earliest Yiddish translation appeared in 1919 (in New York); the Warsaw Kultur-Lige republished this edition in 1923.[11]

Bergson argues that the one reality available to us by means of intuition is "our own person in its flowing through time."[12] He tracks the process of the intuition of the self through various stages, beginning with perceptions that come from the outside world and the motor actions that arise in response to them. But the picture changes "if I pull myself in from the periphery toward the center." By completing this inward turning motion, a different picture emerges: "a succession of states each one of which announces what follows and contains what precedes." While the flow of life is ongoing, the states are not separate; as Bergson explains, "They do not constitute multiple states until I have already got beyond them, and turn around to observe their trail."[13] The entire narrative of *Descent* is the trace of something that happened, the trace left behind by the passage of one human being through the world. Every character, every object, every natural phenomenon, every space, and every building reflects and reflects on what happened to Meylekh, who arrived in the town of Rakitne a few years before the novel begins, opened a little drugstore, and then died mysteriously of no apparent illness.

The trace is part of the fabric of this work and its reception. Writing in 1922, Bergelson's friend the literary critic Nakhmen Mayzel describes the author's work generally in terms that suggest a familiarity with the language of the French philosopher Bergson:

> The surrounding world, nature, the characters, and the relationships among them do not grow from the outside, they do not come from the periphery and move toward the center, but the contrary, they come from within, from the center, from the artistic center toward the periphery. And life and the people in the work shed their superficial mechanical laws and move instead by the force of the author's inner drive . . . the characters are as if astounded by the author's intuitive art.[14]

Intimations of Bergson emerge in Mayzel's description of the flow of Bergelson's creativity from the periphery toward the center. The characterization of the "mechanical laws" driving the characters as "superficial" resonates with Bergson's description of the "mechanical encrusted over the living" that is key to humor. Finally, Mayzel's description of Bergelson's art as "intuitive" likely stems from his acquaintance, directly or indirectly, with Bergson's theories.

Mayzel's description of *Descent* generally is imbued with the notion of the trace: "*Descent* from beginning to end is in its entirety a story that is dreamed, imagined, more echo than sound, more reflection than light, more mirror than image."[15] An echo comes after the original sound, just as a shadow trails behind a figure. The echo, shadow, and reflection all hint at the phenomenon of the aftereffect. It is important to distinguish between the continuity of the past in the present (which in Bergson's scheme would appear as one unbroken whole) and the present as the afterlife of the past. To reiterate Bergson's argument from "Introduction to Metaphysics," only after we go beyond the multiple states that constitute the inner self can we turn around to see their trail. The time lag and the gap are necessary for the trail to become visible. The emphasis on the trace, as opposed to the event, is part of Bergelson's deliberately difficult style, by which he impedes recognition and the forward motion of the narrative.

The very first word of *Descent* is "late" (*shpet*): "Late in the afternoon Meylekh was buried in the small-town cemetery of Rakitne."[16] Meylekh's funeral empties the town, which is "as quiet as though no one lived there any longer." The town itself and the stones that are part of its landscape and the rain that falls there all remember that Meylekh died: "As it slept, the town of Rakitne heard the gutters tranquilly dripping water . . . the drops awakened the remembrance that one human being had passed away from the town."[17] To reiterate, the drops of rain remind the town that one person is now missing from it (*hot zikh gefelt a mentsh*). The remembrance is not of Meylekh as he was in life but rather of his passing. The emphasis is on the passage from one state to another, from the living to the dead.

Bergelson suggests the overarching pattern of the narrative as a whole in a dream sequence. The withdrawal from action, the will to dream, as the French philosopher Bergson says, makes dimensions of the past available in the form of images. Khaym-Moyshe converses with his dead friend and suddenly finds himself "transported" to a strange city. Khaym-Moyshe enters an unfamiliar house and sees jackets hanging near the front room: "'Good,' he thought, 'signs of people.' But the people themselves weren't there. He waited a minute and went into the dining room. But no one was there either. Drained glasses of tea stood on the table with a samovar on one side; it was still warm to the touch; an open book was on the table: apparently someone had just dipped into it and scrutinized its lines."[18]

The jackets, the "drained glasses," the still-warm samovar, and the recently read book are traces, signs, or clues (*remozim*) left behind by the actions of people no longer present. While English does not normally permit descriptive phrases to serve as adjectives placed before nouns, I use this awkward syntax to highlight the extent to which the objects bear the imprint of the actions performed on them, thereby serving to indicate temporal passage. In *Creative Evolution* Bergson argues that our habitual view and utilitarian use of objects in the surrounding world blinds us to the traces that time leaves on them: "All of our beliefs in objects rest on the idea that time does not bite into them."[19] Instead of spatialized movement (the transfer of objects from location to location), Bergelson's description of Khaym-Moyshe's journey through the dining room of the abandoned house emphasizes what Bergson calls "time's bite." Khaym-Moyshe arrives too late to see the inhabitants of the house drink their tea and read the book. All he has are the traces they have left behind. The objects that they used are thus *remozim*, clues. The entire novel is a set of clues.

The trace of the past inserts itself into the present along multiple pathways; for example, the first time Khaym-Moyshe enters his dead friend's room

> It reeked of sharp carbolic acid, of mildewed gutta-percha, and of some other odor, an odor that lingered in every house from which a corpse had been recently removed. There was nothing to see. Only in the second, smaller room, where Meylekh had spent his days and nights, he [Khaym-Moyshe] encountered a shaft of golden sunlight that played with dust on a little table covered with black cloth, a shaft of golden sunlight that only reached in well after midday and called to mind the low, late-afternoon sun, a clay tiled roof that gleamed prettily, like fine gold from the distance, and Meylekh himself, lanky bashful Meylekh, who was present here no longer.[20]

Smell, like sound, crosses boundaries; the lingering smell of the dead body is a remnant of the immediate past, as is the beautiful image of the little ray of sunlight, an afterglow of Meylekh himself. Bergelson prolongs the force of the aftereffect by delaying the arrival of the ray of sunlight, which only has managed to reach this inner room in the afternoon and yet also seems like the sun at twilight. Warmth and light are still present after they should have been gone; thus the trace is not only a trace of death, but also of time's expansion.

Time, Counting, Clocks, and Calendars

In *The End of Everything*, Mirl lives out her life as if it were her afterlife; dreary weekday time dominates, unredeemed by festive holiday time. In *Descent*, in contrast, the motif of festive time (*yontev*) and new birth, not confined to religiously marked holidays, abounds. Khaym-Moyshe feels "newborn" the first time he awakens in Yitskhok-Ber's house in the woods; there is a place in the woods, in a valley, where it is "always Sabbath"; when Khaym-Moyshe encounters an older relative in the poor section of the town, she takes him to her house, walking as if dancing "an intricate wedding dance"; "festive" (*yontev*) gold mingles with shadow; finally, the dead Meylekh tells the living Khaym-Moyshe that the dead will be reborn.[21] Disparate moments of individual experience are awash in the sensibility of holiday and possibility: there are days on which it seems that "anything could happen."

As in other works, distinct temporalities coexist in the same space, including big city time, weekdays and Sabbaths, "the noisome excrescence of outworn generations," the two months that Etl Kadis kept silent, and the moment when Khaym-Moyshe learned that his father was dead.[22] Each of these temporal sensibilities belongs to someone and is imbued with a particular individual experience. For example, Khaym-Moyshe learns of his father's death at about three in the afternoon, "and he swore that he'd always remember that day more than all the other days of his life."[23] For the school principal Preger, "the clear hot summer days all bore the name of Khave Poyzner," because he is full of unrequited love for her.[24] The diversity of privately marked times and public clocks and calendars is one of the preconditions of the creative futurity of memory. The multiple temporalities mitigate uniformity and repetition.

In *Descent* as in other works by Bergelson, particularly beautiful moments of expansive time are found in the lives of characters not otherwise attractive or praiseworthy. These are purely contingent moments. Zaynvl Zalker the Singer sewing machine salesman is in "ecstasy" over a beautiful summer day. In the following scene, to give another example, the disgruntled Preger, goes swimming on the Sabbath, when bathing—and smoking—are prohibited:

> He was content. He carried a towel in his hand and was going to bathe. But as he went through the end of the town past the widely opened windows of the synagogue, he heard the Sabbath liturgical chant, borukh she-omar, "Blessed be He who spoke." What an old, unyielding chant! It denied the validity of all the modern changes the world had undergone. And suddenly Preger was irked that this liturgical chant was so stubbornly unyielding and that he himself was not a smoker. . . . [H]e deliberately bathed at a spot in the narrow stream where they could see him clearly . . . Let those over there see how he soaped himself and splashed about for a long, long time until he grew weary. And the narrow stream dazzled his eyes, gleamed and beamed, and his ears murmured as though they'd been filled with water.[25]

As the scene continues, Preger dresses and makes a mental note of the point that the synagogue service has reached; "noticing something shimmering," he feels his heart pound and realizes that a young woman from the town, who used to be in love with him, is also swimming: "Her beautiful slender hands scattered rays of light with every stroke."[26] Preger becomes confused when he hears another fragment of liturgy, and he realizes that the service is not as far advanced as he originally thought. He is glad that he can prolong his stay at the river. He gains time.

In this passage, the author conveys the character's interior monologue without quotation marks. Preger's consciousness bleeds into the narrative. Objects similarly lose their distinctness; sounds "murmur" and things "shimmer." The rules of gravity no longer apply: "Both the red silk parasol and the green jacket seemed to be floating, floating on air.[27] Shimmering or flickering in Bergelson generally signals a shift in attention and perception. Emotion colors perception to such a degree as to change the quality of what is being seen. Proximity and distance shift and change. Later in *Descent*, for example, during a Christian holiday, as the sound of the church bells "chase each other," Khanke looks away from the town toward the distance where "the dense beginning of the great wood rose blue to the sight . . . in the great heat, exuding a blue haze around itself . . . and the place seemed so near now, and yet so far" [ellipsis added].[28]

Bergelson introduces movement and qualities into space by means of a specific character's emotional response. The woods emanate a blue color from the heat, and the blue travels across the distance to Khanke (*hot zikh aher aroysgebloyt*).[29] The distant woods seem close because Khaym-Moyshe lives there and Khanke is in love with him. Emotion changes space and time. In the scene where Preger goes swimming, the Hebrew Sabbath service functions as a clock, in which this or that prayer indicate earliness or lateness. The Sabbath, in contrast to the everyday function of a clock, commemorates the creation of the world and looks forward to its redemption. Bergelson is playing with the transformation of religiously ordained moments of time into the vagaries of individual experience. Preger loses track of time as his desire increases. His emotions shift from contentment to spite, curiosity, lust, and finally back to spite (the woman refuses to acknowledge him).

Idol Worship

Khaym-Moyshe, the visitor to Rakitne, arouses interest not only because he was Meylekh's closest friend but also because he is a native of the town who went on to become a mathematician and the author of several books on mathematics. For all his mathematical knowledge, however, Khaym-Moyshe is strangely inattentive to the passage of time—this is a count that he fails to track properly. Mirl fails to notice that she is pregnant; Khaym-Moyshe is seemingly unaware of his own age, and he is unpleasantly surprised when an old man reminds him that he is no longer the young man he thought he was. Meylekh, Khaym-Moyshe's dead friend, accuses him of counting other people's sorrows and joys without feeling any of his own, thus resembling the devil. In the Bible, David was convinced to conduct a census by Satan. Counting Jews is generally frowned upon in the biblical and rabbinic tradition, and alternative means of arriving at a number were used (e.g., to determine whether the necessary quorum had been reached for prayer). In Bergelson's novel this allusion must be considered ironic, since the number of inhabitants of the shtetl is given as seven thousand. It is also significant that *Descent* includes a young girl with what we would call developmental disabilities who spends her time playing a counting game, and the numbers always come out as she wishes them to. Khaym-Moyshe's friend accuses him, fairly or not, of a lack of emotion.

Like Mirl Hurvits, Khaym-Moyshe's failure to live and feel an emotional attachment to the present comes from his attachment to the past, in the form of his relationship to the dead Meylekh. For Khaym-Moyshe, "One thing was certain, though: now, after his death, Meylekh had unquestionably acquired more substance."[30] Earlier in the story, in the narration of Meylekh's and Khaym-Moyshe's time together in the big city, the narrator observes that "both remembered that they bore small, barely noticeable humps on their shoulders" and that these humps were the legacy of their "small-town Jewish fathers."[31] After he dies, Meylekh replaces the small-town legacy; the nearly invisible hump on Khaym-Moyshe's shoulder has changed its form, taking on the likeness of his dead friend Meylekh. An art student has crafted a small statue of Meylekh, which Khanke Lyuber tries to give to Khaym-Moyshe, but she does not find him at home. She is compelled to carry the statue back and forth between the town and the house in the woods where Khaym-Moyshe is staying. The statue has the same "bashful smile" that characterized Meylekh during his life. In *War and Peace*, Andrei Bolkonski's wife, Lise, has an overbite, which makes her smile all the more charming. After her death, the statue at her grave bears the same charming smile, which serves as a reproach to the living. Bergelson's eternally smiling Meylekh, in contrast, serves another purpose.

The epigraph of the novel, taken from Ezekiel 8, helps to explain its significance. The entire passage is as follows: "And he brought me to the entrance of the court; I looked, and there was a hole in the wall. Then he said to me, 'Mortal, dig through the wall'; and when I dug through the wall, there was an entrance" (Ezekiel 8:7–8). When the prophet enters, he sees the "abominations" that are practiced within and "all the idols of the house of Israel" (Ezekiel 8:9–10). In Ezekiel the "abominations" are sexual; in *Descent* there are no "abominations" as such, but there are hints that Mey-lekh had intimate relations with more than one young woman in Rakitne. Furthermore, the town gossip is that Meylekh and Khaym-Moyshe "were singularly close, like one person: some how like brothers, yet not brothers" (*epes brider un nisht brider*).[32] "Brothers without being brothers" suggests a homosexual relationship.

Bergelson explicitly uses the motif of idols, the form of abomination specifically named in Ezekiel. After a sleepless night, Khaym-Moyshe experiences something like a hallucination, during which he sees not one but "many, many" Khave Poyzners, each one of whom has her own "little idol" (*getele*). The multiple Khave Poyzners sing lullabies to their idols, who fall asleep, "but one of them wore a bashful smile on his open pale face: Meylekh's bashful smile."[33] Meylekh's transformation into a thing begins to take place even before he dies. He visits Etl Kadis as if he were "a tall, bashful shadow" that could "glide" from one place to another. He sits down and remains speechless, and when he finally does speak "he emitted such a bizarre crackling sound, as though not a human but a table or a bench were suddenly starting to speak."[34] Meylekh, a "shadow" before he is dead, undergoes a process of de-animation .

In a letter from 1912, a year before he began work on *Descent*, Ber-gelson wrote a letter to Sh. Niger that discussed false gods and messianic expectations in the broader historical framework of the time. Bergelson described the aftermath of the failed Russian revolution in terms of height-ened expectation and tension. He had seen the "outer fire of the revolution" (a reference to the Russian revolution of 1905), which was driven inward, where it was burnished to the highest degree, but sparks remained in the air and exploded every now and then. The mystical terms of this description are unmistakable; Bergelson refers explicitly to "merkave mysticism" in the letter. It is possible that Jews were creating "a belief without a doctrine, and the present moment is as important as the one when the prophet said that one can 'know' God in one's heart, but the Greeks did not understand this, because they had to touch their god's hands and feet."[35]

Idol worship and the appearance of false messiahs occur at times of pol-itical and metaphysical uncertainty. Bergelson compares the early twentieth century with its temptations, false gods, and empty doctrines to the time of the prophets, who exhorted Israel to avoid idol worship and superficial piety. Jeremiah, living at the time of the destruction of Jerusalem, describes God's future restoration of Israel based on a new covenant: "But this shall be the covenant that I will make with the house of Israel; After those days, saith the LORD, I will put my law in their inward parts, and write it in their hearts; and will be their God, and they shall be my people" (Jeremiah 31:33). The new covenant is an inward and not an external bond; it is of the "heart." The turn of the twentieth century was a time of messianic expectation similar to the earlier epoch and just as easily waylaid by false gods.

In the embedded narrative of the empty house that I discussed earlier, Khaym-Moyshe arrives too late to meet the people who have already departed, just as in the frame narrative where he arrives too late to meet Meylekh, who is already dead and buried. Khaym-Moyshe asks the dead Meylekh what he should do, and the answer is that he should wait and guard the house until the master returns. It is significant that the word *meylekh* means "king" in Hebrew. The master or king has departed but will return; his servant must wait for him. The exchange has the feel of a parable, but the master or king in the parable usually refers to God, and Meylekh is a false god.[36] His suicide indicates his loss of faith not only in God but also, and more importantly, in the world. Meylekh, with his bashful smile, is a temptation more than anything else.

Khaym-Moyshe unknowingly repeats Meylekh's actions, retracing his steps through the town and revisiting the people that Meylekh had visited. Visiting Khanke Lyuber and sitting in the room with its many portraits of her dead mother, he finds himself drawn to one in particular. Khanke cannot "fail to notice that Meylekh had also looked closely at this very same portrait."[37] He stays late at the fete for the Talmud Torah, just as Meylekh did, and then he prepares to "depart" (*opgang*, the title word). Bergelson emphasizes how close Khaym-Moyshe comes to duplicating Meylekh's last act: "A year before, at this very same gala, Meylekh had passed exactly the same kind of night."[38] Khaym-Moyshe recalls that there is "another way out" (*oysveg*): the little container marked with skull and crossbones. He contemplates repeating Meylekh's suicide.

Khaym-Moyshe unwittingly repeats his dead friend's actions but finally frees himself from the "compulsion to repeat." The potential for renewal has to do with the cluster of concepts pertaining to *shtimung*, including music, musicality, and addressivity. Music embodies change and the transformation of one thing into another. In its representation of musical performance,

Descent conjures up fleeting images of harmony among human beings and between human beings and the world. Addressivity, or dialogic interaction, takes place at rare moments in the novel when a speaker directs speech at another concrete human being who is side by side with the speaker.

Metamorphosis

Bergelson's text is musical because he uses rhythm and repetition; he also makes musical performance part of the story.[39] His texts animate the "melodies" that coexist and contend with the innovations of the modern world: the multiple and disparate temporalities carried from the past into the present and the virtual futures that they contain. Melody is a significant metaphor for both Bergson and Bergelson, also related to *shtimung*, sensibility, mood, rhythm, and sensation. Bergelson used the notion of *shtimung* in *"Arum vokzal"* ("At the Depot"), as I discussed in chapter 1, and he directly reflected on the "mood" that a literary work creates in his portrait of Mirl Hurvits in *The End of Everything.*

In *Descent*, *shtimung* emerges as a broader concept. The scene in which a musical performance takes place arises as if by chance, and the characters involved are peripheral to the main action. Khaym-Moyshe appears at the scene also by accident, in pursuit of something else. On the day of the fair, a man who works as a repairer of musical instruments arrives in the town. He is asked to play the accordion. His playing fills the room with "animated sounds that dancingly chased after one another, artfully arranged themselves, and somersaulted and tumbled, tumbled and somersaulted, like tiny jolly mocking clowns."[40]

This remarkable passage transforms sound into visual impressions. Bergelson used this technique in "At the Depot," as I discussed in chapter 1: the flames in the depot lanterns become little nodding heads who listen to the testimony of witnesses. Here, in contrast, the mood is playful: we are transported to the circus, and we watch as the clowns chase each other. The music and the musician become one being. When the musician opens the accordion, he first pulls on its straps and then turns his head from side to side "as if he didn't know yet which ear to listen with: the right or the left."[41] The word in Yiddish for the straps is *oyern*, which can mean "ears" as well as "handles," such as the handles on a jug. The musician's ears and the accordions "ears," so to speak, create a visual echo, drawing out the fusion between the musician and his instrument. There is a comic exchange of qualities between the two. Bergelson sustains the fusion in the next image: "He breathed with no less difficulty than the huge, infinitely wrinkled instrument itself, chomping and snuffling in time with the sounds."[42] The pleats of the accordion look like the wrinkles on the musician's face, and his nasal snuffling sounds echo the instrument's sounds. And the music transforms the listeners: "all were enraptured" (*ale zenen geven nispoel*).[43] This is an example of Bergelson's sense of joy and comedy.

The scene offers a striking contrast to the musical performance in *The End of Everything*. A young woman plays Beethoven's Piano Sonata No. 1, and its "first hushed, haunting tones" are "embarrassed by the crude buffoonery that had preceded them"—and these same notes ask the chords that follow them whether they are "disgusted" by the listeners.[44] Mirl's own disgust and embarrassment clearly infect the mood of the music. Distance, isolation, and separation mark this music, unlike the scene from *Descent*, in which harmony, joy, and transformation are the key motifs.

In *Descent*, the musician is referred to as *der gilgul*, (the "transmigratory soul").[45] Earlier in the novel, Meylekh's unexpected appearance in Rakitne is referred to as *megulgl gevorn* ("*megulgl gevorn a fremder yungerman*").[46] In the dreamlike sequence in which Khaym-Moyshe finds himself at a house full of "traces" of people, the same phrase is also used. *Gilgul* refers to the transmigration of the soul.[47] Discussion of the transmigration of souls occurs in the Zohar, a compilation of texts on Jewish mysticism composed in the late thirteenth and early fourteenth centuries, although the first appearance is much earlier. The Zohar was printed in the sixteenth century, and most scholars agree that the peak of interest in it took place at this time and in the seventeenth century, as a partial response to the expulsions. According to the seventeenth-century kabbalist Isaac Luria, the soul of Adam, which contained all future human souls, was made of 613 parts—the number 613 corresponds to the 613 commandments. Adam's sin fractured his soul and introduced a cosmic fall. In order for individual souls to achieve perfection, they must fulfill all the commandments, and failure to do so leads to the soul's transmigration, which gains the soul another chance to perfect itself. *Gilgul* thus participates in the larger, overarching process of cosmic restoration, or *tikkun*. In *Descent*, Khaym-Moyshe is asked whether he has "set something to rights."[48] The term in the original Yiddish for "set something to rights" is *mesakn*, which is related to *tikkun*; in addition to the idea of repair, *mesakn* carries the mystical meaning of finding repose for a soul in torment. Souls that have fulfilled the commandments wait for their reintegration with Adam's soul. Bergelson was familiar with the notion of the 613 parts, referring to them in a comic vein in a letter. It is possible to see this view of the soul's cosmic journey as offering a parallel to the French philosopher Bergson's view of the life force, which materializes itself in the multiplicity of organic forms. By evoking *gilgul* in the figure of the musician, Bergelson suggests the possibility of a world full of evolving and changing form—the antithesis of the pattern of repetition and imitation that dominates the world of *Descent*. Other authors working in the first part of the twentieth century—including Der Nister and Sh. An-sky in his play *The Dybbuk*—turned to the Jewish mystical tradition as a source of secular cultural expression. Bergelson was doing something similar. Indeed, the dialogue between Khaym-Moyshe and the dead Meylekh offers a parallel to the *dybbuk*: Meylekh's soul transmigrates into his friend's.

The use of the term *gilgul* can also be read as a gloss on Bergelson's own narrative technique, which transforms one quality into another, as in the example of musical notes metamorphosing into acrobats. In a 1926 article, "Sholem-Aleichem and Folk Language" ("Sholem-Aleichem un di folks-shprakh"), Bergelson criticizes Sholem Aleichem's putative inability to depict the individual characteristics of distinct human beings. Bergelson goes on to suggest the correct method: "The face and character [of a literary personage] are felt through detail and ornament" (*a ponim un a kharakter vert derfilt durkh an eyntslheyt, durkh an ornament*).[49] Ornament is usually understood as precisely what is not critical in a work of art, in terms of overall structure or plot, because it is merely decorative, repetitious, pleasing to the eye or ear but not crucial to meaning—which is appropriate for a modernist work that goes around meaning to influence the audience more directly. "Ornament" is an extremely capacious term that can encompass quotation, repetition, sound repetition, rhyme, hyperbole, and circumlocution.[50] It corresponds to "arabesque" in visual art: the repeating formal detail that rhythmically unites the otherwise disparate elements of the work and, according to Riegl, overcomes the emptiness of space by lending it qualities of rhythm.[51] Bergelson's method in *Descent* and other works, which may be termed ornamental or arabesque, creates a kind of literary *gilgul*, or, transmigration.

I and Thou

As I discussed in chapter 1, one of the crucial notions of "mood" or "atmosphere" (*Stimmung* in German) that Alois Riegl discussed in his writings and his classroom lectures has to do with the response that the work of art evokes in the spectator. The Dutch group portrait, according to Riegl, generates an active process of attention and compassion in the beholder. Van Ruisdael's landscapes look back at the viewer. Scholars have attributed the development of Buber's "I–thou" model in part to Riegl's emphasis on the active exchange of attention and emotion between viewers and what they view—the "addressivity" set in motion by the artwork that looks at its beholders. Buber's *I and Thou* was published in 1923, after Bergelson's *Descent* had already appeared in print. It is likely that Bergelson was familiar with Buber's ideas, since he refers to him as a possible contributor to the journal *Di yidishe velt* in a 1912 letter.[52] Buber's notion of "I and thou" was in part based on his earlier concept of intersubjectivity.[53] The dialogic encounter between myself and another enacts an immediate and concrete relation between us. It is not designed for any purpose other than the meeting between the "I" and the "you."[54]

Mikhail Bakhtin's notion of dialogue emerges in his writings from the late teens and early twenties; its full elaboration appeared in the early version of his study of Dostoevsky, published in 1929. Bakhtin, like Buber, drew on Riegl.[55] Bakhtin argues that "I" emerges only in relation to "you"; according to Bakhtin, Dostoevsky's innovation was to create characters oriented toward the "other's word."[56] Addressing the other in dialogue radically differs from describing the other in objective, abstract, or universalizing language. As in previous discussions of the question of influence, the notion of contiguity offers a more productive way of tracing the parallels and overlaps between Bergelson and other figures of this time. Using the framework provided by these concepts, an analysis of *Descent* reveals that the occurrences of addressivity—the first-person orientation toward a second person "you"—mark significant turning points in the novel.

In order to examine these instances, a preliminary discussion of Bergelson's use of reported speech will be helpful. Daniela Mantovan has analyzed Bergelson's style in detail.[57] Mantovan shows that in *The End of Everything* the author makes no firm distinctions between the narrator, "the direct speech of a character, and that character's unexpressed thoughts."[58] She concludes that while this fluidity creates multiple possibilities for the meaning of any particular utterance, it also impedes communication between characters. In reporting a conversation between two characters, Bergelson typically has both speakers using the third person to refer to themselves. Mantovan attributes Bergelson's use of this style to Flaubert, who had initially used it in *Madame Bovary*, a text that the Yiddish author knew well. The third-person report of first-person speech, as Mantovan shows, contributes to the sense of alienation and isolation from which Bergelson's characters suffer, even when they are in the same space at the same time. Speaking about yourself as if you were someone else corresponds to Mirl Hurvits's conclusion that "someone else lived out" the springtime of her life. Mantovan does not discuss *Descent* specifically but reasonably argues that Bergelson uses the indirect method of reported speech in other works. I agree with this assessment, but I will go further and say that other, more positive interpretations also emerge.

The indirect style, or reference to oneself in the third person, is only one element of the overall speech situation in Bergelson's novels in general and *Descent* in particular. An equally important phenomenon is speech that belongs to no one: generalized discourse that includes statements on the order of "one says," "they say," or "people say." In Yiddish these variants can be expressed by the use of the pronoun *men*, in the passage below, appearing in the contraction *m'hot*. The narrator cites the truisms circulated about Etl Kadis—who was supposed to marry Meylekh—after his death:

> Comments were passed:
> —Someone without luck is better off dead.[59]
> M'hot geshmuest:
> "Oyb a mentsh geyt nisht, iz glaykher, er zol shoyn gor nisht lebn af der velt."[60]

No one in particular is affirming this banality, and it is not directed explicitly at Etl but rather stated about her. Idle talk creates the illusion of a community of speakers but in fact does the opposite: it creates alternative versions of individuals, according to its own demands and predilections, based on what "everyone" knows and says.[61]

In *The End of Everything*, Bergelson transforms gossip into a miniature narrative:

> Short, damp days followed in quick succession, driving the shtetl ever more deeply into winter. Neither indoors nor outdoors offered anything to awaken interest, stirring instead the same indifferent discontent toward everything around, so that one might as well stop every overgrown girl who occasionally strolled down the main street in smartly dressed self-importance, vent one's frustration on her, and rebuke her in the voice of an older, deeply discontented woman—Why are you so choosy, you?[62]

The "short, damp days" (the quality of time) lead to collective dissatisfaction, which in turn becomes embodied in a person who accosts Mirl

Hurvits on the street to demand to know why she does not get married. No one is actually speaking, and there is in fact no one there next to Mirl, only this illusion of a person—the distillation of the dreary mood in the shtetl. Bergelson transforms a mood into a ghostly image of a person who then melts away, returning to the general atmosphere of the place. This is another instance of where Bergelson plays with *gilgul*, the transmigration of souls.

In *Descent*, he uses generalized discourse in Khanke's exchange with a group of disgruntled guests at the fête. They feel slighted because they have no place to sit down, and she reassures them by saying,

> —A place would be made available to them at that special table.[63]
> Me vet zey opgeben an ort ot bay yenem bazundern tishl.[64]

Khanke's statement effectively removes her from the conversation altogether: it is not she but some other unknown and abstract agent who will address the other's problem. And the recipients of this statement are not addressed directly with the second person but are instead referred to in the third person: "they" instead of "you." The same result obtains. It is as if the addressee were not present in the conversation. No one is speaking.

A similar effect is produced by questions that remain unanswered; even when an answer is forthcoming, it is not addressed to anyone in particular. Yitskhok-Ber asks Meylekh's sister where the key to the cottage is, but she does not answer him. Later the narrator answers the question by explaining that the key was wrapped up in a handkerchief in Etl Kadis's bag; however, this utterance is not directed to Yitskhok-Ber but rather addressed to the reader, if it can be said to have an addressee at all.

Self-reference in the third person occurs with high frequency in *Descent*. Khanke, for example, hedges about leaving a lit candle in Meylekh's cottage after his death: "She was ninety percent certain that she herself hadn't kindled it."[65] When Yitskhok-Ber, who usually relies on the third person, addresses Khaym-Moyshe and Meylekh in the second person (*Hert-zhe oys*), he announces that there is nothing further to say: "The world's been discussed for good and all by now."[66] The use of the passive here corresponds to the use of "they" or "people" elsewhere, by creating the effect that no one in particular has finished discussing the world. Statements made in this fashion serve to remove speakers from their statements, emptying the world of speakers. When Meylekh (while still alive) speaks to Etl Kadis, he uses the first person to refer to himself and the second person to address her, but as in the examples above, he states anti-climactically that he has nothing to say: "'I nearly, nearly had something to say to you.'"[67]

Direct address, in which speakers refer to themselves in the first person and their interlocutors in the second person, does take place in *Descent*, but significantly the greatest number of cases of this type of speech occurs in Khaym-Moyshe's conversations with the dead Meylekh. In the following philosophical exchange, for example, the two address one another by name:

> —What exactly is a human being, Meylekh?
> —Nothing, Khaym-Moyshe: an experiment or a passing chance.
> —And a human being's sufferings?
> —In the same category, Khaym-Moyshe.[68]

Khaym-Moyshe is addressing his interlocutor directly, but his interlocutor is not there, and what is more, his addressee, the dead Meylekh, says that human beings and their sufferings are of no concern. While the form of the conversation outwardly conforms to a dialogue—an exchange between two persons who address one another—the content of the exchange denies the reality of human existence and the meaning of human suffering.

In *Descent* the use of the third-person indirect speech style occurs most frequently in reference to Khanke. It appears when she admonishes her little brother ("never again would she ever take him"), when she speaks to Khaym-Moyshe, and even when she writes a note to him to tell him that she wants to give him Meylekh's statue ("She'd brought him Meylekh's small bust").[69]

Even when Khanke is alone together with Khaym-Moyshe and proclaims her happiness, the report of this intimate speech remains in the third person:

> —She was content . . . at this particular moment she was content with everything, even with the fact that Motik [her little brother] had no mother. . . . How odd that was! . . . She only wanted to tell him that she required nothing of him [ellipsis in original].[70]

A more conventional narrative style would have the character say, "I am content . . . At this particular moment I am content with everything." The impact of the use of the indirect style is the same as the impact of the use of generalized discourse ("one said"). Even though we are to imagine that the original speech was in the first person (as in "I am content") and it is only the report of the speech that transforms it into the third person "she was content," the end result is the same. The effect is that the speaker is separated from her statement, as if she were absent while making it. The requirement of English grammar that puts verbs in reported speech in the past tense adds to this effect, but it is nonetheless powerful in the original Yiddish.

Bergelson's use of free indirect style, however, does not always signify alienation and separation or the failure to communicate, because it does not always refer to prior direct speech. The use of this style does not always signal a reenactment of oral communication but instead may signify "various unspoken consciousnesses," as Ann Banfield puts it.[71] Banfield's analysis of free indirect style allows for a greater range of interpretation, suggesting a more radical experimentation with the depiction of characters and their consciousness. Her discussion is based on Woolf and D. H. Lawrence, but her conclusions work for Bergelson as well.

After Khanke expresses her satisfaction with everything, the narrative continues in the free indirect style, indicating both Khanke's and Khaym-Moyshe's state of mind. I give the passage in both the translation and the original:

> The essence of it all was that, apart from little Motik, now, in the middle of the hot summer, a great new life had come upon her. Apparently she was happy, intensely happy.
> Later, when Khaym Moyshe returned to the woods, he thought of her in conjunction with this new life that had come upon her.[72]
> Der iker iz geven, vos khutsn kleynem Motikn iz ir itst in mitn heysn zumer tsugekumen a nay un groys lebn. Ir iz, a ponim, geven gut, shtark gut.
> Az Khaym-Moyshe hot zikh nokh dem umgekert tsurik in vald arayn, hot er zi gedenkt in eynem mit ot dem nayem tsugekumenem lebn irn.[73]

Bergelson plays with the boundary separating one consciousness from another. As is typical for free indirect style, adverbs of time and place are retained as they would occur in direct speech. In the statement above attributed to Khanke, the adverb is "now." The fuzziness of time, place, and speaker arises from the phrase "a great new life had come upon her." Whether Khanke actually utters a statement expressing this feeling aloud is uncertain, because "she was unable to speak." Furthermore, the very next line is from an external point of view: "apparently she was happy." For whom her happiness is apparent is unclear, as we would expect from free indirect style; we can assume, however, that it is Khaym-Moyshe who is drawing the conclusion about her apparent happiness. In the very next line, which is marked by the time expression "later" (*nokh dem*) and a description of another place, not the road that the pair is taking but "in the woods," Khaym-Moyshe "thought of," or, "remembered" (*gedenkt*) her and also the "new life that had come upon her," repeating the formulation that may or may not have been uttered aloud. The overall pattern is that what one person said or perhaps merely thought at some prior moment becomes what someone else "remembers" elsewhere and later. Instead of isolation, alienation, and failure, the use of free indirect style in this passage suggests something approaching a merger of consciousnesses, which makes separation in time and place unimportant. Thus far in the novel, the two consciousnesses that have been merged are Khaym-Moyshe's and Meylekh's; the new merger is between Khaym-Moyshe and Khanke.

In a speech world emptied of speakers, as in the examples of gossip and third-person statements, instances of direct address are all the more meaningful and significant. The vocative, the form of speech that signifies direct address, instantiates the meeting of the "I" and the "you" that both Buber and Bakhtin describe. The first significant instance of direct address occurs approximately halfway through the novel, in chapter XVII, when Khanke and Khaym-Moyshe bump into one another at the fair and then go off on their own. The exchange is worth quoting at length:

> Khaym Moyshe led Hanke a little to one side and stopped to talk to her:
> —Well?
> And suddenly something concealed in the unspeaking depths of her wistful pale-blue eyes made itself manifest; as she gazed dumbly up at him, her eyes were suddenly filled with the trembling perturbation of her heart and breast.[74]

The abrupt and awkward interjection "well?" (*nu?*), the demand for speech, provokes an overwhelming emotional response in Khanke, who cannot speak, and her failure to respond in turn leads to Khaym-Moyshe's use of the vocative "Khanke." The vocative says, in effect, "I am speaking to you" or "I am naming you as the other to whom I am speaking now." It can be an announcement of a shift in attention on the part of the speaker—"I am turning (away from something or someone else) to you." Or it can be a demand that the other turn her attention to the speaker: "You, listen to me now." In the context of the conversation above, however, the use of the vocative is also a continuation of the phrase "What is the matter?" as if Khaym-Moyshe had said instead, "What is the matter with you, Khanke?" The use of the direct address refutes the claims made by various speakers to the effect that there is nothing to say, that everything that could be said about the world has been said already, and that human beings and their sufferings are nothing. Khaym-Moyshe is saying, in effect, "Tell me what you are suffering from." Calling Khanke by name may also be a way for Khaym-Moyshe to express his own disquiet and agitation, a petition that she address him.

Calling the other by name is a new thing that has not yet been said; Khaym-Moyshe has not yet addressed Khanke, and when he does, he and she create something new in the world. This new thing, the relation between them, is created outside the public space of the fair—in other words, in a space that is not constituted by the "idle talk" of what "they say." Khaym-Moyshe has taken Khanke off to the side. As the pair leave the town and walk toward the woods, they are even farther removed from the shtetl and its gossip. They sit in the grass, and Khanke finally replies to Khaym-Moyshe's direct address with her own use of the vocative—"Khaym-Moyshe." This new form of exchange between the two continues right through and even beyond the ending of the novel. At the fete, Khanke waits all evening for Khaym-Moyshe to approach her, and when he leaves without speaking to her, she finally decides to go to the woods where he lives. She knocks on his locked window shutters, and his response, the last words of the novel, is once again the vocative address: "Oh, Khanke . . . [ellipsis in original]."[75] The ellipsis underscores openness, possibility, and the suspension of the repetition that has dogged Khaym-Moyshe's actions from the time he first arrived in Rakitne.

When Khanke, alone with Khaym-Moyshe in the woods, calls him by name for the first time, she is overcome with the strange sensation of having already sat with him and having already spoken with him. She experiences déjà vu, the sense that we have already lived through an event, which we remember, and then undergo it again. But in the passage I discussed in relation to the free indirect style, the repetition of the scene creates the feeling that a "great *new* life" has begun for her. This is a concrete instance when memory and even apparent repetition indicate the possibility of a new future, and not merely the repetition of the past.

In his discussion of what he called "memory of the present," Bergson argues that déjà vu is the coming to consciousness of the experience of memory simultaneously with the experience of perception. The normal attentiveness to the immediate requirements of life is temporarily slackened, and we become aware of a process that was already ongoing but that we usually do not perceive: the laying down of memory itself. To put it another way, we take a break from the present and from the anticipation of the future and float, as if in a dream state, so that we experience the present as already past. It is a slackening of attention to the next object coming at us that enables an opening of the perceptive aperture to include the already forming memory of the present.[76] It is the potentiality of the present experienced as already past and returned that gives rise to Khanke's feeling that a "great new life" has begun. The great moments of life feel as if they've begun earlier, because we haven't noticed them, but when they begin to be actualized in the present, it seems that this is a repetition.

Repeating without remembering is the symptom of traumatic war neurosis, according to Freud; this pattern, however, is also found in dreams, the games of children, and indeed in the very foundation of organic life, which seeks only to die its own death and thus return to (or repeat) its former state. For Bergson, in contrast, life may sink into repetition and uniformity, but life's desire is to create itself anew. For both Bergson and Freud, the tendency toward repetition became increasingly evident during World War I.

At the end of *Descent*, Bergelson offers an alternative to both Freud and Bergson. Khanke remembers the past without repeating it, thus moving beyond the aftereffect of Meylekh's death. In other works begun before the World War I, including "In a Backwoods Town," "Impoverished," and "Joseph Shur," the ending repeats the leitmotif of the narrative as a whole. For example, the last line of "In a Backwoods Town" is the repetition of the hero's motto "The world stinks." The last line of "Joseph Shur" is the eponymous hero's phrase about his beet mill, which recurs throughout the narrative whenever he feels the need to assuage his hurt feelings. The last words of *Descent* introduce something new—"Oh, Khanke." It is significant that in an earlier version of the novel, Khaym-Moyshe's words to Khanke contain an additional utterance: "Why had she come so early?" (*nokh vos iz zi azoy fri gekumen*).[77] Reported in the third person, they return to the failure and missed opportunity that dominate *Descent* to this point. Bergelson's decision to omit this line in favor of the much briefer and more direct form of address is important. Whatever the brief address to Khanke means, whether it speaks of love, disappointment, joyous greeting, or resentment, these words have not yet been spoken; they do not repeat a prior utterance. They thus constitute a departure, and here I call upon the other meaning of the novel's title word *opgang*. Addressing the other is an opening into futurity. This is Bergelson's form of "breaking through," to quote the same language with which I began this chapter—there is no earth-shattering new revelation, no drastic remaking of human beings or society. The same petty resentments, jealousies, and conflicts that animate ordinary human life will continue, only with one small difference: a man and a woman will address each other.

Notes

1. See Letter to Niger, 1916, RG 360, Shmuel Niger, Box 7, Folder 9e, YIVO Archive.

2. David Bergelson, "Materyaln tsu D. Bergelsons bio-bibliografye," *Visnshaft un revolutsye* 1–2 (1934): 71.

3. For a discussion of Bergson on war, see Soulez, "Bergson as Philosopher of War and Theorist of the Political," in *Bergson, Politics, and Religion*, ed. Alexandre Lefebvre and Melanie White (Durham, NC: Duke University Press, 2012), 99–125.

4. Henri Bergson, *The Meaning of the War: Life & Matter in Conflict* (London: T. F. Unwin, 1915).

5. Sigmund Freud, *Beyond the Pleasure Principle* (New York: W. W. Norton, 1961), 31.

6. Freud, *Beyond the Pleasure Principle*, 32.

7. Freud, *Beyond the Pleasure Principle*, 32

8. Henri Bergson, *Creative Evolution*, trans. Arthur Mitchell (New York: H. Holt, 1911), 128.

9. Scholars do not agree about the influence of the war on Freud's formulation of a death instinct. For a discussion that discounts this influence, placing *Beyond the Pleasure Principle* in the context of Freud's thought as a whole and emphasizing instead the importance of biology in his work, see Frank J. Sulloway, *Freud, Biologist of the Mind: Beyond the Psychoanalytic Legend* (New York: Basis Books, 1983), 395–413.

10. N. Losskii, "Nedostatki gnoseologii Bergsona i vlianie ikh na ego metafiziku," *Voprosy filosofii* 3, no. 118 (1913): 224–35. See also I. Grossman, "Bakunin i Bergson," *Zavety* no. 5 (1914): 47–62.

11. Henri Bergson, "Araynfir tsu metafizik," *Shriftn*, Summer 1919.

12. Henri Bergson, *An Introduction to Metaphysics: The Creative Mind* (Totowa, NJ: Littlefield, Adams, 1965), 163.

13. Bergson, *An Introduction to Metaphysics*.

14. The Yiddish: "Un di svive, di natur, di tipn, di farheltenishn tsvishn eynem un dem tsveytn vaksn nisht fun oysn, kumen nisht fun di periferye in a tsentr, nor farkert fun ineveynik, fun tsentr, funem kinstlerishn tsenter tsu der periferye. Un dos lebn un vezn in verk farlirt di mekhanishe gezetsn fun oysn un vert getribn fun inerlekhn drang funem kinstler . . . un di tipn zaynen vi farbleft fun dem oytors intuitiver kraft." Nakhmen Mayzel, "David Bergelson: Tsum ershaynem fun ale zayne verk in Berlin," *Bikher-velt* 1 (1922): 239.

15. Ibid., 242. The Yiddish: "Der *Opgang* funem onheyb bizn sof iz ingantsn an oysgekhloymte, ogysgetroymte sipur-hamayse, mer opklang vi klang, mer opsheyn vi sheyn, mer opbild vi bild."

16. David Bergelson, *Descent*, trans. Joseph Sherman, (New York: Modern Language Association of America, 1999), 3.

17. David Bergelson, *Descent*, 7.

18. David Bergelson, *Descent*, 123. I have modified the translation. I wish to thank Zachary Baker for his help with this interpretation. The Yiddish: "'Gut,' hot er a trakht getun,

'remozim af mentshn.' Nor di mentshn aleyn zenen nishto. Er vart a bisl un kumt aroys in estsimer. Nor oykh dartn iz keyner nishto. Opgetrunkene glezer tey afn tish. Un a samovar in der zayt; du tust im a top, er iz nokh varem; an ofener bukh ligt afn tish: emetser hot, a ponim, in im nor vos geleyent, nor vos gezukht mit di oygn tsvishn di shures." David Bergelson, Joseph Sherman, and David Goldberg, *Opgang*, Texts and Translations. (New York: Modern Language Association of America, 1999), 118.

19. Bergson, *Creative Evolution*, 11.

20. Bergelson, *Descent*, 64–65. The Yiddish: Dortn hot geshmekt mit sharfn karbol, mit shimldikn gutapertsh un mit nokh epes a reyekh, a reyekh, vos blaybt in yeder shtub, fun vanen m'hot nisht lang aroysgetrogn a toytn. S'iz dortn nisht geven af vos tsu kukn. Nor inem tsveytn klenern kheyder, inem kheyderl, vu Meylekh hot getogt un genekhtikt, hot er getrofn a goldn shtralkhl, vos shpilt mit shtoyb af a shvarts batsoygn tishl, vos dergreykht ahin ersht shpet nokh halbn tog un dermont in an nideriker farnakhtiker zun, a tsherepenem dakh, vos shimert sheyn, vi gingold fun der vayt, un on Meylekhn aleyn, dem langn shemevdikn Meylekhn, vos iz do itst shoyn nishto." Bergelson, Sherman, and Goldberg, *Opgang*, 62–63.

21. Bergelson, Sherman, and Goldberg, *Opgang*, 21, 30, 131, 108.

22. Bergelson, *Descent*, 38.

23. Bergelson, *Descent*, 40.

24. Bergelson, *Descent*, 175.

25. Bergelson, *Descent*, 168.

26. Bergelson, *Descent*, 168,

27. Bergelson, *Descent*, 167.

28. Bergelson, *Descent*, 135.

29. Bergelson, Sherman, and Goldberg, *Opgang*, 131.

30. Bergelson, Sherman, and Goldberg, 69.

31. Bergelson, Sherman, and Goldberg, 15–16.

32. Bergelson, Sherman, and Goldberg, 100.

33. Bergelson, Sherman, and Goldberg, 73.

34. Bergelson, Sherman, and Goldberg, 62.

35. Shmuel Niger, "Briv fun Dovid Bergelson," *Zamlbikher* 8 (1952): 96. This is my translation. The original Yiddish: "a gloybn on a katekhizim, un der itstiker moment iz aza vikhtiker vi yene, beshes der novi hot gezogt az m'ken 'visn' got bay zikh in hartsn, un der grek hot es nisht farshtanen, vayl her hot badarft tapn zayn got bay di hent un bay di fis."

36. For example, Mark 13:33, the parable about the master of the house who departs, warning his servant to be on the alert for his return.

37. Bergelson, *Descent*, 53.

38. Bergelson, *Descent*, 237.

39. For a discussion of melody in *Opgang*, see Itsik Kahan, "Melody in Dovid Bergelson's Yiddish Prose Style," *Zukunft* 74 (1969): 430–34.

40. Bergelson, *Descent*, 178. I have slightly modified the translation. The Yiddish: "umruike klangen, vos farloyfn tantsndik eyner farn tsveytn, shteln zikh hinterfislekh un kulyen zikh, kulyen zikh vi di kleyne freylikh shpetndike komedyantlekh." Bergelson, Sherman, and Goldberg, *Opgang*, 174.

41. Bergelson, *Descent*, 178.

42. Bergelson, *Descent*, 178.

43. Bergelson, Sherman, and Goldberg, *Opgang*, 175. This is my translation; "deeply impressed" does not convey the emotional response to the music.

44. David Bergelson, *The End of Everything*, trans. Joseph Sherman, New Yiddish Library (New Haven, CT: Yale University Press, 2009), 77.

45. Bergelson, Sherman, and Goldberg, *Opgang*, 177.

46. Bergelson, Sherman, and Goldberg, *Opgang*, 20.

47. I base my account on Gershom Scholem, *Major Trends in Jewish Mysticism* (New York: Schocken Books, 1971), 280–84; Lawrence Fine, *Physician of the Soul, Healer of the Cosmos: Isaac Luria and His Kabbalistic Fellowship* (Stanford, CA: Stanford University Press, 2003) .

48. Bergelson, *Descent*, 211.

49. David Bergelson, "Sholem-Aleichem un di folks-sphrakh," *Frayheyt*, August 29, 1926.

50. I am relying on the introduction to Rae Beth Gordon, *Ornament, Fantasy, and Desire in Nineteenth-Century French Literature* (Princeton, NJ: Princeton University Press, 2014), 3–28.

51. See Michael Gubser, "Time and History in Alois Riegl's Theory of Perception," *Journal of the History of Ideas* 66, no. 3 (July 2005): 451–74.

52. Niger, "Briv fun Dovid Bergelson," 99.

53. See Paul Mendes-Flohr, *From Mysticism to Dialogue: Martin Buber's Transformation of German Social Thought* (Detroit, MI: Wayne State University Press, 1989), 45.

54. I rely on Michael Gardiner, "Alterity and Ethics: A Dialogical Perspective," *Theory, Culture & Society* 13, no. 2 (1996): 121–43.

55. For a study of Bakhtin and Riegl, see Margaret Olin, "Forms of Respect: Alois Riegl's Concept of Attentiveness," *Art Bulletin* 71, no. 2 (1989): 285–99.

56. For a comparison of Buber and Bakhtin, see Nina Perlina, "Mikhail Bakhtin and Martin Buber: Problems of Dialogical Imagination," *Studies In Twentieth-Century Literature* 9, no. 1 (1984): 13–28.

57. See Daniella Mantovan, "Language and Style in *Nokh alemen* (1913): Bergelson's Debt to Flaubert," in *David Bergelson: From Modernism to Socialist Realism*, ed. Joseph Sherman and Gennady Estraikh (Oxford, UK: Legenda, 2007), 89–112.

58. Ibid., 98.

59. Bergelson, *Descent*, 12.

60. Bergelson, Sherman, and Goldberg, *Opgang*, 11.

61. I am relying on Heidegger's discussion of gossip in Martin Heidegger, *Being and Time* (New York: Harper and Row, 1962), 210–19. I am grateful to Bruce Rosenstock for directing me to this source.

62. Bergelson, *The End of Everything*, 32.

63. Bergelson, *Descent*, 231.

64. Bergelson, Sherman, and Goldberg, *Opgang*, 226.

65. Bergelson, *Descent*, 10.

66. Bergelson, *Descent*, 19. The Yiddish: "Di velt iz shoyn arumgeshmuest." Bergelson, Sherman, and Goldberg, *Opgang*, 18.

67. Bergelson, *Descent*, 62. The Yiddish: "Shier, shier hob ikh aykh epes gehot tsu zogn." Bergelson, Sherman, and Goldberg, *Opgang*, 60.

68. Bergelson, *Descent*, 69.

69. Bergelson, *Descent*, 51, 148.

70. Bergelson, *Descent*, 183. The Yiddish: "Ir iz gut . . . fun alts iz ir itst in ot der rege gut, afile fun dem, vos Motik hot keyn mame nisht . . . Vi modne dos iz! . . . Zi hot im nor gevolt zogn, az zi fodert fun im gornisht." Bergelson, Sherman, and Goldberg, *Opgang*, 179.

71. Ann Banfield, "Narrative Style and the Grammar of Direct and Indirect Speech," *Foundations of Language* 10, no. 1 (May 1973): 35.

72. Bergelson, *Descent*, 183.

73. Bergelson, Sherman, and Goldberg, *Opgang*, 180.

74. I have modified the translation. Bergelson, *Descent*, 180.

75. Ibid., 240.

76. Bergson discusses memory of the present in Henri Bergson and Herbert Wildon Carr, *Mind-Energy: Lectures and Essays* (New York: H. Holt, 1920), 83–115.

77. David Bergelson, "Opgang," *Eygns* 2 (1920): 115.

PART 2

BODIES, THINGS, AND MACHINES

Introduction

Part 2 examines Bergelson's various "machine ensembles" by revisiting *The End of Everything* and *Descent* as well as introducing other work—most significantly, Bergelson's first story, "The Deaf Man" ("*Der toyber*"), written in 1906 but not published until 1910. I discussed the machine ensemble of the train in chapters 1 and 2, but given the importance of the larger issue in Bergelson's time and in his writing, a fuller analysis is called for. Chapter 4 centers on the body's mistakes and miscalculations in relation to the surrounding world of things and machines, and chapter 5 focuses on the body's desire, filtered through delay and visuality. Although some of the work to be examined in part 2 was written after Bergelson left Russia in 1921, I reserve my discussion of the historical context of the Russian revolution and civil war for the introduction to part 3.

The first part of the twentieth century saw broad debates about the body and its capacities. The reduction of the body's abilities, its growing similarity to mere things, or its shutdown and reversion to a more primitive state could indicate an overall decline, as in Max Nordau's theories of degeneration. But these shifts could also pave the way for a new relation between things and humans—if properly appropriated and manipulated. In different ways, Futurism, biomechanics, Taylorization, and Russian avant-garde art movements in the first quarter of the twentieth century were optimistic about the potential that could be released if the human body and human society could be reorganized to more closely align with mechanical laws and properties. These developments have been widely discussed in the scholarly literature.[1] How these new modes of work and new movements in art relate to Bergelson's literary experiments in particular and Yiddish literature generally has received far less attention. Yiddish print culture took note of the central importance of technology in all realms of human endeavor. An essay by the Yiddish poet A. Almi published in *Literary Pages* (*Literarishe bleter*) in 1930, dramatically titled "The Last Days of Theater and Opera," raises the possibility that live performances will become obsolete. According to Almi, while various leading figures debate whether technology is a messiah or an Antichrist and who will ultimately rule whom, humans over machines or the opposite, science has begun to consider the possibility of a new synthetic form of life that combines human and mechanistic elements.[2] Cinema had already imagined this new form. Dziga Vertov announced that his cinema-eye could create a new more perfect human being by assembling the best parts of multiple individuals into one cinematic image.[3]

The common point of departure for much early twentieth-century experimentation with the body and its relation to the word and the world was Bergson's essay on laughter, *Le Rire: Essai sur la signification du comique*, first published in 1899. For Bergson, animate life and the inanimate are on one continuum; there is no sharp opposition between them, because my body is an image among the other images that I find in the surrounding world. The affective and dynamic body is at the center of my relation to objects and things; for Bergson, perception is nascent action tinged with memory and not a mental representation. Since the body conditions attention to life, the manipulation of the body changes consciousness. Different forms of attention to the world could emerge from work on the body, including posture and movement, for example. Bergson argued that the body's failure to respond to change is the foundation of the comic. His essay was widely read and translated into most European languages, including Russian and Yiddish.[4] I have already touched on David Bergelson's publication of Stepan Rudyanski's "Henri Bergson vegn estetik," which appeared in *Di yidishe velt* in 1913. The Yiddish poet Meylekh Ravitsh wrote a critical essay about the 1928 Yiddish translation of Bergson's study of laughter, *Der gelekhter, an ophandlung vegn der badaytung fun komizm*. Since Ravitsh attacked the quality of the translation, it can be assumed that he read the original French. The Polish Yiddish journal *Literarishe bleter* also ran a review of the Yiddish translation of Bergson's essay on the comic, also noting the beauty of the style in the original (attributing the author's Nobel Prize in part to this quality) and its lack in the translation.[5]

The comedic has to do with a lack of flexibility or elasticity in the body. When we see someone continue to perform one movement even though another response is called for, we find this funny. The unchanging, automatic response of the body resembles a machine, and this resemblance is the essence of the comic: "The attitudes, gestures, and movements of the body are laughable in exact proportion as that body reminds us of a mere machine."[6] The comedic is something mechanical "encrusted over the living."[7] Lack of adaptability in the body can cause sickness and injury; in the mind, "mental deficiency." The breakdown and loss of flow can also, however, indicate a pathway toward recovery. Bergelson's treatment of the sensory motor misfire or "glitch" is the subject of chapter 4. Other Yiddish writers before Bergelson had attributed various pathologies to the Jewish body, but Bergelson used creative devolution, the loss of flow in movement and gesture, and disabilities in hearing and speech as modernist devices to explore new forms of decentered subjectivity. The same set of devices also allowed him to experiment with the material properties of language, privileging sound over meaning. In so doing he created a Yiddish approximation of Russian Futurist "trans-sense" (*zaum*) language.

Bergson's understanding of the condition of alienation as the result of mechanization and abstraction was transformed by a host of theorists and artists who saw the machinal body as a platform for future positive development into a new synthesis of technology and the human being. Bergson's theory of the body and its elasticity in relation to the world and his understanding of the multiple rhythms condensed into bodily action had ramifications for theater, dance, and movement theorists and directors including Meyerhold in Russia and Les Kurbas in Kiev.[8] The Yiddish author Bergelson, one of the founders of the Kiev Kultur-Lige, served for a time as the head of its theatrical division.[9] This position gave him access to discussions of the new trends and tendencies in the arts.

Bergelson's attitude toward the new technologies of his day is complex. As I discussed in chapter 1, in "At the Depot," a cloud of sorrow gets stuck at the horizon where the telegraph and railway lines meet. The human emotion materializes in such a way as to distort the symmetrical grid created by technology, but it was human beings who drove their own emotion away, pushing it outside, not their trains and telegraphs. The grain traders at the depot, the trains, and the depot itself are part of one machine ensemble. Technological mediation can allow for the emergence of new forms of emotion. Technology may make possible an exchange between subjects otherwise cut off from each other. The voice of God may no longer be audible in the synagogue but may reappear in the most unlikely of places, as I will show in chapter 4. The related issues of seeing and being seen, desire and its mediation through technology, and the resulting delay and postponement of fulfillment are the focal points of chapter 5. I explore Bergelson's interest in the new visual art of his time and his verbal recreation of the sights and surfaces of interwar Berlin.

Notes

1. For Russia, see for example Sara Pankenier Weld, *Voiceless Vanguard: The Infantilist Aesthetic of the Russian Avant-Garde* (Evanston, IL: Northwestern University Press, 2014); Julia Vaingurt, *Wonderlands of the Avant-Garde* (Evanston, IL: Northwestern University Press, 2013). For a broad discussion of bodily efficiency and energy in relation to work and modernity, see Anson Rabinbach, *The Human Motor: Energy, Fatigue, and the Origins of Modernity* (New York: Basic Books, 1990).

2. A. Almi, "Letste teg fun teater un opere," *Literarishe bleter*, April 4, 1930, 1-2 . "A. Almi" was the pseudonym of Elihu Khayim Sheps.

3. See Oksana Bulgakova, *Fabrika zhestov* (Moscow: NLO, 2005), 131.

4. For a discussion of the essay in the context of other theories of laughter, see Jan Walsh Hokenson, "Comedies of Errors: Bergson's *Laughter* in Modernist Contexts," in *Understanding Bergson, Understanding Modernism*, eds. Paul Ardoin, S. E. Gontarski, and Laci Mattison (New York: Bloomsbury, 2013), 38–53.

5. See Meylekh Ravitsh, "Di filosofye fun lakhn: Anri Bergson: Der gelekhter," *Naye folkstsaytung* 3, no. 261 (1928): 6; Nakhmen Blumental, "Anri Bergson's Gelekhter in yidish," *Literarishe bleter* 247, no. 4 (1929): 78.

6. Henri Bergson, *Laughter: An Essay on the Meaning of the Comic*, trans. Cloudesley Brereton (New York: Macmillan, 1914), 29.

7. Bergson, *Laughter*, 37.

8. For Meyerhold, see Spencer Golub, "Clockwise–Counterclockwise (The Vowelless Revolution)," *Theatre Journal* 56, no. 2 (2004): 183–203; Nick Worrall, "Meyerhold's Production of 'The Magnificent Cuckold,'" *Drama Review* 17, no. 1 (1973): 14–34. For Kurbas, see Irena R. Makaryk, "Dissecting Time/Space: The Scottish Play and the New Technology of Film," in *Modernism in Kyiv: Jubilant Experimentation*, ed. Irena R. Makaryk and Virlana Tkacz (Toronto: University of Toronto Press, 2010), 443–77.

9. Gennady Estraikh, "The Yiddish Kultur-Lige," in *Modernism in Kyiv: Jubilant Experimentation*, ed. Irene R. Makaryk and Virlana Tkacz (Toronto: University of Toronto Press, 2010), 197–217.

4

THE GLITCH

MISSING THE TRAIN—BOTH LITERALLY AND FIGURATIVELY—IS SIMILAR
to missing the chair you are about to sit on. Both failures reflect a
disjuncture with the surrounding world. Missing the chair is a symptom
of a routinized relation to the world and hence the incapacity to recognize
change. The chair was not in its usual place, and therefore I missed it. When
the encounter between the body and the world stops working smoothly,
however, the pause and readjustment can also suggest a new form of attentiveness and a pathway to the recovery of the world. In *Descent* bodies do
not respond properly to the objects that surround them; they become inflex-
ible and disaggregated. Distinct parts of the body function as if they were
independent entities. While critics have noted the importance of gesture in
Bergelson's depiction of the internal, psychological state of his characters,
my emphasis is on the broader significance of gestures that fail to serve
their purpose.[1] The glitch or mistaken response to a change in the external
world is an important feature of Bergelson's representation of the body.[2]

The sensory motor misfire is only one feature of Bergelson's broad interest in what can be called "creative devolution," a breakdown in the flow of
motion that connects me to the objects and people around me. In *Descent*,
"The Deaf Man" ("*Der toyber*"), "In a Backwoods Town," and *Judgment*,
Bergelson includes figures suffering from physical and mental disabilities
or diseases that impede their functioning and response to the world. In "At
the Depot" contingent circumstance episodically interferes with hearing
and sight, in *Descent* a more generalized distraction emerges, but in "The
Deaf Man," as its title indicates, the narrative as a whole unfolds from the
perspective of someone with severely limited capacities who hears almost
nothing and cannot utter coherent speech. The narrative shifts attention
away from meaning and thought and toward gesture and movement, and
the barrier that prevents the title character from hearing becomes a barrier

to sense more generally. The text moves from impaired hearing to a general cognitive disarray.

Protagonists from earlier Yiddish literature, particularly in work by Abramovitsh, also suffer from various disabilities; the title character of *Fishke the Lame*, first published in the 1860s, is an example. Fishke not only is lame but also has a speech impediment; his wife is blind. The pair had a "cholera wedding," a match made according to the superstitious custom that marriages made between the lowest of the low would spare a town from the disease. Through his marriage Fishke falls in with a gang of beggars, all with fake ailments except a hunchbacked girl, who is beaten and abused. In the middle of telling his own story, Fishke delivers a tirade arguing that Jewish society in its entirety is based on nothing more than various forms of beggary. As this example shows, descriptions of the pathology of the Jewish body and the Jewish body politic are not original to Bergelson. Unlike Abramovitsh and Peretz, however, Bergelson's disabled and diseased characters do not serve a didactic purpose. They function rather in the service of play with language and representation. Disability in Bergelson functions as a modernist device that decreases the importance of semantics and increases the tactility of the text by emphasizing the physical process of articulating speech. Disability makes ordinary experience unfamiliar in "The Deaf Man."

Furthermore, impairment in sight and hearing plays a role in Bergelson's experimentation with the limits of individual human subjectivity. Sensation, perception, and emotion are removed from the individual and distributed across groups of people and appropriated by things. The hero of "The Deaf Man" and the other workers at the flour mill, like the grain brokers at the depot, form a machine ensemble in which individual consciousness, will, and action are absorbed by the mechanized whole. While Bergelson's greatest innovation in reproducing the effect of the machine would come later, his fascination with the interaction of human beings and technology started at the beginning of his writing career, appearing in early works including his 1913 *The End of Everything*. This chapter explores the dysfunctional and machinal body in Bergelson, focusing for the most part on fiction and essays from before 1921.

Since I am arguing that Bergelson is experimenting with "creative devolution," a brief discussion of the author's familiarity with Darwin is appropriate, especially since Bergelson refers to Darwin in an unexpected way, with reference to art and aesthetics. In *The Descent of Man* (1871), Darwin argues that the similarities between human beings and other mammals, the "rudiments, homologies, and reversions," show that "man is descended from some less highly organized form."[3] Darwin's theories were widely circulated, and popularized versions appeared in many languages, including Yiddish.[4]

Bergelson's awareness of Darwin is evident from his 1919 essay "Belles-Lettres and the Social Order" (*"Dikhtung un gezelshaftlekhkayt"*). Bergelson describes the chaos of the post-revolutionary moment, the "void and formlessness" that prevails, and the need for "rebuilding the life of society."[5] The author calls upon an evolutionary model to make his point: "Society has finally come to the inmost conviction that it lives within a far less organized structure than some animals or even than some insects."[6] Bergelson could have gathered some understanding of the complexity of animal societies, including insects, from a number of sources.[7] In *On the Origin of Species*, for example, first published in 1859, Darwin discussed the "castes" and "division of labor" found in ant communities.[8] Bergelson's characterization of the simple state of human social structure in 1919 as "less organized than some animals and even some insects" suggests a moment of crisis. The underlying premise is that the more evolved a society, the more complex its organization, thus in the aftermath of the Russian revolution, which destroyed the old forms, society was abruptly thrown back to a simpler, more primitive configuration.

Darwin's theory of reversions itself evolved in various early twentieth-century arguments about degeneration, including Nordau's argument about individuals of the "fin de siècle type." Nordau expanded the idea that certain aberrations from the norm could be transmitted to offspring, until the point when the offspring could no longer reproduce. Some theorists at this time argued for a notion of degenerate species that had descended from a more complex to a simpler form.[9] While Nordau saw evidence of overall human decline and decay at the turn of the twentieth century, in part due to the precipitous advance of technology, Henri Bergson saw evidence of continued change and development, not only in human intelligence but also in other human capacities; hence his notion of *creative* evolution.[10]

Nordau famously applied various theories of degeneration to the art of his time, characterizing as degenerate those who "lisp and stammer instead of speaking" and "those who draw and paint like children ... and confound all the arts, and lead them back to the primitive forms they had before evolution differentiated them" [ellipsis added].[11] In contrast to Nordau, Aleksey

Kruchenykh, one of the founders of Russian Futurism, characterized various imperfections and mistakes in the production of language, including "ethnic accents" and stuttering, as a form of "word creation" and a tool for inventing a new, trans-sense language.[12] Stammering and other speech impediments characterize several Bergelson protagonists, including the hero of "The Deaf Man."

Bergelson explicitly refers to Nordau both in *The End of Everything* and "The Deaf Man," in which one character asks another whether he knows "what Max Nordau says" (*vos Maks Nordau zogt*).[13] While Bergelson's images of disability may indicate to some degree that he believed the Jewish community was in a state of decline, they more importantly suggest his artistic interest in a return to the body and the potential for a new relation to it and the surrounding world. In Bergelson's works, the body's loss of flexibility, its reversions to more primitive forms of movement, and other glitches in sensory motor coordination are better understood under the rubric of creative devolution and a modernist decentering of intellect and intention.

Creative Devolution

In the opening of *Descent*, Meylekh's sister, who has come for the funeral, has a problem seating herself in a carriage. Bergelson devotes considerable attention to the scene, describing in minute detail the individual actions that go into the overall movement:

> When she was offered assistance by Hanke Lyuber and by Ethel Kadis, the university student who should soon have been married to Meylekh, she refused their help, made a few stubborn, uncertain movements, and finally threw herself forward into the britzska like someone mounting a horse. While the other young women waited for her last word, the umbrella suddenly slipped [*aroysgeglitsht*] from her grasp. Up above, on the sodden driver's seat, she abruptly jerked her head into her shoulders, hunched herself up so that the felt coat took on the appearance of being stuffed with a bundle of rags, and emitted a wildly despairing shriek:
> —Oh, Meylekh! . . . Meylekh! [ellipsis in original][14]

The word term I am using for sensory motor misfire, "glitch," occurs in the Yiddish for "slipped" (*aroysgeglitsht*); notice that the umbrella seemingly performs this action of its own accord. The translation omits the ugly detail that Meylekh's sister throws herself into the carriage *mitn boykh*, belly first, as if she has lost the use of her arms and legs or has none.

There are other occasions when a character miscalculates how to complete a physical act. Khaym-Moyshe turns back to have a look at Khanke Poyzner and makes a strange movement, "as if he had forgotten to bring something with him"; the movement is abrupt and is cut off midstream.[15] Later, when Khaym-Moyshe visits Khanke Lyuber for the first time, he sits "in a posture so peculiar it seemed as if at any moment he might suddenly slide off the bench [*tut er zikh mit a mol a glitsh arop funem benkl*] and be left squatting on all fours on the velvet-smooth carpet under the table."[16] The key term "glitch" appears in the original Yiddish.

What is surprising about episodes such as these is their ugliness and dehumanization. Meylekh's sister scrunched up in her felt coat looks like a bundle of rags, and the otherwise sophisticated Khaym-Moyshe suddenly and inexplicably does not know how to sit in a chair properly and might end up like an animal or an infant on all fours on the floor. In the episode of Meylekh's sister and the uncooperative carriage and umbrella, as well as in the scene when Khaym-Moyshe almost slides from his seat, Bergelson's narrative technique heightens the vividness of the physical gesture for the reader. Instead of seeing the action as we normally would, without interruption, the action is jerky and abrupt; both passages use *mit a mol* and *plutsem* (both mean "suddenly"). There is nothing to motivate the abrupt motions Meylekh's sister and her umbrella make; the use of "suddenly" serves only to impede the action. The act of seating oneself in a carriage is broken down into three distinct motions with no connection between them: the belly forward, followed by a pause created by the young women "waiting to hear" Meylekh's sister's "last word," then the umbrella slipping from her hand, and then the final motion of hunching the head into the shoulders, which takes place in a seemingly different location, above on the driver's seat. A separate body part performs each motion: belly, hand, head, and shoulders). The forward motion of Meylekh's sister's departure cannot take place in the way it normally would have.

The cause of the sensory motor breakdown is presumably the sister's overwhelming grief, although Bergelson does not make this explicit. In the carriage scene in *Descent*, physical action is shown in its decomposition, lacking in the necessary relation between the component parts. The passage from the carriage scene leaves readers no choice but to visualize gesture and motion; the "last word" that readers and the two young women Khanke Lyuber and Etl Kadis expect to hear never comes. Instead the bereaved sister "lets loose with a squeal, 'Oy, Meylekh.'" This alternative, less elegant translation better captures the devolution in the scene. The squeal cannot be described as a deliberate, articulate utterance.

The motions that Meylekh's sister performs, thrusting herself forward belly first and hunching her head down into her shoulders, suggest a kind of limbless form of locomotion, something far more primitive than we would expect from upright *Homo sapiens*. This gesture hints at something like Darwin's reversion (the throwback to what Darwin called a "lower member" of the same group of animals). Elsewhere in the work Bergelson uses the phrase *toyevoye*, which suggests primordial chaos. In a flashback to the prehistory of the novel, during which Khaym-Moyshe and Meylekh lived in the city, Khaym-Moyshe expresses the wish that the city, which consists of nothing more than "formlessness and void," should be smothered by a snowstorm.[17] Visual artists of the time, including Wyndham Lewis and Marc Chagall, portrayed the human form in primitive fashion, as a great hulking body that hardly seemed separate from nature itself. Bergelson's friend and colleague the painter and illustrator Issachar-Ber Rybak also created a primitive visual Jewish style.[18]

Bergelson also uses devolution in his novella "In a Backwoods Town" ("*In a fargrebter shtot*"), first published serially in 1914. The protagonist, Burman, has repeatedly missed opportunities for mobility, having become the "state rabbi" (a government position) out of sheer inertia. In Irving Howe and Eliezer Greenberg's translation, he is perpetually "drowsy" and has "let his chance to finish the university go by forever."[19] Burman, like Beynish Rubinshteyn of "At the Depot" and Preger in *Descent*, has let the future go by without him. An old widow considers him as a match for her daughter, his former student, and tries to remember how engagements are celebrated: "When you have an engagement party, you invite the rabbi, the slaughterer, the cantor, and all the relatives, and by the light of a lot of candles you break a dish. However, she was too lazy to think these three separate thoughts and could not do so. . . . she had long since lost the desire to think in an orderly fashion."[20] The widow has lost the the capacity for rational thought. This is not suspension of reason for the sake of creativity or Bergsonian intuition, however. Bergelson uses the character's senility as a prism through which the customs pertaining to engagement appear as bizarre and incoherent. These acts, which used to mean something and which once were part of a coherent lifeworld, no longer cohere; they make no sense. This passage is another example of Bergelson's use of defamiliarization: making what would have been perfectly familiar and ordinary to his readers strangely meaningless and absurd.

Disability as Modernist Device

In the work I have discussed thus far, the moments of sensory motor or cognitive failure appear episodically, but in "The Deaf Man," in contrast, all the forms of the glitch emerge as a whole to dominate the work. Bergelson wrote "The Deaf Man" in 1906, before "At the Depot," but could not find a publisher for it. The story was first published in 1910 in the Kiev periodical *Yiddish Almanac* (*Yidisher almanakh*); then in 1914 as a separate imprint and finally republished in collected editions that came out in 1922–1923 and 1928–1930.[21] The title character (who remains nameless) is a worker at a flourmill. The boss's son, Mendl, has sex with the deaf man's daughter, Esther—the circumstances suggest that she was an unwilling partner. The deaf man wants to help his daughter, but before he can, he suffers an accident, falling from the fourth story of the mill. After he recovers, he learns from Esther that their boss is trying to cover up his son's misdeed by marrying her off to another man, an unsavory character. Esther kills herself. This unhinges the deaf man, who in a bizarre act of revenge first mutilates the boss's cow (by cutting off its tail) and later kills it. His frozen body is found dead next to the animal's carcass.

The story also became the basis for a play performed in Gomel in 1929 and then at the Moscow State Yiddish Theater in 1930 with Solomon Mikhoels in the leading role.[22] Another production was performed under the direction of David Herman in Warsaw.[23] In an interview he gave at the time of the Warsaw theatrical production, Herman said that he emphasized the dynamism of the play, particularly the vertical space from which the deaf man falls and the rapid transition from scene to scene, commenting that his treatment approached a "cinematic tempo" in the depiction of the action.[24] The Moscow State Theater production transformed the deaf man into a socialist hero who leads the mill workers in a strike against the owner.[25]

The original novella, in contrast, avoids overt political statements. Instead, Bergelson explored modernist themes—including the machinal body, the "primitive," and the physiological production of speech. He also experimented with modernist narrative techniques, using cognitive and sensory motor failure as a stylistic device and decoupling words from their meaning, subsequently shifting the emphasis toward the sonic properties of language. Of course he was not alone in this stylistic and thematic experimentation. These dimensions of Bergelson's work were central to the artistic, philosophical, and scientific work conducted in early twentieth-century Russia and Europe, and especially among Russian Futurists. It is important, however, to distinguish the Italian Futurist link between art, politics, technology, and violence from other forms of Futurism that drew more from Bergson's theory of intuition, creativity, and musicality.[26] Bergelson flirted with an aesthetic of violence in work produced in the 1920s, which I will address later. In "The Deaf Man"—in contrast to this later work and in continuity with "At the Depot," *The End of Everything*, and *Descent*—the past encroaches on the present, shattering the unity of time. For Bergelson, the disjunctive rhythms of any given moment include voices from the past. Even when proclaiming the triumph of the future, he does so from the perspective of those who perpetually miss its arrival. He does not revel in the destruction of the past.[27]

The deaf man's most remarkable feature is his ears, which are "like two rags" (*tsvey shmotes*) that hang on both sides of his head.[28] The story opens with rumors about Esther and Vove Biks's son, Mendl, which the deaf man cannot hear. When his daughter's dead body is discovered, the deaf man cannot hear what people tell him; instead he sees the reaction on their faces. He "peered with this lead-colored eyes and noticed: the faces of the newcomers were terrified, their mouths were gaping and their eyes were gawking fearfully."[29] In *Descent* the accordion player's music metamorphosed into the image of "clown acrobats." Here, the sounds of crying and exclamations are transformed into the sight of gaping eyes and wide-open mouths. One occasion is joyful and the other tragic, but on both occasions the functions of hearing and sight exchange qualities; the human being is reorganized in a new way. For the deaf man, the silent gaping mouths are purely gestural forms of communication.

Displacement (*sdvig* in Russian) was a fundamental tenet of Cubism, wrote David Burliuk, the so-called father of Russian Cubism. Displacement in visual art could mean a disorienting shift in the relation of figure and ground or other significant elements of the image, including the alternative placement of the features of the human face. Drawing on his own theories of synesthesia, Mikhail Matiushin planned for the music and acoustical effects of *Victory over the Sun* to complement what the audience saw. He called upon the audience to be "a spectator with a large ear."[30] In "The Deaf Man," David Bergelson is exploiting similar notions: his protagonist is a listener with a large eye, so to speak; he has ears that see and eyes that hear.

The deaf man's impediment has consequences for his verbal capacities; his speech is a chaotic and violent process: "He began to talk in his deaf, incoherent way, making crude gestures with a round, bent arm and violently tearing single words from his broad and powerful chest."[31] In the Moscow State Yiddish Theater production, Mikhoels used this action as a "gesture leitmotif of his performance.[32] The deaf man pulls the wild, roaring sounds of his speech out of his body. In a later essay written after the Russian revolution, Bergelson will explicitly link the new, harsh sounds of poetry to the revolutionary era and the new forms of art it helped to create. Bergelson characterizes his own language as harsh and grating, well suited for the violent upheaval in life and politics, "the present chaos."[33] He will use physiological imagery in describing the speech of another hearing-impaired character in his 1929 work *Judgment* (*Mides-hadin*). The emphasis on the material nature of language and its physiological and not intellectual production has much in common with both scientific and artistic experimentation at this time. New technologies that revealed the physical and kinetic production of speech went hand in hand with artistic innovations in poetry and prose that stressed movement and dynamism. As Friedrich Kittler writes, work on the causes of speech pathology showed that "language breaks down into individual elements: into optical, acoustical, sensory and motoric nerve impulses."[34] The Yiddish author's representation of hearing- and speech- impaired characters and his comparisons of the human mouth to inanimate things exploit this notion to engage in play with the material qualities of language beyond rational meaning.

Bergelson uses the deaf man's pathology to explore the relation between words, thoughts, and things. The disjointed elements of the plot replicate the cognitive disconnectedness in the title character. Words and phrases repeat without joining together to make sense. The deaf man wants to tell others about what happened ("something about a bolting mill that kept shaking, about a plank bed with a corpse, and about a hook with a rope"), but all he can do is repeat the boss's name, Vove Bik. It is significant that the Yiddish name Bik corresponds to the Russian word for bull (*byk*). After it loses its tail, the cow thinks, "My tail is gone forever and ever," while at the same time, the members of Bik's household try to figure out who the perpetrator is.[35] The cow's lament about the loss of its tail for all eternity and the boss's name contain sounds that mirror and rhyme with one another: *eybik*, *ek*, and Bik.[36] A similar mirroring effect occurs earlier, in the warning that fails to save the deaf man from his accident. The words for "whisper" and "too late" produce the sound (whispering) that they name and also mirror each other acoustically: *sheptshet* and "*tsu shpet . . . tsu shpet.*"

There are parallels to be drawn between Bergelson's use of sound in this text and elsewhere and Russian trans-sense (*zaum*) experiments that were part of the Futurist movement. The 1913 opera *Victory over the* Sun and Kruchenykh's trans-sense poem "Dyr Bul Shchyl" from the same year are generally considered the foundational texts of the Futurist movement. In "On Poetry and Trans-Sense Language," published in 1916, Shklovsky referred to Aleksey Kruchenykh's 1913 "Declaration of the Word as Such," which argued for the artistic use of personal, nonmeaningful language. Shklovsky emphasized the capacity of "sound-language" (*zvukorech'*) to communicate emotion beyond meaning and thus also to act upon the emotions of the reader or spectator. For Shklovsky, the preeminence of musicality in artistic language served as a point of departure for trans-sense language; he refers to Schiller's description of the "musical state of mind" that marked the creation of each new work. Bergelson, as we recall, used the term *shtimung* (mood, tone) to describe the starting point of the creation of his own works. Shklovsky also drew upon Bergson and William James to argue that the physical condition of the body determines emotion. The reception of language depends on a physiological rehearsal of the same movements of articulation that go into the production of language.[37]

Bergelson was familiar with Futurism both from Russian-language and Yiddish-language sources.[38] In "Art and Society," written while he was still in Kiev, he predicted "cheap, rather than genuine futurism will assuredly come as much to us as to Greater Russia."[39] He distinguished the two on the basis of intellect as opposed to intuition; "cheap" futurism acts only intellectually, but genuine futurism influences readers "intuitively." Intuition, one of Bergson's major concepts, is a transrational form of knowledge that is key to the apprehension of durative time. The Yiddish author's emphasis on intuition is significant in light of the central role of this concept in Russian Futurist visual and literary art. Nikolai Kuzmin, Malevich, Mikhail Matiushin, Kruchenykh, and others argued for the significance of intuition, musicality, transrational forms of knowledge, memory, and the past in the production and reception of a work of art, and Henri Bergson's work on the interrelation between consciousness and the surrounding physical universal directly influenced Matiushin.[40]

One of the sources for Bergelson's knowledge of Futurism was Max Weinreich's essay on the topic published in *Di yidishe velt* in 1914, the same journal and the same year in which "In a Backwoods Town" appeared.[41] Weinreich alluded to Mayakovsky's call to discard the old "idols" Pushkin and Tolstoy; he explained that according to the Futurists, the word is greater than its meaning (*pshat*), and that sense (*zin*) is not the primary purpose of literary art. "The sum of the sound combinations," Weinreich wrote, and not the meanings of individual words, provides the reader with the images that the poet wishes to convey. He went on to explain the emphasis on sound characteristic of Futurist texts and concluded by citing fragments of Elena Guro's 1910 "sound poem" "Finland," which contains repeating patterns built on the sounds "la," "li," "tere," and "dere." Guro was an active participant in Russian Futurist circles; her husband was Mikhail Matiushin.

Bergelson's emphasis on the organs of speech in "The Deaf Man" and elsewhere and his extensive use of sound play suggest a significant convergence with Russian *zaum*. Unlike the Futurist poet Khlebnikov, he does not engage in neologism, and the passages I have discussed do not abandon representation for pure language, hermetically sealed off from the reality beyond the text—the aesthetic favored by some Futurist writers.[42] His insertion, however, of trans-sense play into his otherwise realist narrative resembles the examples of trans-sense that Shklovsky discovered in Knut Hamsun, folklore, and episodes described in Korolenko's and Gorky's memoiristic writing.

Man and Machine

For the French philosopher Bergson, as I discussed earlier, the appearance of the human automaton (the person who misses the chair because it was moved) symptomized the mechanical encrusted over the living; the sensory motor mistake reveals a body out of sync with the rhythm of the world. In "The Deaf Man," the men who work on the machinery of the bolting mill lose their human qualities, assuming instead the characteristics of inanimate moving parts. They can no longer speak or think, having become part of the machine. I quote at length:

> Calm and wistful, the mill chanted its ancient, monotonous roar, shaking together with its forty workers. Amid the roaring and the tumult, the workers labored mechanically, earnestly, mutely like the machines and the wheels turning all round them, and the workers never talked, never thought, as if the huge, wheat-packed sheds were located in their brains, robbing them of their minds.

. . .

At rare moments the mill suddenly trembled, cutting through with an oracular voice:

Stop! . . . Stop!

But no one responded, and it was as if the oracular voice were remote and forlorn, straying into this alien, unfamiliar world, seeking something and unable to find it [ellipsis added].[43]

In this modernist image of the union between the human and the machine, the machine takes over, not by extending the capacities of the workers, but rather by reducing them. The synergy of man and machine does not yield a super body, as in other modernist and Futurist works, or the fusion that would yield a new synthetic person, as in Vertov's cinematic experiments. The workers have lost their capacity for speech, thought, and independent movement because the vast machinal body of the mill "shakes" and "roars" (*brumt*) in their stead. This characteristic "brum" is the noise the deaf man makes when he tries to speak. Everyone at the mill is deaf and mute, like the title character of the story.

Even though his representation of the mill in "The Deaf Man" emphasizes the dehumanizing effect of the machine, Bergelson elsewhere is clearly fascinated by the new technologies of his era, especially those that modify specific organs and functions. When Mirl Hurvits in *The End of Everything* confronts the gravity of her father's condition, both financial and physical, for the first time, she is shocked by his appearance. Mirl "suddenly" sees Gedalye in a darkened room:

Hunched over and markedly shrunken, he sat there with his back toward her, his head thrown oddly forward and his mouth open, gasping like a fish before the medicinal steam he was pumping from the nickel vaporizer he'd brought back with him from abroad. In the deepening gloom of late twilight, the little machine burned before him with a blue-green flame, a turquoise light that barely illuminated his face, wet with countless drops of sweat and condensed steam.[44]

Although the vaporizer is supposed to be therapeutic, the position of Gedalye's neck and head and his open mouth suggest that there is no earthly cure for him. Bergelson describes Mirl's parents' house as a place where "it was, apparently, too late, everything had had already ended," and Gedalye's life is included among those things that have "already ended." Already dead and temporarily revivified by the artificial breath of the vaporizer, he has been transformed into a strange new creature, part fish, part human, and part machine, with an external breathing apparatus. The suddenness with which Gedalye becomes visible, his distorted appearance, and the strange color of the vaporizer flame all contribute to the uncanny impact of his figure. The bizarrely futuristic fusion of man and *machindl* (the vaporizer) in this scene underscores all the more vividly the obsolescence of its human protagonist. His time has past.

Citation as Temporalization

What makes the scene of the bolting mill so striking in "The Deaf Man" is not only Bergelson's use of the modernist trope of the machine ensemble but also his allusion to a Talmudic passage: the *bas-kol* ("oracular voice" in Neugroschel's translation) that stumbles into the mill and tells it to "stop." The Yiddish term *bas-kol* is usually translated as "divine voice," "voice from heaven," or "echo." In a section of the Talmud devoted to a discussion of the appropriate times of prayer, there are several descriptions of the sound of God's voice. The night has three watches, each guarded by God, who "roars like a lion." R. Jose recalls walking in the ruins of Jerusalem, stopping to pray, and being asked by Elijah what he heard there: "I heard a divine voice (*bas-kol*) cooing like a dove, and saying: 'Woe to the children, on account of whose sins I destroyed my house and burnt my temple and exiled them among the nations of the world.'"[45] The divine voice coos, roars, and also laments the destruction of the Temple and the exile of Israel.

Bergelson transforms these motifs in his description of the bolting mill. Why he would characterize the noise of the mill as "ancient" is inexplicable unless we bear in mind the hidden quotation from the Talmud and its reference to the destruction of Jerusalem. The "roaring" noise that it makes is reminiscent of God's roaring presence in the watches of the night, and the appearance of the *bas-kol* in the mill also derives from the passage in the Talmud. Bergelson's interest in this passage is evident from another use he makes of it. In *The End of Everything*, the midwife Schatz's grandmother, who remains silent for months at a time, suddenly speaks: "Her hollow voice could be heard across the entire room, a lethargic, plaintive voice materializing from some distant, crumbling ruin."[46] The Talmudic intertext undergoes a significant change in Bergelson's hands. In the Talmud, God laments that he has exiled his people and destroyed his city; in "The Deaf Man," in contrast, it is God's voice that has been exiled. Lost and alone, it stumbles into the alien world of the mill, where no one listens to it.

Bergelson was not alone in using citations from the Talmud and other canonical Jewish texts in his literary work. Nearly everything Tevye says contains quotations from the Jewish sacred tradition. Sholem Aleichem's work as a whole is oriented toward oral forms, including folklore, sermons, and proverbs. Bergelson's deaf man is the antithesis of Tevye, however, not only because of the most glaring difference between them: Bergelson's deaf man, in contrast to the verbose Tevye, cannot speak. In evoking the Jewish textual tradition, Sholem Aleichem embeds the social upheaval and violence of the Jewish experience in late Imperial Russia in a network of meaning, and he embeds his own oeuvre in the context of the "Judaic literary tradition."[47] For Bergelson, in contrast, the folksy narrative of classic Yiddish fiction is something to overcome and the fabric of biblical meaning is shredded. All that remain are the "threads," as he said, that unhappily bind characters like Mirl Hurvits to a past that is already dead.

The bolting mill, with its wheels, cogs, and dehumanized workers, like the intersection of the telegraph lines and railroad ties in "At the Depot," represents a modern time and space in which machines change how human beings interact with one another. It is precisely, however, in these markedly modern times and spaces that Bergelson interjects human emotions, suggesting that technological mediation makes the emotion legible. The grain dealers' almost palpable *troyer* (sorrow) finds its way into the horizon where the telegraph and railroad meet. In "The Deaf Man," the haunting voice lamenting the exile of the Jews and the destruction of Jerusalem stumbles into the bolting mill. The memory and emotion of something past and lost intrudes as an apparition from a discarded world. Bergelson, however, is not lamenting what has been lost but rather using it to create a multilayered and richly textured literary image. The Talmud citation represents one of many different rhythms that Bergelson's text animates in a new way.

The deaf man also resembles other Bergelson characters insofar as the author uses temporality to describe his emotions. Mirl Hurvits feels that someone else lived out the springtime of her life. When Khanke Lyuber in *Descent* realizes that she is in love with Khaym-Moyshe, she experiences déjà vu. Belatedness and déjà vu are also characteristic of the key moments of the deaf man's unhappy life. When he falls from the fourth story of the mill, it seems to him as if "someone were pitying him and were whispering into one of his deaf ears: 'Too late . . . Too late.'"[48] Later, when he goes to the boss's house to see what happened to his daughter, it seems to him that "everything was trembling and quaking quickly, like the sieves at Bik's mill.

After he recognizes Esther's corpse and understands that she hanged herself, "it was as if he'd already stood by this very same bed with the very same corpse. It had been long ago, long, long ago, but it had really happened. The very same people had stood about."[49]

The deaf man, no matter how lowly or "primitive" he may seem, is no mere cog in the machine. The terrible discovery of his daughter's suicide thrusts the deaf man beyond sequential, linear time. When he recognizes his daughter's corpse, that instant splits into two distinct episodes, each mirroring the other. The deaf man, like Mirl Hurvits and Khanke Lyuber, is one of Bergelson's untimely heroes. The gap in time that he experiences mirrors the disjuncture of his historical epoch.

Missing the Chair on the Stage of History

I have thus far discussed the glitch or sensory motor failure in the context of daily life. The failure to execute physical action effectively and the incapacity of the senses demonstrate both the problem in relation to the surrounding world and the potential for recovery, because of the shift from mere recognition to perception and hence a different relation to the newly revealed world. Sensory motor incapacity, as in the case of the deaf man (both the story and its protagonist), also serves to realign the sensorium and redistribute its functions; intellectual and physical disabilities reframe human subjectivity and move language beyond meaning to sound and emotion. In "The Hole Through Which Life Slips" ("*Der lokh, durkh velkhn eyner hot farloyrn*"), published in 1930, Bergelson uses the glitch to depict the aftermath of cataclysmic political change. The hero's failure to support the revolution manifests itself as a psychophysical dysfunction, a kind of limp.

Some historical and biographical contextualization provides the necessary backdrop for the story. From 1917 until 1919, there were at least five different political regimes in Kiev. The socialist RADA (Council) lasted until 1918, when power went first to the Bolsheviks, then to Pavlo Skoropadsky, and finally to the Directory, headed by Symon Petliura. In 1919, the Bolsheviks retook Kiev. Bergelson was in Kiev from 1919 to 1920. In "The Hole Through Which Life Slips," Yona [Jonah] Grigorevitsh, a formerly prolific left-wing journalist, finds himself alone in his apartment in Kiev. The year is 1918. A year earlier, at the time of the Bolshevik revolution, his wife left him, as did his desire and capacity to write. Yona, like the prophet Jonah, refuses to perform his function.

In a few broad brushstrokes, Bergelson sketches the new cityscape: airplanes overhead, bombs dropping, automobiles draped in banners, new governments, breadlines, and demonstrations. During the chaos of regime change, crowds of people wait in line for bread. They lift their heads in unison "as if for slaughtering" (*vi tsu shkhite*) to look at the airplanes flying overhead; "killings take place on the streets in the early morning."[50] There is death in the air and on the ground. When the Bolsheviks finally retake Kiev, the entire city celebrates. While all of this is taking place, Yona Grigorevitsh remains in his apartment, moving, thinking, and feeling as little as possible. It is axiomatic for him that "all his thoughts and feelings must remain in their former place."[51] He comforts himself with a philosophical quest: "At a time when many men like me have become nothing more than paradoxes—at such a time, when a three-ruble note gets lost, it is sufficient to find the hole through which it slipped."[52] There is no hope of recovering the money itself.

Yona resembles an inanimate being; he is a "hulk" (*makhinye*). Yona is like the "frozen and congealed" train depot in Bergelson's first published work. As Yona's story progresses, he begins to swell, stiffen, and grow dusty, as if he were a thing and not a person. He moves as little as possible so as not to appear comical, but in avoiding motion and increasingly resembling a thing, he achieves exactly the opposite result. A remarkable transformation then takes place: his body becomes separated from his intellect. His body independently begins to find pleasure merely from existing (*hanoe tsu hobn*), and then its pleasure takes on a political overtone: "Driving away his intellect, his body felt independent, celebratory, excited, exactly as if together with the Bolsheviks, every kind of joy had returned to the city."[53]

Yona's body feels Bolshevik joy. In order to show his body that there's nothing to get excited about, Yona takes it for a walk, "as one would a child." While Yona has failed to keep up with the "earth-shattering" (*veltoyftreyslung*) events of his time, his body has gone ahead without him—and this split manifests itself in the sensation that he has developed a limp: "It seemed to him that he was limping—that was the extent to which it was difficult for him to drag behind his body."[54] Beset by physical, emotional, and political immobility, Yona lags behind in all senses of the term. In his case, in contrast to other Bergelson protagonists discussed earlier in this chapter, the all-encompassing sensory motor misfire is the direct result of the failure to apprehend large-scale political change. Events leave him behind, like his wife did. Or, to quote the story, "Living with the times is more interesting than living with a man."[55] While Yona is the target of Bergelson's satire, it is significant that no one else in the story is capable of "living with the times," except the nameless crowds on the street. No one in particular speaks the line above; it is instead a quotation of a quotation: one of Yona's relatives reports having heard a woman say it. "Living with the times" is an aspiration; from the perspective of the characters around whom the story revolves, "the times" are ungraspable. From Bergelson's point of view, untimeliness and obsolescence are more interesting to think with than timeliness.

A key feature of Bergelson's modernist art is the body, with its misfires and processes of fragmentation. The body's autonomy from the intellect, and hence the decentering of the sovereign individual, creates the potential for the reorganization of human beings into a new, mass subject who builds socialism. In "The Hole Through Which Life Slips," Bergelson describes the transformation from individual to mass subject in his depiction of the street demonstrations in Kiev after the Bolshevik takeover: "Each separate person there was a nothing, an airhead, a hick, but together they were weighty, important, full of determination, their gaze steely and threatening."[56] It is this collective actor that humiliates one of the speakers at the demonstration, a middle-aged woman in an old-fashioned hat who makes the mistake of talking about pity for the tsarina. Heads in the crowd shake, and "a pair of hands" tosses her hat into the river:

> The woman wept. Her wrinkled cheeks emphasized her gaunt face, but also at the same time showed how very wide her mouth was—this mouth that wept independently from her face, and without any pity. It didn't bother anyone that aside from this wide, weeping mouth there were also weeping eyes, and a weeping nose, and as a whole—a face.[57]

In passages like these, Bergelson retreats from his embrace of the mass subject. The morselization of the individual into separate parts prevents anyone in the crowd from feeling pity for the "face"—that is, the person— or even acknowledging that there is a person there in the first place.

In "The Hole Through Which Life Slips," the facial features of the woman speaker weep separately and each wants to be treated with mercy. The appeal to be heard and responded to echoes Bergelson's earlier work. None of the workers at the mill in "The Deaf Man" hears the echo of God's voice (the *bas-kol*); no one listens to the blind man in "At the Depot." Mirl Hurvits in *The End of Everything* protests the world's silence. In all these instances, a demand is made from a subject to a missing interlocutor: "Answer me, listen to me." The presumption of the dialogic exchange is the integral human subject. In "The Hole Through Which Life Slips," the tension between the subjectless assemblage of parts and the holistic unity of the speaking voice takes a startling direction. The fragmentation of the body into autonomous parts—and thus the increasing resemblance between the human being and a mere mechanism—should produce a comic effect, according to the French philosopher Bergson. The transformation of separate individuals into a mass subject, indicated by the hands, mouths, eyes, and other features that act independently of any single consciousness, suggests the reorganization of individuals into a collectivity that is capable of an array of affects distributed across a range of facial features and gestures. Bergelson uses the body's breakdown and autonomy to comic and grotesque effect in "The Hole Through Which Life Slips." Nonetheless, he interrogates this transformation by explicitly questioning the indifferent response to the new, morselized face. He will keep asking the question in a series of episodes in which distorted, unattractive features and faces return to haunt those who harmed or were merely indifferent to them. The modernist penchant for displacement and decentering is itself the object of an uncanny transformation in Bergelson's use of the human face that demands to be answered.

Notes

1. See for example Meir Wiener, "David Bergel'son," *Literaturnaia gazeta*, April 26, 1940, 1.
2. The Yiddish term is *glitsh*. Since the word, whether from Yiddish or German, has entered English as "glitch," I will use the English spelling.
3. Charles Darwin, *The Descent of Man and Selection in Relation to Sex* (New York: D. Appleton, 1897), 606.
4. See for example Y. Blumshteyn, *Darvinizm un zayn teorye* (New York: Folksbildung, 1915).
5. David Bergelson, "Belles-Lettres and the Social Order," in *David Bergelson: From Modernism to Socialist Realism*, ed. Joseph Sherman and Gennady Estraikh (Oxford: Legenda, 2007), 338.
6. Bergelson, "Belles-Lettres and the Social Order," 338.
7. In *Creative Evolution* Bergson described the complexity of insect society in order to distinguish animal instinct from human intellect. I doubt that Bergelson's notion of animal communities was drawn from this source, however.
8. Charles Darwin, *On the Origin of Species* (Cambridge, MA: Harvard University Press, 1964), 239, 242.
9. For a succinct discussion of the range of theories linking degeneration to psychology, see Jennie Bourne Taylor, "Psychology at the Fin de Siècle," in *The Cambridge Companion*

to the Fin de Siècle, ed. Gail Marshall (Cambridge Companions Online, 2007), 13–30, http://dx.doi.org/10.1017/CCOL9780521850636.

10. For a discussion of Nordau and others who argued for decay, see Stephen Kern, *The Culture of Time and Space* (Cambridge, MA: Harvard University Press, 1983). , 125–26.

11. Max Nordau, *Degeneration* (New York: Appleton, 1895), 555.

12. Aleksei Kruchenykh, "Declaration of Transrational Language," in *Russian Futurism through Its Manifestoes, 1912–1928*, ed. Anna Lawton and Hebert Eagle (Ithaca, NY: Cornell University Press, 1988), 183.

13. David Bergelson, "Der toyber," in *Geklibene verk*, vol. 1 (Vilnius: B. Kletskin, 1929), 95.

14. David Bergelson, *Descent*, trans. Joseph Sherman, (New York: Modern Language Association of America, 1999), 7–8. The Yiddish: "Az ir hobn gevolt helfn Khanke Lyuber un Etl Kadis—di kursistin, vos hot in gikhn gezolt a kale vern far Meylekhn—hot zi zikh fun zeyer hilf opgezogt; gemakht a por farekshnte, nisht keyn zikhere tnues un zikh sof-kol-sof arayngevorfn in britshke arayn mitn boykh, vi eyner, vos zetst zikh raytn af a ferd. Nor beshas di meydlekh zenen geblibn vartn af ir letstn vort, hot zikh plutsem aroysgeglitsht der shirem fun ir hant. Oybn on, afn ongenetstn kishele, hot zi mit a mol gegebn a tsi arayn dem kop in di akslen, zikh arayngehoykert, azoy az di burke hot genumen oyszen vi ongefilt mit a bintl shmates, un zi hot oysgeshosn mit a meshune yieshdikn kvitsh: "oy, Meylekh! . . . Meylekh! . . ." [Ellipsis in original.] David Bergelson, Joseph Sherman, and David Goldberg, *Opgang*, Texts and Translations (New York: Modern Language Association of America, 1999), 7.

15. Bergelson, *Descent*, 30.

16. Bergelson, *Descent*, 55. For the Yiddish, see Bergelson, Sherman, and Goldberg, *Opgang*, 53.

17. Bergelson, *Descent*, 18.

18. See Nathalie Hazan-Brunet and Ada Ackerman, eds., *Futur Antérieur: L'avant-Garde et Le Livre Yiddish, 1914–1939* (Paris: Skira Flammarion, 2009), 150.

19. David Bergelson, "In a Backwoods Town," in *A Treasury of Yiddish Stories*, ed. Irving Howe and Eliezer Greenberg, trans. Bernard Guerney (Penguin Books, 1989), 471.

20. Customarily, the two mothers-in-law broke a dish. David Bergelson, "In a fargrebter shtot," in *Geklibene verk*, vol. 3 (Vilnius: B. Kletskin, 1929), 9. The Yiddish: "Az men makht a knosmol, ruft men tsunoyf dem rov, dem shoykhet mitn khazn un mit ale kruvem, un bay der shayn fun fil ongetsundene likht brekht men teler. Tsunoyfbindn ober ot di dray bazundere gedanken hot zi zikh gefoylt un hot nisht gekent. . . hot zi shoyn lang farloyrn dem kheyshek tsu trakhtn mit a seyder." I am using my translation of the passage; for the entire story in English, see Bergelson, "In a Backwoods Town."

21. For the English translation, see David Bergelson, "The Deaf Man," in *No Star Too Beautiful: Yiddish Stories from 1382 to the Present*, trans. Joachim Neugroschel (New York: W. W. Norton, 2002), 424–43.

22. See Joseph Sherman, "David Bergelson (1884–1952): A Biography," in *David Bergelson: From Modernism to Socialist Realism*, ed. Joseph Sherman and Gennady Estraikh (London: Legenda, 2007), 47.

23. For Herman, see Zalmen Zylbercweig, ed., *Leksikon fun yidishn teater*, vol. 1 (New York: Elisheva, 1931), 634–35.

24. An interview with Herman appeared in "Far der premyere fun David Bergelsons 'Der toyber,'" *Literarishe bleter*, April 11, 1930, 294.

25. For a discussion of the production, see Jeffrey Veidlinger, *The Moscow State Yiddish Theater: Jewish Culture on the Soviet Stage* (Bloomington: Indiana University Press, 2000), 121–25.

26. An account of Russian Futurism and the Russian reception of Marinetti that sharply distinguishes the former from the latter can be found in Benedikt Livshits, *Polutoraglazyi strelets* (Leningrad: Sovetskii pisatel', 1989), 144–49. Lifshits muses about Marinetti's nationalism and comments that his own racial theory of culture was more metaphysical than political.

27. Jordan Finkin similarly remarks that Peretz Markish's Futurism does not seek to destroy the past but rather to invest it with "newness." See Jordan Finkin, "Constellating Hebrew and Yiddish Avant-Gardes," *Journal of Modern Jewish Studies* 8, no. 1 (2009): 1–22.

28. Bergelson, "The Deaf Man," 424. For the Yiddish, see Bergelson, "Der toyber," 98.

29. Bergelson, "The Deaf Man," 433.

30. Margareta Tillberg, "'Be a Spectator with a Large Ear': Victory over the Sun as a Public Laboratory Experiment for Mikhail Matiushin's Theories of Colour Vision," in *Victory Over the Sun: The World's First Futurist Opera*, ed. Rosamund Bartlett and Sarah Dadswell (Exeter, UK: University of Exeter Press, 2012), 208–23.

31. Bergelson, "The Deaf Man," 426. I have modified the translation. The Yiddish: "Hot er genumen redn af zayn toybn opgerisenem shteyger, makhndik nisht keyn oysgearbete havayes mit eyner a kaylekhdikn eyngeboygter hant un reysndik mit gvald eyntsike verter fun zayn breyt-beynerdiker un kreftiker brust." Bergelson, "Der toyber," 97.

32. Veidlinger, *The Moscow State Yiddish Theater: Jewish Culture on the Soviet Stage,* 123–24.

33. The essay "Der gesheener oyfbrukh" (The present upheaval) was published in the first volume of the Berlin art magazine *Milgroym*, which Bergelson coedited with Der Nister. For another discussion of this essay, see Joseph Sherman, "David Bergelson (1884–1952): A Biography," in *David Bergelson: From Modernism to Socialist Realism*, ed. Joseph Sherman and Gennady Estraikh (London: Legenda, 2007), 32–33. Sherman translates the title as "The awakening has occurred."

34. Friedrich A. Kittler, *Discourse Networks 1800/1900*, trans. Michael Metteer (Stanford, CA: Stanford University Press, 1990), 216. Bergson argued that contemporary investigations into speech pathology confirmed his hypothesis that the brain was the clearing station for motor activity and not the storage house of memory. Recognizing and understanding words (acoustic images) require a rehearsal of the movements of the tongue, larynx, mouth, teeth, and chest that went into producing them, and an injury to certain centers of the brain would impede the proper tracing out of these movements, hence preventing the patient from discerning that a word had been uttered.

35. Bergelson, "The Deaf Man," 435.

36. Bergelson, "The Deaf Man," 111, 112, 113.

37. For the Russian text, see Viktor Shklovskii, "O poezii i zaumnom iazyke," in *Poetika*, ed. Osip Brik (Petrograd, 1919), 13–26. For the English translation see Viktor Shklovsky, "On Poetry and Trans-Sense Language," *October* 34 (Autumn 1985): 3–24. For a contextualizing discussion, see Gerald Janecek, *Zaum: The Transrational Poetry of Russian Futurism* (San Diego, CA: San Diego State University Press, 1996), 1–48. The need to do something in order to understand it derives from Bergson. In lectures and essays from the early 1900s, Bergson used the analogy of reading to get at the distinctive nature of intuition as a mode of access to absolute knowledge. The formulations of scientific discourse ignore the "rhythm, the

structure, the temporal relations between the various sentences" of the "great book of the world," whereas the intuitive process enables the observer to merge with "the direction of a movement." Henri Bergson, *An Introduction to Metaphysics: The Creative Mind* (Totowa, NJ: Littlefield, Adams, 1965), 87.

38. For more on Bergelson's take on Futurism, see Seth Wolitz, *Yiddish Modernism: Studies in Twentieth Century Eastern European Jewish Culture* (Bloomington, IN: Slavica, 2014), 356–63.

39. Bergelson, "Belles-Lettres and the Social Order," 345.

40. For Matiushin's Bergsonian theories, see Tillberg, "Be a Spectator with a Large Ear," For a general discussion, see Charlotte Douglas, "The New Russian Art and Italian Futurism," *Art Journal* no. 3 (1975): 229–39.

41. Max Weinreich, "Fun der eyropeisher literatur: Futurizm," *Di yidishe velt* no. 4 (1914): 145–47.

42. For a discussion of Khlebnikov, see Adrian Wanner, *Russian Minimalism: From the Prose Poem to the Anti-Story* (Evanston, IL: Northwestern University Press, 2003), 104–09. For a discussion of modernism's embrace of the autonomy of art and its insistence on the separation from reality, see Stephen Hutchings, *Russian Modernism: The Transfiguration of the Everyday* (Cambridge, UK: Cambridge University Press, 1997), 226–30.

43. Bergelson, "The Deaf Man," 427. The Yiddish: "Ruik, vi farklert, hot zi gebrumt ir uraltn monotonishn brum un zikh getreyslt tsusamen mit ire fertsik mentshn arbeter. Tsvishn geroysh un tuml hobn mentshn gearbayt mekhanish un ernst-shtum, vi di mashines un reder, vos hobn zikh arum zey gedrayt, nish geredt un nish geklert, glaykh vi bay zey in moyekh voltn gelegn di groyse gepakte mit veyts mil-shafn un bay zey dem seykhl opgenumen."

    < . . . >

Nor zeltn ven hot der mil-geroysh a plutslingn tsiter geton un zikh mit a troyern bas-kol durkhgeshnitn:

'Stop! . . . Stop! . . .'

Nor keyner hot zikh af dem nisht opgerufn, un gedakht hot zikh shoyn, az dos bas-kol iz a vayts un farloyerns, farblonzhet gevorn aher, in a fremder umbakanter velt, zukht emetsn un ken nisht gefunen." (Bergelson, "Der toyber," 98–99.)

44. David Bergelson, *The End of Everything*, trans. Joseph Sherman, New Yiddish Library (New Haven, CT: Yale University Press, 2009), 93. The Yiddish: "Ayngehoykert un shtark farklenert iz er dortn gezesn tsu ir mit di pleytses, der kop etvos farvorfn arunter un dos moyl ofn, vi bay a fish, un ongeshtelt akegn der refue-dampf, vos er hot zikh gelozt funem oyslendishn niklnem mashinl. In der shpeter bin-hashmoshosdiker luft hot dos mashindl akegn im mit a kleynem bloy-grinlekh flam gebrakht, un mit derm bloy-grinem flam iz zayn ponem koym-koym baloykhtn geven, oysgezen nas un badekt mit fil shveysike dampf-tropns." David Bergelson, *Nokh alemen*, vol. 2 (Vilno: B. Kletskin, 1929), 120.

45. Hayyim Nahman Bialik and H. Ravnitzky, eds., *Sefer Ha'agadah*, trans. S. Epstein (London: Soncino, 1948), 6–7.

46. Bergelson, *The End of Everything*, 41.

47. See Ken Frieden, *Classic Yiddish Fiction: Abramovitsh, Sholem Aleichem, & Peretz* (Albany: State University of New York Press, 1995). For a discussion of Tevye in particular, see Michael Stern, "Tevye's Art of Quotation," *Prooftexts* 6, no. 1 (1986): 79–96. Broader

discussions of Sholem Aleichem's use of oral forms can be found in Dov Sadan, "Three Foundations: Sholem Aleichem and the Yiddish Literary Tradition," *Prooftexts* 6, no. 1 (1986): 55–63 . See also David Roskies, "Sholem Aleichem: Mythologist of the Mundane," *Association for Jewish Studies Review* 13, no. 2 (1988): 27–46.

48. Bergelson, "The Deaf Man," 427.

49. Bergelson, "The Deaf Man," 427. The Yiddish: "S'dakht zikh im: er iz shoyn do amol bay ot dem zelbn taptshan mit dem zelbn toytn geshtanen. Shoyn lang iz dos geven, zeyer lang, not s'iz dokh geven. Afile di zelbe fil mentshn." Bergelson, "Der toyber," 100.

50. Bergelson, "Der lokh, durkh velkhn eyner hot farloyrn," 83–84.

51. Bergelson, "Der lokh, durkh velkhn eyner hot farloyrn," 82.

52. Bergelson, "Der lokh, durkh velkhn eyner hot farloyrn," 83.

53. Bergelson, "Der lokh, durkh velkhn eyner hot farloyrn," 87.

54. Bergelson, "Der lokh, durkh velkhn eyner hot farloyrn," 88. The Yiddish: "Im hot zikh gedakht, az er hinkt—af azoyfil iz im geven shver zikh nokhtsushlepn nokh zayn kerper."

55. Bergelson, "Der lokh, durkh velkhn eyner hot farloyrn," 92.

56. Bergelson, "Der lokh, durkh velkhn eyner hot farloyrn," 87.

57. Bergelson, "Der lokh, durkh velkhn eyner hot farloyrn," 89.

5

DELAY, DESIRE, AND VISUALITY

Bergelson's short story "the dynamic moment" ("*di dinamishe rege*," 1927) describes the radical practice of a young painter: "For the sake of mischief he stumbled into the history of art to show that in painting, as in life, there were no stable relations between things and people. As soon as you move them from their place, they create a dynamic moment of new relations."[1]

The mischievous painter likely refers to Marc Chagall, whose canvasses set in motion a dynamic interplay of light, color, and movement. The boundary between figure and ground disappears, and human figures float in the air or appear, as Bergelson says, "with their feet up and their heads down." Chagall's murals for the Moscow State Yiddish Theater, for example, included images of acrobats walking on their hands. Chagall and Bergelson knew each other, and Chagall visited Bergelson in Berlin.[2] The "dynamic moment" recalls Bergson, who argued that conventional notions of time ignore the reality of constant change. The painter, in love, is free from clocks and calendars; he experiences time as dynamic change. As Bergelson puts it, "Time, with its divisions into hours and minutes no longer had any influence over" the artist.[3] At the story's end, the painter experiences "the dynamic moment" in the life-altering experience of the birth of his first child "with feet up and head down." Bergelson's son, Lev, was born in 1918, and his emphasis on birth in this and other stories from the twenties reflects this event. "The Dynamic Moment" is a playful, joyous story.

The loss of "stable relations between things and people" is a good way to describe the major shift in perspective central to visual and narrative art in Bergelson's work and his milieu. The body and emotion shape perception; there is no objective, mathematically calculable perspective capable of describing the truth. It is significant that Bergelson linked artistic creativity, play, and birth in 1927, a time when cataclysmic, destructive change was the leitmotif of numerous discussions of art and poetry—including the author's own theorizations of art, as I will show.

The figure of the artist appears frequently in Bergelson's stories from the late teens and twenties. Aside from "The Dynamic Moment," the artists include the painter who falls in love with the fourteen-year-old Murre and then her twenty-eight-year-old sister Polye in the story "Sisters" ("*Shvester*," 1926), the painter Babo in "One Night Less" ("*Mit eyn nakht veyniker*," 1927), the famous painter visiting Kiev who is admired by Joseph Shur's never-to-be fiancée in "Joseph Shur" ("*Yoysef Shur*," 1922), and the hunchbacked sculptor Nesi in the same story. Bergelson was also interested in another kind of visual art, one akin to today's performance art, in which the artist's manipulation of his or her own body is the artwork. Inspired by Kafka's "Hunger Artist," Bergelson created his own version of a similar figure in the 1926 "For 12,000 Bucks" ("*Far 12 toyzend dolar fast er 40 teg*").

Bergelson wrote about art in a 1919 in an essay that I have previously quoted:

> Art, however, also possesses even a distinct physiological significance for us: the relaxed auditory nerve, for example, demands sustenance and thus engenders the need to hear music. For some time, the work of certain nerves will be suspended in the new social order, but with the passage of time they will accumulate colossal energy and will demand a great deal of sustenance, and the great regeneration of art will begin.[4]

Bergelson's emphasis on physiology reveals his underlying conceptualization of the intimate relation between art and the body. The human nervous system needs art; art is key to the healthy and normal function of sense perception. In the first period of the crisis in art—created by the social upheaval of World War I and the Russian revolution—the nerves will go slack, but the temporary suspension of art production will build up unmet demand, and the physiological need for art will skyrocket. At that moment, new forms of art will be created and the crisis will move toward resolution. Art, like a missing appendage of a living organism, will begin its regeneration.

Bergelson wrote his essay on art while still in Kiev; he and his family left Kiev for Moscow in 1920. Looking back on Moscow at that time, Bergelson later wrote that the city resembled a ghost town in which former shopkeepers had become "shadows without their property." Moscow in 1921 was thrust back to a time when there were no buildings, no city, and no land, but only water; Moscow's numerous structures had regressed to "frozen waves on the sea" (*heyzer—farfroyrene khvalyes af a yam*). Time went the wrong way: "Higher than all the rooftops, higher than all the sharpest spires of the churches, the large invisible clock turned its hand backwards."[5] Fleeing hardship and embracing opportunity, Bergelson exchanged Moscow for Berlin in 1921, at the invitation of a publisher.

Berlin in the 1920s was a gathering place for the Russian-language diaspora; Vladimir Nabokov, Marina Tsvetaeva, Il'ia Erenburg, and Victor Shklovsky lived there temporarily. Berlin was also a center for Hebrew and Yiddish writing and publication and art production; the Hebrew authors Bialik and Tchernichowsky were in Berlin, as were the Yiddish writers Leyb Kvitko, Moyshe Kulbak, Perets Markish, Der Nister, and David Hofshteyn, among others. Bergelson wrote for the American Yiddish newspaper *Forward* (*Forverts*); he played chess at the Romanisches Café, whose habitués also included the prose writer Alfred Doblin, the critic Alfred Kerr, the visual artists Otto Dix and George Grosz, and the poets Franz Werfel and Else Lasker-Schüler. According to Yisroel Rubin, an observer of the time, Bergelson was nothing less than the master of ceremonies at the Yiddish writers' table. Daniel Charney, Eliyahu Cherikover, Jacob Lestchinsky, David Einhorn, and Hirsh Nomberg were among those in attendance. Bergelson did not so much converse as speak in monologues, reworking stories from his own and other's accounts and in so doing setting out the architecture of his future written work. His table talk was a crucial phase of his writing process.[6]

While in Berlin, Bergelson wrote a number of short stories that explicitly reference the city and its streets, prostitutes, and cheap cafes and restaurants. The fictitious characters Max Wentsl and Dr. Mer, for example, both found in the story "One Night Less" ("*Mit eyn nakht veyniker*"), in all likelihood refer to the real-life poet Franz Werfel and Alfred Kerr, respectively. Dafna Clifford points out that Bergelson's description of Yiddish literature as "a young hag powdering herself with the smoke of big-city cigars . . . could be taken straight from a painting by Otto Dix or Georg Grosz."[7] In "Blindness" ("*Blindkeyt*,"1926) the heroine's dismissive comment about a young blonde, her rival, subtly reflects the automatism and mass phenomena of Berlin. The girl belongs to a certain type about whom "you feel that the big city releases only a very tiny number of them, according to a special order and according to the latest fashion, from a special secret factory."[8]

Bergelson himself participated in the regeneration of art not only with his own literary work but also with various cultural enterprises. He was one of the founders of the Berlin Sholem Aleichem Club, which Doblin visited.

In his article "The Present Upheaval" ("*Der gesheener oyfbrukh*"), published in the first issue of the journal *Milgroym*, Bergelson praises the young generation of Yiddish poets from Russia, citing excerpts from Leyb Kvitko, David Hofshteyn, Moyshe Lifshits, and Arn Kushnirov.[9] The slaughter on the battlefields of World War I, equivalent to the death of a whole generation, gives rise to a new collective voice not bound by any law (*gesets*) or limitation, having abandoned any sense of "wholeness" (*gantskeyt*) and freely given over to the "chaotic life" that resides in everyone.[10] Bergelson seems to embrace a new aesthetic of violence, translating the experience of the trenches—of which he had no direct knowledge—into poetic practice: "The new poem has fired off a shot with its excess, it has opened all its veins nerves, and cells, it drinks, vomits . . . and chokes on itself [ellipsis in original]."[11] The expressionist metaphor of the text as a fleshly corpus is pushed to its physiological extreme in these words; the poem consists of bodily effluvia that gag their creator. The art historian Rokhl Vishnitser-Bernshtayn similarly said that the new art of was participating in the "apocalyptic atmosphere of the destruction of the world" (*di apokaliptishe shtimung funem velt-khurbn*).[12]

The same issue of *Milgroym* included a Cubist painting of an old Jew with a clock, the work of Bergelson's Kiev friend Isaachar-Ber Rybak. [13] The painting is titled "The Old One" (*Der alter*), and it is dated October 1917, suggesting a connection to the Russian revolutions. Unlike other portraits, including Rembrandt's, Rybak's old Jew wears no prayer shawl and does not study a book or even a newspaper. His eyes are shut; his mouth twisted down in a grimace of pain or exhaustion. One hand is thrust in the breast of his coat. The other arm, with its veiny hand, presses against the back of a chair. But the chair doesn't rest on the ground; this is a Cubist painting, and everything is in motion. The sharp angles of the face, coat, and hat, and the overall fragmentation of the space create a sense of dynamism and movement: can the "old one" keep up? A wall clock, decorated with a red flower, hangs above the old man's shoulder. Like everything else in the painting, the clock is positioned at an angle and the numbers on its face, like the features of the man's face, are not aligned properly. Time is out of joint.[14]

Bergelson was deeply interested in the new art of his day. His own work, like the modernist visual art of his time, raises questions about what and how we see, the relation between sight and the other senses, and the role of time, memory, and desire in vision. These issues are important to the stories I mentioned earlier, and they work together in a particularly powerful way in "Blindness" and *Judgment*. Scholars use the term "visuality" to emphasize the historical, psychic, physiological, and political dimensions that inform both seeing and the failure of sight.[15] Bergson, Riegl, and Benjamin are foundational for the study of visuality today.

This chapter explores the relation between visuality, desire, and belatedness, focusing for the most part on work written from 1921 to 1933, while Bergelson was in Berlin. In the aftermath of World War I and the Russian revolution and civil war, Bergelson's narratives reveal the shapes that memory, technology, and history lend to perception and desire. Laura Mulvey's anatomy of the gaze provides the point of departure for my discussion of desire and visuality, the intersection between sight and pleasure, and the gendered positions of the spectator and the spectacle. Bergelson breaks down this fixed structure, however, by translating sight into other forms of perception, including smell and sound, and by showing how technological advances fundamentally change seeing and being seen. Seeing and being seen, an essential feature of desire, are embodied in the entire sensorium and mediated through objects, technologies, and other human beings.

The second half of the chapter focuses on desire and temporality: how memory and catastrophe haunt desire. For Bergelson, the characteristic delay and loss that are constitutive of desire assume a new dimension in light of the overwhelming historical events of the first quarter of the twentieth century. Even within this tragic framework, however, Bergelson remains interested in reanimating what seems to be irretrievably lost, in redeeming the virtualities concealed in the past. In this respect, his fictions are comparable to Benjamin's theory of the suddenly emergent image, the pause in the continuity of history in which some form of redemption may be glimpsed. Bergelson explores "love at last sight," another permutation of belatedness.[16] His own relation to the shtetl may be seen in this light.

The Pleasure of Looking

In her 1975 essay "Visual Pleasure and Narrative Cinema" Laura Mulvey argues that classical Hollywood cinema codes women as objects to be looked at, thereby defining the position of the spectator as masculine..[17] Objectification is a form of violence that keeps the fear of castration at bay; women embody the terrifying consequence of failing to obey the father's law. The pleasure of looking, or scopophilia, that the voyeur and the film spectator share has to do with the power of the masculine gaze to control and also derive enjoyment from the female spectacle. Mulvey's essay emerges from a particular moment in feminism, psychoanalysis, and cinema history—a trajectory that Bergelson does not share, although both his male and female characters enjoy the pleasures of spectatorship.

Bergelson depicts these pleasures in "In a Backwoods Town," which I touched on in chapter 4. The story describes the corrupt practices and violence among a group of butchers in "a backwoods town." Its leitmotif is "the world stinks" (*di velt iz blote*).[18] A wealthy member of the community dies, but his grandson Elishe, a newcomer, refuses to pay the "donation" requested by the burial society in order to bury him. Elishe's new wife, whose reputation is tarnished, attracts the attention of the men and sleeps with Burman. Elishe competes with the local butchers over the right to collect the tax on kosher meat, and the tension between them erupts in violence. The butchers attack Elishe, who dies a few days later.

When Elishe first brings his new wife from Medzhibodzh to the "backwoods town," everyone comes to have a look:

> She was a whole head taller than Elishe . . . and when, clad in her tight black dress, lifted her foot to take a step, all of the surrounding male eyes unwillingly focused on it; as if in this slender foot lay some particular Medzhibodzh art, and it was worthwhile seeing what would happen to it, and to her entire tall figure, when she would once again lift it and again place it on the ground [ellipsis added].[19]

Male desire dilates time in this scene. "Male eyes" fixate on and fix the pointing, lifting, and placing of the women's leg and foot. The longer the delay, the more pleasurable is their experience. Bergelson returns to the motif of the eroticized foot in a subsequent scene in which Elishe's wife and her lover, Burman, play "footsies," "*a gantser ernster shmues af fis-loshn.*"[20]

Burman walks past Elishe's house and notices the curtains that have already been hung:

> From behind one of them, which had been raised and thrown back a bit toward the side, the hammering of a small hammer could be heard; the chill inside the room and the tall chairs, in their newly made covers, and she herself, Elishe's wife—could be imagined. She was standing there near the maid, who had climbed up a table that had been placed there, and ordered her:
> Please put the nail in a little higher . . . higher.[21]

The scene depicts a voyeuristic encounter comparable to Beynish and Klare in "At the Depot." Burman's desire for Fradochka is mediated by the chair, table, picture, nail, and maid. Each serves as a substitute for Fradochka;

each is charged by contact with her in an eroticized metonymic chain. Bergelson translates a sound into an erotic visual element, less seen and more imagined. This sensory translation is important, because the mediation and gaps that the transfer requires destabilize the position of the viewer. Indeed, there is no specific viewer or listener; the sounds "could be heard" (*hobn zikh gehert*) by anyone, everyone, and no one; similarly the chill of the room, and the people and things in it "could be imagined" (*s'hot zikh gemolt*) by anyone and no one.[22]

Viewing the Bride

Cultural context and cultural shifts and discontinuities are part of the fabric of how we see and what seeing and being seen mean. Bergelson explores this broader question by focusing on marriage in "Joseph Shur" ("*Yoysef Shur*").[23] The publication history of this work resembles the fate of *Descent*, which was begun in 1913 but not published until 1920. The earliest form of "Joseph Shur" was titled "In Darkened Times" ("*In fartunklte tsaytn*"), begun in 1913. A portion appeared in 1915; reworked, another version was published in Bergelson's short-lived journal *Our Own* (*Eygns*); the full novella was published in 1923.[24] Bergelson draws on his readers' knowledge of marriage customs in his depiction of the failed engagement of his title character. Even in stories written and set before World War I, there are no instances in Bergelson in which two sets of parents engage their children without their consent (unlike Sh. An-sky's *Dybbuk*). Nonetheless, engagement and wedding ceremonies in Bergelson in the early period are traditional. In "Joseph Shur" a sharper change takes place. The marriage broker, traveling on a train during Passover, is shocked to hear Yiddish coming out of the mouths of young people who are cheerfully consuming leavened foods forbidden during the holiday, as if they were non-Jews.

Joseph Shur, misled by the marriage broker, travels by train from his shtetl to Kiev under the mistaken impression that he is the prospective groom for a young woman who lives there at the home of her wealthy uncle. He believes that he going to meet his prospective bride; she, educated and independent, merely "smiled when she was told that he was coming to see her" and went out for the entire evening, avoiding him.[25] The uncle catches sight of the would-be bridegroom, noting to himself, "That is the young man . . . who came to have a look at Sorele" (*onkukn Sorelen*); the uncle further observes, "This is how a young man of today, a rich man, looks—who would make young ladies not even want him to see them."[26] The emphasis on looking and seeing is unmistakable.

On the way to Kiev, however, a chance encounter on the train substitutes for the traditional meeting of the bride and groom. By coincidence, Joseph Shur and the young woman have been traveling in the same compartment, a circumstance known to him but not to her. She sleeps for most of the journey while he gazes at her. At one moment, however, "the girl had a look at him; she opened her eyes, her sleepy, blue eyes stared for a moment at his boyish face and wanted to remember something, and then became once again indifferent and uninterested."[27]

The girl's eyes, separately from the girl herself, perform the actions of looking, attempting to remember, and resuming indifference prior to closing. Bergelson suggests a parallel between the sleeping girl's eyes and the train's night-lights. Joseph Shur switches off the light over the girl's head, but as soon as he does, the train's night-lights come on. The somnambulant opening and closing of the girl's eyes parallels the automatic nighttime illumination of the train compartment. Technology and the sense organs replicate and substitute what we would expect to be the actions performed by a human agent; in the context of the night-lights episode, a similar on/off switch seems to control the girl's eyes. The looks that Shur and Sorele trade in the train compartment do not amount to an intersubjective exchange—that is, a moment of reciprocity—but instead mark only a momentary interruption in the sleep cycle: an organic off/on switch like the lights in the compartment. This moment and the episode at the uncle's house reveal that even before he arrived in Kiev for the supposed meeting with his prospective bride, Joseph Shur had already been looked over and dismissed without knowing it.

Looking Back

In a set of stories featuring women protagonists, including "In the Boarding House of the Three Sisters" ("*In pansion fun di dray shvester*," 1927), "Payment" ("Skhar-tirkhe,"1928) and "Blindness," ("*Blindkeyt*,"1926), Bergelson reverses the direction and therefore the power of the gaze: women look at men, deliberately inviting their sexualized stares; in "Blindness" the female protagonist is the source of her own pleasure. Whether the boardinghouse of the three sisters is a boardinghouse or a high-class brothel is left unclear.

The three women who run it abandoned their husbands somewhere on the way from Russia to Berlin and use the promise of sex to lure boarders to their lodgings and then charge them excessive fees. The walls of the boardinghouse are covered with "pictures and photographs of women [that] peer down, with pious faces . . . and misty, passionate eyes" [ellipsis added].[28] The youngest sister, Yulya, has a body that "tears off her clothes with invisible hands."[29] Allison Schachter argues that "In the Boarding House" reveals the tension between Jewish traditional values and the sexual freedom of Weimar Berlin. The women in the story wield economic and sexual power as well as the pleasure of spectatorship: they assess each male customer, deciding what he likes and what he needs. By figuring the reader as masculine, Schachter goes on to say, the story challenges the traditional gender norms of Yiddish literature, according to which readers were typically women.[30]

Bergelson had already begun experimenting with sexual norms before the Berlin period. In *The End of Everything,* published in 1913, the Hebrew poet Herts sends Mirl a book "like the fruit of sin"; she spends an evening with Nosn Heller; she aborts the pregnancy resulting from sex with her husband. Mirl's unwanted marriage, made to save her bankrupt father, is a manipulation of sexual economic exchange not so very different from the sisters who run the boardinghouse or the adulterous couple in "Payment" ("*Skhar-tirkhe*"). Mirl, however, remains more innocent than the women in the Berlin-era stories. In the period after 1917, sexuality and other appetites in Bergelson's female characters can also indicate the wrong attitude toward socialism.

The story "Payment," first published in 1928, is an example. "Payment" is set in a Sovietized shtetl. Private houses and businesses have been nationalized or confiscated. Rute Kuptshik's husband has been exiled for withholding grain from the authorities, and their house has been taken. She expects the attorney Shpolyanski, married to a sickly wife, to recover her property, adding that she will stop at nothing to achieve her end. Her cheeks are always aflame, her look resembles that a woman on her wedding night, her lips are those of an *aguna* (Hebrew for "abandoned woman"), and worst of all she wears "seductive high-heeled shoes" (*yeytser-horedik khoykhe optsasn*) that set in motion the entire affair.[31] The attorney forges a document granting the return of the house and receives payment in the form of sex with Rute Kuptshik. Sex is a commodity that can be traded like any other item. The story represents the illicit contract between Rute and the lawyer as part of the corrupt old world to be rooted out by the new regime.

Bergelson often figures feminine desire as excessive. He interweaves violence, desire, and treachery in his civil war narrative *Judgment* (*Mideshadin*), published in part in 1926 and published in full in 1929. Set on the border between Ukraine and Poland, the novel tells the story of the heroic self-sacrifice of a Bolshevik leader as he battles various enemies, including smugglers, socialist revolutionaries, and a femme fatale known as "the blonde" (*di blonde*), whose first name and patronymic are the same as Tolstoy's adulterous heroine Anna Arkadevna Karenina. I will discuss this novel in the context of the interwar period and the theme of justice in chapters 6 and 7, but for now focus on the extraordinary figure of "the blonde." She is "drop-dead gorgeous" (*treyf-sheyn*)—the Yiddish suggests there is something "unclean" about her beauty. She attempts to steal across the border with a young child who turns out not to be her own; documents sewn into the child's dress reveal that she is a courier for the enemy of the Bolsheviks, the Whites.

Her eyes are peculiar. Instead of seeing others or even reflecting images of the surrounding world, her pupils reflect only her image of herself. The torn photograph of Beynish Rubinshteyn's dead wife in "At the Depot" looks back at her husband, reflecting him and his desire for forgiveness, but the blonde's eyes in *Judgment* offer no reflection of anyone else. Instead, in each pupil there is a woman with a crucifix on her breast, and the image of each woman contains the image of yet another woman, and so on. Late in the novel, as she makes a last effort to get across the border to Poland, she prays to an icon of the "Holy Mother" and believes that Mary has slipped out of the icon frame to enter her own body. She believes that no one will thwart her journey across the border, because no one will want to thwart the mother of God. Through the figure of "the blonde," Bergelson imagines an endless projection and proliferation of surfaces without anything behind them and without an inner connection that would link them. Even though *Judgment* is set in Ukraine, it was written in Berlin, and the blonde, like the fantastical factory girls, reflects the gleaming surface culture of Berlin, with its advertising, neon lights, and shop mannequins.[32]

Waiting in prison to learn whether she will be shot for espionage, the blonde asks her body whether it senses imminent death:

> She lay down on her mattress . . . shut her eyes and, with all of her inner feeling, queried her hands, her feet, and her breasts about this. The answer her robust limbs promptly gave her made her feel calm. All the muscles in her body presented their report together:
> "We feel the same way—we aren't the ones they have in mind" [ellipsis added].[33]

The blonde is comparable to a researcher in a turn-of-the-century psychology laboratory investigating the physiology of the mind.[34] She breaks down her body into its constituent anatomical parts and then tallies the results of an imaginary experiment testing the sensitivity, reaction time, and responses of her muscular system. Her muscles receive information independently of her mind, brain, and senses. In the "backwoods town," male desire separates the beautiful young woman's foot from the rest of her body; in *Judgment*, the blonde separates her limbs from her own body. The independent existence of the blonde's body and limbs parallels the experience of the protagonist of "The Hole Through Which Life Slips": "driving away his intellect, his body felt independent, celebratory, excited, exactly as if together with the Bolsheviks, every kind of joy had returned to the city." Politics separate the blonde and Yona Grigorevitsh, but what is of more interest to their creator is the play with the fragmentation of their bodies in the absence of any notion of a unified self. Political upheaval contributes to the milieu in which this kind of experimentation is possible.

Belatedness

The force of desire freezes time: the male eyes leave Fradochka's foot suspended in the air as they stare at it. The inverse is also true: time mediates desire, slowing and speeding its urgency and also suspending and delaying it. The mediation of desire through objects and other human beings contributes to delay.[35] Lack and delay are constitutive of desire. If I possessed the thing I want, I would desire it. From the psychoanalytic perspective, the constitution of the subject and hence the subject's desire is bound up with the loss of and separation from the mother. While the experience of desire always includes delay and mediation, in work written after World War I and the Russian revolution and civil war, Bergelson amplifies loss by adding the historical brokenness of a present that is the aftereffect of a violent past.

As in *The End of Everything*, the "pain that comes afterward," *nokhveyenish*, flows into the pleasure of desire. Mirl Hurvits was a mourner (*shivezitserin*) but not in relation to any particular death, including the death of her father, whom she does not mourn. In the period after World War I, there is something concrete to mourn. The prewar world of progress and opportunity has exploded. History has conspired to make retroactively concrete the intangible sense of loss on which characters like Mirl Hurvits and Meylekh (the dead hero of *Descent*) are based. The mechanization that was supposed to shrink space and time and liberate human beings from the drudgery of work failed. Technological progress gave rise to the suffering of the "tiny, fragile human body" isolated in a force field of destructive torrents, confronting the overwhelming force of mechanized warfare.[36]

Belatedness and delay are part of the sensory motor experience of the people who inhabit Bergelson's fictitious world; the glitch, discussed in chapter 4, is an example. Belatedness is also the central theme of Bergelson's representation of the shtetl, which lags behind and is sunk in obsolescence. Bergelson's characters are perpetually at the wrong place at the wrong time; they arrive too late and too early for the meeting that never takes place and for the new opportunities that happen somewhere else and for someone else. Missing the moment takes on cosmic dimensions in the inserted allegories of *The End of Everything* and *Descent:* the savior arrives too late in Herts's story of the dead town, and the woman who waits for God all her life steps out the moment before he arrives.

Belatedness is thus an experiential, existential, and historical condition in Bergelson's works and the world in which he lived. In the Berlin stories in particular, characters in the midst of the frantic pace of modern urban life experience a pervasive sense of belatedness. The past persists in the present, erupting all of a sudden, unforeseen and uncanny. The confrontation with the alienated past combines pleasure and dread.

Benjamin's notion of the "suddenly emergent image" sheds light on this dimension of Bergelson's Berlin stories. The suddenly emergent image is the unforeseen appearance in the present of a phenomenon that has already disappeared in the past: "the relation of what-has-been to the now is . . . not progression, but image, suddenly emergent" [ellipsis added]. [37] The image becomes visible suddenly, "in a flash," and is gone. It could be a forgotten bit of the past subject to psychological or political repression, written out of the history of a person or a nation. The new type of history that Benjamin sought to write with his *Arcades* project would redeem these discarded moments. [38] Suddenly emergent afterimages from previous times appear in two Bergelson stories of the Berlin period. Both "Among Refugees" and "Blindness" weave together the destruction of the shtetl with the eruption of a new, strange form of belated desire that crystalizes around images of the discarded past. The suddenly emergent image, beautiful in its passing, offers Begelson a way to negotiate his own relationship to abandoned moments of his own history.

In "Among Refugees," a young Jewish man, a World War I veteran originally from Ukraine who previously traveled to Palestine and now lives in Berlin, discovers that a Ukrainian leader, notorious for his role in anti-Jewish violence, is staying in the same boardinghouse as he.[39] This is a boardinghouse without the three charming sisters. The young man decides that he must assassinate the Ukrainian leader, and having failed to find support from the Jewish community, who try to put him under the care of a psychiatrist, he turns to the writer, the first-person narrator, for help. The story opens with a description of the impression the visitor makes on the writer and his family: "Coming home from the streets of Berlin one hot July day, I found my family tense and agitated. Their faces were pale and very frightened."[40] The source of their anxiety is the visitor: the young man who sits curled up in a chair in a corner of the writer's study, waiting for him. What is striking about his description is not his strangeness but, on the contrary, his familiarity: "His whole body reminded me of the gray dust on the far roads of small towns [*kleynshtetldike vegn*], and he gave the impression of someone who had breathlessly traveled a long distance."[41]

After a few words with his visitor, the writer leaves him in his study but finds himself compelled to think about the young man. The narrator emphasizes the strange sensation that the compulsion produces: "Sitting the other room, I felt very ill at ease."[42] In the original Yiddish, "ill at ease" is *umheymlekh*, which can also mean "uncanny."

The violence of Jewish history, the shtetl destroyed during the Russian civil war, reappears in the figure of the visitor, the self-styled "Jewish terrorist." In the line I have already quoted, Bergelson stresses the association between the stranger and the shtetl, setting up a series of associations: the figure of the young man connects with the gray dust that connects with the faraway roads linking the small shtetlekh. The most familiar, well-known object, the small shtetl where Bergelson grew up and about which he made his reputation as a writer, is practically buried in the metonymic chain. Berlin and its streets are the setting for the writer's home and all those who are dearest to him, his "own," and the small shtetl, the place of his origin, is the farthest away and the most remote—only this farthest away and most remote place is now embodied in this unsettling young man who has succeeded in penetrating the most intimate corner of the writer's new home in Berlin, the place where he writes, his study. Almost more hallucination than reality, the strange yet familiar visitor embodies the suddenly emergent image.

The visitor's face is bizarre and grotesque:

> He had high cheekbones, which were uneven and made his cheeks look disparate. The right cheek the same as on all faces—a cheek that wanted to enjoy the world, that says: "I want to be with people."
>
> His left cheek, however, was crooked; as if it were his and not his. It was like a cheek at war with the world—it had fallen out of favor with life, and therefore life had fallen out of favor with it. The left cheek made the young man look ugly, but as it seemed to me, the young man had sided with it. He reminded me of a mother who has a beautiful child and a monster—for justice's sake he was on the side of the hideous left cheek, bearing its meanness in himself [*getrogn in zikh*]. Because of the ugly cheek he had a mustache—to hide its ugliness a bit. I spotted the mustache instantly and thought to myself: "The right cheek isn't pleased with the mustache because it has the unusual color of dirty brass. It commands your attention and it announces: 'Don't bother me. I'm nasty. Better you go your way and I go mine.'"[43]

Refusing the cohesiveness and stability of a conventional portrait, this image resembles a surrealist collage of disaggregated parts. Fragments of personal history appear on the surface of the visitor's face. Years of accumulated spite have left their trace. A more deeply buried Freudian family history also plays out in the rivalry between the two halves of the face: the mother who neglects her good-looking, successful child, preferring instead her freakish, ugly child. The young man assumes the mother's role, not only siding with the left cheek but also "bearing" or "carrying" (*getrogn*) its features within himself as a mother bears her child in pregnancy (to be pregnant is *trogedik*, from the same verb used in the passage). The archeology of the past is written on the surface of the visitor's facial features.

Bergelson's verbal collage strikingly resembles Otto Dix's "Skin Graft," an etching and aquatint done in 1924 as part of his series called *Krieg* (War). In the portrait above, the left cheek is "at war with the world" (*iz tsekrigt mit der velt*). In both images, the left side of the face is distorted. Bergelson's hero is a veteran of World War I; Dix fought in the trenches and was wounded twice.[44] Facial injury was a terrible new development of the technology of combat at this time, connected to trench warfare. The suddenly emergent image of the visitor's face also conjures up the recent past of the war. Dix's portrait, like Bergelson's verbal image, unites narrative and static description: a horrifying scene of violence unfolds on the young man's face, transformed into a landscape of destruction.[45] The fact that Bergelson named the blind war veteran "Otto" in another Berlin story "Blindness" suggests a link between the painter and the Yiddish author, both of whom were

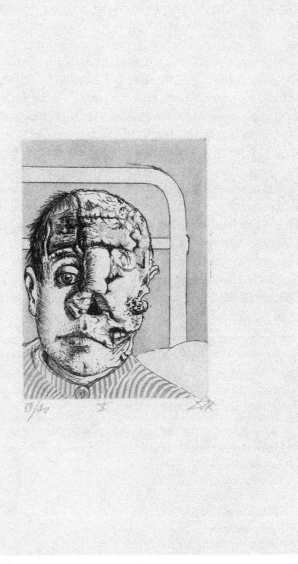

Figure 1. Dix, Otto (1891–1969) © ARS, NY. *Skin Graft (Transplantation) from the War (Der Krieg)*, 1924. Etching, aquatint, and drypoint from a portfolio of fifty etching, aquatint and drypoints. Publisher: Karl Nierendorf, Berlin. Printer: Otto Felsing, Berlin. Edition: 70; plus 1 proof each of states I and II; and 16 (state IV) published by the artist in 1961. Gift of Abby Aldrich Rockefeller. Digital Image © The Museum of Modern Art / License by SCALA / Art Resource, NY.

habitués of the Romanisches Café, as I have already mentioned. Bergelson in all likelihood encountered veterans with facial injuries, the so-called "broken men" in Berlin, where special benches were designated exclusively for them.[46] In "The Tribe of Gedalye" ("*Sheyvet Gedalye*"), written and published during Bergelson's stay in Berlin, the hero observes a man with a crude wooden prosthetic and finds himself attracted to "cripples."[47] Viktor Shklovsky, who briefly lived in Berlin in 1922–23, noted that the "streets are filled with terribly subdued cripples."[48] Facial and bodily disfigurement featured prominently in everyday life in Berlin, as in other European cities after World War I. The mutilated face was central to avant-garde art in the 1920s; El Lissitzky, who like Bergelson left Ukraine for Berlin, created photomontages that reconstructed the human face.[49]

The new wave of Yiddish poetry of the 1920s also featured images of the mutilated human body on the battlefield. In his essay on the new aesthetics of the revolutionary era, which I discussed earlier, Bergelson praises a poem by Arn Kushnirov, "Af shlakht-felder viste volgert ir zikh" ("You Wander in Empty Battlefields"). Kushnirov (Aron Davidovich Kushnirovitsh, 1890–1949) served in the tsarist army during World War I and was awarded the St. George Cross; he later enrolled in the Red Army. In addition to poetry, he wrote dramatic works including the play *Hirsh Lekert*, translated nineteenth- and twentieth-century works from Russian to Yiddish, and edited Soviet-era Yiddish journals.[50] Kushnirov included his war poem in his first volume of poetry, *Vent* (*Walls*), published in Kiev in 1921. The first stanza of "You Wander in Empty Battlefields" focuses on the maimed body of a dead soldier who has come back to life to haunt the scene of his own destruction:

> You wander homeless in empty battlefields. . . .
> Pierced by bayonets
> And bullets
> Your guts spilling out
> Af shlakht-felder viste volgert ir zikh
> Geshoktene
> Dershtokhene,
> Mit aroysgefalene gederes.[51]

In contrast to this and other similar portraits of the war, the young man's crooked face in "Among Refugees" is not the result of World War I or the anti-Jewish violence of the civil war. Although the protagonist of "Among Refugees" is a war veteran, he was already injured before his military service. He always resembled the Dix portrait. "From childhood on, my face has been flattened, crooked, as if run over . . . I am not very good looking . . . you think I don't know?"[52] The source of his crooked and split face is unknown: "It runs in the family." While disfigured heroes run in the family of Yiddish literature, so to speak, Bergelson's Jewish terrorist is more a figure for time gone astray. Bergelson transposes the violence of the immediate past into a more remote past, undermining conventional notions of causality. World War I and the Russian civil war have already mutilated the young man's face before these events took place. Events catch up to him, and he catches up to the future he already lived. The deferred action of history leaves its mark on the left cheek of the self-styled "Jewish terrorist."[53] There is a strange and horrifying rightness about his crooked face; he is particularly well suited for the task of murdering the pogromist.

What previously felt wrong in his life finally feels right: for the first and only time in his life, the visitor is in the right place at the right time. When he learns that the pogromist has arrived at his boardinghouse, he feels that a piece of himself has been restored to him. His accustomed feeling of spite against everyone else drops away, and he is ready to embrace everyone he sees. Anticipating the assassination makes him happy. In contrast to every other time of his life, he experiences joy, especially when the pogromist is at home in his room, together with him in the boardinghouse—the homey intimacy not of the lover and the beloved but rather of assassin and victim. Bergelson transposes the emotions and impulses typical of a love story into a story of hatred. Who is the assassin and who the victim becomes confused. The self-styled "Jewish terrorist" with his hideous face who uncannily appears in the writer's study is a figure for the unjust violence of the recent past that is already fading from view. He is a "suddenly emergent image" of a history that was in danger of never being written.[54]

Blindness

In "Among Refugees" the untimeliness that marked an entire life almost gets righted but fails to do so; the longed-for meeting never takes place, because the assassination turns into suicide. In "Blindness," in contrast, the longed-for meeting happens; the two people are in the same place at the same time, but they miss each other nonetheless. The two stories similarly feature an unnamed first-person writer/narrator who introduces the embedded narrative of the protagonist. Like "Among Refugees," in "Blindness" unmet desires from the past reappear in the present, belatedly.

The story begins when the first-person narrator notices a blind young man hovering around the entrance to his apartment building. When he discovers a notebook left behind by one of the previous tenants, Sonya Grayer, he realizes that she and the young man must have had a relationship. In addition to the notebook, the only other remnant the woman has left behind is a slip of paper from the city anatomical museum confirming the receipt of her corpse. The device of the found document is not new, of course, but the juxtaposition of the museum receipt and the notebook is nonetheless shocking. The young man, we learn, was blinded during the war; Sonya Grayer came with her husband from a shtetl in Ukraine, where she was called Khane. The notebook contains her diary, written in neat Russian letters, but we read the diary as if it had been translated into Yiddish, embedded in the frame narrative of its discovery. Educated young people would have spoken and corresponded with each other in Russian, not Yiddish (Mirl inserts Russian phrases in conversation with her peers, for example). At the end of the story, the narrator attempts to return the notebook to Sonya's husband, but he refuses it.

The story is built around the aftereffect, *nokhveyenish*: it is after the war, after Otto's terrible injury, after the revolution and civil war, after the departure from a shtetl in Ukraine (*a yidish shtetl*), after the affair, after the "bad ending" the protagonist came to (*zi hot shlekht opgeshnitn*), after the discovery of the notebook, after its translation into Yiddish, and after the failure to return it to the widower. In "The Task of the Translator," Benjamin writes, "A translation proceeds from the original. Not indeed so much from its life as from its 'afterlife' or 'survival' [*Überleben*].[55] Bergelson realizes the metaphor of translation as emanating from the afterlife of the original: the author of the text that is translated is dead. The frame structure and the fiction of translation in "Blindness" heighten the effect of mediation and delay. The found notebook and the receipt from the anatomical museum mediate the voice and body of the dead woman. The gaps, slips, and multiple infidelities ripple out from the events and their narration in an ever-widening series of circles. The frame device of "Blindness" makes readers complicit in a kind of voyeurism, granting us access to the intimate details of a woman's life and the guilty pleasure associated with seeing what otherwise would have remained hidden.[56] What is hidden and revealed to whom and by whom is a key element in the narrative structure of "Blindness."

The diary begins with a nested memory. The heroine recalls a spring day in Berlin that reminds her of a spring day in the shtetl, before Passover, when the smell of burnt dough from matzo baking was in the air. The "lively noise" of the "gigantic city" of Berlin reminds her of the pre-Passover noise in her shtetl. This mnemonic experience is jarring, because in another Berlin story, "One Night Less" the sounds of Berlin are utterly different from the sounds of the shtetl. Here is Berlin: "roaring iron wheels . . . a tangled, whirling throng of automobiles, trolleys, bicycles, trucks, and pedestrians" [ellipsis added].[57] In *The End of Everything* and other works set in the shtetl, noise is quieter and each sound is distinct and attached to a particular craft or activity: the hammering of the blacksmith that can be heard at a distance, the pedal of a sewing machine, the cutting noise of a tailor's shears, and plates being washed, for example.

The discontinuity between the present in Berlin and the memory of the shtetl that it provokes is important. The past does not flow into the present; it is rather cut off from the present and suddenly reappears unexpectedly. It is also significant that the heroine's memory of the shtetl in "Blindness" is aural and olfactory—a "blind" memory that resonates with Otto's blindness.

In the shtetl, the heroine was young and her name was Khane, not Sonya. The memory provokes an overwhelming desire to clean her Berlin apartment—in other words, to reanimate the time when she was young, it was spring, and Passover preparations were under way. For Mirl Hurvits, Passover had no meaning. The elaborate preparation for the holiday was just some empty ritual that her father and mother performed; for Mirl Peysekh was *pakh*, nothing. And for Mirl there was no springtime; someone else had lived out the springtime of her life. For Sonya Gayer, in contrast, Passover, the spring, and the springtime of her life are all of a piece. The object of her desire is not another human being but rather the self she left behind in another time and place, to which it is impossible to return. The text elides the story of what happened in the "Jewish shtetl" and how the heroine ended up in Berlin. There is a gap between the two parts of her life.

The sudden impulse to clean and scrub the Berlin apartment as if it were Passover in the shtetl is accompanied by another, equally powerful impulse: the wish to delay its satisfaction: "That urge grew in me from day to day like a secret craving, which it would be a pity to satisfy immediately and which therefore would be better to postpone until later, later."[58] Delaying the satisfaction of the urge is better than fulfilling it immediately, because the more it is put off, the more it grows and the greater the pleasure in the anticipation of its fulfillment. The heroine's articulation of her desire, with its accompanying delay, provides the context for her account of the encounters she has with a series of men, including her husband, the pharmacist Adolph, men in nightclubs and on the street, and finally the blind officer Otto, with whom she forms a relationship.

Sonya is the instigator of her own erotic adventures. After the sudden breath of springtime and the reawakening of the memories of her youth, especially the smell of matzo baking, she returns to her apartment and stares at herself in the mirror. Her eyes tell her that she is aging, but when she smells her own body, "it smells young" (*es shmekt yung*). She goes out of the apartment and strolls along unfamiliar backstreets, where she sees young couples secretly in love and feels an unclear sense of waiting for something. She thinks of the young German man in the drugstore (Adolph) and fantasizes their life together in a cottage at the edge of the woods near her shtetl. The blinds of the cottage would be drawn in the middle of the day, "they absolutely will be drawn" (*umbadingt aropgelozt*)—she and the young man will enjoy themselves free from prying eyes.

The motif of seeing and being seen occurs in nearly every scene of the story. The heroine visits the drugstore and believes that the young man is interested in her. Her flirtation with the druggist is a matter of what their eyes say to each other as their mouths discuss her purchase: "Meanwhile, our eyes were having a second conversation—quite independently of the conversation of our mouths."[59] Reality, however, is less kind than the heroine's fantasy. When she subsequently returns to the drugstore, she realizes that the pharmacist was not flirting with her but with another woman, a young blonde "who was behind a curtain in a second room"—the motif of the secret behind a screen.

After this disappointment the heroine returns home, the laughter of the young couple behind the curtain sticking in her memory. She suddenly feels something streaming from around her heart to her throat and wants to tear off everything that she is wearing and expose her breasts; she lies on a chaise longue face down, breasts uncovered. I provide a modified version of the English translation to highlight the intensity of the experience:

> And then my entire body shook convulsively with deep, hysterical sobs while I listened with a special, still unfamiliar pleasure to the echoes of my own weeping, and I gorged myself with the pleasure [*hob gefresen dem genus*] of the new streams gushing out of me as if weeping, as if from a wellspring. My chaise longue creaked under me, my body trembled and shook.[60]

The heroine wants to be naked and alone, and she satisfies her own desire and experiences the pleasure her own body provides. No one sees her at this moment face down on the chair; sound, movement, and sensation take the place of visual spectacle—except in one regard. The narrative places the reader in the position of spectator, intruding on this intimate moment.

Both Sonya and Mirl stage their appearances to provoke the gaze of men. Sonya enjoys going out on the street and inviting the lewd stares of male passersby. Arriving at a party, Mirl feels the "attractive power" of her graceful, corseted figure. In "Blindness" Sonya drags her husband along with her to nightclubs, where she dances with strange men, her arms and shoulders bare, and wants to tell her dance partners about her "innermost unfulfilled desire."[61] She informs one of them that she has never felt "female" desire in herself so powerfully as then.

Belatedness dominates the heroine's erotic encounters, including the autoerotic episode. They are part of the reanimation of her youth. Her memory of herself in the shtetl, her secret desire, its postponement, and the flare-up of other, more overtly sexual desires and pleasures take place when she realizes her youth is gone. The minute she marks the passing of her youth also marks its reappearance: "And precisely because the feeling was so strong, it suddenly seemed to me that I had become young again . . . very young."[62] The fleeting return to youth brings with it the sense that everything is new; the buildings, automobiles, and pedestrians "looked as if they hadn't existed an hour ago." The heroine herself feels as if she has "suddenly been placed on earth, new fully grown, with my inmost, unfulfilled passionate yearning, as if I were permitted to do anything."[63]

The heroine's discovery of her youth is at the same time a signal of its disappearance. The same temporal structure of a return to something that is lost, the recovery of something that is over, defines the chief torment of Otto's life. He cannot remember any other day of his previous sighted life except the day when he lost his sight: "It's only that final day that gave him no peace, like an extraordinary brightness before the sun goes down . . . 'If it hadn't been for that bright day,' he said, 'I'd be happy'" [ellipsis added].[64]

If Otto could forget the extraordinary brightness on the last day of his sighted life, he would be happy. The flaring up of the phenomenon or experience is tormenting, because it is a swan song. Never before had Otto seen such a bright light as the time when he was about to lose his sight; never before had Sonya experienced such desire as the time when she was about to lose it. Otto, who studied law before he became an officer in the

German army, now sits on a park bench, one of Berlin's "broken men," only his injuries, unlike the hero of "Among Refugees," are invisible. A significant transformation in Bergelson's use of disability may be seen here. In "At the Depot," the blind spots were temporary and contingent: it was night, the hero was in an unfamiliar setting, and an impediment blocked his view. Beynish could not see or understand the sounds he was hearing, and they had to be translated for him. The hero of "The Deaf Man" was deafened by years of working at the mill. World War I caused Otto's blindness. Bergelson historicizes what he formerly rendered as contingent. History catches up with the vision he already had.

With Otto, the heroine of "Blindness" loses the pleasure of seeing; the conversation of the eyes is silenced. Otto reinvests her eyes with their material corporeality, as part of her body that can receive the pleasure of touch. He kisses her on the eyes, and she watches with one eye how his lips find her other eye without any trouble. She becomes half-blind in his embrace. Unlike the other men, who see her, Otto hears the subtly different qualities of her voice, touches her, and senses her presence even when she does not speak or signal in any way that she is there. Typically for Bergelson, Otto's emotion of expectant waiting is transferred to an inanimate object: the heroine senses his anticipation in the folds of his silk pocket handkerchief. Her cruelly silent presence causes his entire body to shudder as if she were pulling a string attached to him, and her decision not to announce that she will no longer see him causes him to wait for her even beyond her death. This is another in the long string of meetings between Bergelson characters that never take place. Both are present at the same time and at the same place, in a purely external sense. Only Sonya is not who she says she is; it is too late for her; she is already married and already mourning the past she lost; she is present physically but in another time zone, not on the same clock as Otto. "Blindness" is a story about two "afterhistories" that fleetingly coincide.[65]

Sonya uses Otto's blindness as a blank screen on which she enacts a younger, more desirable version of herself. She is not Sonya Grayer, wife of Grayer the broker; she is not Khane, who left a shtetl, but another person entirely. She tells Otto she is a young student living with her brother, "a foreign professor," in Berlin. Sonya becomes who she wants to be because Otto cannot see her. At the end of the story, no matter how intimate readers have been with Sonya, they still have not discovered what happened to Khane, possibly the victim of sexual violence during the pogroms. Having intruded into the intimate details of a woman who committed suicide, having seen much, it turns out nonetheless that we know little. The widower's refusal to accept his late wife's diary makes sense: better not to be deceived by the illusion of knowledge. Better to accept blindness.

In fiction written in the aftermath of World War I and the Russian civil war, "suddenly emergent" flashes of memory create a jarring moment in which the shtetl, the past, unexpectedly reappears in Berlin, the city "on the edge of time."[66] The self-styled Jewish terrorist brings the dust of faraway shtetl roads into the writer's Berlin study. The nameless visitor grew up in a house in which nearly everyone died prematurely, and his face, split into a friendly right and a hostile and horrifying left side, bears the traces of family history and the history of trench warfare during World War I. A nanny's call to a child in a Berlin park makes the heroine of "Blindness" smell the odor of burnt matzo dough and sets in motion her memory of Passover, the spring holiday of rebirth and redemption. The memory of the shtetl also reanimates her desire. The obsolete and "frozen" (*farglivert*) shtetl retroactively transforms into a space of youth and passion.

Bergelson's relocation to Berlin creates a "dynamic moment" of new relations between things, people, and bodies, transforming voyeurs into sexualized objects, victims into aggressors, and the past that never was into a present that is already over. The failures and missteps that mark Bergelson's shtetl characters continue in their new lives in Berlin. The Jewish terrorist does not assassinate the pogromist but kills himself instead. The "love at last sight" that the protagonists of "Blindness" experience also reflects Bergelson's relation to the past that has been destroyed and that his own art resurrects, albeit in estranged form. The Jewish terrorist's failure to carry out revenge is also significant in light of Bergelson's overarching theme of postponement and delay. Putting off revenge, as I will argue in chapter 6, may open the possibility of justice.

Notes

1. David Bergelson, "Di dinamishe rege," in *Geklibene verk*, vol. 6 (Vilnius: B. Kletskin, 1929), 116. There is no English translation; all translations are my own.
2. Both Chagall and Bergelson knew Bialik, Mayzel, Niger, and Opatoshu, among others. See Benjamin Harshav, *Marc Chagall and His Times: A Documentary Narrative* (Stanford, CA: Stanford University Press, 2004).
3. Bergelson, "Di dinamishe rege," 123.

4. David Bergelson, "Belles-Lettres and the Social Order," in *David Bergelson: From Modernism to Socialist Realism*, ed. Joseph Sherman and Gennady Estraikh (Oxford: Legenda, 2007), 345.

5. David Bergelson, "Moskve," *Frayheyt*, September 5, 1926.

6. See Yisroel Rubin, "Bay di tishlekh fun Romanishn kafe: Dovid Bergelson," *Literarishe bleter* 3 (January 17, 1930): 53–54.

7. Dafna Clifford, "From Exile to Exile: Bergelson's Berlin Years," in *Yiddish and the Left*, ed. Mikhail Krutikov and Gennady Estraikh (Oxford: Legenda, 2001), 247.

8. David Bergelson, *The Shadows of Berlin: The Berlin Stories of Dovid Bergelson* (San Francisco, CA: City Lights, 2005), 90.

9. For another discussion of this essay, see Joseph Sherman, "David Bergelson (1884–1952): A Biography," in *David Bergelson: From Modernism to Socialist Realism*, ed. Joseph Sherman and Gennady Estraikh (London: Legenda, 2007), 32–33. Sherman translates the title as "The awakening has occurred."

10. David Bergelson, "Der gesheener oyfbrokh," *Milgroym* 1 (1922): 42.

11. Ibid., 41. The Yiddish: "Hot dos naye lid a shot getun mit neyn mas reyd, geefent bay zikh ale odern un nervn, ale kemerlekh, vos zoyfn eyn un brekhn oys un . . . zikh farkhlyunet."

12. Rokhl Vishnitser-Bernshtayn, "Di naye kuntst un mir," *Milgroym* 1 (1922): 7.

13. The Yiddish poet Perets Markish was extremely critical of *Milgroym*; he pointed out that the Jewish emigrants had copied what the Russian emigrants had done in their journal *Firebird*; Rybak was the only fresh feature of the journal, but it was nonetheless annoying that the editors had selected Rybak when they could have chosen Lissitzky, Falk, or Altman. Peretz Markish, "Milgroym," *Bikher velt* 4–5 (1922): 396–401.

14. For the image, see the book jacket of this volume.

15. For the collection of essays that initiated the trend, see Hal Foster, ed. *Vision and Visuality* (Seattle, WA: Bay Press, 1988).

16. Benjamin used this phrase to characterize Baudelaire's urban experience. See Walter Benjamin, *Illuminations* (New York: Schocken Books, 1969), 169.

17. The essay can be found in Laura Mulvey, "Visual Pleasure and Narrative Cinema," *Screen* 16, no. 3 (1975): 6–18. For a discussion of the limitations of Mulvey's approach from a feminist perspective, see Gertrud Koch, "Ex-Changing the Gaze: Re-Visioning Feminist Film Theory," *New German Critique* 34 (1985): 139–53. Eric Naiman discusses Shklovsky and Mulvey in Eric Naiman, "Shklovsky's Dog and Mulvey's Pleasure: The Secret Life of Defamiliarization," *Comparative Literature* 50, no. 4 (1998): 333–52.

18. David Bergelson, "In a fargrebter shtot," in *Geklibene verk*, vol. 3 (Vilnius: B. Kletskin, 1929), 59. I am using my own translation here and henceforward; the published English translation is found in David Bergelson, "In a Backwoods Town," in *A Treasury of Yiddish Stories*, ed. Irving Howe and Eliezer Greenberg, trans. Bernard Guerney (Penguin Books, 1989), 471–504.

19. Bergelson, "In a fargrebter shtot," 14. The Yiddish: "Zi iz geven mit a gantsn kop hekher fun Elishen . . . un az zi hot in shvartsn shmoln kleydl ongeshtelt a fus af a shpan tsu ton, hobn zikh tsu im nisht-vilndik aropgelozn ale arumike mansbilishe oygn; glaykh in ot dem hipshn un shlankn fus ligt epes a gantser Mezhibzher kunts, un s'iz keday tsu zen, vos vet farkumen mit im un mit ir gantser vuksiker figur, beshes zi vet dem fus nokhamol a heyb tun un vet im nokhamol af der erd aropshteln."

20. Bergelson, "In a fargrebter shtot," 30.

21. Bergelson, "In a fargrebter shtot," 15; the Yiddish: "Fun hinter eynem fun zey, an untergehoybenem un a farvorfenem abisl on a zayt, hobn zikh gehert di klep fun a kleynem hant-hemerl; s'hot zikh gemolt di kilkayt, vos inveynik, in kheyder, di hoykhe shtuln, vos in di frishe ongetsoygene tshekholn, un zi, Elishes vayb aleyn. Zi iz dortn geshtanen lebn dinst-meydl, velkhe iz aroyfgekrokhn af a kleyn tsugeshtelt tishl, un hot ir bavizn: 'Shlog im, zayt moykhl, abisl hekher, dem tshvok . . . nokh hekher.'

22. Allison Schachter discusses this and other Bergelson stories from the perspective of gender and exile in *Diasporic Modernisms: Hebrew and Yiddish Literature in the Twentieth Century* (New York: Oxford University Press 2012), 93–101.

23. For a discussion of this work in the context of Bergelson's earliest writing as a whole, see Avraham Novershtern, "Hundert yor Dovid Bergelson: Materialn tsu zayn lebn un shafn," *Di Goldene Keyt* 115 (1985): 44–58.

24. I am relying on Joseph Sherman's account in Sherman, "David Bergelson (1884–1952): A Biography," 18.

25. David Bergelson, "Yoysef Shur," in *Geklibene verk*, vol. 3 (Vilnius: B. Kletskin, 1929), 115.

26. David Bergelson, "Yoysef Shur,"115. For the English translation, see David Bergelson, "Joseph Schur," in *A Treasury of Yiddish Stories*, eds. Irving Howe and Eliezer Greenberg, trans. Leonard Woolf (New York: Viking Penguin, 1989), 504–45. I am using my own translations.

27. David Bergelson, "Yoysef Shur," 93.

28. Bergelson, *The Shadows of Berlin: The Berlin Stories of Dovid Bergelson*, 45. I have modified the translation.

29. Bergelson, *The Shadows of Berlin*, 50. I have modified the translation.

30. Allison Schachter, "Modernist Indexicality: The Language of Gender, Race, and Domesticity in Hebrew and Yiddish Modernism," *Modern Language Quarterly: A Journal of Literary History* 72, no. 4 (2011): 493–520.

31. David Bergelson, "Skhar-tirkhe," in *Geklibene verk*, vol. 6 (Vilnius: B. Kletskin, 1929), 258–59. The story has not been translated into English.

32. See Siegfried Kracauer, *The Mass Ornament: Weimar Essays* (Cambridge, MA: Harvard University Press, 1995); Janet Ward, *Weimar Surfaces: Urban Visual Culture in 1920s Germany* (Berkeley, CA: University of California Press, 2001). For a discussion of this phenomenon in relation to Russian literature, see Luke Parker, "The Shop Window Quality of Things: 1920s Weimar Surface Culture in Nabokov's *Korol', dama, valet*," *Slavic Review* 77, no. 2 (Summer 2018): 390–416.

33. David Bergelson, *Mides-hadin*, vol. 7, Geklibene verk (Vilnius: B. Kletskin, 1929), 254.

34. A discussion of late nineteenth-century psychology can be found in Jonathan Crary, "Unbinding Vision," *October* 68 (Spring 1994): 21–44.

35. I am developing ideas presented in Martin Häglund, "Chronolibidinal Reading: Deconstruction and Psychoanalysis," *New Centennial Review* 9, no. 1 (2009): 1–43.

36. Benjamin, *Illuminations*, 84.

37. Walter Benjamin, *The Arcades Project* (Cambridge, MA: Harvard University Press, 2002), 463. For a discussion, see Max Pensky, "Method and Time: Benjamin's Dialectical Images," in *The Cambridge Companion to Walter Benjamin*, ed. David S. Ferris (Cambridge, UK: Cambridge University Press, 2004), 177–98. See also Susan Buck-Morss, *The Dialectics of*

Seeing: Walter Benjamin and the Arcades Project (Cambridge, MA: MIT Press, 1989), 216–27. There is a discernably Bergsonian architecture to Benjamin's "suddenly emergent" image, since it occurs when thought comes to a standstill. In *Matter and Memory* Bergson argues that when habitual action is thwarted and the template formed by perception is not immediately filled by action, an image may appear.

38. Benjamin's dialectical image derives in part from earlier notions of the afterimage. Prominently discussed by Goethe in the early nineteenth century, afterimages became the object of scientific experimentation and calculation in the latter part of the century and also became the basis for technological innovation leading to the cinema. The persistence of retinal afterimages suggested that the temporal and spatial unity of the individual and the perceived object was an illusion. Individual experience and the body became the mediator of perception, and time lag played a key role. For discussions of the importance of Goethe's intervention, see Jonathan Crary, "Techniques of the Observer," *October* 45 (Summer 1988): 3–35.

39. Neugroschel's translation of the title "*Tsvishn emigrantn*" is "Among Refugees." The most common English rendering of *emigrantn* would be "emigrants," but in using "refugees" Neugroschel rightly emphasizes the displaced, exilic, and minority status of Bergelson's hero and all the "mute, haunted ghosts" that surround him in Berlin.

40. Bergelson, *The Shadows of Berlin*, 21. For the Yiddish, see Bergelson, "Tsvishn emigrantn," 175.

41. Bergelson, *The Shadows of Berlin*, 21–22; Bergelson, "Tsvishn emigrantn," 176.

42. Bergelson, *The Shadows of Berlin*, 23.

43. Bergelson, *The Shadows of Berlin*, 22–23. I have modified the translation. For the Yiddish, see Bergelson, "Tsvishn emigrantn," 177.

44. For more on Dix's antiwar art, see Dora Apel, "'Heroes' and 'Whores': The Politics of Gender in Weimar Antiwar Imagery," *Art Bulletin* 79, no. 3 (1997): 366–84.

45. For a brief discussion of the Dix portrait in the context of European art of the time, see Wendy Baron, "Art and the First World War," *Burlington Magazine* 136, no. 1099 (1994): 715–16.

46. A discussion of facial injuries and prosthetic masks used to conceal them can be found in David M. Lubin, "Masks, Mutilation, and Modernity: Anna Coleman Ladd and the First World War," *Archives of American Art Journal* 47, no. 3/4 (2008): 4–15.

47. David Bergelson, *Geklibene verk*, vol. 6 (Vilnius: B. Kletskin, 1929), 25–26.

48. Viktor Shklovsky, *Zoo, or Letters Not about Love* (Normal, IL: Dalkey Archive Press, 2001), 136.

49. For a discussion of the role of the fragmented body in avant-garde theater, see Stanton B. Garner, "The Gas Heart: Disfigurement and the Dada Body," *Modern Drama* 50, no. 4 (2007): 500–516. For a discussion of the use of the prosthetic in art and daily life in interwar Germany, see Mia Fineman, "Ecce Homo Prostheticus," *New German Critique* 76 (Winter 1999): 85–114.

50. Hirsh Lekert was executed for assassinating the governor general of Vilnius and became a hero of the revolution. I base my account of Kushnirov on Gennady Estraikh, "Kushnirov, Arn.," 2010, http://www.yivoencyclopedia.org/article.aspx/Kushnirov_Arn. See also Khone Shmeruk, ed., *A shpigl af a shteyn* (Jerusalem: Magnes Press, 1964), 745–47.

51. Arn Kushnirov, *Vent* (Kiev: Kultur-Lige, 1921), 29.

52. Bergelson, "Tsvishn emigrantn," 180.

53. For a discussion of deferred history in Benjamin, see Susan Buck-Morss, "Walter Benjamin: Between Academic Fashion and the Avant-Garde," *Pandaemonium Germanicaum* 5 (May 2001): 73–88.

54. Cherikover lead the effort to preserve the documentation of the civil war pogroms; Bergelson also participated in the attempt. For the documents in relation to the assassination of Petliura, see David Engel, *The Assasination of Symon Petliura and the Trial of Scholem Schwartzbard 1926–1927: A Selection of Documents* (Gottingen: Vandenhoeck & Ruprecht, 2016).

55. Steven Rendall, "The Translator's Task: Walter Benjamin," *Traduction, Terminologie, Redaction* X, no. 2 (1997): 153.

56. Verbal narrative even without frame devices also places readers in key positions in the "plot space," creating and withholding access to hidden knowledge. See Teresa de Lauretis, *Alice Doesn't: Feminism, Semiotics, Cinema* (Bloomington: Indiana University Press, 1984).

57. Bergelson, *The Shadows of Berlin*, 111.

58. Bergelson, *The Shadows of Berlin*, 88. I have modified the translation. The Yiddish: "Der doziker farlang hot in mir nokhdem angehoybn tsu vaksn fun tog tsu tog, vi a farborgene glustenish, velkhe es iz zeyer a shod tsu bafridikn bald un es iz deriber besser optsulegn es af shpeter."

59. Bergelson, *The Shadows of Berlin*, 89. I changed the translation. Neugroschel has "the conversation of our voices," but the Yiddish has *mayler*, "mouths."

60. Bergelson, *The Shadows of Berlin*, 91. I have modified the translation.

61. Bergelson, *The Shadows of Berlin*, 93. I have modified the translation.

62. Bergelson, *The Shadows of Berlin*, 88.

63. Bergelson, *The Shadows of Berlin*, 94.

64. Bergelson, *The Shadows of Berlin*, 97–98. The Yiddish: "Nor yener letser tog lozt im nisht ruen, vi epes an umgeveynlekhe likhtkayt, eder di zun geyt unter. . . . 'Ven nisht yener heler tog,' hot er gezogt, 'Volt ikh geven glikhlekh'" [ellipsis added]. David Bergelson, "Blindkeyt," in *Geklibene verk*, vol. 6 (Vilnius: B. Kletskin, 1929), 71.

65. I take the term "afterhistory" from A. Auerbach, "Imagine No Metaphors: The Dialectical Image of Walter Benjamin," *Image [&] Narrative* 18 (2007), http://www.imageandnarrative.be /thinking_pictures/auerbach.htm.

66. Hans Ulrich Gumbrecht, *In 1926: Living at the Edge of Time* (Cambridge, MA: Harvard University Press, 1997).

PART 3

A STRANGE NEW WORLD

Introduction

In 1918, Bergelson's friend the critic and playwright A. Vayter used the term *khurbn* to describe the consequences of World War I for the Jewish community:

> It is not yet possible to measure the destruction [*khurbn*], which the war produced in our national life. The terrible impetus of its devastating might has not yet ceased, and it can very well be that the horrendous five and a half years of external war that have just passed are nothing less than the beginning of an entire epoch of internal wars, which will destroy and uproot all the foundations of the present world order.[1]

Originally referring to the destruction of the two Temples, *khurbn* came to signify Jewish national disaster, especially the Holocaust. Vayter's apprehension stemmed from the massive death toll, displacement, and large-scale economic upheaval of the war but also the splintering of the Jewish population into the disparate nation-states formed after World War I. The low estimate of the number of Jews forcibly expelled from their places of residence in the Russian Empire is 500,000; Vayter compares this event to the Spanish expulsion of the Jews in 1492.[2] Jews were considered a suspect population, secretly loyal to the enemies of Russia, and the tsarist army took Jewish hostages in order to prevent Jewish attacks against Russian soldiers. Jews were not the only victims of murder and deportation during World War I; the Armenian genocide of 1915 is another tragic example at an even greater scale. Bergelson's acquaintance Franz Werfel, another habitué of the Romanisches Café, published a novel about the Armenian genocide in 1933.

The passage I have quoted comes from Vayter's essay "Our Time" ("*Unzer tsayt*") published in Vilnius in 1918. His words about an epoch of internal wars proved true. He became a victim of a conflict that arose in the wake of the collapse of the tsarist empire. In April 1919, Vayter was dead, shot by Polish soldiers who mistakenly believed that he was a Bolshevik.[3] While other Jewish intellectuals also registered the national catastrophe caused by World War I, Vayter's sense of foreboding about a future global political collapse stands out.

In his Berlin-era fiction Bergelson raises questions about the consequences of the massive violence of World War I and the Russian civil war. For Bergelson, as for others, the destruction *(khurbn)* had implications beyond Jews and even beyond the global political order; World War I and the Bolshevik revolution touched on the meaning of human history, the end time, and the possibility of messianic redemption. Bergelson's interwar fiction, like the work of his German Jewish contemporaries Gershom Scholem, Martin Buber, and Walter Benjamin, profoundly engages with questions of political theology. I use this term to refer to the question of whether and how human history reflects a plan of divine salvation. While fascinated by the prospect of a clean sweep and an utterly new beginning, Bergelson did not embrace or seek to hasten the end. Bergelson proposed deferred judgment in response to the massive, unprecedented injustice of the Russian civil war. He can thus be brought into dialogue with his German Jewish intellectual counterparts, especially Scholem, as I will show in chapter 6. Although the prevailing scholarship finds no mutual influence between Yiddish writers and German Jewish intellectuals, my readings of Bergelson, Scholem, and Buber reveal significant contiguities among them.[4]

After a period of independence following the collapse of the Russian Empire, a series of regimes took power in Ukraine, including the Skoropadsky government, sustained by the German army, Petliura's Directory, and the Bolsheviks, who took Kiev, lost it, and retook it. The armies of Zeleny and Denikin resisted Bolshevik power, and smaller military units and gangs also attacked Bolsheviks; these armies and units conducted a steady campaign of anti-Jewish violence, associating Jews with Bolsheviks. The Red Army and other groups were also responsible for pogroms. One of the issues raised in 1921 at a session of the statistical division of the Jewish section of the People's Commissariat of Nationalities had to do with the problem of tallying the number of pogroms if they took place in a continual fashion, or to use the language of the 1921 meeting, "the question of permanent pogroms."[5] Murder, rape, maiming, looting, and the destruction of stores, workshops, and homes meant that entire areas were decimated, leading to massive dislocation, disease, and "an army" of children separated from adults or orphaned.

Tens of thousands of Jews were killed during the pogroms of 1918–22.[6] Most of the deaths took place in Ukraine; the Kiev District Commission of the Jewish Public Committee for Relief to Victims of Pogroms reported 48,000 victims in Kiev province during 1919—the term "victim" (*pogromlennye*) includes the displaced and injured.[7] Precise numbers of pogrom deaths may never be established, because documentation at the time of the violence and prosecution of its perpetrators was incomplete and scattershot. The Holocaust has long overshadowed the events of 1918–22, and it is only recently that historians are turning their attention to the earlier period.[8] Bergelson was interested in the preservation of the historical record. In 1924, he participated in a collective effort to publish a multivolume Yiddish-language archive of the civil war pogroms.[9] In this context, artistic literature serves as a particularly important historical register of the events. But as I will show, more than merely reflecting what took place, fiction about the civil war reframed its significance not only in light of broad theological and political issues but also in day-to-day human terms. David Hofshteyn, Perets Markish, Leyb Kvitko, Itsik Kipnis, and other Yiddish authors responded to the violence of the Russian civil war and the pogroms in Ukraine.[10] Bergelson's work explicitly confronts the problem of injustice for the murdered victims.

Bergelson lived in Kiev from 1919 to 1920 before taking his family to Moscow and then Berlin. In May 1920 he participated in an appeal to "friends of Yiddish" in America, seeking help in relocation to the United States. His letter described the circumstances in which Jewish artists and writers found themselves, "[dragging] out what is left of their lives," surrounded by "ruined towns and villages, razed, drowned in blood, and now obliterated," and "distracted by those most beloved and closest to them among the murdered victims."[11] The loss of Bergelson's archive from this time makes it difficult to determine whether the author himself suffered such a loss.[12] The emotional and sensationalistic language of the appeal is not characteristic of Bergelson's published work. Depicting the aftermath of violence in muted tones is more typical, as in the story "Blindness" discussed in chapter 5.

Jewish researchers of the time documented the violence and its impact on Jewish life in the former Pale of Settlement. In addition to Cherikover and Dubnov, another prominent figure involved in the work of documentation was the economic historian Jacob Lestchinsky (1876–1966), a friend of

Bergelson's. The two men saw each other in Berlin and exchanged letters when Bergelson traveled to Romania and Lithuania to write about Jewish life for the Yiddish journal *Forward*. In a letter from 1924, Bergelson describes his sense of unreality—it was as if he were "dreaming" and had been "buried and raised from the dead in the world to come" because "so many aspects of Jewish life here [in Romania] are copies of our life at home before the war."[13] The language that Bergelson uses indicates the extent to which he felt that Jewish life in Russia had been utterly and irrevocably destroyed: only in a dream or "the world to come" could it be realized again. Experiencing prewar Jewish life in the flesh produced the effect of an uncanny return. The state of "permanent pogroms" in Ukraine, Bergelson's personal plea, and his reference to the world to come suggest that the notion of the end of time and messianic redemption, while not matters of religious belief, were not merely ideas but had taken on flesh and blood in the writer's experience.

In his fiction Bergelson raises the question of his own responsibility as a writer in relation to the violence in Ukraine. In "Among Refugees", the "Jewish terrorist" explains that he told the writer his story "because you are as responsible [*farantvortlekh*] as I am, and even more than I am because you're a writer."[14] At the end, the young man asks the writer to turn on the light so that he can see his face. Turning on the light turns the tables on the writer: Who is he? What is he concealing? In the face-off between the Bergelson figure and the "Jewish terrorist," the young man takes the position of the interrogator and the writer becomes the accused, charged with responsibility to the "murdered shtetl," called upon to answer for and answer to the dead.

Bergelson attempts to discharge his responsibility as a writer by interrogating the problem of judgment and justice. The stories to be discussed in part 3 raise questions of sin, crime, justice, judgment, courts, trials, and retribution. Bergelson makes frequent references to the prophets, the Bible, and Jewish legal commentaries having to do with human and divine judgment. He paints a picture of violent destruction and raises the question of judgment and justice, both human and divine, but can't find an answer. He does so not as a believer but instead as a secular intellectual and artist who makes use of an extraordinarily broad range of texts, images, and metaphors drawn from Jewish canonical texts (including the Bible and its commentaries) and works of mysticism. He adjusts his narrative focus so that the problem of justice and judgment expands beyond the lives of particular individuals to reach a universal and even cosmic scale. The world is out of sync; vast devastation and injustice have already taken place. What will happen next? Bergelson's broad-ranging inquiry takes place artistically, not systematically. Contradiction and paradox abound.

Among the contradictions, Bergelson's 1926–29 novel *Judgment* (*Mideshadin*) is the most important. Scholars have argued that this work attests to Bergelson's new allegiance to the Soviet Union. Bergelson made public statements to this effect in 1926. When placed, however, in the context of other fiction with similar themes, a different picture emerges. The image of the harsh, unyielding Filipov, the head of the Bolshevik outpost at the center of the story, may seem particularly important for Bergelson's alleged new ideological commitments. I have found, however, a nonfiction autobiographical story that Bergelson published in 1925 that suggests that the author's sympathies were far from this type of figure. Chapter 7 explores the problem of judgment in Bergelson's novel in the context of political theology.

Bergelson is consistent with regard to one central aspect of his post–civil war fiction: there is a direct continuity between his earliest works and the Berlin period when it comes to the theme of time lag and delay. In the pre–World War I fiction generally, postponement characterizes the existential and experiential encounter between the self and the world. Interwar Berlin was a place where intellectuals found themselves "between the times"—this was the phrase the German Protestant theologian Friedrich Gogarten used to describe his generation's position; it became the title of a journal he launched in in 1922 with other prominent churchmen.[15] The sense of crisis and rupture was commonplace among Weimar's writers; Benjamin described the crisis of experience (in "The Storyteller") and the precipitous reemergence of the lost past. Messianism in various forms characterizes the entire generation of Jewish intellectuals even before World War I. Bergelson, who had already created an asynchronous world in which characters were perpetually too late and too early, might have felt strangely at home in the atmosphere of temporal dislocation that surrounded him. Before the Berlin period, he had written about delay and postponement as a phenomenological experience and psychological and existential problem. In the interwar years, the interval—the time in between—assumed new historical and cosmic significance.

Notes

1. A. Vayter, *Ksovim* (Vilna: B. Kletskin, 1923), 114. Sh. An-sky also wrote about these events, in *Khurbn Galitsye*, using the same traditional religious term *khurbn* as Vayter. A discussion of this dimension of An-sky's writing can be found in Polly Zavadivker, "Blood

and Ink: Russian and Soviet Jewish Chroniclers of Catastrophe from World War I to World War II" (PhD diss., University of California at Santa Cruz, 2013), 88–127. See also Gabriella Safran, *Wandering Soul: The Dybbuk's Creator, S. An-Sky* (Cambridge, MA: Harvard University Press, 2010). For a discussion of World War I and Jewish writers, including An-sky, see David Roskies, *Against the Apocalypse: Responses to Catastrophe in Modern Jewish Culture* (Cambridge, MA: Harvard University Press, 1984), 93–123.

2. See Eric Lohr, "The Russian Army and the Jews: Mass Deportation, Hostages, and Violence during World War I," *Russian Review* 60, no. 3 (2001): 404–19.

3. For a detailed discussion, see http://www.haynt.org/chap04.htm.

4. An example would be Dafna Clifford, "From Exile to Exile: Bergelson's Berlin Years," in *Yiddish and the Left*, ed. Mikhail Krutikov and Gennady Estraikh (Oxford: Legenda, 2001), 242–58.

5. Kiev District Commission of the Jewish Public Committee for Relief to Victims of Pogroms, Fond 3050, opis 1, delo 123, "Protokol zasedaniia statisicheskogo otdela pri upolno-mochnnym evotdela narkomatsa RSFSR, 23 August 1921."

6. Estimates of the number of Jewish deaths range from 35,000 to 150,000. For a discussion and for a documentary history, see L. B. Miliakova, *Kniga pogromov: Pogromy na Ukraine, v Belorussii, i evropeiskoi chasti Rossii v period grazhdanskoi voiny 1918–1922 gg.* (Moscow: Rosspen, 2007). For an essay that links the anti-Jewish violence of the Russian Imperial Army during World War I with the anti-Jewish violence of the civil war pogroms, see Oleg Budnitskii, "Shots in the Back: On the Origin of the Anti-Jewish Pogroms of 1918–1921," in *Jews in the East European Borderlands: Essays in Honor of John D. Klier*, ed. Eugene M. Avrutin and Harriet Murav (Boston: Academic Studies Press, 2012), 187–201.

7. Ibid.

8. At the time of the writing of this study, Jeffrey Veidlinger and Elissa Bemporad were both working on a history of the pogroms.

9. David Engel, *The Assassination of Symon Petliura and the Trial of Scholem Schwartzbard 1926–1927: A Selection of Documents* (Gottingen: Vandenhoeck & Ruprecht, 2016), 148–50.

10. For a discussion, see Harriet Murav, *Music from a Speeding Train: Jewish Literature in Post-Revolutionary Russia* (Stanford, CA: Stanford University Press, 2011), 21–65.

11. See Joseph Sherman, "David Bergelson (1884–1952): A Biography," in *David Bergelson: From Modernism to Socialist Realism*, eds. Joseph Sherman and Gennady Estraikh (London: Legenda, 2007), 7–78. For the Yiddish original, see Gennady Estraikh, David Bergelson, and Balmakhshoves, "Gefunene manuskriptn: A kol-koyre tsu Amerikaner kolegn," *Forverts*, 2006.

12. Khone Shmeruk, ed., *A shpigl af a shteyn* (Jerusalem: Magnes Press, 1964), 734.

13. YIVO 339, Collection of Jacob Lestchinsky, Box 1, Folder 7, letter dated September 18, 1924.

14. David Bergelson, *The Shadows of Berlin: The Berlin Stories of Dovid Bergelson* (San Francisco, CA: City Lights, 2005), 42.

15. See Friedrich Gogarten, "Between the Times," in *The Beginnings of Dialectic Theology*, ed. James Robinson (Richmond, VA: John Knox, 1968), 277–82. I thank Bruce Rosenstock for pointing this out to me. A discussion can be found in Stephen R. Haynes, "'BETWEEN THE TIMES': German Theology and the Weimar 'Zeitgeist,'" *Soundings: An Interdisciplinary Journal* 74, no. 1/2 (1991): 9–44.

6

JUDGMENT DEFERRED

A LTHOUGH IN HIS EARLIER FICTION BERGELSON HAD HINTED at the cosmological significance of the missed meeting between humans and God, his writing after World War I and the Russian revolution and civil war brings the problem of history and redemption to the foreground. Bergelson takes his inquiry about impeded action and slowed motion from the realm of experience and extends it to the sphere of law, judgment (*din*), and justice. Instead of the delayed encounter between one character and another (or with a physical object, as in the glitch), it is the execution of judgment, both human and divine, that gets put off. This chapter examines the postponement of judgment as the solution to injustice. In "At Night" ("*Bay nakht*"), "Old Age" ("*Altvarg*," 1926), "Among Refugees," "Two Murderers" ("*Tsvey rotskhim*," 1926), the 1928 story "Birth" ("*Geburt*"), and other work, the central theme is the deferral of judgment. Bergelson shows some interest in apocalypticism, but for the most part sustains his interest in slowed time. Against the backdrop of Jewish national disaster, the impending collapse of the world order, and the prevailing mood that the end of history had been reached, Bergelson proposes delay and postponement, embracing the potential of the time in between the times.

Interwar German Jewish thought is key to the argument, and the chapter begins by comparing Scholem, Buber, and Bergelson. I introduce Fischel Schneersohn, whom Bergelson knew personally, as another figure, less well studied than Scholem and Buber, who also transformed concepts imported from Hasidism into a secular philosophical context. An overview follows of some of these concepts that are important for work to be discussed in both this chapter and the next. I then turn to Bergelson's flirtation with apocalypticism and his fiction of judgment deferred.

The Philosophical Context: Scholem and Buber

The "standard account" of Yiddish–German relations puts the two groups at odds, asserting that emigrating Yiddish writers in the interwar years fall into the category of *Ostjuden*, an exotic other that is both romanticized and reviled.[1] As David Biale has shown, Scholem tended more toward the former.[2] I have found a significant parallel between Bergelson and Gershom Scholem, one having to do with the relation between justice and the time of postponement. This is an instance of "contiguity," the term Dan Miron uses to describe encounters and confluences that take place in ideas and art, without direct influence. Scholem, the founder of the study of Jewish mysticism, the one responsible for bringing kabbalah to the forefront of Jewish thought, was thinking about time, delay, and justice in the period immediately following World War I.

Judgment delayed is not necessarily justice denied—on the contrary. Scholem's 1919 essay "On Jonah and the Concept of Justice" explains how.[3] Scholem theorizes that postponing divine judgment grants more time to human beings, and thus the possibility for change and future redemption. By refraining from acting in human history God permits human history to continue. God has not abandoned human history. He is waiting. In order for justice to emerge, time—and thus delay, holding back—is necessary. Originally part of the correspondence between Scholem and Benjamin that had begun a few years earlier, Scholem uses the Jonah story to contrast human and divine notions of justice. Jonah, tasked with warning Nineveh that it must repent or be destroyed, is disappointed when God suspends the execution of judgment. The instant he uttered his prophecy, Nineveh's fate was sealed, or so Jonah thought. Jonah's mistake, according to Scholem, was to assume that the past and the future are synchronous. From this perspective, the passage of time makes no difference. God's perspective disrupts the symmetry, because the future can be different from the past, and in the case of Nineveh, it was. Nineveh repented and ought not to have been destroyed. Judgment is the issuing of the sentence, but justice is the deferral of its execution.[4] Scholem notes that in the Talmud, the conditions necessary to carry out the death sentence are nearly impossible to fulfill. He defines deferral as "the being of justice" because in the suspension of the sentence, there is the possibility of transformation. Law (understood as human law) seeks to carry out the sentence, but the possibility of justice, which transcends law, requires a pause. God rebukes Jonah for lamenting the destruction of the date tree and not the near-destruction of Nineveh, because the whole point of prophecy is to put off divine judgment, to avoid retribution.[5] Justice, as opposed to judgment, has a futural, not yet realized dimension that is destroyed in the execution of the sentence.

Scholem explains in other unpublished notes that divine judgment necessarily means judgment against the entire world. He writes, "The idea of divine judgment over the world means: the Last Judgment." When divine judgment comes, it will end time. Nineveh repented, and thus divine judgment was deferred; but Scholem is saying something more radical about time. The very fact of time means forgiveness, the kind of impossible forgiveness that humans are nearly incapable of, because no repentance is required for it to be extended. Forgiveness returns to the past to annul the wrongdoing that took place; it changes the past and thus creates the possibility of something new. Time is a form of divine forgiveness extended to all creation; in the face of the end of time and divine judgment for all, delay is a form of mercy. Henri Bergson similarly considered the essence of time to be delay or holding back, because if everything happened at once, it would be the end of time. The deferral of divine punishment, even in the absence of repentance, opens up the present to the future, because it allows life to continue. Many years later, in *The Messianic Idea in Judaism*, Scholem returned to the significance of deferral in Judaism in far more ambivalent terms.[6] Significantly, Bergelson's perpetrators do not repent; rather, his would-be avengers suspend their sentence of death against them. They remain nonetheless under judgment. I argue that this is not a failure but rather an embrace of the potential of the time in between.

Scholem uses the story of the prophet Jonah to mount his argument; Jonah is the central motif of Bergelson's "Old Age" (to be discussed later) and "The Hole Through Which Life Slips," which I introduced in chapter 5. Yona (Jonah) Grigorevitsh, a formerly prolific left-wing journalist, finds himself alone in his apartment in Kiev in 1918. Like the prophet Jonah, Bergelson's Yona refuses to prophesy: he does not come out in favor of the new regime. Although Scholem and Bergelson use the biblical story to raise different questions, both find in Jonah a text that is good to think with, especially in regard to the catastrophes of their shared recent past and the meaning of these catastrophes for the continuation of human history.

Bergelson did not participate in the same circles as Scholem.[7] However, he knew the kabbalistic and Hasidic concepts that the German Jewish figures debated in the interwar period and was personally acquainted with other figures, including Meir Wiener and Fischel Schneersohn, who, like their German Jewish counterparts, adapted religious concepts, pieces of the Jewish lifeworld, and Jewish practices in new forms suitable for secular life, philosophy, and art, establishing their significance for the interwar period and beyond.[8] The reservoir of common texts was shared, but the use to which they were put and the conclusions reached were strikingly different.

Although it is my larger purpose in part 3 to show how Bergelson's intervention in political theology depends in part on concepts imported from Jewish mysticism, it would be misleading to suggest that he regarded mysticism or Hasidism with any particular reverence. In *Judgment* the femme fatale is a devout Christian: "She was a Christian and very severe— as if Christians, like Hasidic Jews with their rebbes, had dynasties among their clergy, and their daughters, pious and strict, held forth among their own disciples [*shtrenger tekhter, vos praven tishn*]."[9] Bergelson mocks both Christianity and Judaism by using Hasidic practice to describe the piety of his seductress.

Aside from the biographical fact that his father belonged to a Hasidic sect, Bergelson's relation with Hasidism may be gleaned from his correspondence, especially a letter he wrote to Shmuel Niger during World War I, in which he argued that the next phase of Yiddish literature was going to result from its new synthesis with biblical Hebrew, which would reinvigorate it without losing its broad appeal. After the war, major new Yiddish talent would arise. Yiddish had already given rise to Peretz and Sholem Aleichem; it "had created a space for the artistic spirit of our broad masses, who had created the charming legends of the Hasidim."[10] In the same letter, he argues the importance of a single language for the entire Jewish people, pointing to the creation of the "literature of Hasidism" as an example of what could be accomplished in periods of linguistic unity. In his 1926 essay "Three Centers," in which Bergelson maintained that Yiddish in the future would flourish only in Moscow, he said, "We have no need of a second Hasidic era."[11] The "first" Hasidic era had already had a far-ranging influence on the development of Yiddish literature. Bergelsonwas not interested in personal or national renewal through the practice of Judaism; for him, Hasidism had served its purpose as a source of Yiddish literature and could do not so again.

Indeed, by referring to the "charming legends of the Hasidim," Bergelson likely had in mind Buber's German translation and adaptation of R. Nakhmen's Yiddish tales, which was discussed in the Yiddish press. One such discussion reflected broadly on the significance of a new form of Judaism whose ecstatic practices had overcome the split between authority and belief. Hasidism had also helped to create a new theology based on a conception of God as infinitely uniting all things in himself.[12] This evaluation of Hasidism is far from Bergelson's emphasis on Hasidism and literary creativity. When he was editing the culture and literature section of *Di yidishe velt* (*The Jewish World*), Bergelson published excerpts from Buber's lectures on Jews and Judaism, which were first published in 1911.[13] Buber and Bergelson differ widely in their attitudes toward the meaning of the Jewish people and the relation between human and cosmic history. For Buber, Jews are the fulcrum of a history that begins on earth and ends in the realm of metaphysics. For Bergelson, the Jewish people do not play the same role; while he is appalled at the devastation they suffered during World War I and the Russian civil war, theirs is not the fate of humankind, let alone anything approaching the Promethean and cosmic significance Buber accords them. Buber embraces the absolute, the "unconditional," the unmediated, the absolute; he seeks total, "sudden and immense" renewal; Bergelson, as I show in this chapter and the next, toys with these ideas with regard to the Bolshevik revolution but sets them aside. His literary art emphasizes mediation and deferral above all else. Unlike Buber, however, he does not lament the loss of authentic Jewish experience. Far from striving toward oneness and unity, Bergelson is interested in multiplicity. He depicts the manifold permutations of a single ray of sunlight that arrives too early and too late; he shows the multiple temporalities that extend a single moment in different ways to different people.

While in Berlin, Bergelson met with a friend from his Kiev days, Fischel Schneersohn, a member of the Hasidic Lubavitcher dynasty who was ordained as a rabbi but also had received a medical degree and published fiction in Yiddish. Schneersohn was interested in psychology and psychoanalysis, and his theories included an important role for religious devotion in healing psychic illness.[14] The monotony of everyday conscious life, with its focus on pragmatic affairs to the neglect of the whole personality, could lead to psychic imbalances of various kinds. Schneersohn, like Bergelson, was in Kiev in 1919 and remarked that the "overwhelming tempo of events . . . the menacing peril of riots" and "psychical shocks" that resulted could in certain cases restore balance to those suffering from a loss of interest and inability to respond properly to the stimuli of normal life. "Riots" refers to what in a Russian- and Yiddish-language environment were called "pogroms." Unlike Freud, Schneersohn maintained that psychic shocks could be restorative. In addition to the orientation toward daily life, the human psyche has another dimension that Schneersohn characterized as the "spherical soul-life," including under this term "primitive eroticism" as well as art and religion.[15] In language revealing the influence of Bergson, Schneersohn argued for the restoration of the irrational, nonpurposive impulses and desires that the necessities of daily life keep at bay. Like Bergson, Schneersohn thought that dreamy, purposeless mental states were important because they provided the capacity for a free, intuitive, holistic life. And again, like Bergson, Schneersohn argued that artists could stimulate psychic processes in their audience parallel to the ones that engendered the production of the artwork in the first place. The result would be "the co-vibration of similar potential feelings."[16] He also emphasized the significance of religious experience in nurturing the holistic "spherical-intimate" life of the psyche and restoring harmony to unbalanced psychological states. Schneersohn used as an example the "Chassidic ecstasy (*Dvekuth*) [*devekut, dveykes* in Yiddish], an intimate ecstatic concentration" that could be a "source of healing" both for individuals and for society. The limitations and isolation of modern life could be overcome in such moments of connection with the "eternal" and "infinite" source of life. Gershom Scholem's discussion of this practice stresses its emotional, nonrational basis as well as its accessibility without reflecting on its practical therapeutic possibilities. Schneersohn transformed the Hasidic practice of *dveykes* into a secular medical therapy that could assuage the fragmentation and monotony of modern life. Schneersohn was a guest in Bergelson's apartment in Berlin; we can imagine discussions of the usefulness of *dveykes* in psychiatric care.[17] Indeed, in "Among Refugees," the would-be "Jewish terrorist" meets with Jewish community members in Berlin, one of whom is a psychiatrist. The prototype for this figure could have been Schneersohn.

Schneersohn, no less than Benjamin, recognizes the "crisis of experience." The larger issue is that Bergelson and his circles, like that of the better known German Jewish intellectuals in the same period, also reimagined Jewish texts, thought, and practice was in order to address the crises of the time. Unlike the generation of German Jewish intellectuals before the war and in the interwar period, whose messianism was apocalyptic and catastrophic, Bergelson focused on the messianic potential of the suspension of action—the pause before violence is met with more violence.

Bergelson's writing attests to his interest in rethinking Hasidic and mystical concepts and practices in light of the catastrophic upheaval of World War I and the Russian revolution and civil war. He cites key texts and Hasidic and mystical terms in his fiction and nonfiction of this period. I have already mentioned *din*, judgment. To give another example, the hero of "Old Age" reads from *Sefer haredim* (*Book of the Pious*), written by a student of Isaac Luria, Eliezer ben Moshe Azikri (1553–1600), who was known for his concept of the mystical communion with God, or *devekut*, the practice that Schneersohn believed could help restore balance to the otherwise atrophied "spherical" life of the psyche in modern times.[18] In a nonfiction piece from 1926, Bergelson humorously uses the term *oylem-hatoye* (world of chaos) to describe Moscow in 1921; the phrase was used in kabbalistic writing to describe the cosmic disorder that resulted from the "breaking of the vessels." Bergelson also refers to *tikkun*, the process of cosmic restoration, in a 1922 story.

Given the importance of these concepts in Bergelson's work in this period, some more detailed discussion will be helpful.[19] Creation, the first phase of cosmic history, is understood as a concentration and contraction of God into himself; the process is known as *tsimtsum*. There is continuity between this understanding of creation and Scholem's notion of justice. In order for the world to come into existence, God withdraws; in order for existence to be sustained after catastrophe, God withdraws from human history, so as not to execute judgment against it. God's concentration into a limited space allowed for the dispersion of divine light, which was supposed to be caught in specific containers or "vessels," but the vessels shattered. The light (or divine) elements became intermixed with the lower world, with evil. The reunion of the divine sparks or the restitution of order (*tikkun*) is the function and purpose of human life. Judgment, *din* (which can also mean "sternness" or "rigor"), is one of the qualities or emanations of the divine revealed and released in the process of creation, and it is considered "the source of evil."[20] There are two differing views of its appearance. The first is as a byproduct of creation in which "the forces of *din*, like a sort of waste product" were eliminated from the essence of the Godhead.[21] The second view is that the demonic realm, as Eliot Wolfson puts it, is "a link in the continuous chain of being."[22] Regardless of the different emphases in the two theories of the origin of the demonic realm, the "common denominator is that the demonic left side has its root in the left side of the divine."[23] Significantly, judgment (*din*), untempered by other divine attributes, especially mercy, is associated with evil, the demonic realm, and the condition of exile. Judgment alone without mercy does not result in restoration. My argument in this chapter and the next is that for Bergelson as for Scholem, *din* is not some sort of cosmic correction to the world of injustice. The left, as Wolfson says, must be contained in the right side. This has significance for Bergelson's emphasis on the deferral of judgment.

Noah's Ark

"At Night: A Half-Imagined Tale" ("*Bay nakht: a halb-oysgetrakhte mayse*"), first published in 1916 in the journal the *Jewish Word* (*Dos yudishe vort*) and later included in various editions of Bergelson's collected works, is a humorous sketch of a few pages, in the tradition of train stories by the trio of classic Yiddish writers Abramovitsh, Peretz, and Sholem Aleichem.[24] There is no English translation.

As the title indicates, it is nighttime, and the first-person narrator is traveling in a train crowded with snoring passengers. He is drawn to an old Jewish man whose expression demands something. The man's voice seems very old, "older than the time that I remember" (*elter fun der tsayt, vos ikh gedenk*).[25] The scene juxtaposes two different time frames: the new, modern train, which accelerates time, and the old man, who seems to come from an earlier, distant epoch. The narrator also notices a young man who complains about insomnia, and when he reveals his illiteracy, the old man tells him to repeat word for word as he, the old man, reads from Genesis—thereby recreating heder (Jewish elementary school) on wheels. A symphony of snoring, whistling, and snorting humorously punctuates the narration of the creation of the world. The reading of Genesis continues to the point when God regrets having created humankind and wants to "blot out" the world. Noah, however, pleases him. The text quotes Genesis 6:8, "And Noah found grace in God's eyes," in Yiddish (*Un Noyekh hot gefunen kheyn in di oygn fun Got.*) The old man says the line, and the young man repeats it, and as the first-person narrator falls asleep, he muses, "It's good, 'Noah found grace,' that's what saved the world" (*A gut vort: 'Un Noyekh hot gefunen kheyn,' s'hot matsl geven di velt*).[26]

Besides this sketch and rewriting *Descent*, Bergelson produced no new works of fiction during World War I. In remarks made in the 1930s, Bergelson said that he could not write during this time, "when blood was gushing everywhere—that seemed far more important than any literary 'theme.'"[27]

In this context, the reworking of the Noah story is all the more significant. Bergelson repeats the line about Noah finding grace three times in a story of three pages. Noah found favor in God's eyes, and thus God did not destroy the world. God made a judgment against the world but did not execute it. He changed his mind. The time structure of "almost but not yet" that is characteristic of other works of fiction leaves Bergelson's protagonists unhappily stranded between the times. Here in the Noah story (both the Bible's and Bergelson's), the same temporality is of great positive significance for the created world in general and Bergelson's immediate world in particular. The total destruction that almost took place during World War I did not happen, and it is a good thing.

The images of Noah and the old world in "At Night" starkly contrast with their representation in the essay "The Present Upheaval" that I discussed briefly in chapter 5. In this piece, Bergelson argues that the demands of the past should be ignored. Noah's ark is full of dead animals: "From time to time yesterday still appears to demand its due—the old uncle comes with his pairs of dead animals."[28] Bergelson is referring to a poem by Leyb Kvitko in which Noah's ark, full of dead beasts and birds, is carried along by the troubled sea. Kvitko, a protégé of Bergelson's, was in Berlin at this time and published in *Milgroym*; his work had also appeared in Bergelson's journal *Eygns* (*Our Own*). Among the works that Kvitko was best known for in this period was his pogrom cycle titled *1919*.[29] In the poem "Uncle's Voyages" ("*Fort mayn feter*"), the biblical Noah is a peddler who tries to sell the dead pairs of animals from his ark to imaginary customers in far-flung places, unaware of the folly of his doomed enterprise.[30] He has the power to summon the shadows of the dead from the sea and "old children" from long-deserted fairs, who exhort the poet, Noah's nephew, to help the old man. Noah is not the sole human being to "find favor" in God's eyes and thereby to save creation from divine destruction. Rather, he is a madman who cannot distinguish the living from the dead, and he and his ark full of dead animals are a remnant of a world that has already been destroyed. As his comments about Kvitko's poem reveal, Bergelson's attitude toward the past changed in the interval between 1916, when "At Night" was published (in which Noah saved creation), and 1922, when his programmatic essay appeared and Noah was transformed into a shadow from a world that no longer exists.

With a stroke of his pen, Bergelson seems to render his earlier preoccupation—the presence of the past—irrelevant. "Every now and then the past still comes to demand its due" Bergelson writes, but the new poets drive it away.[31] Memory, he continues, is perpetually flat and "empty" (*nikhter*). Memory yields nothing. In this single phrase Bergelson apparently negates the fundamental proposition of his entire oeuvre from "At the Depot" to *Descent*. In "At the Depot," the ghost of *troyer* (sorrow) unaccountably haunts the rational grid of railway ties and telegraph lines—the empty, homogeneous time of modernity. Indeed, in all of Bergelson's work until this point and subsequently as well, memory is overfull; the past is alive in the present; the emotions of the present well up from often unseen sources in the past.

The new orientation toward eschatology had consequences for Bergelson's notion of time. Instead of multiple clocks and calendars that expand and contract time, allowing for the realization of virtual pasts, and in the place of the Jewish calendar that alternates between weekday, Sabbath, and holiday, Bergelson seems to have embraced Buber's "once and for all" eschatological destruction and redemption.[32] The "waves of destruction" give way to renewal and redemption for all. This language suggests the "apocalyptic messianism" that Anson Rabinbach finds characteristic of German Jewish intellectuals generally in this period.[33]

This conclusion, however, is too simple. Although Bergelson seems to engage in a Nietzchean revaluation of all values in this essay, other work indicates the opposite. In the very same issue of *Milgroym* as "The Present Upheaval," Bergelson also published the short story "Onheyb kislev TaRAT" ("The Beginning of December 1919"). The title relies on the Jewish calendar both to indicate the month and the year—an unusual specification for Bergelson—signaling that the narrative to follow has a specifically Jewish resonance.[34] December is the month in which Christ was born, thus marking a time of rebirth and salvation for Christians; however, in this story Kislev, the corresponding month in the Jewish calendar, is a time of calamity. A Jew thrown from a train lies dead on the frozen ground. One of the more chilling details of the 1921 session of the statistical division of the Jewish section of the People's Commissariat of Nationalities in Kiev has to do with the problematic classification of victims killed "by trains"—should they be considered "pogrom" victims?

Bergelson's very short story focuses on precisely this type of victim. He abandons the celebratory standpoint of the "wedding for all humanity," painting instead a bleak picture of a Jewish space during an interlude between violent attacks:

From the large Jewish shopkeepers' quarter right across the entire area around this locality an acrid old world lingers, a God-forsaken world, exposed to the chill of winter, to the wind that might gust down from the north, and to the trouble that had yet to erupt and sweep down from very far away, from a God-forsaken town in the furthest distance where it had already erupted and come to pass: a massive slaughter had taken place there.[35]

The Yiddish words for "time" (*tsayt*), "north" (*tsofn*), and "trouble" or "calamity" (*tsore*) all begin with the letter "ts"; the repetition in the sound of the words thus underscores the semantic connection between them. In this passage, what has already "erupted" (*hot oysgebrokhn*) can erupt (*oysgebrekhen*) again. The essay on poetry revels in the "awakening" or "eruption" into a radically new condition of festivity and joy. Here, in contrast, "eruption" revers to war and revolution that bring calamity and grief. The violence, characteristically, is offstage; the present moment in the story is an interval between past and future violent events.

Word and World Up for Grabs

Bergelson similarly uses the Hebrew term *hefker* antithetically in the two pieces. When used with regard to objects and property, it means "owner-less, up for grabs"; with regard to the new Yiddish poetry, *hefker* signals freedom from poetic convention, norms, and traditions; Bergelson proudly proclaims that the new poetry is *hefker*. Yiddish poets of the time, including Moyshe Leyb Halpern, Moshe Kulbak, and Perets Markish, used the term as a fundamental tenet of their modernist aesthetic.[36] The 1922 essay I quoted earlier celebrates the utter breakdown of the foundation of the world; Bergelson writes that there is "no longer any law, limit, and order" (*nishto mer keyn gezets, keyn roymen, un keyn seyder*). In contrast, in the passage from "The Beginning of December 1919," the loss of limits and order means that both God and man have abandoned the world, hence it is *hefker*, a no-man's-land unsuitable for human habitation where acts of violence can be perpetrated with impunity. The frozen corpse of the Jew lying on the ground near the train lines is also *hefker*: claimed by no one and with no one to account for his death. The solution, however, is not divine punishment on a cosmic scale, as I will show later.

In the typical plot of a Bergelson narrative, everything significant has already happened in the past. In *The End of Everything*, the heroine lives her own life belatedly, after everything has already ended. When Khanke falls in love with Khaym-Moyshe (in *Descent*), she feels as if she has fallen in love with him before. This is an instance of the potentiality of the past realizing itself in the present. In "The Beginning of Kislev," déjà vu is not personal but rather reflects the larger pattern of Jewish history; the calamity that has already occurred reflects the calamity that is about to come, and these calamities are a link in a chain of calamities that extend into the entirety of Jewish history: "the nightmares of two thousand years." Time itself comes to a stop: an "old wall-clock" chimes the wrong hour in its "drawn-out death-agony," each new day arrives "stillborn," the Sabbath is "murdered." The cyclic alternation between Sabbath and weekday has ceased; there is no reprieve and no "restoration" (*tikkun*). The last line of the story reads, "Everything stood without any restoration [*tikkun*] —eternally, everlastingly, without any restoration."[37] *Tikkun*, restoration, corresponds to the kabbalistic concept of the restoration of the harmonious order of the world. To remain eternally without *tikkun* is to be condemned to a world without the possibility of transformation. This is the most absolute sense of an ending in Bergelson's entire corpus.

"The Beginning of December 1919" is a work of fiction that reflects a specific historical reality, while "The Present Upheaval" is a programmatic aesthetic piece. Bergelson suggests that art should be *hefker*, free; human life, on the other hand, should not be up for grabs, available for the taking. But the contradiction between on the one hand delighting in rupture and the pleasures of the God-forsaken world (*hefker-velt*) and lamenting the loss of life and an entire way of life on the other is too great to be dismissed merely by compartmentalizing two distinct realms of human activity. As a writer, Bergelson typically chose his words with the utmost care; I cannot imagine that the gap between exalting and mourning the *hefker* word, world, or corpse is anything less than deliberate, in order to draw attention to the sharpness of the contradiction and the anguish of its emotional weight.

In "Art and Society" ("*Dikhtung un gezelshaftlekhkayt*," 1919), Bergelson notes approvingly that "together with the whole of humanity [the Jewish intellectual] is now treading over an entire dead world." The question is whether the Jewish intellectual named Bergelson can make the leap so easily. One foot remains in the not yet dead world, and the other never quite lands in the new one. Bergelson is suspended between the revolution in art and the revolution in life, a difficult but also highly productive position artistically. The tension between embracing the eruption that destroys and the eruption that creates leads to a series of works that imagine one or the other side of the dilemma and the interval between them. Bergelson is saying "both and." The new Jewish artist is both a product of the new world created by the revolution and a witness to the violence of its creation. He or she both celebrates and laments and lives in and artistically evokes the temporalities of both celebration and lament. Bergelson will use the new, *hefker* word to describe the *hefker* world.

"Old Age" and the Cry That Cannot Be Heard

"Altvarg" ("Old Age," also referred to as "Old Folks" or "Obsolescence") beautifully exemplifies the fraught, rich contradictions of Bergelson's position in the interwar period. Having dismissed memory and the past in 1922 and having described the complete destruction of the shtetl, Bergelson nonetheless returns to these themes in "Old Age," published in 1926, the year that he publicly signaled his allegiance to the Soviet Union and began publishing *Judgment*. "Old Age" is one of the last works that Bergelson published in the New York *Forverts*; in 1926 he became a regular staff writer for *Morgen-frayheyt*, a communist daily. I will discuss this shift in chapter 7. The story, like "Blindness," relies on the suddenly emergent image, because it too reveals the flaring up of something already gone, repressed, historically and politically overcome. What is already gone is the world of the shtetl, its economic and social structure, and its various belief systems, all of which were destroyed. Like "Blindness" the story reconfigures the timescape of Berlin with the timescape of the shtetl, drawing upon the Bible and other canonical Jewish texts. Just as "At Night" is a commentary on Noah, "Old Age" is a commentary on Jonah interwoven with references to Genesis 18, the story of Sodom. Both biblical stories concern God's judgment and its deferral. God tells Jonah to warn Nineveh that it is about to be destroyed. The prophecy is effective, and God suspends the sentence. In Genesis 18 (Sodom), God considers putting off destruction because of Abraham's intervention, and although he demolishes Sodom, he saves Lot and his family.

Moyshe Greyvis, a recent refuge from a shtetl in Ukraine, lives in Berlin with his grown children. He finds himself alone one evening and enters a dreamy state in which he interprets both his own history and world history in light of Jonah and Genesis 18. He remembers his past and remembers a way of remembering the past: by linking events from his own time and space to biblical events. The story intertwines reading, interpretation, and memory. Moyshe Greyvis reads the Bible and other books, compares Berlin to Nineveh and Sodom, and concludes that he is responsible for everything that happened in Europe and Russia in the past few years: the "great wind" that destroyed his shtetl and that "rent mountains." He divorced his second wife without asking her forgiveness, and "at that very moment the war had broken out."[38] He believes that World War I, the revolution, and the civil war took place because of his sin against the woman, "for because of a girl's cry (according to the Biblical exegetes), God had once destroyed Sodom."[39] The Yiddish original contains no reference to "exegetes" (*vorim iber dem veygeshray fun eyner a meydl hot got amol ibergekert Sodom*).[40]

The link between the "girl's cry," the destruction of Sodom, and Moyshe Greyvis's story requires some explanation, however, and the Talmudic exegetes provide it. God tells Abraham that since "the cry of Sodom and Gomorrah is great," he will see what has happened there and whether he should destroy the cities. Abraham intercedes, asking whether God is willing to put off the destruction if fifty righteous men can be found there, and God agrees; Abraham keeps asking, reducing the number by ten each time, until God agrees to spare Sodom and Gomorrah for the sake of ten righteous men. Abraham does not ask beyond ten, and as it turns out, only Lot is saved. In a section of the Talmud, wordplay on the term "great" (as in the phrase "the cry of Sodom and Gomorrah is great") allows for a different explanation of why the cities were destroyed. For the word "great" (in Hebrew, *rabah*) the word *ribah* is substituted, transforming the entire phrase to mean that God will destroy Sodom on account of the girl and not the great cry. The reason that God would be willing to do so is this: the girl gave a poor man some bread, and to punish her, the wicked inhabitants of Sodom stripped her and covered her in honey, and a swarm of bees "consumed her."

In "Old Age" Bergelson explicitly refers to the Talmudic variant, transforming it into the psychological motivation that guides his protagonist. The silent, tearless cry of Moyshe Greyvis's second wife corresponds to the girl's cry. Bergelson also alludes to the Talmudic story indirectly by introducing the motif of bees. As he reads his sacred books, Moyshe Greyvis "hummed like a bee that has wandered into the narrow space between double windows and keeps banging and banging into the panes without managing to escape."[41] The metaphor of the buzzing bee trapped between two windowpanes arises from the bizarre story of the girl's death in the Talmudic variant of the story of Sodom and Gomorrah. This story in turn derives from the substitution of a single letter—*rabah* to *ribah*—so that instead of the "great cry" that goes up to God from Sodom it is a "girl's cry" that God hears. Bergelson's use of literary metamorphosis displays some continuity with Talmudic interpretation.

Moyshe Greyvis, like other characters from Bergelson's earlier fiction, is a pious, self-deluded man who believes that his former prosperity was a sign of God's special favor to him and that his present misery in exile is a sign of God's disfavor. Moyshe listens to the sounds of the breaking day, the clatter of trams and trains, and the whistles of the factories. He fears that there is no one to repent for Berlin, which will be destroyed as if it were an unrepentant Nineveh. He escaped the previous destruction (of his shtetl), and now, fearfully waiting for the next eruption, he hides from God, like the prophet Jonah. Like the protagonists of Bergelson's early fiction, Moyshe Greyvis remains in his dreamy state; he hears and sees but does not and cannot act. Moyshe Greyvis experiences the stratification of time, whose layers—the accelerated pace of modern urban life and the timeless, cosmic, and transcendent eternity of biblical narrative—do not overlap. The clock that ticks loudly in the quiet apartment after Moyshe Greyvis's children have gone out takes no cognizance of the meaning of the past for the present. It is like all clocks in all apartments where the owners have gone out: it merely indicates the next moment of time, just as the racket outside the apartment indicates "a new day of work." Bergelson does not espouse the view that the destruction of Jewish life in Ukraine was a just punishment for all the sins of all the Moyshe Greyvises. Even though Bergelson's protagonist in "Old Age" applies the story of Nineveh to the history of the shtetl in Ukraine as well as to Berlin, the modern-day Nineveh, it is clear that the author and his character Moyshe Greyvis should not be confused. In characterizing his hero as *altvarg* (someone or something that has outlived its usefulness), he frames Moyshe Greyvis's interpretation of history as obsolete. Having done so, however, he is free to explore its beauty. This is another instance of "love at last sight." Because of a girl's cry, a city was destroyed; Bergelson adds, "Worse than anything else is the crying of a mute person."[42] For Scholem, the significance of the Jonah story is the postponement of divine judgment; Bergelson, in contrast, shifts the emphasis to the causes of divine retribution. Sodom was not destroyed because of the failure to find the necessary quota of righteous men but rather for the sake of the inaudible cry of a single girl. Bergelson, "the new Jewish artist," affirms that the writer's responsibility means responding even to a cry that cannot be heard. Withholding judgment transcends the limits of human justice; assuming responsibility for the cry that human ears cannot detect similarly pushes against the limits of the possible.

Not Pulling the Trigger

The tension between exalting in and lamenting the destruction of the shtetl is a problem for Bergelson. There is another possibility, however, that avoids both extremes: putting off the end, deferring punishment for the perpetrators of the unjust murder of tens of thousands of Jews, even without repentance. Poised at the brink of the end of the world, Bergelson avoids condemning it to further destruction. He suggests the alternative of living with its messes and even its evils—continuing life in the world still unredeemed by God or Bolshevism, with the hope that seemingly insignificant gestures might contain something resembling redemption. This is a world that takes time to unfold, in which people wait, time flows, and sometimes nothing happens. Another term for this alternative could be the messianism of the interval.[43]

In 1926, the same year as he published "Old Age," Bergelson also published "Two Murderers" ("*Tsvey rotskhim*"), also in the New York Yiddish *Forward*. This and other stories focusing on anti-Jewish violence in Ukraine do not use Jonah, but they nonetheless stage moments when judgment is put off. Bergelson's perpetrators do not repent, but they suffer no consequences from their actions. "Two Murderers" is the story of a German war widow, her dog, and her lodger, a Ukrainian named Anton Zarembo, whom the narrator describes as "the leader of a small group that plundered and murdered shtetls in Ukraine."[44] The three protagonists share overlapping fates in the aftermath of the Russian civil war and World War I. After the war, the widow, Hilde Ginter, had adopted a seven-month-old orphan; the dog Tel, however, is jealous. When Frau Ginter steps out to get a few things from the store, she returns to find the baby with its throat ripped out. Because Tel did not have rabies, he was not destroyed. There was no further outcome; as Frau Ginter remarks with regret, "there was no trial"—but whether for herself or the dog is not clear. What is clear, however, is that her regret is not for the child.

The story of Frau Ginter's dog reminds Anton Zarembo, her Ukrainian lodger, of other, very similar stories:

> The story with the bloodied child that lay there on the floor of the room with its throat ripped out reminded him of many similar stories in the shtetls in Ukraine, where he with his group murdered and plundered. He remembered

blood . . . blood in all the Jewish houses, blood on the street, where amid broken glass and all kinds of other rags and Jewish guts. Bloodied bodies lay with chopped-off heads—here was a head with a salt-and-pepper beard.[45]

This dispassionate account, almost a list of separate bloodied items, contrasts sharply with the description of the pogroms that Bergelson used in his appeal to friends of Yiddish in America. The appeal uses emotional language ("in great anguish and pain," *in groys angst un payn*) to describe the psychological state of the artists and writers in Kiev in 1919–20. In contrast, Zarembo shows no emotion. Strangely disconnected from his own actions, he remembers blood on the streets as if he had no role in putting it there. In previous work, Bergelson had used a similarly disjointed modernist style to emphasize the fragmentation of his untimely characters. In this story, the separation of cause and effect especially from the perspective of perpetrators, has a strikingly chilling moral impact.

A similar disconnect characterizes Frau Ginter's response to her lodger's story. She fails to understand "who is guilty" (*ver iz shuldik*) and "why blood was shed." What is clear to her, however, is that in Zarembo's homeland, there were a lot of murdered children, "children with their throats ripped out." She asks with particular interest whether there was a trial (*gerikht*), and when she learns there was not, she expresses her compassion—not for the victims but instead for the perpetrator. She addresses him in German as *"armer, armer"* ("you poor man"; the Yiddish would be *oremer*) and exclaims over the similarity between the fate of her dog and that of her lodger. According to Frau Ginter, Zarembo's and Tel's stories of the failure of the legal system are "exactly the same." The unexpected shift to compassion for the perpetrators—the "two murderers" who never got their day in court—raises the question of justice even more pointedly than an emotional plea for compassion for the victims. The story suggests a syllogism: If it is unjust to deprive perpetrators of their day in court, how much more unjust is the situation of victims who will never get theirs? Could there be justice for the dead if Zarembo and Frau Ginter were imprisoned and the dog put down? Would the world be put to rights? The unspoken question the story raises about justice and restoration echoes the theme of *tikkun* (restoration) that is so categorically denied in "The Beginning of Kislev." There is neither restoration for the victims nor judgment for the "two murderers." Human judgment would be inadequate, and divine judgment would have to sentence and punish the entire world of human beings. The problem is left unsolved.

In other works, in contrast, there is no question of a court trial. Judgment for the perpetrators of anti-Jewish violence is deferred because at the eleventh hour, the self-appointed executioners fail to pull the trigger. In "Among Refugees," the self-styled Jewish terrorist changes his mind about killing the Ukrainian leader and hangs himself instead. I discussed the peculiarities of the young man's face in chapter 5, but one crucial dimension remains. It is "out of justice" (*fun yoysher*) that the visitor "takes the side of his ugly left cheek." As I discussed earlier, in the kabbalistic tradition with which Bergelson was familiar, *din* appears on the left side of the tree figure used to represent the attributes of God. *Din* is the divine quality or emanation that includes judgment, punishment, and destruction. Acting on behalf of his left side corresponds to inflicting judgment on the world by assassinating the Ukrainian leader. The young man thus is not merely a psychological case or a victim of trauma suffering the consequences of the multiple deaths of his family members. His failure to assassinate the Ukrainian leader and his subsequent decision to kill himself ought not to be read as symptoms of a psychological imbalance of the type Schneersohn would cure. The uncanny visitor is additionally an allegorical figure: the embodiment of *din*, punishment. The kabbalistic dimension of Bergelson's portrait of the "Jewish terrorist" suggests that he is raising the same question in "Among Immigrants" as he did in "Two Murderers." The question about pulling the trigger should be viewed as a philosophical problem particularly acute in the era "between the times," when the past is over and the future postponed. Even in the absence of repentance, the deferral of judgment and punishment better serves justice than the execution of the sentence, because in allowing human time to continue, the possibility of transformation is left open. Divine judgment would solve the problem for human beings but would also catastrophically change human history. Human beings have to solve the problem themselves, and judgment alone will not bring justice into the world.

The analysis of justice and judgment in Bergelson's Berlin-era stories would be incomplete without at least a brief discussion of the real-life case of Shlomo Schwartzbard. Schwartzbard was a Ukrainian refugee living in Paris; he had become a French citizen and had served in the French army during World War I. In May 1926 in Paris, Shlomo Schwartzbard killed Symon Petliura because he believed Petliura was responsible for the pogroms in Ukraine. A French jury acquitted Schwartzbard in October 1927. One of the witnesses for the defense was Henri Bergson, although he did not make an appearance at the trial. There is a question regarding the first publication date of Bergelson's "Among Refugees": 1923, 1924, and 1927 appear in the scholarship.[46] When he began and finished writing is difficult to say, because so little of Bergelson's archive survives and no manuscript drafts remain. Whether he wrote "Among Refugees" in response to Schwartzbard's act or had anticipated some version of it cannot be determined. If the later date is correct, there can be no doubt as to Bergelson's awareness of the event, given its wide reporting in the press. Regardless of the problematic date of publication, the fact of the murder and the acquittal makes Bergelson's fiction of an aborted assassination all the more striking and significant.[47] Schwartzbard was not the only national avenger to achieve fame in Europe in the 1920s. Soghomon Tehlirian assassinated Talaat Pasha in 1921 and was acquitted by a German court.

Bergelson raises similar questions about justice for perpetrators and survivors in the disturbing story "*Geburt*" ("Birth," 1928), which has not been translated into English. In this work, as in "Among Refugees," a would-be Jewish avenger plans to murder the Ukrainian he believes responsible for Jewish deaths during a pogrom, but he fails to pull the trigger. The publication date of this story indicates very strongly that Bergelson already knew about Schwartzbard's acquittal for the murder of Petliura. Even though Schwartzbard was acquitted, Bergelson stuck to his guns: deferring the execution of judgment better served the larger cause of justice.

Dr. Moti Shteynberg, a surgeon, has been out of sorts with the world from the beginning, like the young man in "Among Refugees." After the civil war breaks out, and after the pogrom in Proskurov, he sends his blonde, pregnant wife and their four-year-old child to her father in Teriev for safety. (Proskurov, now Khmelnitsky, was a real city in Podolya, the site of a massive pogrom in 1919; Teriev is likely a reference to Tetiev, some seventy miles from Kiev, also the site of a mass killing of Jews.) Dr. Shteynberg later learns that his wife sought refuge at the house of his colleague, the non-Jewish Dr. Pshibulski, who had examined her a few days earlier, warning of possible complications with her delivery. Dr. Shteynberg imagines the other man palpating his wife's pregnant belly. At the greatest moment of need, however, the gentile doctor refused to open his door to his patient and her child, and at ten in the morning, they were shot on the steps of his porch.

The plot of "Birth" touches on real-life events in the Bergelson family, as recounted by Lev Bergelson.[48] During the civil war, Bergelson traveled with his pregnant wife from Odessa to her hometown of Haysyn (Gaisin), approximately 125 miles from Kiev. He apparently thought that the small town would be safer. He went on to Kiev, where he helped to found the Kultur-Lige. But Haysyn turned out not to be safe, and Lev Bergelson was born during a pogrom in August 1918; his father was unable to journey to Haysyn in time for the birth. Train travel for Jews in the region at this time was dangerous, as Bergelson's story "The Beginning of December 1919" describes. In order to get the family out of Haysyn, Bergelson hired a peasant who agreed to say that Tsipora and Lev were his wife and child. The journey by horse and cart took several weeks, and it was doubtless terrifying. The personal story had a fortunate outcome; the fiction does not.

The murder of his wife and child creates a crisis for Dr. Shteynberg. Serving in a Red Army field hospital, he loses the capacity to view his patients as human beings. They have become "pieces of wood, garbage, shit" (*tinef*).[49] He begs his commander to release him, but before leaving he receives a reproach for his dismal view of other human beings. Dr. Shteynberg sets off for Tetiev with his revolver and one goal in mind: killing Dr. Pshibulski, the man he considers responsible for the deaths of his pregnant wife and child. The confrontation with his enemy turns out differently than he planned. Disgust, not hatred, overwhelms him as he aims his revolver at Dr. Pshibulski, and he fails to pull the trigger.

In a daze, Dr. Shteynberg sets off for Kiev, where he has one more confrontation. He sees a barefoot peasant in the market holding a crying child; the child wants chocolate, and his penniless father goes to vendor after vendor, but no one will give him a piece. Dr. Shteynberg grabs some chocolate, gives it to the child, and pays for it, all without saying a word. A woman, a complete stranger—not a beautiful woman, but not a madwoman, either—accosts him, moved by his act, but not for the reason we might expect. She is the survivor of a pogrom, she tells him; she saw people killed before her eyes, and she came to Kiev to kill herself. Watching the peasant, the crying child, and the refusals of the sellers, it became easier to fulfill her plan, but Dr. Shteynberg ruined it for her with his good deed. She doesn't know whether to curse or bless him. Dr. Shteynberg decides for her, by telling her that if she were beautiful, she would not have noticed him or the crying child. Kissing his hand in gratitude, she leaves to commit suicide.

Like the would-be assassin in "Among Refugees," Bergelson's protagonist in this story also has a physical mark on the left side of his body. He received a bullet wound on his left calf while serving in the Russian army during World War I. The left side is associated with *din*—judgment, punishment, and destruction; the right side is connected with mercy. Bergelson makes Dr. Shteynberg's allegorical role even more explicit, however. Whereas earlier his sense of "mercy" (*rakhmones*) was never well developed, he has stopped feeling its absence altogether; he has become stony, like his name (*shteyn* means "stone"). His unclear image of himself since the death of his wife as a "creature as heartless as the angel of death" (*malkehamoves-dik-trukener bashefenish*) grows stronger and clearer.[50] In the kabbalistic texts that I discussed earlier, the angel of death emanates from the left side. But this story's self-appointed agent of divine retribution makes a mistake. He lets the man he considers his wife and child's murderer live but encourages the suicide of a witness to a pogrom with his cruel observation about her ugliness and its role in her sensitivity to the pain of others.

In an inversion of Deuteronomy 30:9 ("I have set before you life and death, blessing and curse/Choose life"), he has helped the woman choose death. He has become one of the executioners and for a petty reason: the woman provided a mirror of himself; he too came to Kiev to take his own life. Only afterward does he recall his commander's words back when he complained that his surgical patients seemed to him to be nothing more than wood and even worse. What did he expect, "gold"? For this, you have to "first prepare . . . you have to do a little work."[51] It is important to note that the commander's words of admonition rest on a kind of evolutionary, incremental notion of change and not the revolutionary elimination of enemies.

Presumably Dr. Shteynberg understands that the language about the necessity of a little work applies to him as well as to others. Recalling his commander's words after he has already condemned the unfamiliar woman to death, Dr. Shteynberg's newfound understanding comes too late to save her but possibly not too late to change himself. Transformation cannot be instantaneous; it requires time. Even though the world contains human beings who kill for pleasure, it ought not to end. This is another instance of the messianism of the interval.

In both programmatic essays written in 1926, Bergelson described the difficulties of his own role as a "Jewish artist." In "Moscow" and "Three Centers" he said that the new Jewish artist has to listen to the heart-rending cries of *khurbn* (destruction) that ascend to heaven. Dr. Shteynberg too assumes this responsibility: he listens to the unfamiliar woman as she tells her story.

What the woman tells Dr. Shteynberg is a form of testimony about the pogrom, but not because it contains an account of the actions of a perpetrator, a gang, or a military unit and not because it names the victims, their ages, and professions or how they died. This was the kind of information that the Jewish Public Committee collected and recorded. Unlike Bergelson's appeal to "friends of Yiddish in America," there is no blood or guts in the woman's account and no direct expression of emotion. All these details are omitted, and what the woman says instead is dry and abstract. Animals kill because they have to eat; humans kill for pleasure; they are "vipers." She has run away from them, come here to the city to kill herself, and what she has seen here has made it easier for her, until she encountered Dr. Shteynberg. Until he arrived, many passersby ignored the man and the crying child, who went to eight different kiosks, and no one would give them a piece of chocolate. Dr. Shteynberg made things difficult for her, however: his act of mercy caused her "such pain." The consequence of the pogrom is a loss of faith in the world and the absolute decision to reject it completely. Dr. Shteynberg caused the woman pain because he made her hesitate—at least for a few minutes, before he restored her belief that there was nothing to believe in.

Not pulling the trigger condenses into a single dramatic moment the larger pattern of inaction that typifies the protagonists of Bergelson's prewar fiction. His early characters, like the train depot itself in his first published work, are *farglivert* (frozen, congealed). Beynish Rubinshteyn ("At the Depot"), Burman ("In a Backwoods Town"), and Mirl Hurvits (*The End of Everything*) do not act. Having failed to grasp the new ideologies and economic opportunities of their epoch, they fall behind. Their failure does not make them better people. It does, however, allow them to see and hear what others do not. Mirl notices an absence. She is the only one who notices that the world has fallen silent. She protests the world's silence, but not in response to catastrophe or mass death. From Mirl's perspective, the new beliefs and new forms of economic opportunity are merely a way of passing time, comparable to a habit of reading novels or chewing sunflower seeds. The world is silent because there is nothing to do and no one to do it, and if there is something to be done, no one knows what it is or how to do it.

Not pulling the trigger is also a form of ceasing action. It does not immediately put the world to rights or redeem the dead, but neither does pulling the trigger. Pulling the trigger is worse, because it precludes any other possibility emerging. The human effort to assume the divine role of avenger only brings more death, piling destruction on top of all the other destruction that has taken place and may take place again. Divine judgment (*din*) is enveloped in mercy; "the left contained by the right." Acting as judge and executioner in one fell swoop, without pause and thus without mercy, eliminates the possibility of transformation because it demolishes time. In contrast to human judges, God pauses before executing judgment. From the human viewpoint, the pause may seem like abandonment; hence the *hefker* world. God has ceased rewarding and punishing. The temporality of hesitation and the suspension of judgment will be particularly important for my discussion of Bergelson and Bolshevism in the following chapter.

Bergelson's interwar fiction stresses the importance of delay and inaction as a crucial element of justice and a precondition of transformation. Bergelson marks his would-be avengers on the left side of the body, corresponding to *din* (rigor and judgment), and situates these embodiments of *din* in plots that suspend the execution of the sentence. The use of these concepts suggests that mediation and deferral play as important a role in his fiction of experience and the body as they do in his fiction on justice and political theology. Bergelson transforms his modernist aesthetic of mediation and slowed motion—and the literary effect of slowed and impeded perception—into a philosophical inquiry about delayed judgment, even in the terrible face of violent injustice. Bergelson's emphasis on judgment postponed, like Scholem's, offers a striking counternarrative to the apocalyptic messianism of interwar Berlin intellectuals and to the similarly eschatological strains in the new Bolshevik order, the subject of the next chapter.

Notes

1. For an account that turns the standard version on its head, see Jeffrey A. Grossman, "Yiddish Writers/German Models in the Early Twentieth Century," in *Three Way Street: Jews, Germans, and the Transnational*, ed. Jay Howard Geller and Leslie Morris (Ann Arbor: University of Michigan Press, 2016), 66–90.

2. The time Scholem spent in Berlin in 1917 in close contact with Eastern European Jews was particularly important for the development of his interest in mysticism. See David Biale, *Gershom Scholem: Kabbalah and Counter-History* (Cambridge, MA: Harvard University Press, 1982), 24–28.

3. For the English text, see Gershom Scholem and Eric J. Schwab, "On Jonah and the Concept of Justice," *Critical Inquiry* 25, no. 2 (1999): 353–61. For a discussion of this and other work by Scholem in the context of messianism and violence, see Eric Jacobson, *Metaphysics of the Profane: The Political Theology of Walter Benjamin and Gershom Scholem* (New York: Columbia University Press, 2003). I depend on Jacobson for an explication of Scholem's difficult text.

4. Benjamin's language about the "messianic cessation of action" is comparable. See Walter Benjamin, *Illuminations* (New York: Schocken, 1969), 263.

5. For a broad-ranging discussion of the role of deferral and its antithesis, see Bruce Rosenstock, "*Palintropos Harmoniê*: Jacob Taubes and Carl Schmitt 'Im Liebenden Streit,'" *New German Critique* 41, no. 1 (2014): 55–92.

6. "Thus in Judaism the Messianic idea has compelled a *life lived in deferment*, in which nothing can be done definitively, nothing can be irrevocably accomplished." See Gershom Scholem, *The Messianic Idea in Judaism and Other Essays on Jewish Spirituality* (New York: Schocken, 1995), 35.

7. For the attitudes of German Jewish intellectuals to Yiddish literary figures including Bergelson and Der Nister, see Jeffrey Grossman, "The Yiddish-German Connection: New Directions," *Poetics Today* 1–2 (2015): 61–110. For a volume of essays on Yiddish writers in Berlin, see G. Estraikh and Mikhail Krutikov, eds., *Yiddish in Weimar Berlin: At the Crossroads of Diaspora Politics and Culture*, Studies in Yiddish (London: Modern Humanities Research Association, 2010). Another study of Russian Jewish life in Berlin is Oleg Budnitskii and Aleksandra Polian, *Russko-Evreiskii Berlin 1920–1941* (Moscow: Novoe literaturnoe obozrenie, 2013).

8. The only English-language study of Wiener is Mikhail Krutikov, *From Kabbalah to Class Struggle: Expressionism, Marxism, and Yiddish Literature in the Life and Work of Meir Wiener* (Stanford, CA: Stanford University Press, 2011).

9. David Bergelson, *Judgment*, trans. Harriet Murav and Sasha Senderovich, Northwestern World Classics (Evanston, IL: Northwestern University Press, 2017), 15. For the Yiddish, see David Bergelson, *Mides-hadin*, vol. 7, Geklibene verk (Vilnius: B. Kletskin, 1929), 19.

10. Undated Russian language letter, YIVO archive RG360, Shmuel Niger, Box 7, Folder 9e.

11. David Bergelson, "Three Centres: Characteristics," in *David Bergelson: From Modernism to Socialist Realism*, ed. Joseph Sherman and Gennady Estraikh (Oxford: Legenda, 2007), 349.

12. A. Koralnik, "R. Nakhmen's mayses," *Dos yidishe folk* 1, no. 30 (1906): 1–4.

13. Martin Buber, "Di yehudes un di menshhayt," *Di yidishe velt*, no. 2 (1913): 91–101. The original work, *Drei Reden über das Judentum*, was published in 1911.

14. For his theory, see Fischel Schneersohn, *Studies in Psycho-Expedition*, trans. Herman Frank (New York: Science of Man, 1929). John Dewy wrote one of the prefaces. For more on Schneersohn, see Mikhail Krutikov, "Unkind Mirrors: Berlin in Three Yiddish Novels of the 1930s," in *Yiddish in Weimar Berlin: At the Crossroads of Diaspora Politics and Culture*, ed. Gennady Estraikh and Mikhail Krutikov (London: Legenda, 2010), 239–61.

15. Ibid., 184.

16. Ibid., 93.

17. The fragmentary nature of Bergelson's Berlin archive only allows for speculation.

18. Gershom Scholem, "*Devekut*, Or Communion with God," in *Essential Papers on Hasidism: Origins to Present*, ed. Gershon David Hundert (New York: New York University Press, 1991), 275–298.

19. I rely on Scholem for my account, with the awareness that the nuances of Bergelson's own understanding of these ideas may not be the same as Scholem's. See Gershom Scholem, *Major Trends in Jewish Mysticism* (New York: Schocken, 1971). For a critique of Scholem's historicizing, see, for example, Jacob Taubes, "The Price of Messianism," in *From Cult to Culture: Fragments Toward a Critique of Historical Reason*, ed. Charlotte Elisheva Fonrobert and Amir Engel (Stanford, CA: Stanford University Press, 2010), 3–9.

20. Ibid., 13, 363, 267. See also Elliot R. Wolfson, "Light Through Darkness: The Ideal of Human Perfection in the Zohar," *Harvard Theological Review* 81, no. 1 (1988): 73–95.

21. Gershom Scholem, *Sabbatai Sevi, The Mystical Messiah* (Princeton, NJ: Princeton University Press, 1973), 30.

22. Elliot R. Wolfson, "Light Through Darkness: The Ideal of Human Perfection in the Zohar," *Harvard Theological Review* 81, no. 1 (1988): 93.

23. Wolfson, "Light Through Darkness," 93

24. While the title *"Bay nakht"* could point to Peretz's play *Bay nakht in altn mark*, Abramovitsh's *"Shem un Yafes in a vagon"* includes a partial recitation of creation and refers, as its title indicates, to the two sons of Noah. For a discussion of Abramovitsh, see Leah Garrett, *Journeys Beyond the Pale: Yiddish Travel Writing in the Modern World* (Madison: University of Wisconsin Press, 2003), 96–105. Peretz, who died in 1915, was on Bergelson's mind at this time.

25. David Bergelson, *Geklibene verk*, vol. 3 (Vilnius: B. Kletskin, 1929), 179.

26. David Bergelson, *Geklibene verk*, 183.

27. David Bergelson, "Materyaln tsu D. Bergelsons bio-bibliografye," *Visnshaft un revolutsye* 1–2 (1934): 67–73.

28. The Yiddish: "Fun tsayt tsu tsayt kumt nokh alts monen zayn khuv der nekhtn—der alter feter kumt tsuforn mit di toyte porn." David Bergelson, "Der gesheener oyfbrokh," *Milgroym* 1 (1922): 41.

29. For a discussion, see Sabine Koller, "'The Air Outside Is Bloody': Leyb Kvitko and His Pogrom Cycle *1919*," in *Yiddish in Weimar Berlin: At the Crossroads of Diaspora Politics and Culture*, eds. Gennady Estraikh and Mikhail Krutikov (London: Legenda, 2010), 105–22.

30. The poem has not been translated into English. For the Yiddish, see Khone Shmeruk, ed., *A shpigl af a shteyn* (Jerusalem: Magnes, 1964), 358–67.

31. Bergelson, "Der gesheener oyfbrokh," 41.

32. I take the phrase from Martin Buber, *The Origin and Meaning of Hasidism* (Atlantic Highlands, NJ: Humanities Press International, 1988), 40.

33. Anson Rabinbach, "Between Enlightenment and Apocalypse: Benjamin, Bloch and Modern German Jewish Messianism," *New German Critique* 34 (Winter 1985): 78–124.

34. A discussion of this issue can be found in Mikhail Krutikov, "Narrating the Revolution," in *David Bergelson: From Modernism to Socialist Realism*, ed. Joseph Sherman and Gennady Estraikh (Oxford: Legenda, 2007), 167–182.

35. I am using the English translation in Joseph Sherman, "The Beginning of December 1919," in *From Revolution to Repression: Soviet Yiddish Writing 1917–1952*, ed. Joseph Sherman (Nottingham, UK: Five Leaves Publications, 2012), 61–65. The Yiddish: "Ibern gantsn shetekh fun vinkl do, fun yidn-kant dem kremershn un groysn, nogt an alte velt a zoyere, an hefker-velt fray far kelt fun vinter tsayt, far vint, vos kan fun tsofn blozn un far tsore, vos darf nokh oysgebrekhn un kumen fun vayt, fun a hefker-shtot an ekster, vu alts hot shoyn oysgebrakhn un getrofn: a groyse shkhite iz dort geshen." For the original Yiddish, see David Bergelson, "Onheyb Kislev TaRAT," *Milgroym* 1, no. 1 (1922): 25.

36. See for example Ravhel Seelig, "A Yiddish Bard in Berlin: Moyshe Kulbak and the Flourishing of Yiddish Poetry in Exile," *Jewish Quarterly Review* 102, no. 1 (2012): 19–49. For a discussion of the concept of *hefker*, see Naomi Brenner, *Lingering Bilingualism: Modern Hebrew and Yiddish Literatures in Contact* (Syracuse, NY: Syracuse University Press, 2015), 63–71.

37. Sherman, "The Beginning of December 1919," 65.

38. David Bergelson, *The Shadows of Berlin: The Berlin Stories of Dovid Bergelson* (San Francisco, CA: City Lights, 2005), 16.

39. Bergelson, *The Shadows of Berlin*, 17.

40. David Bergelson, *Geklibene verk*, vol. 5 (Vilnius: B. Kletskin, 1930), 169.

41. Bergelson, *The Shadows of Berlin*, 10.

42. Bergelson, *The Shadows of Berlin*, 19.

43. I am modifying Taubes's characterization of Martin Buber's "messianism of continuity"; see Jacob Taubes, "Martin Buber and the Philosophy of History," in *From Cult to Culture: Fragments toward a Critique of Historical Reason*, ed. Charlotte Elisheva Fonrobert and Amir Engel (Stanford, CA: Stanford University Press, 2010), 11–27.

44. This is my translation. The original: "Ataman fun a kleyner bande, vos hot barabevet un gekoylet yidishe shtetlekh in Ukrayne." David Bergelson, *Velt-oys velt-eyn*, vol. 6, Geklibene verk (Vilnius: B. Kletskin, 1929), 209.

45. Bergelson, *The Shadows of Berlin*, 7. The Yiddish: "Di geshikhte mitn farblutikn kind, vos iz do in tsimer gelign, af der podloge mit an ibergebisn helzl, dermont im in fil enlekhe geshikhtes in yene Yidishe shtetlekh af Ukrayne, vu er mit zayn bande hot gekoylet un gerabevet. Blut . . . blut in ale Yidishe hayzer gedenkt zikh im, blut af der gas, vu tsvishn tsebrokhn gloz un tsvishn alerlay anderere shmotes un Yidishe bebekhes valgern zikh farblutikte kerpers mit epes an opgehakte kop—a kop mit a grolekh-shvartser bord." Bergelson, *Velt-oys velt-eyn* 6: 211–12.

46. The source for the 1923 date is Shmeruk, *A shpigl af a shteyn*, 773. Shmeruk simply gives the date 1923 for "*Tsvishn emigrantn*" without providing additional bibliographic information. Other scholars who similarly refer to 1923 without giving a citation include Allison Schachter, *Diasporic Modernisms: Hebrew and Yiddish Literature in the Twentieth Century* (New York: Oxford University Press, 2012). For a reference to 1924 as the date of the composition of the story, see Shachar Pinsker, *Literary Passports: The Making of Modernist Hebrew Fiction in Europe* (Stanford, CA: Stanford University Press, 2011), 136. Nineteen twenty-seven is the date given for the first publication of the story in Roberta Saltzman, "A Bibliography of David Bergelson's Works in English and Yiddish," in *David Bergelson: From Modernism to Socialist Realism*, ed. Joseph Sherman and Gennady Estraikh (Oxford: Legenda, 2007), 306–336.

47. For discussions comparing the trial to the story, see Anna Schur, "Shades of Justice: The Trial of Sholom Schwartzbard and Dovid Bergelson's 'Among Refugees,'" *Law and Literature* 19, no. 15 (2007): 15–43; Sasha Senderovich, "In Search of Readership: Bergelson among the Refugees," in *David Bergelson: From Modernism to Socialist Realism*, ed. Joseph Sherman and Gennady Estraikh (Oxford: Legenda, 2007), 150–66.

48. Lev Bergelson, "Memories of My Father: The Early Years (1918–1934)," in *David Bergelson: From Modernism to Socialist Realism*, ed. Joseph Sherman and Gennady Estraikh (Oxford: Legenda, 2007), 79–88.

49. David Bergelson, "Geburt," in *Geklibene verk: Tsugvintn*, vol. 8 (Vilnius: B. Kletskin, 1930), 104.

50. David Bergelson, "Geburt," 108.

51. Bergelson, "Geburt," 104.

7

THE EXECUTION OF JUDGMENT

IN 1926, BERGELSON PUBLICLY SHIFTED HIS ALLEGIANCE TOWARD the Soviet Union. He expressed this new commitment in several ways. He wrote an apologetic letter to Aleksandr Chemeriskii, at the Soviet Yiddish newspaper *Der emes*. He started a journal, *In shpan* (*In Harness*), in which he published "Three Centers." Bergelson visited Moscow in 1926 and described his enthusiasm for it, using the metaphor of "time forward." The clock hovering invisibly on Moscow's horizon had sped up dramatically since 1921, when time ran backward. He also published the first few chapters of *Judgment* in his new journal; the complete novel came out in 1929.

The year 1926 thus may be considered a turning point, although how decisive is another matter. An attentive reading of the fiction and nonfiction post-1926 reveals significant continuity with the past. Bergelson shared the desire for a new future promised by the revolution. The revolution opened a space beyond the shtetl—a link to the whole world and all of humanity. In 1922 Bergelson characterized his own historical moment as "a wedding for all humanity" and the world as "festive, washed clean, and new."[1] The revolutionary future meant new space, new time, and a new community: Jewish festive time extended beyond Jews. The embrace of all of humanity resonates with utopian notes in Marxist thought about the breakdown of boundaries and the access to the whole world that the revolution would give previously isolated individuals.[2]

Bergelson's public pronouncements in 1926, however, do not mean that he adopted Marxism-Leninism as an ideology. Although the Bergelson archive is incomplete, there is no statement about Marxism in the available letters and papers. Bergelson's public stance in 1926 shifted, but he was in no rush to return to Russia. Just three years earlier, he had written to

Abe Cahan, the editor of the *Forward*, desperate to get out of Berlin and demanding more money so he could take his family to Switzerland.[3] The anti-Jewish riot of November 1923 and the Munich beer hall putsch were undoubtedly factors in Bergelson's sense that life in Berlin was untenable.[4] He did not receive the money, though, and did not leave Berlin until 1933. In the manner of his fictitious characters, he hesitated. Instead of taking Bergelson's public position as the sole basis for interpreting his *Judgment*, a closer examination of the text itself reveals far greater ambivalence. Bergelson's commitments were more artistic than political; his lifelong project was building Yiddish literature, not socialism; his lifelong love was the Yiddish language, as he said during his secret trial in 1952.

The question of politics is of course important nonetheless. My approach toward Bergelson and Marxism asks how Marxism meshes with—and collides against—other elements of his literary project. Framing the question this way means asking how Marxism could appeal to Bergelson the writer—and more specifically, Bergelson the writer interested in *shtimung*, a concept that embraces mood, atmosphere, and also the embodied qualities of textuality, including rhythm. It means attending to the inevitable conflict between revolutionary Marxism–Leninism and Bergelson's interest in the presence of the past and the temporality of the interval.

To approach these issues, it is better to begin more broadly. There are points that Bergson, Bergelson, and Marx share, because each is responding to the conditions of capitalist modernity. Materiality serves as a common point of departure. Marx argues that the material conditions of life determine consciousness; Bergson, in *Matter and Memory*, argues that the body conditions perception. Bergelson's decentering of the intentional self, fragmenting it into parts of the body, and his exploration of the physiological production of speech indicate a similarly materialist tendency, but not in terms of class struggle. Both Marx and Henri Bergson register the diminution of experience, the loss of the world, and the evisceration of the present, although their explanations of the causes and cures for the problem differ. Under capitalism, says Marx, "the past dominates the present" because of the constant drive to produce more capital. The past consists of the accumulated weight of labor transformed into objects and capital, which sets in motion the need to create more. Under communism, in contrast, "the present dominates the past."[5] For Bergson, the pragmatic needs of daily life and the scientific cast of mind cause us to merely "read the labels" and thus fail to experience duration, the fullness of the present. Although Bergson did not explicitly critique capitalism, his theories were used for such a critique. Capitalist temporality is mechanical because of its instantaneousness and repetition. Capitalism destroys the differences among objects, people, and the quality of time. The cliché "time is money" gets to the heart of the problem; equation of the two reduces the multiple and subjective qualities of time to a single common denominator.[6]

The similarities between Marx and Bergson only go so far, of course. Marx and Bergson both identify the problem of alienation of self from self, self from other, self from world. Marx affirms the reason of history in the form of inevitable class struggle, whereas Bergson rejects reason in history and its corollary notion of predictability. There is no unity in the history of nature or humankind but instead endless unpredictable differentiation— "creative evolution." Even after his 1926 shift, the Yiddish writer Bergelson interrogated the reason of history by weaving it into the fabric of daily life, asking how life is lived despite history's dictates. As I will show later, "spite" is the operative word even in *Judgment*, largely considered an openly pro-Bolshevik novel. In the case of *Judgment*, the results of the experiment are bleak; as one of the characters says, "It was like an absurd nightmare from which you want to awaken but can't."[7]

Bergelson had criticized the economic structure that dominated shtetl life in work that predates the Russian revolution. In "At the Depot" (1909), Beynish Rubinshteyn is a bad capitalist because he focuses on the past instead of the future; he pauses, remembers, and sees what others do not, an experience he shares with other protagonists in Bergelson's post-1926 fiction. The successful capitalist, in contrast, looks toward the next deal. Beynish listens to a conversation critical of capitalism as he waits in the house of a wealthy man: the capitalist exploits the labor of the worker by profiting from a product he has not produced. Beynish's own "source of capital," he admits, is the dowry he received on the occasion of his second marriage.[8]

The implicit critique of capitalism in "At the Depot" and other early works does not mean that Bergelson became a Bolshevik ideologue in 1926. Nonetheless, there is a shift that can be traced in the temporal patterns of his revolutionary texts—revolutionary both aesthetically and thematically. The protagonists of "Among Refugees," "Birth," and "Two Murderers" fail to act. Their failure corresponds to a philosophy of judgment deferred. In these stories the action of the plot slows down. In contrast, *Judgment* picks up the pace. The rhythm of the plot, the details of the description, the structure of the grammatical sentence, and the execution of the legal sentence speed up. Bergelson's philosophy of justice seems to have changed. Unlike the other Berlin work on justice, discussed in chapter 6, *Judgment* allows for no delay: penal sentences are executed immediately.

In *Judgment* and the other narratives of revolution and the civil war to be discussed in the pages that follow, including "Gusts of Wind" ("*Tsug-vintn*," 1922) and "Civil War" ("*Birger-krig*," 1927), the violent political upheaval of 1917 fundamentally changes experience. Characters experience the world as strange not primarily because of their routinized response, and hence lack of attention to it, but mainly because the world created by the Bolshevik revolution is new and strange, lacking its familiar markers and signs. Defamiliarization is no mere device artfully contrived so that depending on contingent circumstances, individual characters may experience the familiar as strange. Rather, the revolution has made the world strange for everyone.

The process of intensified defamiliarization and fragmentation in "Gusts of Wind," "Civil War," and *Judgment* also contaminates the revolution itself. Bergelson makes the word "revolution" and the event of the revolution a problem. To anticipate the argument, Bergelson's revolutionary text is ultimately unstable, its meaning postponed. The temporality of waiting is as important in the post-1926 fiction as anything he wrote earlier. The 1926 shift toward the Soviet Union is thus more tentative and precarious than otherwise might be assumed. Bergelson's supposed literary pledge of allegiance to the new Bolshevik order is lined with uncertainty, more Kafka than Lenin. I begin with Bergelson's letters and nonfiction and then turn to the experimentation with time and space in his fiction about the revolution and civil war. Reopening the question of political theology sets the stage for an examination of the enigmas of *Judgment*.[9]

1926: Looking Back, Looking Forward

Bergelson's 1926 letter expressed regret for the mistakes he had made in attacking the Evsektsiia (the Jewish section of the Communist Party) in articles he had written in 1923.[10] He had lambasted these Jewish activists, comparing their "struggles" against Yom Kippur, circumcision, and Elijah the prophet to the work of the nineteenth-century *maskilim* (reformers); the writers in control of *Der emes* had come late to the revolution and were merely playing at it; they were completely cut off from the masses. All of this was in 1923.[11] In 1926 Bergelson explained that he could not realistically contemplate returning to the Soviet Union, because his previous misunderstanding made good relations with his fellow Soviet writers difficult and spoiled relations would depress him. Mood is a consistent theme throughout Bergelson's writing; personal animosity and resentment dominate the relationships between the characters in *Judgment* as well. The letter ends enigmatically with the half-serious mention of the Jewish practice of wandering as a form of penance (*oprikhtn goles*). Bergelson said that his penance, his exile, was because of his misunderstanding of the difficult position of Evsektsiia in the early 1920s.[12] The editors of *Der emes* took Bergelson's language literally: the author was not in exile; he had left Russia of his own will. The letter is hardly a ringing endorsement of the Soviet Union or Jewish literary life in Moscow; the apology for past errors is lukewarm, and the reason for postponing his return (he would be depressed) is pathetic. The letter was published in the newspaper, even though this was not Bergelson's intention.[13]

Other correspondence reveals a more serious interest in the new world being created in the new Russia. In another letter written in 1926, Bergelson tries to persuade his friend Nakhmen Mayzel to write for his new journal *In Harness*. He wants to attract "the best writers, who feel responsible to the time in which we live" (*velkhe filn af zikh di farantvortlikhkeyt far dem tsayt, in velkher mir lebn*). In the 1926 story "Among Refugees," the responsibility is to the past and to people, the murdered victims of the pogroms; in the 1926 letter, in contrast, the emphasis is on the future, the "new Jewish reality" being constructed in post-revolutionary Russia. History is making demands on Bergelson, and his new journal would train the next generation of Yiddish writers struggling for the new reality.[14] Acting responsibly for the sake of the future requires attunement to it. Bergelson says he wants to set the right mood or atmosphere (*shtimung*) for his new journal; thus in 1926 he calls upon the same concept that he had used in 1910.

Bergelson visited Moscow for an extended period in 1926 as a correspondent for *Frayheyt*. His article compares the city he left in 1921 with the new Moscow of 1926.[15] In 1921 "the world of chaos" had overtaken Moscow. The term *oylem-hatoye* refers to the universe before creation and also means a kind of purgatory, a way station in which atonement is made for prior sins; Bergelson hints at this meaning in his reference to the bourgeoisie deprived of their livelihood. His comparison of Moscow 1921 with the remote past can be contextualized in light of other authors working at the same time who used similar tropes of the archaic and the primitive to describe what was utterly new.[16]

In contrast, the "world clock" that hangs over Moscow 1926 is modern: "reliable, precise, its solid steel hands turn from ten to eleven and from eleven to twelve indicating the time of tomorrow and the day after—the time of the future."[17] The focus on the future eliminates the present; there is no timepiece that indicates "now." Instead of ghosts from the past, Bergelson finds "joyful youngsters" in 1926 Moscow, a city that "heals by making people younger."[18] His depiction of Moscow as the city of the future is consistent with the emerging templates of what was to become socialist realism.[19] Socialist realism did not become an officially promulgated aesthetic until 1932; Bergelson's essay is from 1926. He was, like the city he described, ahead of his time.

Bergelson observes that the people around him are so interested in the new construction that they stop on their way to work in the morning to watch its progress, and even though they look as if they will never forgive themselves for arriving late at work, they will commit the same sin on the following day, which will set in motion the same cycle of delay and regret. It is ironic that the love Muscovites feel for their future compels them to fall behind. The same components of anticipation, delay, and regret dog the lives of Bergelson's shtetl characters, who are perpetually late. The doomed engagement between Velvl Burnes and Mirl Hurvits drags on for four years before it finally ends; even though Meylekh's funeral is late in the afternoon, his friend Khaym-Moyshe arrives too late for it. The condition of being late and left behind is the distinctive feature of Bergelson's characters, even when they turn out to be inhabitants of Moscow, the city of the future. Bergelson takes the shtetl with him to the new capital, thus setting in motion a paradoxical relation between futurity and the past. On the way to the future, Muscovites are late: Will they ever arrive?

Even though Bergelson describes Moscow time as "time forward," it is nonetheless not free from the past. He writes euphemistically about shadows in Moscow, "shadows connected to the hardships that arise from not being afraid to start history over again, if necessary."[20] The gangs of children begging on the streets for a puff of his cigarette represent just one of the aftereffects of the violence and dislocation that came from resetting the clock in 1917. The revolution may not be the decisive, once-and-for-all event that changes time forever. There may well be another revolution and another "world of chaos."

The tension between progress and the past, creativity and destruction is also apparent in "Three Centers" (*"Dray tsentren"*), another programmatic essay from 1926. While Moscow is to be the center of the next phase of Yiddish literature, in the Soviet Union the "new Jewish artist" would witness terrible "destruction" (*khurbn*) around him, unavoidable destruction crying to the heavens—"the full severity of the law, the rod of social justice" (*mides-hadin, rut fun sotsialier gerekhtikeyt*).[21] This is not the destruction caused by World War I or the pogroms of the Russian civil war; this devastation is the result of Bolshevik economic restructuring and Bolshevik justice. By 1919, the Cheka (All-Russian Extraordinary Commission for Struggle with Counter-Revolution and Sabotage) had replaced the short-lived "revolutionary tribunals" formed immediately after the revolution. In 1918, the Cheka had been given the power to shoot criminals on the spot; by 1919, its purview expanded to include economic crimes, including the withholding of goods from government appropriation and all forms of economic activity not explicitly sanctioned, the term for which was "profiteering." In 1918, the Cheka shot 5,381 people.[22] Internment in concentration camps—the fate of one of the characters in Bergelson's *Judgment*—was a lesser punishment, although it extended to entire families.[23]

The new Bolshevik system accorded legal rights and material sustenance, shelter, health care, and other benefits only to workers; hence high numbers of Jews, who were primarily traders and brokers, fell into the category of the disenfranchised (the *lishentsy*).[24] In "Three Centers" Bergelson does not directly name Jews as the victims of economic and social restructuring, but in another version of the same material, published in the New York Yiddish *Frayheyt*, he refers to "the Jewish masses," who "have been thrust out of their economic positions because of the new life."[25] Economic conflict between the shtetl and the new Bolshevik government is as important to *Judgment* as political opposition. Filipov tells the Jews that if they don't find other ways to make a living, he will burn their shtetl to the ground.

Bergelson had hinted vaguely at the need for large-scale Jewish "penance" almost a decade earlier. In a letter from January 1917 to Shmuel Niger, he remarked that the Jewish people were characterized by both "beauty" and "ugliness," repeating Buber's argument about a fundamental Jewish duality. Bergelson went on to say mysteriously that the Jews would have to undergo some sort of "purification" and penance after the war, but he wondered who would have the strength to compel them to do so.[26] It may be that in 1926, he had decided that Jewish purification would come at the hands of the Bolsheviks, many of whom were, of course, Jews. As one of the characters puts it in *Judgment*, "Jews fleecing Jews."[27]

In the 1926 essay, Bergelson promised that renewal would follow the time of woe but would come very slowly. In using the language of severity, Bergelson also indulges in a bit of self-advertising. He had already depicted life under the "full severity of the law" (*mides-hadin*) in his novel of the same name (*Mides-hadin*, or *Judgment*), the first few chapters of which appeared in *In Harness*.

Making the World Strange

In Bergelson's milieu, artists working in various media employed deliberately opaque texts and images, including found material. The hieroglyph had broad currency in the 1920s. According to Shachar Pinsker, Hebrew and Yiddish writers in Berlin, including Bergelson, encountered the city as a hieroglyph-like surface to be deciphered.[28] For Siegfried Kracauer hieroglyphs were visible codes, part of the built environment but inaccessible to consciousness.[29] Sergei Eisenstein interpreted the hieroglyph as a form of montage. Its distinct elements resemble cinematic shots; the perception first of their separateness and then "collision" leads to the apprehension of the hieroglyph's meaning.[30] In his 2015 book *Mashiny zashumevshego vremeni*, Ilya Kukulin develops the notion of montage beyond film to embrace literary works. He argues that fragmentariness, a shifting narrative perspective, defamiliarization, parataxis (verblessness), the uncanny, and the introduction of heterogeneous materials (documents, newspaper articles, reports, and letters) create a literary effect similar to cinematic montage.[31] In addition to Eisenstein, Lev Kuleshov, and Dziga Vertov, a broad range of writers and groups, including James Joyce, Vladimir Mayakovsky, the Kultur-Lige, the German writer Alfred Döblin, and the Yiddish author Moshe Kulbak and other Yiddish writers in Berlin variously used montage in their works, according to Kukulin. Bergelson's revolutionary texts—"Currents," "Civil War," and *Judgment*—may be added to the list. In contrast to Eisenstein, Bergelson's textual montage does not direct his readers' consciousness to a unitary understanding of the world. The various disparate elements of the text instead destabilize conclusions about the meanings of the events the text describes.

The primary categories of experience, including time and space, are destabilized. In "Civil War" the country has had no tsar or gentry for seven months. In "Gusts of Wind" it is the beginning of 1918. The Bolsheviks have just fled Kiev, and the Germans have also left; as Bergelson says in a letter, during these "bloody days" there was no strong central power in Ukraine.[32] Naming the date only underscores the larger chaos. Bergelson measures the revolution's impact as a sea change in his protagonists' phenomenological experience, not in their beliefs. He thereby also creates a similar effect in his readers. Dislocation and disorientation are features of the world and the product of deliberate strategies of the text.

"Gusts of Wind" and "Civil War" share a pair of non-Jewish Bolshevik characters, Botchko and Zik. Bergelson published a few chapters from the latter work in 1922, the same year "Gusts of Wind" first appeared; the two chapters were titled "Fragments of a Novel." As in the earlier fiction, the emphasis in both works is less on plot than atmosphere; here it is mute horror. "Gusts of Wind" opens with the "sin" (using the Hebrew term *eveyre*) committed by Botchko and Zik's associate Andryuk, who kills a Jew and steals his horse and wagon. The use of the Hebrew term by a non-Jewish character adds to the disorienting experience of reading the text. It ends with the rape of a gentry woman; Botchko arrives at the scene to prevent further violence and looting. In "Civil War" Botchko and Zik continue to wander the countryside; in a flashback readers learn that Botchko was chosen leader of his regiment after it rebelled against its tsarist commander; he is in love with a Christian wet nurse who worked for a Jewish family, but instead of going north to see her again, he goes south and never sees her again. Eventually Botchko and Zik unite with another Bolshevik, a Jew named Leyzerke, in a small shtetl beleaguered by Ukrainian gangs bent on anti-Jewish violence. Rape and looting have already taken place. The last line of the novel, far from a proclamation about revolutionary solidarity, is Leyzerke's expression of hate for another Jew.

Bergelson's depiction of offstage violence relies on metonymy, defamiliarization, and emotional displacement, comparable to "Two Murderers." The two gentry women alone in their manor house in "Gusts of Wind" express delight at the news that Petliura's men are killing Jews. Yet they are also victims. Andryuk and Zik enter their house and take everything of value; Andryuk rapes one of them. The description suggests that it is not people who do these things but rather disparate parts of their bodies acting independently. In the beginning of the scene, a hand turns the handle of the door; a "stony hard" forehead, not eyes, stares at the woman; a shoulder pushes her aside. Bergelson uses metonymy elsewhere. In "The Hole Through Which Life Slips," for example, the laughing crowd fails to register that the weeping features of a woman's face express the grief and outrage of the woman weeping. They see the parts but fail to grasp the whole. Here naming the part for the whole intensifies the overall effect of fragmentariness and thus violence: performing acts of violence violently dismembers the body performing the acts, severing it from consciousness.

The aftermath is as follows: "In the quiet darkness as if anew the wall clock struck, slowly measuring out the nocturnal moments of the old violated house. It accompanied the woman's crying, the nagging, unending whimpering that came from some distant room: tick-tock, tick-tock."[33]

The victim's protest is repetitious and bothersome, making it difficult to feel pity for her. Readers experience the acoustical texture of the crying and the ticking of the clock but not emotion for the victim. Clock time, however, cannot adequately measure what has happened. Everything else is left unsaid.

As the protagonists wander the countryside in "Civil War," they cannot determine who is an enemy and who is a friend. Hieroglyphs abound, and like the book's characters, readers must decode their meaning. Botchko and Zik flee from a seeming enemy who turns out to be their own comrade decked out to look like a Ukrainian soldier. They stumble across a corpse in a ditch and can't tell whether it's a horse or a human being. The corpse is "abandoned" (*hefker*) just like the corpse in "The Beginning of December 1919," but something else has also been lost. The distinction between animal and human, a basic category of knowledge, no longer obtains. Labels do not serve their purpose. Place names have been "blotted out" (*zenen geven opgemekt di shildn*), and as Botchko and Zik tried to "decipher what was defaced, it seemed to say, 'There are no more place-names here or people, either.'"[34]

The earth gives birth to strange new "creatures" (*bruim*). One of Botchko and Zik's associates, Porets, kicks at an abandoned dugout, and out spring eight Chinese soldiers; they've been holed up for seven days, feeding on a dead horse, and are covered in a sticky, greasy film. They resemble the hands of an old Jewish woman who's been cleaning chickens. Bergelson juxtaposes the familiar image from daily life with the bizarre image of the unfamiliar Chinese men. Their unnatural rebirth takes place in a world dominated by unnatural, premature death. Botchko and Zik encounter other traces of violence: blood and ink spattered on the walls of an abandoned gentry house. The ink is from a clandestine Bolshevik printing press, and the blood is from raped women. The post-revolutionary "God-forsaken" (*hefker*) landscape is littered with indecipherable remnants of terrible violence.

The cognitive disarray in Bergelson's prewar fiction is the result of a routinized response to the world, a constriction of the ebb and flow of life that leads to sensory motor misfire. These failures, however, also indicate the possibility of a creative recuperation of a new, more fluid relation to ongoing change. Bergelson also uses defamiliarization to indicate broader changes in Jewish life and the world beyond it. Botchko and Zik in "Civil War" are not the first Bergelson characters faced with the necessity of deciphering clues. In *Descent* Khaym-Moyshe, in a strange, dreamy state, finds himself transported to an unfamiliar city, where he enters a house that has just been abandoned by its inhabitants; he notices "signs" (*remozim*) of people. He collects bits of tangible evidence (including a note, a fragment of whalebone, and a small box), but fails to assemble them into a coherent account of Meylekh's death. In this instance, the moments of strangeness are isolated and particular to the individuals who experience them.

In contrast, in "Gusts of Wind," "Civil War," and *Judgment* the world is strange for everyone; its strangeness extends to the basic categories of experience and history as well. Shklovsky's phrase "the world is montaged" is particularly apt, because time and space have broken apart into discrete episodes, moments, and scenes that conflict and collide with one another without yielding a meaningful whole. Time loses the continuity of accumulating change. Porets, one of the characters in "Currents," has no short-term memory. As soon as he goes to sleep, "yesterday's Porets dies . . . the Porets of today is newborn" (*der hayntiker Porets iz nay-geboyrn*).[35] Porets lives in a perpetual now in which food, drink, sex, and killing are pleasures to be consumed without consequence. That his name means "landowner" suggests Bergelson's nod to socialist morality. Raping a woman and killing an enemy leave no mark on him. Time has no duration for Porets, because he lacks all sense of his own past. He resembles a mechanical device that switches on and off, living in a now that reappears again and again.

Bergelson uses Porets to imagine the radical flattening of time to the single plane of the present uninflected by the past. Botchko and Zik experience an equally radical shift in the quality of space. As they look for their comrades, they are "frightened by an unexpected valley and a sudden village" (*zikh geshrokn far an umgerekhtn tol un far a plutsimdik derfl*).[36] It is more typical to use "sudden" to refer to an action, even if the action is expressed with a noun; for example, "sudden rain" means the unexpected beginning of a downpour. Bergelson could have used a verb to say that the two men "suddenly saw a village" or that "a village suddenly appeared" but did not, and the choice is significant. Neither perception nor space is neutral or objective. Botchko and Zik are terrified of any encounter in which their identities as Bolsheviks could be revealed. Any space is potentially a space from which they will have to flee; hence they perceive space as having the capacity to be "sudden," because it is the source of their own sudden motion. One of the most powerful instances of Bergelson's temporalization of space occurs in his 1913 novel, *The End of Everything*. Mirl Hurvits moved out of her parents' house temporarily, and when she returned, "[s]omething, it seemed, was too late here, had already ended."[37] The space of Mirl's home was "too late" (*shpet*) and "had already ended" (*nokh alemen*)—just as in the example from "Gusts of Wind" in which the village and valley are too early, "sudden." In the 1913 novel time's otherness is confined to a specific place and a single character, but in the civil war fiction, time's otherness spreads out to include entire regions. It is "too late" in the "most expansive expanse" in "Civil War," because "the worst devastation had already occurred" (*dem vaytikdikn arumikn arum iz di greste eveyre shoyn opgetun gevorn*).[38] In "At the Depot," the surrounding space is steeped in the emotion of longing; the depot itself longs for salvation from some distant, unknown point. Here, in contrast, space has been the victim of the greatest possible "devastation" and "transgression" (the Hebrew term *eveyre* means both). This is an important instance of the absolute and total destruction of order and limit.

In *The Communist Manifesto*, Marx and Engels famously said that capitalism melts "all that is solid into air." Marshall Berman borrowed this phrase to encapsulate the experience of modernity as a whole.[39] Like other modernist writers, Bergelson unleashes objects and people from their stable moorings in already established lifeworlds. The release, even when destructive, is not wholly negative. Bergelson's imagination of the world beyond its given qualities of space and time is a way of reanimating the human relation to the world, bringing things, spaces, and human beings into a zone of maximal interaction. He had done so before 1917, as had other modernists, including, for example, the Russian Cubo-Futurist artist David Burliuk, who had proclaimed the new doctrine of "displacement" (*sdvig*) before World War I. There is continuity, in other words, between Bergelson's work before and after 1917. The Russian revolution made the aesthetic that Bergelson had developed earlier more radical, its scope all-encompassing.

Revolution as Hieroglyph

Of all the hieroglyphs of the civil war fiction, the revolution is the most important. In a difficult passage from "Civil War," Bergelson suggests the possibility that 1917 is only the precursor of another catastrophe: "Now slippery little crimes were taking place. They fell together with the sticky dripping rains of autumn, and everything was permitted in the innocent land, although something was brewing in its dirty folds: either an unprecedented crime was in the making there, or a good deed, the greatest ever."[40]

The minor crimes (*eveyres*) that continued unabated could refer to events recounted in "Civil War" and its related tale, "Gusts of Wind." The "unprecedented crime" that may yet take place is more difficult to parse. The revolution already occurred seven months earlier, as the narrator makes clear at the outset of the story. The monumental event that may yet take place could be another revolution. In his essay on Moscow, Bergelson talked about shadows that resulted from not being afraid to start history over. In "Civil War" he suggests the possibility that history could be restarted yet again. The greatest crime or the greatest good deed is yet to come. Again, Bergelson's imagination of the world puts us in a time zone after and before—and not face to face with—the decisive single moment, the revolution. The world is still waiting for transformative change. The temporality of the interval in between events strikingly contrasts with the once-and-for-all world-historical significance attributed to the revolution by its more committed adherents in 1917 and beyond.

Judgment

Set in 1920 during the civil war, *Judgment* tells the story of the non-Jewish Filipov, who presides over an outpost of the Cheka near the Polish border. Ill and unloved by most of his own men, he faces opposition from peasants, Ukrainian groups, well-organized Socialist Revolutionaries, and various Jewish and non-Jewish smugglers, "speculators," and spies. A former monastery functions as the prison, interrogation center, and place of execution where Filipov serves as the arbiter of "judgment" (*din*). Yuzi Spivak, arrested for his anti-Bolshevik activities on behalf of the local Socialist Revolutionaries, sits in his cell, waiting for death. Aaron Lemberger, a wealthy and smug tannery owner, celebrates his last Friday night in prison. Other characters include the elderly Dr. Babitsky, who wants to remain on the sidelines but cannot; Sofia Pokrovskaya, a leading Socialist Revolutionary and the seductive "blonde" with eyes "kosher as two crucifixes," a courier for the Whites. By the end, Spivak experiences a change of heart: he confesses that he is not a worker, and his life is spared. Filipov heroically sacrifices himself.

A few words about the historical context are in order. Bergelson's focus on Socialist Revolutionaries (SRs) well reflects the uncertainties of early Bolshevik rule. The Socialist Revolutionaries comprised the largest political party in 1917; in the early part of the twentieth century, they perpetrated numerous acts of terror against the tsarist government. The SRs were the leading opposition to the Bolsheviks, and a group of SRs were the defendants in the first show trial in Russia in 1922, accused of plotting against the Bolsheviks with the aid of foreign powers, among other charges. Their death sentences were commuted.[41] The ethnographer and author Sh. Ansky was an SR, as was Viktor Shklovsky. Both fled Russia in the early 1920s to avoid prosecution.

Economic tensions simmered just below the surface of the political conflict. The ban on private trade meant that the primary occupations of the shtetl became illegal. The economic collapse of the shtetl preoccupied statisticians and researchers on both the pro- and anti-Bolshevik sides. Jacob Lestchinsky, Bergelson's friend, published many articles and several books on this topic.[42] Although *Judgment* is not a realistic depiction of the economic collapse of the shtetl in the early 1920s, the fear and uncertainty expressed by the shtetl inhabitants in the novel reflect the ongoing economic hardship experienced by Jews at the time, "the cries of woe reaching to the heavens," as Bergelson said in "Three Centers."

Since its publication, most critics have viewed *Judgment* as Bergelson's literary oath of obedience to the Bolshevik order. In 1930 Isaac Nusinov wrote in the most important Russian-language literary encyclopedia of the time that the novel "proclaimed the justice of the fact that the revolution had to judge not by mercy, but according to the cruel deeds of the past, for only then could it fulfill its great historic tasks."[43] Nusinov rightly names the crucial terms of the debate—history, judgment, mercy, and justice—but formulates the relation between them incorrectly. Judgment without mercy is not justice, not in the religious tradition that Bergelson used as the source for his imagery, as I showed in chapter 6, and not in the world evoked by Bergelson's novel, as I show in this chapter. The entry for Bergelson in the influential *Lexicon of Modern Yiddish Literature* (*Leksikon fun der nayer yidisher literatur*), published in New York in 1956, also concludes that with *Judgment*, Bergelson "openly declared his recognition of the dictatorship of the proletariat."[44] The Soviet government, in contrast, was far more ambivalent about Bergelson's novel. The Russian-language translation of the novel, prepared by the theater critic Isaac Aronovich Kruti (1890–1955), was never published.[45] Although it was staged in October 1933 at the Moscow State Yiddish Theater, the libretto changed the plot significantly. More recent scholarship has seen *Judgment* in a more nuanced light, and my discussion contributes to the alternative view.[46]

In his 1919 essay "Art and Society," Bergelson praised revolutionary poetry for disrupting previous literary conventions by replacing the individual with a collective author, introducing harsh and unpoetic sounds, and celebrating violence as the source of creativity. *Judgment* comes the closest to fulfilling this literary mandate. Bergelson's play with language reaches an extreme, to the point where the connection between one word and another is lost. Shmuel Voltsis and his wife try to make sense of a conversation they overhear, but it is impossible: "A word would try to stand up on its own two feet, but then another word would arrive, and both collapsed in a heap."[47] This playful image of language as human bodies—clowns that tumble and fall, reminiscent of the clown acrobats in *Descent*—here underscores the constructedness of the text. Instead of immersing readers in the illusion of an ongoing reality, revolutionary art that "lays bare the device" requires that readers participate in the construction of a new, revolutionary reality.

In the context of the work as a whole, revealing the artifice of narrative exposes the failure of the revolution to lend coherent new meaning to the world. It is not only the words that collapse into a heap; the sounds that make up words suffer the same fate. This is especially striking when the word in question is "revolution." A severely deaf character speaks only the word "revolution," which he uses for all interactions with others. Bergelson emphasizes the physiological processes that go into the production of the all-purpose word:

> His mouth opened very wide, as if he were going to throw up all his innards, his intestines, heart, and lungs. Honking and snorting noises erupted out of him, a honk and a snort, one after the other, from somewhere in his neck, deep, deep in his throat. The honks and snorts now intermingled, now wrestled with each other deep in his throat, under his palette, and only a well-trained and familiar ear could make out the word:
> "Rrrrree . . . vv . . . vv . . . vo . . . o . . . o . . . lluu . . . shshsh . . . un!!!"[48]

Far from elevating the revolution into a transcendent and transformative event, this description lowers it to a mere physiological acoustical effect, with comic results. Bergelson subverts the meaning of the revolution as event by rendering the word "revolution" as a set of disconnected animal-istic sounds. In 1919, he had chronicled the process of literary creativity as self-mutilation: "The new poem has fired off a shot with its excess, it has opened all its veins, nerves, and cells, it drinks, vomits . . . and chokes on itself." In *Judgment* there is one all-important word that has the same result. Articulating the revolution is tantamount to self-evisceration. This episode reveals the larger pattern of the text as a whole. The revolution in art allows for more radical experimentation with language, musicality, and rhythm and brings more opportunities to use the material qualities of the text as a medium of creativity. The revolution in life, however, causes pain. The revo-lution in art and the revolution in life are impossibly intertwined.

Body Mechanics

In *Judgment* Bergelson transforms the idiom of Berlin experimental art and Russian constructivism into the strange new world created by the Bolshevik revolution. Supra-individual activity, collective consciousness, and mass phenomena are key to this transformation.[49] In "The Mass Ornament," Siegfried Kracauer interpreted popular entertainment of the 1920s as the intersection of capitalism and technology. For Kracauer the synchronized movements of the dance group "the Tiller Girls" represented "the aesthetic reflex of the rationality" of the capitalist system.[50] The calculation of the movements of factory workers and Tiller Girls relied on parts of the body, arms and legs, as the smallest possible unit. The result is a rational and aesthetically pleasing but nonetheless violent attack on the body's integ-rity. Kracauer would go on to critique the mass ornament as the figure of fascism.

What Kracauer criticized as the negative effect of capitalism on the human body and consciousness, Russian constructivism and biomechanics lauded as a means of producing a new human collectivity and a renewed relation to the surrounding world.[51] In the spirit of Marx and Bergson, the body and physiology could be used to change consciousness. In *Judg-ment*, Bergelson's technique resembles Russian constructivist literature, art, and theater. His syntax changes, producing a new rhythmic effect. He introduces an aesthetic of punctuated action that reflects the tempo of

the conveyor belt. His new literary technologies concretize his new imagination of the relation between the body, the machine, and collectivity.
Individuals appear as appendages of a mass subject, in some cases fused
with objects.

The new collective being moves to the new rhythm. Bergelson experiments with this basic pattern, spinning out various configurations, some
playful, some emotionally charged. In the opening of the novel, for example, Filipov's men sit in a room listening to the accordion one of them is
playing. Suddenly the music stops:

> A series of dull, hard thuds came from the wall. They sounded distant at first,
> as if they came from deep inside the earth. But the longer they continued, the
> more persistently they struck the wall and the more clearly everyone under-
> stood their origin. It was boss, who had fallen ill; he was signaling from his
> room that it was ten o'clock—time for Zubok, Igumenko, and Andreyev to get
> on their horses and head out towards the border.[52]

When the men finally ride out of the courtyard, they are described as "three
dots of the Hebrew vowel *segol*" (the vowel appears as three dots in a tri-
angle).[53] This sequence can be understood as action by remote control. It
is not Filipov who hammers the wall with his fist; it is rather the wall itself
that gives out blows, which substitute for a clock or an alarm. The result
of this remote trigger is the triangle-shaped formation of the three riders.
Each individual rider is merely a point in the figure.

The site of the prison provides opportunities for the exploration of
mass subjectivity. The sleeping prisoners in the general holding cell form a
single body with multiple arms and legs strewn here and there. One of the
prisoners walks stiffly, like a golem, the clay figure of Jewish legend. Bergelson animates the building and renders inanimate the crowd gathered at its
entrance: "From the long delay the peephole in the heavy gates yawned with
its mouth half-open. The gates opened lazily and then shut. They sleepily
grabbed the wife of an arrested man and ten minutes later spit her out back
into the courtyard to make room for another."[54]

The inanimate objects in the passage move, act, and take on human
qualities, including sleepiness and laziness, whereas the human beings
are passive objects moved from place to place not by their own agency.
The whole building is like a giant artificial human being (another golem)
with eyes (the peephole), a mouth (also the peephole), and limbs (the
gates). The functions of the eyes and mouth are deliberately confused:
the peephole, the eyes, open into a yawn, like a mouth. In contrast to the

somnambulant train station of his first published work, the prison building is awake.

Elsewhere in the text, a sewing machine reacts to sound as if it were a human being: "It seemed to hear something . . . but it didn't do anything about it, because it was nothing more than a machine" [ellipsis added]. Bergelson had imbued objects and machines with human capacities in earlier works. In "At the Depot," the lanterns answer Beynish, affirming that they have heard his cry; in "The Deaf Man," the bolting mill speaks with the voice of God. In the strange new world of Kamino-Balke, there is no answer, no response, and what is more, the text explicitly says so. Racing along in a cart driven by Filipov's men, on his way to Kamino-Balke to treat Filipov, Dr. Babitsky wants to call out to someone to help him. The men taking him won't respond; they have been replaced by their shoulders, which are like the bars of a cell. He realizes that "screaming would have been pointless, even foolish, it would not have helped at all."[55]

Bergelson pursues the logic of the alienated human body to more radical extremes in the story of a prisoner who removes his own rubber bridge with five gold teeth to send to his wife before he dies.[56] Turning one's own body into a source of valuable products is a form of self-commodification. Beynish Rubinshteyn lives off his capital, consuming his future, and Bergelson's "Hunger" artist fasts to make money. These figures use themselves up in the most literal sense. The principle of the alienation of one's own labor is extended to grotesque conclusions. For the post-1945 reader, the episode of the gold teeth, together with Shmuel Voltsis's interment in a concentration camp, horrifyingly suggests what is to come in the following decades.

Bergelson's favorite technology, the clock, plays a starring role in another episode involving a machine ensemble. Filipov's medical examination begins with a ticking sound:

> Tick-tock, tick-tock.
> In a dark corner of Filipov's room there was a cheap alarm clock.
> Its ticking was like cold drops dripping in the stillness. And the stillness was hard, like stone . . .
> It seemed that:
> The cheap alarm clock was counting out his last minutes [ellipsis added].[57]

The rhythm created by the sound of the ticking of the clock, *tik-tak* ("ticktock"), is transformed into *tropns tripn* (drops dripping); as the scene continues, the same language about the ticking clock is repeated twice more.

The cold drops dripping become the "cold fingertips" of the doctor as he feels his patient's pulse, an internal bodily rhythm.

Bergelson adds yet another rhythm to the scene as the doctor feels the swellings on the sick man's neck. It seems to the doctor that the patient says, *"Tapst mikh . . . tapst mikh . . . mikh hot men shoyn genug arumgetapt"* (Tap, tap me, you've tapped me out). In both the Yiddish original and the translation, "tap" repeats three times in one line. The tapping rhythm is so overpowering that even when Filipov interrupts the exam by sitting up in bed, the doctor's fingers continue to palpate where his neck had been: "And the doctor's tapping fingers remained hanging in the air, dancing their foolish dance."[58]

What interests Bergelson is the acoustical choreography of the ticking clock and the doctor's dancing fingers—the rhythm created by mechanical repetition and repetitive human action. The French philosopher Bergson defined the comedic as something mechanical superimposed on life. Others interpreted mechanical repetition in more positive terms. One of the most vivid example is the eating machine in Charlie Chaplin's 1921 *Modern Times*. Chaplin, trussed up in a device that mechanically sends food to his mouth, looks both comical and dismayed. Chaplin was extraordinarily well known and widely commented on in the Americas, Europe, Russia, and the Yiddish-speaking world. Marc Chagall's 1929 pen and ink drawing of Chaplin includes the comic actor's bowler hat and cane but also represents Chaplin's feet as chicken legs, suggesting the famous scene from *Gold Rush* in which a starving fellow miner imagines Charlie as a chicken ready to be slaughtered and cooked.[59] Daniel Charney, Bergelson's close associate and friend and a member of the editorial group of *In Harness*, wrote a critical article about the Moscow State Yiddish Theater that strikingly names Chaplin as the image par excellence of "modern times."[60] In the film, Chaplin, a factory worker, steps away from the conveyor belt, but his body continues to perform the same jerky movements as if he were still at the line. For Charney, the automated human body fulfills the new social and political order. The new way of life in Russia is creating the "mass-person," who is both "jerky (*tsapldik*) like Chaplin and cinematographic."[61] The new art and the new society break down the natural flow of human movement into its component parts, recreating them as if they were frames of film, reorganizing them, and thus producing a new form of human collective life. Life itself is like the work of art in the age of mechanical reproduction. The assimilation of the body into the machine was part of the bright socialist future already being enacted in theater, film, and real life.

Bergelson's use of parataxis and weak verbs (for example, "it seemed") and his reliance on the colon as a preferred form of punctuation help create the effect of "jerky" (*tsapldik*) motion. In the bedside scene I discussed earlier, instead of saying that Filipov looks like this or that, the narrator omits the verb entirely, replacing it with a noun and the colon: "Filipov's appearance: [this or that]." A similar pattern occurs whenever there is a description of people, places, or atmosphere. The overall effect can be compared to a series of quick shots in film. The reader is confronted with "this instant" and then "the next instant" without knowing the connective tissue between the instants. The experience of reading *Judgment* can thus be compared to the experience of viewing cinematic montage.

In the opening of chapter 13, Pinke Vayl carries a report back to Kamino-Balke from the distant villages at the border, where insurgents are gathering:

> The day—frozen, slippery-muddy, eyes half closed, as if about to sneeze.
> The road—a five-hour sleepy predawn wakeup one.
> Der tog—a farkaterter, a glitshik-koytiker, a farzhshmureter, vi af a nis tsu gebn.
> Der veg—a fartogik-nishtdershlofener, a finf-shoendiker.[62]

I have preserved as much of the original syntax as possible in the translation. Bergelson attributes qualities belonging to time to space and vice versa; the road was icy, but Bergelson shifts this quality to the description of the interval of time, the day, which was "slippery." Verbs that would normally describe the motion of the human actor are omitted, replaced by adjectives and other modifiers that apply to the space and time in which the action is performed; instead of "Pinke had to get up before dawn," it is the road that is "predawn," the day that is on the verge of sneezing. The dash replaces the missing connective tissue of the sentence. The use of punctuation and the verbless intensified metonymy adds to the staccato rhythm or jerky quality. These features of the text create a supercharged description of the protagonist's action packed into highly condensed and discrete images that rupture the continuity of the narrative.[63]

The changing quality of time is a central feature of Bergelson's work in the 1920s. The clock accompanies an old Jew in Issacher-Ber Rybak's Cubist portrait, published in *Milgroym* in 1922. The clocks in the childhood home of the Jewish terrorist in "Among Refugees" take note of the unnaturally short lives of his family members; each one marks the anniversary of a death. In contrast, the clock that loudly ticks in the quiet apartment after

Moyshe Greyvis's children have gone out cannot know how the violence in Ukraine weighs on the old man; it merely indicates the next moment of time. The clock in Moscow in 1926 moves time more quickly. The clock in "Gusts of Wind" adds its rhythm to the weeping of the woman assaulted by Andryuk. The cheap alarm clock in Filipov's room drives the rhythm of the doctor's dancing fingers; the accelerated tempo and fragmentary style of *Judgment* point to the new pace of time: the rhythm of the revolution.

The Reason of History

The jerky, mechanical tempo of *Judgment* shows Bergelson's experimentation with the new forms of art he had described in his 1919 essay "Art and Society." Notwithstanding his revolutionary aesthetic, his take on revolutionary justice and the revolutionary philosophy of history is another matter. *Judgment* marks the birth of "a new world." The passage containing this key term is worth quoting at length:

> The walls of the monastery were cracked and dilapidated, like the walls of ruins—and yet everything seemed to be infinite, it seemed that there was no "end," but instead, a "beginning."
> The first fires that had been lit appeared there, ascending high in the sky, and they too were no simple, ordinary fires; they were the cold fires of judgment, fires over which "he"—Filipov, a worker from the mines—presided. They were the fires of some strange, new, harsher world [*fayern fun epes a modner nayer shtrenger velt*].[64]

In the era of the Russian revolution, rhetoric about the new world, and the new heaven and new earth—was on everyone's lips. [65] The new world was the creation of Lenin's revolution. In earlier epochs, voyages of discovery, as they were called, revealed marvelous new worlds. In Shakespeare's *Tempest*, Miranda, delighted to see a male figure for the first time, proclaims: "How beauteous mankind is! / O brave new world" (Act 5, Scene 1). Bergelson's "strange new world" is savage, rather than marvelous; it is the demonic realm of *din*: nightmarish, endless punishment.

In the novel and the reality it reflects, Filipov's power, and the dictatorship of the proletariat that he embodies has established itself on earth, sanctioned by nothing on earth except its need to establish itself as the new source and expression of authority. By deciding human fates, the revolution enacts and expresses its authority to decide human fates. A line from Babel's "Gedali" nicely sums up the circular logic: "'The Revolution cannot not shoot, Gedali,' I tell the old man, 'because it is the revolution.'"[66]

The dictates of revolutionary "judgment" (both in Bergelson's novel and the historical reality) overthrow juridical limits; its violence is akin to the divine violence Benjamin theorizes. At Kamino-Balke, the former monastery, Filipov is sovereign because he holds the power of life and death over the prisoners. As Dr. Babitsky says, Filipov is the "ambassador of history." The allegorical language about an "end" that is really a "beginning" and the "cold fires of judgment" (the phrase contains the title word, *mides-hadin*) clothe the Bolshevik regime in quasi-divine authority. The concept of "political theology" received fresh impetus in the 1920s with the writings of Carl Schmitt. Secular notions of the state, Schmitt argued, were derived from theology. The absolute power of the state to decide life and death beyond all juridical systems is what grants the state its sovereignty.[67] Bergelson's novel *Judgment*, however, puts these concepts to work to interrogate the meaning of the new Bolshevik regime—not to proclaim its justice or rectitude.

Language, specifically, the language of the deaf, offers another way to understand Bergelson's defamiliarization of ideology. Earlier I discussed the articulation of the word "revolution" as a self-inflicted wound. In another important scene, Bergelson returns to the device of deafness to further distance the revolution from the realm of ordinary life and its commonplace human understandings. Filipov makes a speech to the inhabitants of Golikhovke, warning them to give up their smuggling. A deaf old man asks what Filipov is saying; another answers, "He says he has the authority," and the Russian word for "authority" appears in the Yiddish text. The deaf man fails to understand and is told that Filipov has the authority from the revolution to turn everyone and everything in the shtetl to "ashes."[68] The new language of revolution is unnatural, not native to anyone; it proceeds from some other location and is articulated by some other speaker, not me. I cannot hear it; it cannot be addressed to me, because its violence is overwhelming.[69] The alien new language helps to create the strange new antiworld.

The revolution authorizes Filipov to destroy the shtetl and its inhabitants by burning everything to the ground. The motif of fire signifies the merciless "rectitude of the revolution." In "Gusts of Wind" Bergelson used the image of a strange fire in the woods. The fire disturbs Botchko and Zik because its unnatural brightness makes it seem both close and far away; the fire cannot be extinguished or approached, the "way to it, eternal." In *Judgment*, in contrast, the fire is simpler and closer; it is the punishment for sins committed against the revolution. Bergelson is clearly calling upon biblical, prophetic, and mystical texts in which divine punishment takes the form of fire that consumes human beings. The realm of the absolute and the unconditioned that was beyond reach in other Bergelson works is front and center here. It seems that Bolshevism incarnated the apocalyptic messianism that he avoided in works like "Among Immigrants" and "Birth." The absolute and inevitable laws of history have finally entered the actual workings of law in human history, but no one knows what this means. The hieroglyphic transformation of the world intensifies, especially in the space of the prison. A set of footsteps approaching could mean death; they turn out to mean transfer to another cell; a commotion in the courtyard could mean the collapse of Bolshevik power; the arrival of a new prisoner could mean salvation but does not. The world is illegible.

In "Civil War" and "Gusts of Wind," as I discussed earlier, the upheaval of the revolution destabilizes space and time. Geography undergoes yet another significant shift in *Judgment* as part of the mystical and religious apparatus of the new form of political power. Up, down, left, and right replace the points of the compass. Kamino-Balke, the local Cheka headquarters, is uphill from Golikhovke ("Sodom"); the corrupt shtetl overrun by smugglers and speculators is downhill. "Down" is associated with the demonic realm. Filipov has ascended in more than one sense; having worked underground in the mines, he now wields terrible power; his original name was Anastasyev, which means "resurrection." Filipov's appearance enhances his fearsome mystical significance: he is gigantic; he suffers from some disease resulting from his time in the mines—something terrifying that a strange futuristic "radiotherapy" would cure. When he speaks, which is rare, his voice is hoarse, and his tag line is in Russian with harsh, grating sounds: "*Chto vy, shutite?*" (What, are you joking?). There is no need for him to make an actual appearance in order to strike terror into others. Kamino-Balke, the realm over which Filipov presides, has an Escher-like surreal topography: prisoners appear from the depths below, dragging straw beds as if they were encased in sacks.

Filipov, the arbiter of *din*, judgment, is associated with the left side, and not only politically. Angry with soldiers who won't obey his orders, he has trouble mastering his emotion. The Yiddish original creates an inner spiritual topography that is difficult to translate into English: "Inwardly his anger turned right and left, and there his iron drop—that came from the revolution—emerged. It hardened and supported him . . . always, in all his difficult moments, prompting him to do what was necessary and just" [ellipsis in original].[70]

It is significant that Filipov's iron "drop" comes from his left side. When, near the end of the novel, Filipov decides to ride to the forest where the enemy is hiding, he turns left near the stables. Later, for no reason other than "spite," "he turned left, towards the forest" where he knows he will be ambushed and killed. Filipov is explicitly associated with the principle of *din*, the emanation that in the kabbalistic tradition is found on the left side; Filipov's left-sidedness adds to the political-theological symbolism of the novel, emphasizing the evil of Bolshevik justice.

Left-sidedness makes Filipov resemble Dr. Shteynberg and the would-be Jewish terrorist, both marked on the left side of the body (the terrorist dramatically so). Both these protagonists are vectors of judgment who fail to pull the trigger. The punishment that they would inflict on wrongdoers is postponed. In "Birth" and "Among Refugees" Bergelson explores the possibilities left open by delaying the execution of judgment, thus providing a parallel with Gershom Scholem's argument that the postponement of judgment is akin to divine justice. More time corresponds to an impossible divine forgiveness, because it confers the gift of life even in the absence of repentance. The world does not end. As Bergelson's narrator remarks in "At Night," it is good that Noah found favor in God's eyes. God postpones judgment; Filipov, in contrast, orders his judgments to be executed in the here and now. This is the opposite of divine justice. Unlike nearly every other Bergelson protagonist, he does not hesitate. Lemberger, guilty of withholding products from government appropriation, is shot. The "blonde" is shot for espionage, together with Sofia Pokrovskaya, guilty of counterrevolutionary activity on behalf of the Socialist Revolutionaries; Shmuel Voltsis, who harbored the blonde, is sent to a concentration camp.

In *Judgment*, Bergelson seemingly abandons his philosophy of delayed execution. In the months before the October Revolution, Lenin started writing about the "fast tempo" of history, the need to end "the most painful thing on earth, vacillation," and the way that the war had "accelerated" the revolution.[71] It is as if, like Lenin, Bergelson had grown impatient, was sick of waiting and vacillation, and was hurrying to bring the next stage of world history to fruition. Several passages in the novel explicitly state that mercy and pity, even for oneself, were no longer to be found in the world.[72] As Dr. Babitsky notes, however, Filipov has no regard, let alone mercy, even for himself. Bergelson emphasizes the point that the Bolshevik revolution made mercy irrelevant. The religious sources from which Bergelson derives the dominant metaphors of his novel associate judgment (*din*) with evil and the realm of the demonic. In the mystical and religious corpus that provides the text's mystical topography, judgment alone is inadequate. Punishment in and of itself does not usher in the messianic age. Executing judgment (*din*) does not restore the proper balance to a world lacking limits and order (the other sense of *din*), or to put it another way, the world riven by sin and devastation (*eveyres*)—the world of "Two Murderers," "Among Immigrants," and "Gusts of Wind"—is not made right by the imposition of the harsh decree. The left is to be contained by the right; mercy must accompany judgment.

Filipov, the embodiment of judgment, has no human interests outside the revolution. His single-minded focus is not necessarily positive. In 1925, a year before he began publishing the first parts of *Judgment*, Bergelson wrote a lighthearted essay about his encounter with the Cheka during the "difficult, merciless years of the Russian revolution" (the subtitle of the article). The author describes his frustrating attempt to travel from a small town back to Kiev. The town, which Bergelson does not name, is in all likelihood Haysyn (Gaisin), where the author had traveled with his pregnant wife to get her out of harm's way. The worst obstacle during the author's return journey was not the persistent gunfire but the burgeoning bureaucracy of the new regime. Without a pass from the Soviet authorities from his point of origin, he could not make the onward journey from a town midway to his destination. He got turned back to his starting point. Things took a turn for the worse when a suspiciously young and hungry-looking "fourth regiment" appeared in the town, even though Bergelson finally received the necessary papers from its commander. At his next stop, instead of receiving permission to travel on, the Cheka arrested him. The stamp on his documents was counterfeit. Bergelson describes the man in charge as someone who was clearly incapable of smiling, "harsh and merciless," the kind of person who believes he is the most "decent, upright, and incorruptible" man in the world and therefore is incapable of listening to anyone else, because he suspects everyone of lying. This is an embryonic portrait of Filipov.

In *Judgment* Filipov is incapable of leading others. Even though the other characters fear him, they do not share his beliefs, and they continue to live their lives full of ordinary passions, interests, and conflicts. Comrade Sasha, for example, who holds a high rank and was responsible for bringing Filipov to Kamino Balke, is in love with him, sends for a doctor against his wishes, and near the end of the novel celebrates her birthday, attaching as much significance to this occasion as if there were no revolution and no conflict with counterrevolutionaries. Shmuel Voltsis bickers with his wife in the same manner as he always had in the past. Igumenko and Filipov had never got on well, and at the climactic end of the work, when insurgents are massing in a nearby wood, Igumenko flatly refuses to obey Filipov's orders, accusing him of reserving the cushier tasks for himself. Pinke Vayl falls in love. Love and hate, resentment, spite, animosity, jealousy, and rivalry—not ideology—dominate the lives of these ordinary people, regardless of the new regime. The strange new world resembles the old familiar shtetl. There is no single and all-at-once change from wrong to right, from transgression, injustice, crime, and sin to rectitude, justice, order, and reconciliation in *Judgment*.

This failure appears in the novel's temporal patterns. The machine-like tempo of the text, corresponding to the inexorable march of history, is but one dimension of its temporal structure. Other, slower time zones persist, and these alternative moments, which reflect both the Jewish past and Bergelson's literary past, disrupt the tempo of the revolution. Mirl Hurvits expresses her despair with the realization that her life will consist only of workdays without festive time. Dr. Babitsky comes to a similar conclusion about the revolution. Bergelson uses the same traditional Jewish alternation between workdays and holidays to describe Dr. Babitsky's attitude toward the revolution: when others woke up, he would go to sleep "to spite the cruel waking hours of the revolution"; he had taught his ward the word "revolution" during its first "festive weeks."[73] The Yiddish preserves the distinction between the week (*vokh*) and the holiday (*yontev*). The revolution has already taken place, yet the festive time is already over and the festive time for all humanity has yet to begin. The note that Bergelson sounds here resonates with Babel's Gedali, who wants the revolution of "happiness" and the "sweet revolution."

The notion of festive time is not limited to the decrepit old doctor. Memory, and specifically memory of the Jewish world and its festive time, is important for other characters as well, and because the perspectives of Bergelson's characters infuse his narratives, these memories bring a halt to the new temporal and political regime. Even though in "Three Centers" Bergelson writes about the "colorfulness of the newly flourishing Jewish life" in the Soviet Union, in *Judgment* the gray world is the revolutionary present, while all color is reserved for the past. The shtetl may well be a "Sodom" in need of purification, but it is nonetheless a source of beauty. After his first, much-delayed interrogation, when Filipov asks Yuzi whether he is truly a "worker" (*rabochii*, in Russian), Yuzi is returned to the cells and searches his memory for how to answer the question; without meaning to, he "suddenly searches too deeply in his previous, past years" and recalls himself as a child on Rosh Hashanah, playing on the steps of the synagogue while his grandfather chanted prayers, and how his grandfather's loud exclamation at one point startled his brother. The memory is so vivid that "the border of the white holiday tablecloth actually sparkled in his eyes and the fragrance of watermelon from that distant Rosh Hashanah morning tickled his nose."[74]

Yuzi experiences this deeply embodied memory as he waits for death. Others wait, but only Yuzi remembers. Time is different for him: it opens up to encompass the past. In another scene of memory, the end of the day comes very, very slowly, "as if somewhere far from the barred window of his cell one and the same sun was taking days to set."[75] Just as in earlier work, the physical laws of the universe suspend their normal operation in *Judgment*. In this strange condition, the thought occurs to Yuzi "that his death had begun with his life, and not only his own life, but also with the lives of the generations before him."[76] He recalls these prior generations: his fiery grandfather, whose income was derived from his lawsuits against a nobleman; his mother, who uncharacteristically for a woman of her time "knew Hebrew"; and his father, who read Torah in a "velvet voice." What is so striking about these memories is that they are not Yuzi's own. The use of free indirect discourse plays a role in the creation of this effect. The narrator switches from Yuzi's perspective to his dead grandfather's. This shift in perspective appears in the use of personal pronouns; thus Yuzi's mother is referred to as his daughter and Yuzi's father as his daughter's husband. In creating the impression that Yuzi is remembering the memories of others, Bergelson makes it seem that the past is reaching forward to the present. This can be understood as a form of time travel in which the other time zone, the past, realizes itself in the images that the traveler sees. The very long sunset in the cell allows for the past to appear there.

Benjamin's concept of the suddenly emergent or dialectical image helps to explicate *Judgment*. Bergelson emphasizes the conflict between the economic life of the shtetl's past, consisting of "speculation," smuggling, and the grandfather's lawsuits, and Soviet productivization taking place in the present; Filipov will raze the shtetl to the ground if the old forms of making a livelihood do not stop. Benjamin writes about the caesura (or pause) in the movement of thought where the dialectical opposition of the discarded past and the present is greatest. The moment of maximal tension is the one in which the image emerges. Yuzi's strange temporal shift back to his grandfather's life is such a moment. Its beauty appears precisely at the moment of its destruction; Bergelson places great emphasis on the horrifying capacity of the past to kill someone in the new Bolshevik present. This is not nostalgia or the desire to live in the past. In its flourishing the shtetl economy is oppressive, even disastrous. Mirl Hurvits agrees to an unwanted marriage to save her father from bankruptcy; the characters in "In a Backwoods Town" beat a man to death for attempting to undermine their monopoly. The dialectic means that beauty and destruction are inextricably linked; there cannot be one without the other. It is in fleeting moments of its afterhistory that the shtetl's beauty appears.[77]

After the End of History

The end of the novel amounts to yet another hieroglyph. Pinke Vayl despairs over the loss of Filipov, searching for ways to honor him in death. He wants to cover Filipov's office, where interrogations used to take place, with red banners, but there aren't enough: "whole swaths of wall remained white."[78] El Lissistzky's 1919 constructivist poster "With a Red Wedge Beat the Whites" also relies on the alternation of red and white shapes to issue its revolutionary call to action. The painter was one of the crucial figures, together with Bergelson, in the Kiev Kultur-Lige; both participated in the creation of avant-garde children's books. Like Bergelson, El Lissitzky spent the early twenties in Berlin, where he exhibited his work and together with Il'ia Ehrenburg founded the art journal *Veshch'*. The poster "With a Red Wedge" was so well known that it is unlikely that Bergelson was unaware of it.[79] Pinke Vayl's summons for more red banners to cover the white walls, the last line of the text, signals Bergelson's link to the revolutionary art and politics of his time, yet it hardly registers the definitive triumph of the workers' and peasants' state. The insurgents are still in the woods; the leader is dead; the borders are not secured. Even revolutionary inspiration is in short supply: there are big patches where the walls are not covered in red. The 1933 Russian-language playbill, including a synopsis of the plot, that accompanied the Moscow State Yiddish Theater performance of *Judgment* radically changed the ending: Filipov remains alive and in charge, and he permits Jews fleeing pogroms to take shelter at the Cheka headquarters. The text reads, "Not a single enemy of the workers' and peasants' state dares to breach the borders of the Soviet Union."[80]

In the novel, in contrast, a mournful note resounds beyond the ending. The revolution, whose festive time has not yet arrived, already has its afterhistory:

> In the deep darkness naked branches clattered. A hoarse cry of pain broke
> from the disheveled trees. The events hidden here in the nooks and crannies of

the countryside seemed to be rifling through their leaves. It sounded as if the rustling was causing someone pain . . . [ellipsis in original].[81]

This perspective belongs to no one and everyone alike; it is part of the *shtimung*, the atmosphere of the work as a whole. The scene in which it occurs begins with Dr. Babitsky, who calls Filipov the ambassador of history. As the aperture of the narrative camera widens and pulls back, however, the individual perspective becomes diffused and the trees and surrounding countryside begin to take part in the human experience; the landscape in *Judgment*, no less than the landscape in "At the Depot," feels not only sorrow but also pain. The events leaf through their own pages, like the wind blowing the leaves on the trees, and it causes someone pain. Sound play in the original Yiddish heightens the effect:

> In der tifer fintster hobn geklapt nakete tsveygn. Af ekste tseshoyberte beymer hot genogt a heyzerik vey-geshray, un gedakht hot zikh: dos bletern zikh di gesheenishn, vos lign oysbahaltn in di faldn fun der gegnt—zey bletern zikh, un es dakht zikh: es tut emetsn vey.[82]

The repetition of the "sh" sound in the words *tseshoyberte* (disheveled), *geshray* (cry), and *gesheenishn* (events) produce the sound of rustling. The "ey" sound in the word *vey* (pain) is broadcast throughout the passage, occurring in *tsveygn* (branches), *beymer* (trees), and *heyzerik* (hoarse); it is found (reduced but still present) in *gesheenishn* (events) and in the repetition of the word *vey* at the end of the passage (*es tut emetsn vey*). The passage compels readers to imitate the cries of suffering that it describes. Jacque Rancière fixes on the loss of individual subjectivity as the key moment of modernist texts: "the movement through which the artistic will loses itself in the impersonality of a milieu."[83] Bergelson is a master at depicting the milieu, but his depiction is deeply personal, full of the pain and loss that accompanies history's inexorable march forward.

Notes

1. David Bergelson, "Der gesheener oyfbrokh," *Milgroym* 1 (1922): 43.

2. Karl Marx, *Karl Marx: Selected Writings*, ed. David McLellan (Oxford: Oxford University Press, 1977), 172.

3. For a discussion of Bergelson's relationship with Abraham Cahan and for an overview of the former's work for the newspaper, see Ellen Kellman, "Uneasy Patronage: Bergelson's Years at Forverts (1922–1926)," in *David Bergelson: From Modernism to Socialist Realism*, ed. Joseph Sherman and Gennady Estraikh (Oxford: Legenda, 2007), 183–204.

4. According to a *Forverts* article from November 7, 1923, the violence was organized by the "leader of the Fascists in Germany"; the source was Bergelson's friend Jacob Lestchinsky. For a recent discussion, see David Clay Large, "Out with the Ostjuden: The Scheunenviertel Riots in Berlin, November 1923," in *Exclusionary Violence: Antisemitic Riots in Modern German History* (Ann Arbor: University of Michigan Press, 2002), 123–41.

5. Karl Marx, *Karl Marx: Selected Writings*, 233. The assumption that Marxist temporality is purely teleological is too simple.

6. As Sanford Kwinter puts it, "Everything that needed to be mastered—after all, capitalism needed a comprehensive system of global correlation, where time could be transformed into standardized units of value, units of value into goods, and goods back into time—could be mastered by spatialization and quantification." Sanford Kwinter, *Architectures of Time: Toward a Theory of the Event in Modernist Culture* (Cambridge, MA: MIT Press, 2001), 22. For more on space and time in Marx, see N. Castree, "The Spatio-Temporality of Capitalism," *Time and Society* 18, no. 1 (2009): 26–61. Some political movements, including anarcho-syndicalism, linked Bergson and Marx.

7. David Bergelson, *Judgment*, trans. Harriet Murav and Sasha Senderovich, Northwestern World Classics (Evanston, IL: Northwestern University Press, 2017), 65. For the Yiddish, David Bergelson, *Mides-hadin*, vol. 7, *Geklibene verk* (Vilnius: B. Kletskin, 1929), 83.

8. David Bergelson, "Arum vokzal," in *Geklibene verk*, vol. 1 (Vilnius: B. Kletskin, 1929), 57. Bergelson was not, however, the first Yiddish writer to critique the economic basis of traditional Jewish marriage. Mendele's *Fishke the Lame* provides a similar critique.

9. An earlier version of my discussion of appears as part of the introduction, cowritten with Sasha Senderovich, to the English translation of *Judgment* (Evanston, IL: Northwestern University Press, 2017).

10. For a study of the Jewish sections, see Zvi Gitelman, *Jewish Nationality and Soviet Politics: The Jewish Sections of the CPSU, 1917–1930* (Princeton, NJ: Princeton University Press, 1972).

11. David Bergelson, "Yidishe komunistn in rusland bashlisn, az es iz shoyn mer nito keyn yidn af der velt," *Forverts*, March 4, 1923, 12.

12. David Bergelson, "A briv fun Dovid Bergelson," *Der emes*, March 3, 1926, 3.

13. For a discussion and another interpretation of the 1926 shift, see Gennady Estraikh, *In Harness: Yiddish Writers' Romance with Communism*, Judaic Traditions in Literature, Music, and Art (Syracuse, NY: Syracuse University Press, 2005), 78–82.

14. YIVO 421, Box 1, Folder 6, Daniel Charney.

15. Olgin published Bergelson's article in *Frayheyt* on September 5, 1926. For a discussion of "Moskve" and the English translation, see Gennady Estraikh, "The Old and the New Together: David Bergelson's and Israel Joshua Singer's Portraits of Moscow Circa 1926–1927," *Prooftexts* 26 (2006): 53–78. For the Yiddish, see David Bergelson, "Moskve," *Frayheyt*, September 5, 1926.

16. For a discussion of this metaphor in the work of Boris Pilnyak, see Michael Kunichika, "'The Scythians Were Here . . .': On Nomadic Archaeology, Modernist Form, and Early Soviet Modernity," *Ab Imperio* 2 (2012): 229–255.

17. Estraikh, "The Old and the New Together," 63.

18. Estraikh, "The Old and the New Together," 65.

19. As Katerina Clark shows, although most socialist realist novels were not set in Moscow, the city, "as the capital of a highly centralized society, was to be an enhanced space, ahead of its time physically as the leaders were politically." Katerina Clark, "Socialist Realism

in Soviet Literature," in *Routledge Companion to Russian Literature*, ed. Neil Cornwell (London and New York: Taylor and Francis, 2001), 174–183.

20. For the English, see Bergelson, "Moscow," 67. The Yiddish: "Shotns, vos zaynen gebundn mit di shverikaytn fun nit moyre hobn ontsuhoybn di geshikhte, oyb men darf."

21. For the English, see David Bergelson, "Three Centres (Characteristics)," in *David Bergelson: From Modernism to Socialist Realism*, ed. Joseph Sherman and Gennady Estraikh (Oxford: Legenda, 2007), 347–354. For the Yiddish, "Dray tsentren," *In shpan* 1 (April 1926): 84–96.

22. Matthew Rendle, "Revolutionary Tribunals and the Origins of Terror in Early Soviet Russia," *Historical Research* 84, no. 226 (2011): 693–721. For a discussion of Bolshevik terror, see Vladimir Buldakov, *Krasnaia smuta: Priroda i posledstviia revoliutsionnogo nasilia* (Moscow: Rosspen, 1997). For a discussion of Bolshevik ideology in relation to Soviet violence, see Peter Holquist, *Making War, Forging Revolution: Russia's Continuum of Crisis, 1914–1921* (Cambridge, MA: Harvard University Press, 2002).

23. Golfo Alexopoulos, "Stalin and the Politics of Kinship: Practices of Collective Punishment, 1920s–1940s," *Comparative Studies in Society and History* 50, no. 1 (2008): 91–117.

24. See Golfo Alexopoulos, "Soviet Citizenship, More or Less: Rights, Emotions, and States of Civic Belonging," *Kritika* 7, no. 3 (2006): 487–528, doi:10.1353/kri.2006.0030. For a discussion of the disproportionate number of Jews in this category, see Golfo Alexopoulos, *Stalin's Outcasts: Aliens, Citizens, and the Soviet State, 1926–1936* (Ithaca, NY: Cornell University Press, 2003), 5, 57–58, 118.

25. David Bergelson, "Vi azoy vet oysen dos yidishn lebn in Rusland shpeter mit etlekhe yor," *Frayheyt*, May 29, 1926: 5.

26. YIVO RG360, Shmuel Niger, Box 7, Folder 9e, letter dated January 14, 1917.

27. Bergelson, *Judgment*, 53. The Yiddish: "M'banemt. Un ver "Yidn!? . . . Bay yidn!?." Bergelson, *Mides-hadin*, 7: 67.

28. Shachar Pinsker, "Deciphering the Hieroglyphics of the Metropolis: Literary Topographies of Berlin in Hebrew and Yiddish Modernism," in *Yiddish in Weimar Berlin*, ed. Gennady Estraikh and Mikhail Krutikov (Oxford: Legenda, 2010), 28–53.

29. Siegfried Kracauer, *The Mass Ornament: Weimar Essays* (Cambridge, MA: Harvard University Press, 1995), 29.

30. Sergei Eisenstein, *Eisenstein: Writings 1922–1934*, ed. Taylor, Richard (Bloomington: Indiana University Press, 1988), 164. For a discussion, see Judith Mayne, "Eisenstein, Vertov, and the Montage Principle," *Minnesota Review* 5 (Fall 1975): 116–24.

31. Il'ia Kukulin, *Mashiny zashumevshego vremeni* (Moscow: Novoe literaturnoe obozrenie, 2015), 20–169.

32. David Bergelson, March 20, 1922, RG 1139, Abraham Cahan, YIVO.

33. David Bergelson, "Tsugvintn," in *Geklibene verk*, vol. 8 (Vilna: B. Kletskin, 1930), 48. My translation.

34. For the Yiddish, see David Bergelson, "Birgerkrig," in *Geklibene verk*, vol. 5 (Vilna: B. Kletskin, 1930), 47. For the English, see David Bergelson, "Civil War," in *Ashes out of Hope: Fiction by Soviet-Yiddish Writers*, ed. Irving Howe and Eliezer Greenberg, trans. Seth Wolitz (New York: Schocken Books, 1977), 110. I have slightly modified the translation.

35. Ibid., 38.

36. Bergelson, "Birgerkrig," 12.

37. For the English, see David Bergelson, *The End of Everything*, trans. Joseph Sherman, New Yiddish Library (New Haven, CT: Yale University Press, 2009), 92–93. For the Yiddish, David Bergelson, *Nokh alemen*, vol. 2 (Vilnius: B. Kletskin, 1929), 119.

38. The English is Bergelson, "Civil War," 110. For the Yiddish, Bergelson, "Birgerkrig," 45. I have modified the translation.

39. Karl Marx, *Karl Marx: Selected Writings*, 224.

40. This could be an inversion of Joel 3:18 and Isaiah 45:8, which describe the mountains as dripping with righteousness. Seth Wolitz translates *eveyre* as "devastation" and not "sin," but "sin" makes more sense as the opposing term for *mitsve* in the last line. See Bergelson, "Civil War," 110–11. The Yiddish: "Itst geyen shoyn eveyres-pitselekh glitshik-klayne. Mit klepik dripindike Tishrey-regns dripn zey un dripn un alts iz muter in antshulndikn land, khotsh epes greyt zikh dokh banayes in zayne mide broyzndike kneytshn: an aveyre greyt zikh dortn, an umgeherte, tsi a mitsve a nisht gevezn groyse." The Yiddish is found in Bergelson, "Birgerkrig," 45.

41. I base my account on Scott Smith, *Captives of the Revolution: The Socialist Revolutionaries and the Bolshevik Dictatorship, 1918–1923* (Pittsburgh, PA: University of Pittsburgh Press, 2011).

42. For a discussion of the larger economic issues and the debate in the scholarship, see Deborah Yalen, "Red Kasrilevke: Ethnographies of Economic Transformation in the Soviet Shtetl 1917–1939" (PhD diss., University of California, Berkeley, 2007), 76–173.

43. Yitskhak Nusinov, "David Bergel'son," in *Literaturnaia entsiklopediia*, vol. 1 (Moscow: Izdatel'stvo kommunisticheskoi akademii, 1930), 455–56, http://feb-web.ru/feb/litenc/encyclop. For a discussion that sees Bergelson's *Judgment* in a similar light, see Susan Slotnick, "The Novel Form in the Works of David Bergelson" (PhD diss., Columbia University, 1978), 233, 330.

44. B. Tshubinski, "Dovid Bergelson," in *Leksikon fun der nayer yidisher literatur*, ed. Shmuel Niger and Jacob Shatsky, vol. 1 (New York: Congress for Jewish Culture, 1956), 381.

45. RGALI f. 622, op. 1, ed. khr. 49. Bergel'son, David Rafailovich. *Vozmezdie* [Povest']. Kruti translated from Ukrainian, edited an anthology of one-act plays, and wrote studies of the theater; I have been unable to find other translations from Yiddish. No reason was given for suspending the translation project.

46. Mikhail Krutikov, "Rediscovering the Shtetl as a New Reality," in *The Shtetl: New Evaluations*, ed. Steven T. Katz (New York: New York University Press, 2007), 211–32. See also Estraikh, *In Harness*, 82–85; and Harriet Murav, *Music from a Speeding Train: Jewish Literature in Post-Revolutionary Russia* (Stanford, CA: Stanford University Press, 2011), 62–65.

47. Bergelson, *Judgment*, 25. Bergelson, *Mides-hadin*, 7: 32.

48. Bergelson, *Judgment*, 22. Bergelson, *Mides-hadin*, 7: 29.

49. A discussion of the importance of simultaneous motion and homogeneous action can be found in Jacques Rancière, "Rethinking Modernity," *Diacritics* 42, no. 3 (2014): 6–20, doi:10.1353/dia.2014.0017.

50. Kracauer, *The Mass Ornament*, 79.

51. For a broad-ranging article that discusses Russian constructivist theater in this light, see Nick Worrall, "Meyerhold's Production of 'The Magnificent Cuckold,'" *Drama Review* 17, no. 1 (1973): 14–34.

52. Bergelson, *Judgment*, 4. Bergelson, *Mides-hadin*, 7: 6.

53. Bergelson, *Judgment*, 7. Bergelson, *Mides-hadin*, 7: 10.

54. Bergelson, *Judgment*, 133. The Yiddish: "Fun langvaylikayt genetst mit a halb moyl der "kuker," vos in di shvere toyern. Foyl efenen zikh di toyern un farmakhn zikh bald vider. Farshlofenerhayt khapn zey arayn a yidene tsu ir arestirtn man un in tsen minut arum

shpayen zey zi fun zikh aroys tsurik afn plats un khapn arayn a tsveyte." Bergelson, *Mides-hadin*, 7: 170.

55. Bergelson, *Judgment*, 61. Bergelson, *Mides-hadin*, 7: 77.

56. Bergelson, *Judgment*, 102. Bergelson, *Mides-hadin*, 7: 130.

57. Bergelson, *Judgment*, 68. Bergelson, *Mides-hadin*, 7: 86.

58. Bergelson, *Judgment*, 70. Bergelson, *Mides-hadin*, 7: 89.

59. The Yiddish press carried articles written by Chaplin and translated into Yiddish; see for example Charlie Chaplin, "In vos bashteyt der sod fun mayn derfolg," *Literarishe bleter* 56 (1925): 3. For a discussion of the Chagall and the significance of Chaplin generally in Russian experimental art, see Yurii Tsivian, "O Chapline v russkom avangarde i o zakonakh sluchainogo v iskusstve," *Novoe literaturnoe obozrenie* 5 (2006): 99–142.

60. For more on Charney in Berlin, see Estraikh, *In Harness*, 69–70.

61. Daniel Charney, "A briv fun Moskve," *Tealit* 5 (1924): 24.

62. Bergelson, *Mides-hadin*, 7: 143.

63. This was a noted feature of Russian futurist and imagist poetry. For a discussion, see Boris Eikhenbaum, *Anna Akhmatova: Opyt analiza* (St. Petersburg, 1923), 19–21.

64. Bergelson, *Judgment*, 61–62. Bergelson, *Mides-hadin*, 7: 78–79.

65. "We are living in a cosmic era—an era of creation of a new heaven and a new earth," Evgenii Zamiatin in *We*, trans. Mirra Ginzburg (New York: Avon Books, 1972), x. The literary journal *Noviy mir* started publication in 1925. Aldous Huxley's novel *Brave New World* was not published until 1932.

66. Isaac Babel, *Complete Works* (New York: Norton, 2002), 228.

67. See Carl Schmitt, *Political Theology: Four Chapters on the Concept of Sovereignty*, trans. Schwab, George (Cambridge, MA: MIT Press, 1985), 16–19, 31–34. A discussion of Bolshevik violence in the context of political theology can be found in James Ryan, "The Sacralization of Violence: Bolshevik Justifications for Violence and Terror during the Civil War," *Slavic Review* 74, no. 4 (2015): 808–31, doi:10.5612/slavicreview.74.4.808.

68. Bergelson, *Judgment*, 56. Bergelson, *Mides-hadin*, 7: 71.

69. Irina Sandomirskaia makes this point with the pun in Russian that plays between *nemoi iazyk* ("deaf language") and *ne moi iazyk* ("not my language"), although her focus is on the Stalinist period. She also links the language of deafness to the concept of defamiliarization. See Irina Sandomirskaia, *Blokada v slove: ocherki kriticheskoi teorii i biopolitiki iazyka* (Moscow: Novoe literaturnoe obozrenie, 2013), 7–50.

70. David Bergelson, *Mides-hadin*, vol. 7, *Geklibene verk* (Vilnius: B. Kletskin, 1929), 240. The Yiddish: "Ineveynik in im hot der kes zikh gegebn a shar af rekhts un af links, un aroysgerukt hot zikh dort der eyzerner tropn, vos ker tsu der revolutsye un hartevet un halt op . . . shtendik, in ale shvere minutn hot im ot der tropn untergezogt dos neytike, dos rikhtike."

71. V. I. Lenin, *Collected Works*, vol. 26 (Moscow: Progress Press, 1977), 29, https://www.marxists.org/archive/lenin/works/cw/pdf/lenin-cw-vol-26.pdf.

72. See for example Bergelson, *Mides-hadin*, 7: 183.

73. Bergelson, *Mides-hadin*, 7: 26, 29.

74. Bergelson, *Judgment*, 107. Bergelson, *Mides-hadin*, 7: 137.

75. Bergelson, *Judgment*, 76. Bergelson, *Mides-hadin*, 7: 96–97.

76. Bergelson, *Judgment*, 76. Bergelson, *Mides-hadin*, 7: 97.

77. For a discussion of Benjamin's concept of afterhistory, see Susan Buck-Morss, *The Dialectics of Seeing: Walter Benjamin and the Arcades Project*, 219.

78. Bergelson, *Judgment*, 209. Bergelson, *Mides-hadin*, 7: 265.

79. For discussions of El Lissitzky and the Kiev Kultur-Lige, see Myroslav Shkandrij, "National Modernism in Post-Revolutionary Society: The Ukrainian Renaissance and Jewish Revival, 1917–1930," in *Shatterzone of Empires*, ed. Omer Bartov and Eric D. Weitz (Bloomington: Indiana University Press, 2013), 438–48. See also Gennady Estraikh, "The Yiddish Kultur-Lige," in *Modernism in Kyiv: Jubilant Experimentation*, ed. Irene R. Makaryk and Virlana Tkacz (Toronto: University of Toronto Press, 2010), 197–217. For information on El Lissitzky in Berlin, see Oleg Budnitskii and Aleksandra Polian, eds., *Russko-evreiskii Berlin, 1920–1941* (Moscow: NLO, 2013), 152–59.

80. David Bergelson and Solomon Mikhoels, *Mera strogosti: Midas hadin, libretto* (Moscow: Der emes, 1933).

81. Bergelson, *Judgment*, 27. Bergelson, *Mides-hadin*, 7: 35.

82. Bergelson, *Mides-hadin*, 7: 35.

83. Rancière, "Rethinking Modernity," 15.

PART 4

TIME CANNOT BE MISTAKEN

Introduction

Bergelson wrote about his sense of responsibility to "the time in which we live" in 1926. The language of obligation suggests a new relationship to time. In the same year, Viktor Shklovsky wrote, "Time cannot be mistaken; the time cannot have wronged me."[1] Events have crystallized in a legible pattern, and the socialist victory has been won. By speaking of the rightness of time, Shklovsky means the rectitude of the revolution and its new order, which makes demands on him. Bergelson similarly expresses his obligation to contemporaneity. In part 4 I discuss Bergelson's attempt in literature and in life to fit the time, which could not be mistaken.

Chapter 8 is devoted to his autobiographical novel, *At the Dnieper*, and other prose and nonfiction work from 1932 to the beginning of World War II. I explore the relation between socialist realist temporality and Bergelson's poetics of belatedness: how Bergelson modified time lag, afterwardsness, and slow time—the temporal elements of the poetics he had developed earlier—and what he accomplished artistically by working with the new aesthetic norms of the 1930s. In a letter from 1933, Bergelson described his own inability to keep up with the heroic pace of socialist construction in Birobidzhan, which was a part of Soviet construction as a whole and part of the "great future." He could not write that quickly; to use his own evocative Yiddish, it was beyond him to write *"khop-lop."*[2] My discussion explores the ways in which Bergelson's modernism intersects with socialist realism, accentuating what the two have in common.

Chapter 9 turns to World War II. Bergelson wrote dozens of articles and stories for the Yiddish newspaper of the Jewish Anti-Fascist Committee; he began publishing *Aleksander Barash* in its pages—a novel that confronts the issue of the postwar survival of Jews and Jewish culture, pitting his generation of Jews against the younger generation that had grown up and been educated in the Soviet time. This novel and most of Bergelson's other work from this period remains virtually untouched in the critical literature, even though Bergelson was among the first writers to respond to the Nazi genocide of the Jews. Reading the fiction against the published and unpublished journalism reveals the ways Bergelson transformed history into literature. By the end of the 1940s, Bergelson would change his mind about time's rectitude and would accuse time of being unfair to the Jewish people. His play *Prince Reuveni*, the last important work he wrote before his arrest in 1948, sets the postwar Jewish crisis of the twentieth century in the context of the Jewish crisis of the sixteenth century.

In a speech given in Warsaw in 1930, Bergelson said that literature from Poland and the United States could be compared to a clock that chimed beautifully but had no hands and thus could not tell the time. To put it another way, Polish and American Yiddish literature lacked contemporaneity, the quality that Bergelson and Shklovsky evoked in 1926. In contrast, literature from the Soviet Union was like a symphony orchestra playing on an express train. Those standing on the platform heard the "interrupted, incomplete sounds" as the train passed and wanted to catch it.[3] Bergelson suggests the fundamental paradox underlining Soviet culture: its actors are always too early or too late for their bright future. It continually eludes them. Bergelson would contradict the laws of physics by being in two places at one time, both on the rushing express train and on the platform with those left behind. He attempted to catch the beat, "get the rhythm of the time," as he says in this speech, but his fundamental perspective remained with those left behind, even in his Soviet-era works that seem to celebrate the triumph of socialism.

Before examining Bergelson's writing, I want to say a few words about his return to the Soviet Union in the terrible year of 1934, when Kirov was murdered, setting off the Great Terror. A great deal has been written about the return, and it is not the purpose of this study to give an account of the author's life decisions, holding him to account. Doing so runs the risk of engaging in an odious posthumous judgment, as if his murder in 1952 were his fault because he made the wrong choice. Daniel Charney wrote in 1956 that if not for Hitler, the entire Russian Jewish émigré community would have remained in Berlin "to this day."[4] Meylekh Epstein, the editor of *Frayheyt*, wrote in 1962 that Bergelson did not accept the offer that had been made to him (referring to 1929) and also noted that Bergelson "liked Berlin, its intellectual life and its closeness to East European Jews."[5] I have not been able to find more detail with regard to this offer, and the gap between the date when it was made and the subsequent reference to it raises some questions about its terms.[6] Financial uncertainty had always plagued Bergelson in Berlin; he had never succeeded in becoming a regular staff writer for the *Forward* or receiving an adequate salary from *Frayheyt*. His wife, Tsipora, supported the family with her secretarial work at the Soviet Trade Commission. When she was transferred to Copenhagen in 1933, the family followed. Bergelson had traveled in the United States from November 1928 to May 1929; he was a close friend of Joseph Opatoshu, a Yiddish writer who had emigrated from Poland to America earlier. According to Charney, Bergelson felt superfluous in America, since two well-established Yiddish authors, Opatoshu and Sholem Asch, had already won the hearts of the American audience. Asch had achieved world renown and had been translated into many languages, including English. His multivolume *Three Cities* appeared in English in 1933.[7] This kind of international stature would elude Bergelson for decades to come.

There were other concerns as well. In "Three Centers," Bergelson had written that Jews in America were assimilating rapidly and abandoning Yiddish; he suggested that language change was tantamount to conversion and even the loss of the ability to produce comprehensible speech. His understanding of the American Yiddish audience was no doubt colored by his uneasy relationship with Abraham Cahan, the editor of the *Forward*, who told Bergelson that his style was inaccessible and his vocabulary too difficult, and who frequently ignored work that Bergelson sent to him from Berlin—leading to the latter's frequent state of depression.[8] As Gennady Estraikh puts it, Bergelson had "concluded that America was one of the places where highbrow Yiddish writers had virtually no readers."[9] In contrast to America, in the Soviet Union, Yiddish was promoted as the official language of the Jewish national minority, and at least for a time, Bergelson was the preeminent Yiddish writer.[10] The performance of Bergelson's work on the stage of the Moscow State Yiddish Theater is one example of a broader trend of state support for Yiddish, as is Bergelson's inclusion in the school curriculum. Bergelson's need for a Yiddish-language audience and the sense that this and his financial needs would be met played a significant role in his decision to return to Moscow. His support for socialism was another factor.

Bergelson was an intensely private person, and even his available correspondence rarely touches on personal decisions. He once complained about having to supply biographical information for a Yiddish literary lexicon, comparing the disclosure of personal data to opening his bedroom to pass-ersby on the street. We will never know conclusively what led the author back to the Soviet Union. It is also possible that Bergelson, like so many other human beings, would have been unable to give a full account himself.

The Russian literary newspaper the *Literary Gazette* (*Literaturnaia gazeta)*, the official publication of the Soviet Writers' Union, heralded Bergelson's return in a May 1934 issue with a front-page picture of the author; the caption described him as the "famous Jewish writer" who had composed "At the Depot," *The End of Everything,* and *Judgment.* Since his return, he had begun to work on a book about Birobidzhan. The year of Bergelson's return, 1934, saw the beginning of a new round of Stalinist show trials. In January 1937, Karl Radek, Yurii Piatakov, and Grigorii Sokolnikov were convicted of conspiring with Germany and Japan to overthrow the Soviet government. Bergelson's Russian-language article attacking the condemned men, titled "The People's Punishing Sword," was published along with similar articles by Perets Markish, Yurii Tinianov, Demyan Bedny, and other prominent Soviet writers in February 1937.[11] Bergelson's article was sent by telegraph from Birobidzhan, where Jews were building socialism, and where I begin chapter 8.

Notes

1. Viktor Shklovsky, *Third Factory* (Normal, IL: Dalkey Archive Press, 2002), 8.

2. Letter to Paul Novick, March 4, 1933, from Copenhagen. YIVO RG 205, Kalman Marmor Collection, Folder 105.

3. David Bergelson, "Problemen fun der yidisher literatur," *Literarishe bleter,* no. 24 (1930): 439.

4. Daniel Charney, "Vi David Bergelson iz farnart gevorn keyn rusland," *Der tog,* August 5, 1956, sec. 2.

5. Epstein cited by Gennady Estraikh, "Bergelson in and on America (1929–1949)," in *David Bergelson: From Modernism to Socialist Realism,* ed. Joseph Sherman and Gennady Estraikh (Oxford: Legenda, 2007), 212.

6. In 1962, Meylekh Epstein wrote that Bergelson "refused our offer to make New York his home." See ibid. According to Marina Bergelson Raskin, her grandfather sought but did not receive a promise of a year's worth of income. Personal conversation with the author, March 27, 2016.

7. For more on Asch in this time period in relation to Russia, see Gennady Estraikh, *Evreiskaia literaturnaia zhizn' Moskvy 1917–1991* (St. Petersburg: Evropeiskii universitet v Sankt-Peterburge, 2015), 111.

8. David Bergelson, Letter to A. Cahan, Berlin, 1924 in YIVO, RG 1139, Abraham Cahan, Folder 54, reel 3.

9. Estraikh, "Bergelson in and on America (1929–1949)," 207.

10. For Yiddish in the Soviet Union, see David Shneer, *Yiddish and the Creation of Soviet Jewish Culture* (Cambridge, UK: Cambridge University Press, 2004).

11. David Bergelson, "Karaiushchii mech naroda," *Literaturnaia gazeta*, February 1, 1937, 5.

8

SOCIALISM'S FROZEN TIME

IN 1932 THE FIRST VOLUME OF BERGELSON'S AUTOBIOGRAPHICAL novel *At the Dnieper* (*Baym Dnyepr*) was published in Moscow; the author was still in Berlin. The second volume, subtitled "Early Years" (*Yunge yorn*), came out in 1940; by then Bergelson had left Berlin and returned to Russia. *Literaturnaia gazeta*, the organ of the Soviet Writers' Union, called the appearance of Bergelson's novel "the most significant event in Soviet Jewish literature."[1] The 1932 work, subtitled *Penek* (the name of the hero), opens with a refusal. Even though the people in this book would like their story to begin with the patriarchs in the Bible, their wishes are not going to be respected. Instead, the narrator simply states that this generation lived "thirty years before the revolution."[2] In other words, it is 1887, and Penek, the child hero of the novel, was born in 1880. The opening of the novel proclaims a break with the Jewish tradition of inserting ongoing history into biblical time. Bergelson had not previously relied on biblical historiography but had more typically begun with "after"—after some unknown but decisive event has already taken place, as the Yiddish title of his 1911 novel *Nokh alemen* (*The End of Everything*) reveals. *Nokh alemen* can be translated as "after everything." The protagonist of *Descent* (1913) arrives too late to see his friend alive and even too late for the funeral. Bergelson's 1932 announcement of his break with tradition thus carries a certain irony while also raising a question: Why announce a departure from something he had never done in the first place?

In November 1929, on the anniversary of the Bolshevik revolution, Stalin announced his "great break": the complete restructuring of every aspect of Soviet society, including the collectivization of labor, industrialization, and vast rearrangements of land, water, and human beings, all of which brought massive economic and social change, dislocation, and destruction including the deaths of millions. The year 1932 constituted a significant new point of departure for Russian literature and the arts; it was the year all literary groups were united into one state-sponsored organization, the Writers' Union, which held its first congress in 1934. This period marks the beginning of socialist realism as an official doctrine: "the truthful, historically concrete representation of reality in its revolutionary development."[3] Bergelson's declaration of a new beginning on the opening page of his 1932 novel demonstrates his participation in the broader phenomenon of the Stalin revolution and his reinvention as a socialist realist Yiddish writer.

This chapter focuses on *Birobidzhan Settlers* (*Birebidzhaner*, 1934) and *At the Dnieper* (1932 and 1940), situating these works in the broader context of socialist realism and the interwar historical novel. The crisis of historical time of the twenties in the aftermath of World War I and the collapse of empires took a new shape in the Stalinist thirties. The quality of time changed again. Whereas earlier, the destruction of the past created an interregnum "between the times," the Stalinist end of historical time was the result of a different premise. History was over, because perfection had already been achieved. Time froze, but the major themes that had preoccupied Bergelson earlier persisted. The warp and woof of Bergelson's fiction still consisted of aftermaths and futurity. My aim in this chapter is to examine how he adjusted his modernist belatedness to the aesthetics of "petrified utopia" and to show what he achieved in so doing. Socialist realist temporality also relied on after-the-fact retrospectivism, as I will show. The relation between the past and the present was not simply a matter of paving the way toward the bright future.

Too Late Again

The goal of socialist realism was the production of socialism in all aspects of life. A transformation in the consciousness of writers and readers was a key part of this project. Socialist realist literature of the 1930s generally featured the theme of construction, and the artist was expected to show—in a clear and accessible style—the emergence of a positive hero, connected to the party, who would guide the people.[4] While scholars differ on the relation between socialist realism and the avant-garde movements of earlier periods and modernism more broadly, there is general agreement about socialist realism's removal from historical time.[5] In Evgeny Dobrenko's resonant phrase, socialist realism offered its spectators and consumers the image of "petrified utopia."[6] The history of Soviet clock time is telling. As Victor Papernyi explains, in the twenties, clock time was moved forward in summer and back in winter, but in 1930, "time lost its plasticity."[7] Time froze. Stillness, the dominant feature of socialist realist temporality, mirrors Bergelson's emphasis on the "frozen" and "congealed" (*farglivert*) time of the shtetl. The train station in his first published work, "At the Depot" (1906), was *farglivert*. The frozen time of socialism's perfection and the frozen time of the shtetl's permanent imperfection mirror each other. Time's halt in Bergelson also signals national disaster. In the second volume of *At the Dnieper*, Olga, a stalwart revolutionary, suddenly loses her sense of time's forward motion when she learns of the 1903 Kishinev pogrom; time "freezes" (*di tsayt iz farglivert gevorn*).[8]

Even though victories had already been won in industrialization and collectivization, Stalin made it clear that thought had not kept up with the practical successes that had already been achieved; theory lagged behind practice. Andrei Zhdanov put the problem slightly differently at the first congress of the Soviet Writers' Union. The teachings of Marx, Engels, Lenin, and Stalin had already become embodied in life, thanks to the work of the party and the soviets; the occasion of the first congress of writers depended on this victory; literature thus would come after the triumphs that had already taken place. In his 1930 Warsaw speech, Bergelson stated the terms of the artist's belatedness directly. "Everything—language, imagery, motifs—has been created by the people. The artist comes afterward."[9]

Petre Petrov identifies the death of the author as the common ground shared by both modernism and socialist realism but distinguishes between modernist and socialist realist temporality. Modernism looks forward to the future world, but socialist realism "looks backwards to a pre-existing state of being."[10] The artist's work confirms, after the fact, the truth of what socialism has already accomplished. At the beginning of the Stalin revolution, the condition of belatedness, so central to Bergelson's modernism and modernism generally, also characterized Soviet thought and literature. Whereas other discussions emphasize socialism's characteristic rush forward, my focus is on the whiplash that comes from arriving too late.[11] In Bergelson, the past is preserved in the traces, both positive and negative, that it leaves on the present. In earlier works, including *Descent* and *The End of Everything*, the protagonists have arrived on the scene of their own lives too late for the decisive events that have already shaped them. The decisive event is loss, and there is nothing to be done except to bear witness to the aftermath. The possibility of transformation is not yet lost, however. Socialist realist belatedness functions, in contrast, in relation to a positive event (the victory of socialism), and there is everything to be done, because the new chimerical reality must be visible in every aspect of life and work and embodied in art and literature above all. Authors must visit and write about the Promethean construction sites where dams, canals, and (fundamentally) socialism were being built.

For Bergelson, this site was Birobidzhan, which he visited several times in 1932 and 1933.[12] The project of Jewish colonization in the Russian Far East targeted several goals at once, including military security and the economic task of making the "disenfranchised" population of the shtetls into productive agricultural laborers.[13] Declared the Jewish Autonomous Region in 1934, Birobidzhan was part of a broader Soviet plan to make socialism indigenous among all the peoples of the new socialist country by promoting culture in the various native languages, in this case, Yiddish. Compact settlement in the Russian Far East offered the promise of Jewish transformation and renewal in the world's first Jewish national homeland since biblical times. The Jewish people, the Jewish body, and the Jewish mentality would change in the new conditions.

Birobidzhan Settlers (*Birebidzhaner*) was published in 1934. Bergelson wrote it while simultaneously completing the second volume of *At the Dnieper*. Set in 1928, it tracks a group of settlers as they travel by train from Minsk to Birobidzhan and describes their early days in their new home.[14] Healthy, muscled Jews cheerfully work the untamed land that surrounds them, spurred on by the posters and newspaper articles featuring Lenin and Stalin, who summon them to do the work of building socialism. They clear land, fell enormous trees, haul tractors through rivers of mud, and dig out of huge snowdrifts. The titanic force of the taiga nearly conquers them. A tiny settlement in the woods runs out of food, but a heroic nighttime rescue in a snowstorm saves the group. The one shirker and doubter among them leaves. At the end, the snow covers the taiga, "hiding all its mud and all its treasures."[15] All traces of socialist accomplishment disappear. The blanket of snow renders socialist accomplishment illegible.

The novel demonstrates that Bergelson could write in the new socialist realist style. The necessary boxes have been ticked. The party builds the entire Soviet Union; if not for the Soviet Union, there would be no settlement in the wilderness, no well, no bright morning, and no nighttime rescue. Gorky and Stalin named the emotions proper to Soviet construction as joy and cheerfulness; Bergelson's protagonists travel on a train that makes cheerful sounds, in contrast to the melancholy unfinished tales Mirl Hurvits hears as the train passes her by, and the work they do is "joyous" (*di arbet—a freylekhe*). Birobidzhan is not unique; it is linked to other Promethean construction, including the hydroelectric dam *Dnieprstroi* and the Turkish–Siberian railway, both mentioned explicitly. Birobidzhan, vitally tied to the "construction taking place on a sixth of the earth's surface," also serves military and strategic purposes as the "outpost of socialism—a giant iron fist" defending the Soviet Union against enemies.[16]

In the world of the novel, as in the world of the Soviet Union in the 1930s, the new consciousness of building socialism is more important than concrete accomplishment or accomplishments in concrete. The socialist realist writer's literary work serves as a transparent window through which the truth of socialism can be seen, whether or not actual buildings, roads, or electric stations have been completed. In *Birobidzhan Settlers* the tiny outpost in the woods lacks a single finished house, a problem that one of the characters loves to point out. Yudl Lifshits has no greater pleasure than telling newcomers that there is nothing there: "It's empty all around" (*Umetum iz pust*).[17] This problem is beside the point, since the settlers travel to Birobidzhan to build socialism, not buildings, as another character explicitly states. To accomplish the task requires that individuals become artifacts of socialism.

This transformation involves more than merely sensing oneself as part of a collective. It also involves bending time, something that Bergelson was good at. Bergelson's modernist belatedness meshes well with socialist realist time lag. To be sure, other dimensions of his modernist poetics necessarily fall by the wayside. Experimental and avant-garde art and literature turned away from sight as the vehicle of truth, bringing the other senses to the foreground. Bergelson used disabilities in hearing as a modernist device to emphasize the material qualities of language. In contrast, socialist realism restores vision to a new central role, As Petrov writes, "To have been permeated and possessed by the force of socialism [is] thus to have been made to see."[18] In Bergelson's earlier work, delay and mediation impede perception, but here the emphasis is on all-consuming, total sight and knowledge. Indeed, what must be seen is often depicted as so bright as to be blinding, as Petrov shows. Bergelson's remarks at the first congress of the Soviet Writers' Union are significant in this regard. Responding to the literary representative from Dagestan, Bergelson said, with some irony, "I did not understand a single word of this speech, but nonetheless this extraordinary poem about Lenin's and Stalin's national policy was written on a piece of paper of blinding whiteness."[19] The truth is so dazzling that it becomes opaque. In *Birobidzhan Settlers* Bergelson translates the unbearable brightness into unbearable heat. The newspapers that arrive from Moscow "hot off the presses" are too hot to handle; in a version of the biblical trope of flame from God's mouth, they "breathe flame" because "they tell the story of the burning blaze of socialist building, the great storm of Bolshevik reality."[20]

Being possessed by the "force and might" (*gevure*, another adaptation of a biblical image) of building socialism means being able to see the already past and future accomplishments of socialism. This is the inverse of "Seeing is believing." Believing means be able to see. In Bergelson's Birobidzhan novel, fantastical visions of socialist glory interrupt the depiction of the characters' struggles against nature. One of them, Engineer Todi, has a vision of a future city built around a mountain. I paraphrase the text. His plan would have the river Bira split the city just as the Seine cuts through Paris. The mountain peak would remain in the center of the great socialist city, whose society would be classless. At the very tip of the mountain would be a workers' sanatorium. Agronomist Shteyn, possessed by the same vision, fills in the rest of the picture. A giant illuminated statue of Lenin, his arm outstretched, would be placed above the workers' sanatorium. If imperialism were still in force on the other side of the border, the gesture would caution the enemy against invasion, but if the revolution had already taken place, the gesture would spur the Chinese on to greater feats of socialism.[21]

As witnesses to a future that has not yet arrived, Todi and Shteyn are strangely parallel to Mirl Hurvits, witness to "the end of everything" that only she knows. There is nothing to be done in the world of *The End of Everything*, and too much time; in contrast, in socialist realism there is everything to be done and not enough time to do it in. Socialist realist temporality is not merely a matter of seeing the future in its present, embryonic form.[22] The socialist realist "now" is caught between an already realized truth and its ever more perfect embodiment in life and consciousness. One must hurry to catch up; time is always short, and the problem of belatedness persists. For example, as two young settlers look out at the mountainous scene before them, "the longing to come here gnaws at their hearts—they were here in this country and still longed for it" (*me gefint zikh in land un me benkt tsu dem*).[23] The satisfaction of their desire is yet again deferred. In a manner similar to other Bergelsonian protagonists who miss the important moment (of encounter, love, or salvation), they too have missed the moment of arrival. The more conscious settlers in Birobidzhan feel that the work of the "great socialist construction is taking place far away, in another country, in another world."[24] Their own settlement was developing too slowly; the work was "barely moving."[25]

The dazzling truth of socialism encompasses the beauty of the natural world. As the train carrying the settlers to Birobidzhan takes them along Lake Baikal, the reflection of the setting sun's rays on the surface of the lake creates a strange, still beauty, and "it seemed that something or someone from the train was left behind at that beauty."[26] The pervasive belatedness jars against the emphasis on Birobidzhan as a place of new beginnings, a garden of Eden with a series of triumphant firsts: the first tree to be felled, the first log sent down the river, the first couple to fall in love, the first step in building the settlement. In Bergelson's socialist realist tableau vivant, notwithstanding the grandiose rhetoric of creation on a biblical scale, delay and mistiming haunt the new socialist world: it has arrived, but his characters have missed it.

New Histories

The need for new beginnings in the epoch of the Stalin revolution, the freezing of time, and the retreat from modernist internationalism made way for an increased interest in the past, including Russian history. The avant-garde sought a complete break with the past for the sake of an utterly new future. While the officials of the new form of revolutionary literature in the 1930s argued the necessity of learning from the classics, their aim was to put the classics to a new use. Biography and the historical novel, especially the "historical revolutionary novel," became important Soviet genres.[27] Maxim Gorky's speech at the first congress of the Soviet Writers' Union in 1934 emphasized the importance of history, including the history of recently built factories, Russia's historical past from feudal times to the construction of collective farms, and the history of the peoples of the Soviet republics. The histories of the new enterprises and the national minorities could be done collectively, to educate beginning writers. All of these histories were to be "illuminated by the teachings of Marx, Lenin, and Stalin."[28]

Alexander Fadeev's *The Last of the Udegs* fulfills Gorky's requirements, because it depicts the revolutionary development of one of the nomadic minority peoples of the USSR, focusing on a native leader who correctly begins to see the socialist future.[29] In a 1935 letter written shortly after he arrived in Moscow, Bergelson described his work assisting with the Russian translation of the first volume of *At the Dnieper*, slated to appear in an inexpensive Russian-language monthly as a serial, noting that this was the "first time a book from one of the national literatures [Yiddish] was being published in *Roman-gazeta*."[30] Fadeev's novel and Alexei Tolstoy's *Peter the First* were also published in the same monthly.

The interwar period was important for the Yiddish historical novel beyond the Soviet Union. Max Brod published his fiction about the real-life sixteenth-century Jewish pretender David Reubeni in 1925, and Israel Joshua Singer and other Yiddish authors also wrote historical novels at this time. Der Nister's *The Mashber Family* (*Di Mishpokhe Mashber*), like Bergelson's novel, was set in the final decades of the nineteenth century. Only the first volume of two volumes was published in its entirety in the USSR, appearing serially in the same journal as *At the Dnieper*. In his preface Der Nister ("the hidden one," the pen name for Pinkhas Kahanovitsh) said that the world of people he portrayed had "disappeared without a trace" and that his novel had temporarily resurrected them in order to allow them to take "their historically necessary last step—to the abyss" (*zeyer geshikhtlekh-noytvendikn letsn gang—tsum apgrunt*).[31] Charting the course of destruction of a life-world can also serve as a means of preserving it in memory, however, and this double gesture characterizes both Der Nister's *The Family Mashber* and Bergelson's *At the Dnieper*.

The historical novel and the novel of the hero's development, the bildungsroman, also attracted the interest of literary theorists. Bakhtin wrote his work on Rabelais and the bildungsroman in the same period. In contrast to the frozen temporality of utopia achieved, Bakhtin emphasizes process and crisis as the hallmarks of the bildungsroman. Bakhtin's lesser-known work from the same period, although unpublished at the time, also sheds light on the temporality of *At the Dnieper*. Bakthin's discussion of the grotesque body in the Rabelais book provides a larger framework for understanding the image of the people in Bergelson's novel; however, in Bergelson's novel, joy and renewal are balanced against grotesquerie and mass death.

At the Dnieper is the bildungsroman of Bergelson's fictitious socialist realist writer, Penek Levin, the unloved youngest child of a wealthy family who grows up against the backdrop of events three decades before the

1917 revolution.[32] The two volumes span the years 1880–1903. The characters associated with the "white house" where the Levin family lives include Mikhoel Levin, the father, who is ungenerous to his own children but whom Penek loves; Penek's mother, Mikhoel's second wife, who loathes Penek; his elder brother and sister, whom he loathes; "Big Sheyndl" (*Sheyndl di groyse*); the domineering oldest daughter; and Yankel the coachman, whose mother nursed Sheyndl. In contrast to the wealthy white house of the Levin family, the backstreets house the poor workers: Nakhmen the painter, Rakhmiel the rag picker, and Alter Meytes, who operates the mill by "dancing" on its steps all day long. Manye and Olga Heysman are daughters of the "apostate" who is the bookkeeper at the family distillery. By the end of the first volume, Mikhoel Levin has died without putting Penek in his will. Penek is twelve years old and has already begun to read secular literature in Hebrew. He is estranged from his family, having realized that his father's wealth depended on the poverty and suffering of others. His father's death liberates him from any remaining sense of obligation to his own family, and his acceptance by the proletarian children of the backstreets marks a new stage in his consciousness. Left out of his father's will and disinherited from the past, he is ready to inherit the socialist future. While socialist realism is a matter of being made to see, what Penek comes to see and what "he would see for his entire life" are the perspectives of "both sides" (*beyde ekn*); that is, the positions of both the wealthy and the poor, the older generation and his own.[33] In the same vein, Bergelson's speech at the first congress of the Soviet Writers' Union mentioned the "multisidedness of our reality" (*mnogoplanovost'*) and thus the "multisidedness" of socialist realist literary composition.[34]

The second volume, set in Kiev, where Bergelson lived as a young man, simultaneously traces Penek's continued development as a writer and the rise of the revolutionary movement directed offstage by Lenin, explicitly named in the novel; Stalin is alluded to in the character conducting strikes in Batumi. The Levin family has relocated to a wealthy neighborhood in the city, but Penek spends more time in the courtyard of a dilapidated tenement house. Space articulates class tensions: the family house is to the tenement courtyard as the "white house" in volume one is to the backstreets. In volume two, a policeman is murdered and the body of his daughter is found in a basement belonging to a Jew; an anti-Jewish campaign based on a trumped-up charge of ritual murder is set in motion. The city is on the brink of pogroms, echoing the real-life events in Kishinev in 1903. Penek forms a relationship with Manye, whose sister Olga has become a revolutionary. In addition to Olga, the revolutionary cast of characters includes Anton; his wife, known as Tetka ("auntie" in Russian), who carries revolutionary literature in her false pregnancy belly; Yosl, Penek's friend from the shtetl; and Klim, an allusion to the eponymous hero of Gorky's *The Life of Klim Sangin* (*Zhizn' Klima Samgina*). Gorky's Klim has to overcome his privileged background and rewrite his biography, like Penek and Bergelson himself. Magidovitsh, who works at a Russian liberal newspaper, an autodidact, ethnographer, and former tutor in the Levin family, is arrested for publishing an article exonerating Jews in the murder of the policemen and his daughter. By the end of the second volume, Penek's first stories have been published with the help of Elkhonon Kadison, a Hebrew writer whom Bialik once praised. This is an allusion to a real-life figure from Bergelson's own youth, Elkhonon Kalmonson (1857–1930).

As this overview shows, the style and content of *At the Dnieper* has changed considerably from the earlier work. The cast of characters is larger, their names and biographies are made clear from the beginning, they are organized into well-defined economic classes, and their consciousness matches their class. In an article published in the Moscow *Literaturnaia gazeta* (*Literary Gazette*), Bergelson said that in his pre-revolutionary work he had not uncovered the social significance of the reality he was describing, an omission that he would attempt to rectify.[35] In previous stories and works of fiction, the emotions of various characters filter the exposition of the plot, thereby creating elliptical, difficult narratives lacking crucial facts. The experience of slowed perception as an effect of reading is a key feature of Bergelson's modernism. At the beginning of *Descent*, readers do not know why Meylekh killed himself, and the novel does little to shed light on the mystery or even the basic facts of Meylekh's life. Here, in contrast, everything is spelled out: who, what, where, when, and why. Instead of the condensed, brief period of time typical of other novels, in *At the Dnieper* years go by, and the number of pages expands appropriately. The two volumes comprise over a thousand pages. The monumental novels of socialist realism, imitations of nineteenth-century critical realism, are palpable evidence of the new socialist reality, just like the monumental construction projects of socialism that they documented. Yet regardless of this impressive bulk, the novel is incomplete. The original plan was to publish five volumes.[36] Gorky's *The Life of Klim Samgin* and Fadeev's *The Last of the Udegs* were also unfinished. The great literary monuments to the triumph of socialism are in fact monumental fragments, inadvertent testaments to an incomplete victory.

Like other work from after 1926, the publication of *At the Dnieper* led to two opposed critical readings: readers outside Soviet Russia tended to see a dramatic decline in the artistic quality of the novel, especially in the second volume, caused by Bergelson's ideological shift, whereas readers more sympathetic to the Soviet cause favor the second volume. Regardless of the political orientation, each group defined a "kosher" and a "treyf" (not kosher) Bergelson. An example of the first tendency is a 1939 essay interpreting *Penek* (the subtitle of the first volume) as a revision of *The End of Everything* and other early work along purely Marxist lines. Whereas Mirl's father appears as a sympathetic figure, Penek's father is as an exploiter of the poor, and the entire way of life represented in the early novels is revealed in the 1932 work to be class struggle in embryonic form.[37] Dafna Clifford more bluntly labels the novel as Bergelson's "passport to Moscow."[38] The poet and essayist Dovid Eynhorn sees *Penek* as the "death rattle of Bergelson's artistic personality." Bergelson had "besmirched" and "debased . . . the traditional beautiful Jewish home" [ellipsis added].[39] Joseph Sherman is more generous to Bergelson as far as the first volume is concerned; even though the novel contains a clear ideological message, it is "the last novel in which he was able independently to merge conception and style."[40] The second volume, in contrast, conforms to "a politically approved version of the events before and after the 1905 revolution," and the "language drifts into official clichés."[41] From the other side of the ideological divide, Yekhezkel Dobrushin (1883–1953), a Yiddish poet, critic, and scholar who, like Bergelson, had a long writing career in the Soviet Union before his arrest in 1948, published a substantive article on the second volume of *At the Dnieper*, praising Bergelson for exposing the hidden mechanisms of the oppression wielded by the ruling class.

In confining themselves to Bergelson's Marxist analysis of the shtetl, these assessments omit much that is important. My reading blurs the boundary between the kosher and the treyf Bergelson, arguing for continuities between the two volumes and for the larger vision of the novel as a whole, which is concerned as much with preservation as destruction. It is not wrong to say that Bergelson "besmirches" the traditional Jewish home in *Penek*. The question is what this gesture means. Penek's growing alienation from his family and the Jewish piety they practice is central to the first volume. Bakhtin's theory of carnival and the grotesque body illuminate the narrative strategy Bergelson uses to free his child hero from the past of Jewish tradition. Carnivalization and parody undermine the cultural value assigned to the belief, practice, or institution that is its target. This dimension of the novel resembles various mock prayers included in publications by the Jewish Section of the Communist Party and the broad-scale effort, directed at Jews and non-Jews, to bring scientific atheism to the population at large. The debased Jewish body of the pre-revolutionary past would become the healthy, muscled, productive Jewish body of the future, as Bergelson's novel *Birobidzhan Settlers*, discussed in the first part of this chapter, would have it.

Bergelson's emphasis on the debased bodies of both Jews and non-Jews casts doubt on the project of Soviet redemption as a whole, however. Filipov, the Bolshevik redeemer in *Judgment* with suppurating sores on his neck, hardly conforms to the emerging template of the civil war hero of the 1920s. Bergelson uses similar tropes in both volumes of *At the Dnieper* to represent the working classes, as I will show, raising questions about their capacity for socialist transformation, regardless of the positive outcome he represents in his fiction about Birobidzhan. Furthermore, *At the Dnieper* is not the first Bergelson work to belittle Jewish practice. In *The End of Everything* Passover is merely an empty sound, *pakh*; its observances mean nothing to Mirl. Penek's development as a writer depends on his capacity to remember everything—including Judaism and Jewish culture. By inserting the Jewish lifeworld in all its detail into the space of a Soviet Yiddish novel, Bergelson's double gesture preserves Jewish culture just as much as it undermines it. This is another example of love at last sight. Although the emphasis on memory connects Bergelson with his fictitious hero, there is also a significant difference between author and hero. The supposedly merely conformist second volume ends with a remarkable image of Jewish memory culture important for the context of the 1930s.

In *Rabelais and His World* Bakhtin defines "carnival" as the inversion of the ordinary world, the overcoming of hierarchy and social stratification. It is the "second world" and the people's "second life" outside the norms and strictures of officialdom.[42] The carnival, or grotesque body, in contrast to the classical body, is open to the world; in it the lower stratum is emphasized, the stratum that unites digestion, birth, and death. "All that is sacred is rethought on the level of the material bodily stratum."[43] The mouth, the bowels, and the genitals form a single plane. "The ever-regenerated body of the people" replaces atomized, individual bodies, and renewal replaces "cosmic terror" and "eschatological expectations."[44] While the grotesque body is very much in evidence in *At the Dnieper,* so are notes of terror and expectations of the end.

The story of how Penek came to be born exemplifies the first tendency. His mother was in love with someone else before she married Mikhoel Levin, and to atone for her sinful desires, she wants to give birth to many children and does, but most of them die in their first months. Her desire is never sated; her "belly is a belly which, as if in great hunger, could not sate itself in pouring children from itself, pouring them out unceasingly" (*boykh—a boykh, vos hot vi in groysn hunger, zikh nit gekont zetikn mit shitn fun zikh kinder, shitn on an afher*).[45] Bergelson's use of synecdoche emphasizes the element of the grotesque in the image of the mother. It is as if her womb is a separate organ with its own desires—to use Bakhtin's language, as if it were "leading an independent life."[46]

We first meet Penek as a little boy of seven with his father:

> Penek was startled to see his father—whose hands, clasped together, seemed to be asking something— among all the upside-down chairs and footstools that he had played with in the summertime chill and dark of the dining room. He had been galloping and giddy-upping, sliding his bottom from one chair to the next with wild shrieks. In the first moment he felt great pity for his father's bewildered, half-festive, half-workday face, for his sorrowful eyes that did not know how good it was to stamp and dance and overturn worlds from great joy.[47]

The portrait of the artist as a little boy is a portrait of unbridled joy.

From an early age, Penek loves "everything that jars against established order."[48] Any hint of disobedience and rebellion gives him pleasure, even including horses that refuse to obey their masters. He hopes for an inversion in the order of things: he wants to see darkness in the daytime and light at night. He dreams of the upside-down world with head down and feet up, the way he loves things to be (*mitn kop arop un mit di fis aroyf, vi er hot lib*).[49] Bergelson's fashionable painter in the 1927 story "The Dynamic Moment," also loved everything upside down. In the 1932 novel, in contrast, Penek's upside-down dreams terrify him. After the death of his uncle, Penek has a nightmare. In the dream, the corpse that has remained shrouded and on the floor of her house for years suddenly bestirs itself and with a "cockle-doodle-doo voice" (*mit a kukureku kol*) demands a Sabbath treat for the boy.[50] Penek screams until he finally wakes up.

During the same long night, Penek tries to understand what it means to die by holding his breath for so long that he no longer felt anything nearby, together with him everyone and everything ceased existing—his father, the house, the city, the distant roads with all the cities and all the people. He frightened himself; he did not want to, could not bear it:

So many dead [*azoy fil toytn*]!!!![51]

The scene begins with the little boy's fear and anxiety caused by the death of someone he knows. As it continues, however, the child's normal reaction changes into something more extreme. He imagines and senses not only the death of a single individual whom he knew but death on a vast scale, the annihilation of hundreds, thousands of people, and his mind revolts at the thought. This new awareness of the possibility of the end of "everyone and everything" causes no pleasure for the young hero. This is more than the world upside down, more than the disruption of routine. This is an image of the destruction of the entire world. There is nothing in the storyline that would justify or explain Penek's sudden terror. While there is no one-to-one correspondence between this episode and any specific trial or newspaper campaign taking place in the Soviet Union that would account for it, there is an emotional correspondence between the general tenor of life in Soviet Russia in the late 1920s and early 1930s and this moment in the novel, set before the Soviet Union came into existence.

Bergelson interweaves the motif of destruction on a mass scale in his account of Penek's experience of Yom Kippur. Yom Kippur becomes a part of the upside-down world that intrudes into the socialist bildungsroman plot of the novel. Penek's growing detachment from religious observance and ultra-pious Jews like his father and his sister unfolds together with his fear of nameless, unknown events. His secret reading of Hebrew books plays a role in his emotions. Penek discovers a cache of Hebrew books among the dead Khaym's belongings and reads about the Spanish Inquisition, including a scene where a family is about to burned at the stake. During the opening *Kol Nidre* service, "the chant illuminated the Inquisition stories—stories of corpses" (*inkvizitsye-mayses—mayses-meysim*).[52] In the Yiddish, the word for "stories," *mayses*, echoes *meysim*, the word for "corpses." The acoustical mirroring creates an unexpected semantic link between "stories" and "corpses," as if the only stories to be told are stories about death. The *Kol Nidre* chant provides a musical accompaniment to the stories of the Inquisition that Penek rehearses in his imagination, based on his reading. This is a visual and acoustical fantasy of death in which Jewish history and Penek's own artistic inventiveness powerfully unite in a single extended scene. Bergelson will return to the Yom Kippur liturgy in his 1946 play, *Prince Reuveni*, a work that links the Nazi genocide to the Inquisition.

Penek's confusion and fear about the destruction of entire areas—"so many deaths!"—constitutes a significant thread in the novel. Penek's *Kol Nidre* fantasy of multiple deaths, like his nightmare, strangely echoes what was taking place in the Soviet Union in the late 1920s: the lethal collectivization and industrialization that created famine in Ukraine. A character articulates the frightening possibility of the deaths of multitudes of children: "The earth could open her mouth and swallow them, all of them, all of them!" (*di erd volt gemegt efenen a moyl un zey aynshlingen . . . ale! ale!*) (ellipsis in original).[53] There are other moments that seem out of place in a novel set in the late nineteenth century and that seem more indicative of the mass deaths of the twentieth century. Bakhtin argues that *Pantagruel* was a "merry rejoinder" to the natural calamities that took place in France in 1532; his own work and the first volume of *At the Dnieper* similarly respond to the catastrophes of their time.[54]

In the opening of the novel, Penek loves his father dearly, but his growing realization of the realities of the world (sexual, economic, and social) changes his image of his father, who makes himself out to be an angel, as Penek says, but who in reality is an ordinary human being. As the novel continues, Levin becomes sicker and sicker, reduced to mere body, and what is worse, the lower part of his body. After his diagnosis, the unseemly words "urine, catheter, and drainage" begin to be used in the house. He is dying from a disease that has to do with "the most shameful organ" (*mitn same shenlekhstn tvishn di glider*).[55] His illness leads to his utter debasement in Penek's eyes.

The process of downward transformation reaches its peak at the end of the novel, when Penek's dream of an upside-down world comes true. The poor and diseased inhabitants of the town gather around the dying man's house, waiting to see the team of doctors treating him:

> Crooked legs appeared, suppurating decayed noses, raw flesh around eyes that had gone blind, broken bones, ancient asthmatic coughs that lasted for hours. One of the blacksmiths came with his wife, who frightened the neighbors with her penetrating hiccoughs—the backstreets encircled the rich man's house with coughing, hacking, the odor of disease, with every kind of grief.[56]

What assembles outside the Levin house is not a group of individuals but rather a dehumanized and collective mass of symptoms, injuries, and abnormalities. The emphasis is on the repulsive sounds, smells, and visual spectacle that this crowd presents. Soviet Yiddish literature used the decaying human body as a trope for the oppression and injustice of bourgeois shtetl life.[57] The crowd storms the Levin house, driven by its intense desire to see what a dying rich man looks like; all of the orifices of the structure are thrown open, and the crowd eventually penetrates through to the dying man's bedroom. Bergelson carries forward the image of the underclass as a grotesque body in the second volume of the novel, raising questions about the capacity of "the people" to be transformed into conscious builders of socialism, as I will show.

By the end of the first volume, Penek realizes that Jewish piety is hypocrisy. As in earlier work, Jewish practice is estranged, but here the punch line is made explicit. In the 1919 novella "In a Backwoods Town," a senile woman tries to remember how an engagement is celebrated but only recalls isolated fragments of the customary practice; readers are left to draw their own conclusions. During a New Year's service, Penek watches rich Jews vying with one another to be called for the honor of reciting the blessing over the Torah (by paying for it with donations), and he wants to flee into the "treyf" (here, "not Jewish") world. Wandering into the section of the synagogue used by the poor, he listens to their comical adaptations of the liturgy. The prayer recited when the Torah ark is opened—"Give praise to God"—becomes "Go tell the lamppost." The shoemaker recites a word-for-word parody of the *asher yotser* (He who creates) prayer repeated after excretion; in referring to this blessing, Bergelson highlights the motif of the lower body. The prayer praises God for creating human beings with the orifices and passages necessary to sustain life. The blessing lauds God's wisdom, but the shoemaker substitutes the satirical comment "it's no great wisdom" (*a kleyner khokhme*).[58]

Even though Penek's development as a socialist and a writer depends on the destruction of his belief in the authority and meaning of Judaism, Jewish practice, and Jewish knowledge, the first volume of *At the Dnieper* (and in some important ways, the second also) serves as a literary repository of all these things. Whereas in his earlier work, Bergelson had "no need for ethnography," in this novel, apparently he does.[59] There is more identifiably Jewish content in *At the Dnieper* than in any other work by Bergelson. While is not exhaustive, the compendium is far-reaching, including an outline of the Sabbath morning prayers, a fable about which animal volunteered to become a human being, and a learned dispute between Mikhoel Levin and his secretary about a passage in the legal commentaries, with lengthy citations and footnotes. Other parodied prayers are also accompanied by explanatory footnotes. The didacticism of the atheist mission bleeds into a didacticism with a salvage mission.

Penek's worldview is thoroughly informed by biblical heroes; when his mother returns after her summer holiday abroad, Penek tells himself that it's the end of the seven good years, referring to Pharaoh's dream in the Joseph story; he thinks of the destitute Nakhmen the painter as the biblical Betsalel, who built the Temple. The narrative of Penek's growing disenchantment with Judaism simultaneously preserves, in a secular and literary framework, knowledge about the very thing that Penek and Bergelson's readers are supposed to discard. There is no parody of Judaism in the second volume, as I will show later; instead of losing more and more authority and importance, Judaism, and especially Jewish memory culture, grows in significance. The return to the past in the form of the historical novel is not merely a revelation of the way forward from delusion to the bright future. The return to the past is an effort to preserve its memory from destruction.

Memory

Most commentators interpret the first volume of *At the Dnieper* as a portrait of the future revolutionary. Susan Slotnick argues that the work is a bildungsroman and, as such, assumes a path of linear progression: the little boy becomes a young man, changing and growing as he does so.[60] A 1936 review of the Russian translation of the novel makes a similar point: *At the Dnieper* is the "multisided and consequential depiction of the child Penek's consciousness."[61] Isaac Bashevis Singer put it this way: *Baym Dnyepr* provides the "psychological genesis" of the hero as a future revolutionary.[62] While Penek's development as a future revolutionary depends on his rejection of the past, his simultaneous development as a writer requires that he remember everything, and in so doing, the rejection turns into its opposite. He repeats in his memory "images, whole mornings, moods [*shtimungen*] from a whole week and from separate inconsequential experiences."[63] Since Bergelson had described the importance of *shtimung* for his own creative process as early as 1910, it is likely that this portrait of the artist as a child is autobiographical: the image of Penek the little boy rehearsing memories is also in some way a portrait of Bergelson. This is not abstract knowledge but knowledge that depends on his body and senses: "Penek's every sense organ was sharpened, had a memory, and demanded to be filled, like the empty stomach of a gourmand."[64] Penek has a deep attachment to his home and the entire world of the shtetl; he feels that he must preserve "deep in the depths of his memory the slightest expression and the tiniest wrinkle" on the faces of the people who surround him. This is more than love, the narrator says; this "comes from Penek's whole body, from each separate limb"; like a wolf cub who senses in advance that he will be "driven mercilessly from his den," Penek feels compelled to commit every detail of it to his memory.[65] This picture of the creaturely, appetitive drive for memory is important. Bergelson's attention to the embodied quality of his hero's memory underscores the material and corporeal qualities of his own narrative art: the emphasis on gesture and the independent action of the parts of the body.

Penek discovers that that "each event had a main feature—a kind of quintessence [*kritshikl*]." Whenever he remembered the critical point, the event in its entirety would emerge: "the day, the morning when it took place, even the air, how it seemed then, even the odor that his nose inhaled." Penek developed the habit of making a "memory sign" (*a simen af tsu gedenken*) for each event.[66] In the second volume, Penek, who is a young man of eighteen, continues his practice. Manye has come to find him for the first time, and they sit together on a bench. In the midst of this, the most important moment of his romance with her, Penek "looks right and left, searching for signs [*simonim*] by means of which he could later remember the street, the tree, and the bench where he had received the greatest reward in his life."[67] In another version of untimeliness typical of Bergelson's protagonists, Penek does not fully experience the moment in which he finds himself, because he is preoccupied with remembering. He seeks for a way to preserve the moment after it has already taken place. This is not a portrait of the artist racing to get on the express train of the future; rather, it is a portrait of the artist struggling to hold on to the past before it passes.

The two scenes about "signs"—one from the "kosher" first volume and one from the "treyf" second volume, both about the work of memory—reveal a key dimension of Bergelson's own creative process and his characteristic orientation throughout his writing life, including the Soviet era, toward aftermaths and traces left behind. In 1940, the Birobidzhan Yiddish journal *Forpost* (*Outpost*) celebrated the thirty-year jubilee of Bergelson's creative work with a special issue devoted almost entirely to the author. Der Nister's contribution, "A Letter to David Bergelson" ("*A briv tsu Dovidn Bergelsonen*"), unlike the other, predictable articles about class warfare in *At the Dnieper* (including Dobrushin's, mentioned earlier), focuses precisely on aftermaths and traces left behind. He praises Bergelson for his "honest memories, which never expire, living eternally, as the people live."[68] The link between eternal memory and the eternal life of the people is important both because it indicates that the people in question are the Jewish people and because Bergelson himself will increasingly draw on this connection. Bergelson's early protagonists, including Mirl Hurvits, Meylekh, and Khaym-Moyshe, had given their author great pain, because although they were the most capable of their generation, they failed to find their place on life's path. Bergelson, Der Nister finds, "empathized with their destruction, their 'departure' . . . which left behind nothing more than the signs [*simonim*] of their passage through the world [ellipsis added]."[69] Der Nister is talking about the failure of Bergelson's heroes to accomplish concrete goals, but his focus on the signs left behind resonates with Bergelson's description of Penek's memory practice and the larger artistic vision crucial to Bergelson's work as a whole, still colored by a Bergsonian emphasis on infinite change, which defers fixed meaning and unitary causation, leaving instead an accumulation of traces (or signs) left behind. Bergelson was more haunted by what had been destroyed than he was inspired by what Soviet socialism was building.

In the first volume, the child Penek starts dreaming of writing a book but is not sure in what language, "like a person who doesn't know what language his life is written in."[70] In the second volume, after a humorous attempt to describe a tenement building in hopelessly flowery Hebrew, he struggles with Yiddish, deciding first that Sholem Aleichem provided the right model, because his Yiddish was simple and clear, "like you speak it" (*ot azoy, ve me redt . . . gring* [ellipsis in original]).[71] Bergelson's written Yiddish was, of course, anything but simple and clear—I will shortly address the divergence between his writing and his hero's. For now, it is important to note the centrality of the language question, which is not merely a choice between two languages, Hebrew and Yiddish; more important is determining the shades and nuances of the Yiddish that Penek will use. He realizes that Sholem Aleichem is wrong for him, because what Penek wants to write about is difficult and sad. Penek's first Yiddish story is about the departure of Yankel the coachman from the Levin house; Yankel leaves to go work on building the railway. "Departure" is another translation of the Yiddish word *opgang*, the title of Bergelson's 1919 novel (translated by Sherman as *Descent*).

Bergelson is restating his commitment to Yiddish, which is more than a literary and spoken language, because it provides the framework for how a life is lived. The writer's life, the compositions he creates, and his constant self-creation, conceived as a process, are intimately connected with one another. When Penek tears up his notebooks to rewrite his stories, he feels as if he is tearing himself up and "beginning a new Penek" (*a nayem Penek*).[72] The creative composition of memory and the creative composition of the self are linked both in Bergelson's *At the Dnieper* and in Bakhtin's work on the bildungsroman. Bakhtin emphasizes the significance of time but not in Stalinist terms of the prehistory of the present as a triumphant march to socialism. The distinctiveness of temporal periods is not absolute; rather, different periods coexist in "historical multitemporality—remnants of the past, and rudiments and tendencies of the future."[73] What comes before leaves its mark on what comes later: Bakhtin describes the *"creative effectiveness* of the past" [emphasis in original].[74] Although Bakhtin's ostensible subject matter in the essay is Goethe, and although the essay was written in the era of socialist realism (it dates from 1936–1937), traces of the past are indeed visible in the essay itself; the "creative effectiveness of the past" suggests Bergson's "creative evolution." That a single epoch contains both remnants of the past and embryos of the future resembles Bergson's comparison of time to the notes of a melody that remember and anticipate one another. Bakhtin criticizes Sir Walter Scott because Scott's notion of the past was contained in remembrance and not an active force. Rousseau's images of beautiful nature and his fantasy of a previous "golden age" were divorced from history; therefore, Bakhtin concludes, time in Rousseau "lacked real duration and irreversibility." Duration is Bergson's key concept, referring to the uncountable, heterogeneous flow of time that "gnaws on things and leaves on them the mark of its tooth."[75] Penek's search for memory signs is a self-portrait of Bergelson's engagement with the creative effectiveness of the past.

The Shape of History

The critics who insist that all that matters about *At the Dnieper* is Penek's development as a future revolutionary fail to see that Penek is not Bergelson. The difference between what Bergelson and Penek write about the tenement courtyard, for example, reveals the difference between Bergelson and his hero. In the beginning of the novel's second volume, Bergelson describes Penek's first encounter with the courtyard: "He heard the groans of people suffering either from constipation or diarrhea. As if to take revenge on the surrounding wealthy life of the city, pornographic graffiti mocking the process of human birth stared at the boy from the doors of the outhouses."[76]

This is not a picture of reality in its "revolutionary development." This is a picture of carnivalesque reality, with emphasis on the grotesque lower body and without a trace of class consciousness. Later, Penek rethinks the courtyard—"outwardly it was broken, in a state of collapse, but inwardly it was pure and whole"—because of the revolutionary commitment of the workers living in the tenement. He realizes that he will have to "completely rework" the description of the courtyard in his notebooks along the lines of "Lenin's teaching" preached by Klim about the coming revolution and the hidden unity of its disparate constituents.[77]

The narrator Bergelson and Penek are not the same, though. The opening of the second volume of *At the Dnieper* (the passage about the outhouses quoted above) does not point to the future transformation of the tenement population into disciplined revolutionary cadres. The opening of the novel, to put it another way, does not change after Penek changes his mind about the tenement courtyard. Penek rewrites his notebooks, but Bergelson did not rewrite his novel.

Moreover, Bergelson's text raises questions about the capacity of Marxist historiography to make sense of history. According to the Hebrew writer Kadison, Penek's story about the departure of Yankel the coachman from the "white house" reveals the shift from feudalism to capitalism. The Marxist interpretation leaves Penek utterly confounded, because for him the biggest issue was finding the right Yiddish for the story. Bergelson's doubts about Marxist historiography also appear in the character Magidovitsh, Penek's former tutor, an autodidact and a Yiddish author who works as a typesetting corrector at a Russian liberal newspaper and who has a phenomenal memory. Magidovitsh reflects on the relation between events—"a greatly tangled piece of life" (*a shver geplontert shtik lebn*)—and the construction of historical narrative. Socialist realist historical narrative typically emphasized linearity and transparency as well as predictability. Bergelson's character paints a different picture: "The massive piece of life, this conglomeration, shatters into pieces for him, and in a sleepy, dreamlike state he sees how what are called 'elemental forces,' 'a pogrom,' 'an uprising,' 'blood-libel'—'history'—will be organized and prepared."[78]

All the events that make up history, including uprisings, pogroms, and the action of elemental forces, are disorganized, chaotic bits and pieces of life that are later transformed into the familiar sequence called "history" (*geshikhte*). The emphasis on the construction of historical narrative and hence the constructedness of history undermines Marxist historiography and the socialist realist aesthetic of being made to see. What Magidovitsh sees is not the truth of victory already achieved but the opposite: how its truth is assembled.

Jewish Memory Culture

The "not kosher" second volume of *At the Dnieper* registers one of the pivotal moments of modern Jewish history in a Jewish way.[79] Although the number of victims was small in comparison to the civil war pogroms and the Holocaust, the 1903 Kishinev pogrom shocked the world Jewish community and propelled a generation of Jews in imperial Russia toward Zionism and other political movements. The significance of Kishinev in *At the Dnieper* can be gauged in comparison to the early work. In *The End of Everything* and *Descent*, Bergelson did not react to 1903 in any obvious way. Departing from this pattern, Bergelson becomes more and not less Jewish in the second volume of *At the Dnieper*, explicitly linking Jewish memory to the survival of the Jewish people.

Hayyim Nahman Bialik's "In the City of Slaughter," published in Hebrew in 1903 and translated into Yiddish and Russian, decried the passivity of the Jewish community, especially its men for their failure to act when Jewish women were raped. The poem sets the poet as a tourist in the "city of slaughter"; God, figured as the poet's guide, instructs him as his prophet as to what to say to the Jewish people.[80] Bialik's God excoriates the Jews for doing what they always do in the face of violence: specifically, reciting Lamentations: "Shall it be also read/ *The Book of Lamentations?*"[81] In *At the Dnieper*, when Penek learns of the events in Kishinev, passages from Lamentations immediately come to his mind, quoted in the original Hebrew: "Though I cry and call for help, he shuts out my prayers" and "Thou has made us offscouring and refuse among the peoples" (Lamentations 3:8, 3:45).[82] Bialik's searing attack on Jewish mourning was provocative when it was first published in 1905; Bergelson's citation of Lamentations is no less so. Merely reading Lamentations in 1903 without making a further demand on God, the Jewish community, and the world is an inadequate response, says Bialik. In 1940 in the Soviet Union, in contrast, quoting lines of Hebrew liturgy in a socialist realist bildungsroman is an extraordinary statement that has gone unremarked in the admittedly meager critical literature. The biblical template of Penek's and Bergelson's childhood exerts a powerful force, both in the world of 1903 when *At the Dnieper* is set and in the late 1930s when it was composed. Penek does not know in what language to write, like a person does not know in what language to live, but Penek and Bergelson know what language best expresses lamentation. Unlike other passages in the text for which footnotes are provided to clarify the Hebrew, the citation of Lamentations is left without explanation. It is not "simple, the way you speak," like Sholem Aleichem's Yiddish; readers in Bergelson's time may have recognized the citation without being able to translate it. I remarked in chapter 7 that Bergelson uses disability in *Judgment* to hint at the revolution's alien and violent language. I may not understand the language of the text called Lamentations, but I am not made deaf when it is recited. The language of lament, unlike the violence of the language of revolution, is not foreign to me. It belongs to the community, as I will show.

Jewish Memory Culture

At the Dnieper ends with two contrasting rituals: a *yizkor* (memorial) service for the victims of the Kishinev pogrom and a May Day demonstration. The memorial service in the novel reflects the actual practice of the 1930s: Jews in the Soviet Union commemorated pogroms well into the 1930s.[83] German anti-Jewish laws and anti-Jewish violence in the 1930s sparked association with tsarist-era violence, including the Kishinev pogrom.

The juxtaposition of the memorial service with political activity might seem at first merely to underscore the impotence of the traditional Jewish response to catastrophe in comparison with the efficacy of political action. Penek, as the narrator reminds us, grew up in the world of traditional Jewish observance; he feels profoundly alienated from the Jews gathered there and criticizes the efficacy of the prayers: "Many of them know that they will achieve nothing with their prayers here."[84] The Torah scrolls are merely "symbols of helplessness." The May Day demonstration, in which Penek participates as his inaugural political act, culminates in a memory. The last sentence of the novel reads, "This is the way that time remained in Penek's memory: the whip lashed out, yet people sang."[85] The present moment, the May Day demonstration, has meaning and value only for the sake of the future, when it will be a memory. "Now" is preserved as a picture for the future—a melodramatic socialist realist piece of kitsch that uses a form of verbal chiaroscuro to contrast the darkness of the tsarist whip with the bright hope of the Communist song. However, in Kiev in 1903, demonstrations planned by Socialist Revolutionaries did not take place, because of fear of a pogrom.[86]

The description of the congregants' emotions provides a sharp counterpoint to Penek's feelings about the Jewish service. As the prayers are recited, the synagogue is filled by a great noise, "as if it were a forest disturbed by a stormy wind," suggesting a divine presence. The congregants grieve for those murdered in Kishinev, and at the same time they remember their own particular sufferings: this one's sick husband, that one's crippled child— "here in this world where extortion and injustice go unpunished" (*do af ot der velt fun umbashtrofter royberay un umrekht*).[87] The world of injustice is the world in which the Jewish people live, both at the time the novel is set and at the time of its publication. Restitution has not yet taken place; perfection is not yet achieved. The bright future remains invisible. Bergelson continues in the same vein: "All remember the great anguish and immense desolation of the people [*folk*] to whom they, the ones gathered here, belong."[88] The language is specific: the individuals gathered there in that place remember the collective suffering of the people to which they belong. In an uncanny image untypical of socialist realism, a ghostly horde appears as if standing "before the eyes" (*far di oygn*) of the congregation, including not only the Kishinev dead but also all those who died since the time pogroms first began. The engineer Todi in Bergelson's *Birobidzhan Settlers* saw and made others see the city of the future, the city on the mountain, but what the congregants see here are the apparitions of the past. The end of volume two thus repeats a motif from volume one, Penek's childhood horror over "so many dead [*azoy fil toytn*]!!!" In "Among Refugees" Bergelson calls East European Jews in Berlin "ghosts"; they wander the streets in the evenings. In his first published work, "At the Depot," a nameless sorrow appears like a cloud disrupting the symmetry of the railroad ties and telegraph wires. The congregants' ghosts are different from the earlier ones because Bergelson uses them to conjure an uncanny people of the dead. The service memorializing the Kishinev victims anchors the community, both as represented in the novel and the readers of the novel in 1940 in a horrific ongoing reality and in a larger Jewish memory culture.

In this chapter, I have tried to provide an account of Bergelson's adjustment to the temporality of socialist realism, emphasizing not so much the promise of a bright future and "time forward" but rather the retrospectivism and time lag built into Stalinism's "end of history." It is significant that in his

1930 speech in Warsaw, Bergelson couched the task of living in a socialist society as attunement to a certain rhythm, "catching the beat." In his first major Soviet novel, *At the Dnieper*, however, other temporalities compete with the building of socialism, in addition to Jewish memory culture. Both have to do with the portrait of the artist as a young man, and both suggest a connection to Bergelson's own creativity and creative process. In volume one, Penek rebels against the Jewish holidays. For him, time is different, or rather, his sense of time is sharper and more intense than for other people (*fil mer vi ba andere zaynen ba im, Penekn, di tsaytn farsheydn*).[89] Time is distinctly variegated into periods when his attentiveness is at its peak, when, "looking at people, he sees something very full, absorbing an infinite number of feelings, and then he becomes festive [*yontevdik*]."[90] At other times he sees nothing, nothing grabs his attention, and he senses nothing but his own "workaday emptiness" (*vokhedik pust-un-pas*). Bergelson translates the organization of the Jewish calendar into workdays and holidays into the artist's secular sensibility of the potential for creativity, and its opposite, the lack of this possibility. A Yiddish critic writing in 1929 had used the term "festivity" to describe Bergelson's work as a whole, and the author's use of this concept to explain his young hero's creative joy is significant. *At the Dnieper* encompasses an array of rhythms and a subtly modulated temporality in which Jewish time plays a central role.

In the second volume, Penek says, "Everything I write begins in the middle, probably because I have no sense in life of what a beginning is and what an ending is."[91] This statement accords with what Yisroel Rubin wrote in 1930 about Bergelson at the Romanisches Café. One of the most characteristic words of Bergelson's table talk was "and," because each story he would recount was a continuation of the previous one; everything belonged to a whole.[92] Penek's strong sense of continuity also reflects what Bergelson said about his own writing and the relation between writing and life. "Each moment is a separate story, but all these moments become one unified story only when they flow into one definite human life."[93] Everything flows; one story leans over into another. This Bergsonian temporal sensibility is distinct from the laws of Marxist history, which demarcate separate phases of development. The story of Penek's development as an artist, like Bergelson's own story, cannot be reduced to the history of a revolutionary or socialist realist writer. The emphasis on continuity shows that Bergelson's emulation of Stalin's great break in the opening of *At the Dnieper* is purely superficial. There is no radical new beginning. In the years of the Nazi genocide and

Stalin's increasing antisemitism, when the continuity of life and story was suspended, Bergelson came face to face with radical and absolute destruction on an unprecedented scale.

Notes

1. "Vecher D. Bergelsona," *Literaturnaia gazeta*, November 14, 1934.
2. David Bergelson, *Baym Dnyepr: Penek*, vol. 1 (Moscow: Der emes, 1932), 5. All references are to this edition, and unless otherwise noted, all translations from the Yiddish are mine. There is no English translation. For another discussion of Bergelson's opening, see Dan Miron, "The Literary Image of the Shtetl," *Jewish Social Studies* 1, no. 3 (1995): 39–40.
3. For a discussion of Stalin's revolution on the cultural front, see Galin Tihanov and Katerina Clark, "Literary Criticism and the Transformations of the Literary Field during the Cultural Revolution, 1928–1932," in *A History of Russian Literary Theory and Criticism*, ed. Galin Tihanov and Evgeny Dobrenko (Pittsburgh, PA: University of Pittsburgh Press, 2011), 43–63.
4. For a discussion, see Katerina Clark, *The Soviet Novel: History as Ritual* (Chicago, IL: University of Chicago Press, 1985); Régine Robin, *Socialist Realism: An Impossible Aesthetic* (Stanford, CA: Stanford University Press, 1992); Lilya Kaganovsky, *How the Soviet Man Was Unmade: Cultural Fantasy and Male Subjectivity under Stalin* (Pittsburgh, PA: University of Pittsburgh Press, 2008).
5. Boris Groys sees a direct link between the avant-garde and socialist realism. See Boris Groys, *The Total Art of Stalinism: Avant-Garde, Aesthetic Dictatorship, and Beyond*, trans. Charles Rougle (Princeton, NJ: Princeton University Press, 1992), 14–74.
6. See Evgeny Dobrenko, "Socialism as Will and Representation, or What Legacy Are We Rejecting?" *Kritika* 5, no. 4 (2004): 675–709.
7. Vladimir Papernyi, *Kul'tura dva* (Moscow: Novoe literaturnoe obozrenie, 2006), 62.
8. David Bergelson, *Baym Dnyepr: Yunge yorn*, vol. 2 (Moscow: Der emes, 1940), 329.
9. David Bergelson, "Problemen fun der yidisher literatur," *Literarishe bleter* 24 (1930): 438.
10. Petre Petrov, *Automatic for the Masses: The Death of the Author and the Birth of Socialist Realism* (Toronto: University of Toronto Press, 2015), 152. One might argue that the literary effect of the author's disappearance is not the same as the actual execution of the author.
11. See for example Marci Shore, "On Cosmopolitanism, the Avant-Garde, and a Lost Innocence of Central Europe," in *Utopia/Dystopia*, ed. Michael D. Gordin, Helen Tilley, and Gyan Prakash (Princeton, NJ: Princeton University Press, 2010), 176–202.
12. For more on Birobidzhan and Bergelson, see Boris Kotlerman, "'Why I Am in Favour of Birobidzhan': Bergelson's Fateful Decision (1932)," in *David Bergelson: From Modernism to Socialist Realism*, ed. Joseph Sherman and Gennady Estraikh (Oxford: Legenda, 2007), 222–35.
13. For discussions of Birobidzhan, see Robert Weinberg, *Stalin's Forgotten Zion: Birobidzhan and the Making of a Soviet Jewish Homeland* (Berkeley: University of California Press, 1998). See also Jonathan Dekel-Chen, *Farming the Red Land: Jewish Agricultural Colonization and Local Soviet Power, 1924–1941* (New Haven, CT: Yale University Press, 2005), 177–78, 182.
14. For a discussion of the novel, see Gennady Estraikh, "David Bergelson: From Fellow Traveller to Soviet Classic," *Slavic Almanac* 7, no. 10 (2001): 210–13.

15. David Bergelson, *Birebidzhaner: Dertseylung* (Moscow: Emes, 1934), 276. There is no English translation.

16. Ibid., 274.

17. Ibid., 155.

18. Petrov, *Automatic for the Masses: The Death of the Author and the Birth of Socialist Realism*, 212.

19. I. K. Luppol and M. M. Rozental', eds., *Pervyi vsesoiuznyi s"ezd sovetskikh pisatelei: stenograficheskii otchet* (Moscow: Sovetskii pisatel', 1934), 271. For more on Bergelson and the Soviet Writers' Union, see Gennady Estraikh, *Evreiskaia literaturnaia zhizn' Moskvy 1917–1991* (St. Petersburg: Evropeiskii universitet v Sankt-Peterburge, 2015), 162–66.

20. Bergelson, *Birebidzhaner: Dertseylung*, 177.

21. Bergelson, *Birebidzhaner: Dertseylung*, 147–48.

22. Meir Wiener, a well-known critic of both Yiddish and Russian literature, explained in 1935 that "to see and recognize authentic reality means to see and recognize the inevitable future in its more or less developed embryo." See "O nekotorykh voprosakh sotsialisticheskogo realizma," cited by Gennady Estraikh, "A Touchstone of Socialist Realism," *Jews in Eastern Europe* 3, no. 37 (1998): 25.

23. Ibid.

24. Ibid., 181.

25. Ibid., 179.

26. Ibid., 43.

27. Evgeny Dobrenko, *The Making of the State Writer: Social and Aesthetic Origins of Soviet Literary Culture* (Stanford, CA: Stanford University Press, 2001), 366–69.

28. Luppol and Rozental', *Pervyi vsesoiuznyi s"ezd sovetskikh pisatelei: stenograficheskii otchet*, 18.

29. For a discussion, see Yuri Slezkine, *Arctic Mirrors: Russia and the Small Peoples of the North* (Ithaca, NY: Cornell University Press, 1994), 292–93.

30. Bergelson to Joseph Opatoshu, January 8, 1934, YIVO Archive, RG 436, Box 1, Folder 24.

31. Der Nister, *Di mishpokhe Mashber*, vol. 1 (New York: Ikuf, 1948), 21. For more on this novel, see Gennady Estraikh, Kerstin Hoge, and Mikhail Krutikov, eds., *Uncovering the Hidden: The Works and Life of Der Nister* (London: Legenda, 2014).

32. For a discussion of the significance of the bildungsroman in relation to the first volume of *At the Dnieper*, see Susan Slotnick, "The Novel Form in the Works of David Bergelson" (PhD diss., Columbia University, 1978). A 1936 review made a similar point; see D. Mirskii, "U Dnepra," *Izvestiia*, 1936.

33. Bergelson, *Baym Dnyepr: Penek*, 1: 457.

34. Luppol and Rozental', *Pervyi vsesoiuznyi s"ezd sovetskikh pisatelei: stenograficheskii otchet*, 270–71.

35. David Bergelson, "Cherta itoga," *Literaturnaia gazeta*, August 18, 1934: 3.

36. In a brief critical article on Bergelson published in 1930, Nakhmen Mayzel describes the first volume of *Baym Dnyepr* as the foundation of a vast building and the subsequent volumes, only one of which was completed, as so many "floors" or "stories" (*shtokn*) in which "the subsequent stories will unquestionably succeed in reaching the high points of the great, complex Jewish existence, the existence of the last twenty years, during which our tragic-fortunate generation experienced such a rich, creative life." See Nakhmen Mayzel, "Dovid Bergelson tsugast in Varshe," *Literarishe bleter*, no. 22 (1930): 402.

37. Aleksandr Pomerants, "Dovid Bergelson: Tsum 30'yorign yubiley zint s'iz dershinen zayn ershte bukh 'Arum vokzal,'" *Morgn-frayheyt*, December 31, 1939.

38. Dafna Clifford, "Dovid Bergelson's Bam Dnieper: A Passport to Moscow," in *Politics of Yiddish: Studies in Language, Literature, and Society*, ed. Dov-Ber Kerler, vol. 4, Winter Studies in Yiddish (London: Sage Publications, 1998), 157–70.

39. Dovid Eynhorn, "David Bergelson's Tsvey romanen *Nokh alemen* un *Baym Dnyepr*," *Der tog* [*The Day-Jewish Journal*], August 27, 1949.

40. Joseph Sherman, "David Bergelson (1884–1952): A Biography," in *David Bergelson: From Modernism to Socialist Realism*, ed. Joseph Sherman and Gennady Estraikh (Oxford: Legenda, 2007), 54.

41. Sherman, "David Bergelson (1884–1952): A Biography," 57.

42. Mikhail Bakhtin, *Rabelais and His World* (Cambridge, MA: MIT Press, 1965), 7.

43. Bakhtin, *Rabelais and His World*, 371.

44. Bakhtin, *Rabelais and His World*, 226.

45. Bergelson, *Baym Dnyepr: Penek*, 1: 15. Unless otherwise noted, all translations are my own.

46. Bakhtin, *Rabelais and His World*, 317.

47. Bergelson, *Baym Dnyepr: Penek*, 1: 7.

48. Bergelson, *Baym Dnyepr: Penek*, 1: 52.

49. Bergelson, *Baym Dnyepr: Penek*, 1: 78.

50. Bergelson, *Baym Dnyepr: Penek*, 1: 84.

51. Bergelson, *Baym Dnyepr: Penek*, 1: 87.

52. Bergelson, *Baym Dnyepr: Penek*, 1: 362.

53. Bergelson, *Baym Dnyepr: Penek*, 1: 385.

54. As Ryklin argues.

55. Bergelson, *Baym Dnyepr: Penek*, 1: 439.

56. Bergelson, *Baym Dnyepr: Penek*, 1: 550.

57. Perets Markish, for example, used a similar technique in his depiction of shtetl life in the screenplay for *Nosn Bekker fort aheym* (*Nosn Bekker Returns Home*) and then later for the novel *Eyns af eyns* (*One by One*).

58. Bergelson, *Baym Dnyepr: Penek*, 1: 320.

59. The phrase comes from Rachel Wischnitzer-Bernstein, cited by Hillel Kazovksy, *The Artists of the Kultur-Lige* (Jerusalem: Gesharim, 2003), 66.

60. See Slotnick, "The Novel Form in the Works of David Bergelson," 44–48, 342–66.

61. Mirskii, "U Dnepra."

62. Isaac Bashevis Singer, "Vegn Dovid Bergelson's Bam Dnyepr (ershter teyl: Penek)," *Globus* 5 (1932): 60. For a positive appraisal of his assessment of Bergelson's novel, see Seth Wolitz, "Bergelson's Yordim and I. B. Singer's," *Prooftexts* 2, no. 3 (1982): 313–21.

63. Bergelson, *Baym Dnyepr: Penek*, 1: 153.

64. Bergelson, *Baym Dnyepr: Penek*, 1: 153.

65. Bergelson, *Baym Dnyepr: Penek*, 1: 55.

66. Bergelson, *Baym Dnyepr: Penek*, 1: 185–86.

67. Bergelson, *Baym Dnyepr: Yunge yorn*, 2: 137.

68. Der Nister, "A briv tsu Dovid Bergelsonen," *Forpost* 2–3 (1940): 34.

69. Der Nister, "A briv tsu Dovid Bergelsonen," 35.

70. Bergelson, *Baym Dnyepr: Penek*, 1: 495–96.

71. Bergelson, *Baym Dnyepr: Yunge yorn*, 2: 119.

72. Bergelson, *Baym Dnyepr: Yunge yorn*, 2: 115.

73. Mikhail Bakhtin, *Speech Genres and Other Late Essays*, trans. Vern McGee (Austin: University of Texas Press, 1986), 26.

74. Ibid., 36.

75. Henri Bergson, *Creative Evolution*, trans. Arthur Mitchell (New York: H. Holt, 1911), 46.

76. Bergelson, *Baym Dnyepr: Yunge yorn*, 2: 16–17.

77. Bergelson, *Baym Dnyepr: Yunge yorn*, 2: 254, 273–74.

78. Bergelson, *Baym Dnyepr: Yunge yorn*, 2: 181.

79. For a brief overview, see Alan Mintz, "Kishinev and the Twentieth Century: Introduction," *Prooftexts* 25, no. 1–2 (2005): 1–7. An important new study of the ramifications of Kishinev is Steven Zipperstein, *Pogrom: Kishinev and the Tilt of History* (New York: Liveright Publishing Corporation, 2018).

80. As Mintz explains; see Alan L. Mintz, *Ḥurban : Responses to Catastrophe in Hebrew Literature* (New York: Columbia University Press, 1984), 150–54.

81. A. M. Klein, "In the City of Slaughter," in Mintz, *Ḥurban*, 139.

82. Bergelson, *Baym Dnyepr: Yunge yorn*, 2: 336.

83. One source comments that Jews in Kiev held a special *yizkor* service on Rosh Hashanah for the sake of the victims of the civil war. See Nisn Rozental', *Yidish lebn in ratnfarband* (Tel Aviv: I. L. Peretz, 1971), 178.

84. Bergelson, *Baym Dnyepr: Yunge yorn*, 2: 532.

85. Bergelson, *Baym Dnyepr: Yunge yorn*, 2: 539.

86. For a discussion, see Natan M. Meir, *Kiev, Jewish Metropolis: A History, 1859–1914* (Bloomington: Indiana University Press, 2010), 122.

87. Bergelson, *Baym Dnyepr: Yunge yorn*, 2: 533.

88. Bergelson, *Baym Dnyepr: Yunge yorn*, 2: 534.

89. Bergelson, *Baym Dnyepr: Penek*, 1: 303.

90. Bergelson, *Baym Dnyepr: Penek*, 1: 303.

91. Bergelson, *Baym Dnyepr: Yunge yorn*, 2:205.

92. Yisroel Rubin, "Bay di tishlekh fun Romanishn kafe: Dovid Bergelson," *Literarishe bleter* 3 (January 17, 1930): 54.

93. Letter to Shmuel Niger, September 6, 1916.

9

THE GIFT OF TIME

TWO MONTHS AFTER HITLER INVADED THE SOVIET UNION in June 1941, Bergelson and other prominent Soviet Jewish figures spoke at a mass rally and radio broadcast from Moscow, appealing to Jews all over the world to join their fight. Bergelson proclaimed the survival of the Jewish people with a quotation in Hebrew from Psalm 118, *Lo amut ki ekhye*, "I will not die, but live."[1] His son Lev served in the army and was decorated for his service; Bergelson was in the Home Guard. Bergelson became a member of the Jewish Anti-Fascist Committee (JAC), formed in 1942, and served on the editorial board of its Yiddish newspaper, *Eynikayt (Unity)*, along with Dobrushin, Kushnirov, Mikhoels, and others. He also was a member of the literary committee for *The Black Book*. The newspaper *Eynikayt* was published three times a week. Bergelson wrote dozens of short stories, articles, feuilletons, novellas, and book reviews about the death camps, killing fields, and ghettoes. Only some of this material was published in *Eynikayt*. He also wrote two plays, one of which, *I Will Live (Kh'vel lebn)*, was considered for adaptation as a film; Bergelson discussed the project enthusiastically in a letter from March 1942.[2] It did not come to fruition, however.[3] The theme of "I will live" pervades everything he wrote about the war, including his last play, the extraordinary *Prince Reuveni*, which ends with the line "You fight my people, that is, you live, my people."

The purpose of the Jewish Antifascist Committee, like other committees formed at the time, was to help mobilize the Soviet population and garner support from abroad. JAC exceeded its brief, coming to resemble a Jewish agency in the USSR. Bergelson's work for *Eynikayt* and his other journalistic prose summon his audience to support the Red Army under Stalin, while also fashioning a Jewish narrative of the war and German occupation.[4] Unlike every other period of his life, Bergelson's archive from the 1940s is available because of the confiscation of his papers during his

1949 arrest. The manuscript versions consistently reveal a greater Jewish orientation than the published work.

Even the censored voice is more Jewish than might otherwise be expected, however, as Bergelson's short piece for the Yiddish-language volume *For the Homeland, to War!* (*Farn heymland, in shklakht*), published by the Emes press in Moscow in 1941, shows. While the essay ends on the rather frenzied declaration that Stalin will save the world, its opening offers a distinctly Jewish perspective on the war. Bergelson quotes from Samuel Usque's sixteenth-century Portuguese text "Consolation on the Tribulations of Israel." Usque, a Portuguese *converso*, explains the causes of the suffering of Jews under the Inquisition and offers words of comfort.[5] Bergelson uses Usque's description of the horrific work of the Inquisition to describe the consequences of fascism under Hitler. The Inquisition is like a monstrous creature whose heart is stone and from whose mouth comes the clangor of violence; whatever living thing it touches withers and dies. Bergelson says these words are too weak to account for the destruction Hitler has wreaked. It is not merely that Bergelson has named Jewish suffering, thereby flying in the face of Soviet policy not to specify Jewish deaths. Bergelson goes further. In framing Hitler's invasion of the Soviet Union in light of events from four centuries earlier, he continues the work of Jewish memory culture, which sees the ongoing present in light of the past. Furthermore, according to Bergelson Jewish history is not merely the fate of a particular people. The fate of the Jews in the sixteenth century is everyone's fate under Hitler; Jewish experience is thus universal. The Soviets called World War II "the Great Patriotic War," invoking Russian Imperial history, but for Bergelson it is early modern Jewish history that provides the prototype.

One of Bergelson's unpublished stories, in all likelihood intended for *Eynikayt*, answers Auden's call to "stop all the clocks."[6] In occupied Belarus a German police captain marches an elderly Jew to an old noble estate. The Jew, Shlomo, is a clockmaker, and he is taken to a room filled with clocks. The German has selected one as a gift for his wife. Shlomo gets three days to fix it; the penalty for failure is death. This is no ordinary kitchen clock like the one Rybak painted in his Cubist portrait of an old Jew. Richly engraved, the clock shows Adam and Eve at the tree of knowledge of good and evil, the flood and Noah's ark, and a bright blue moon with twelve twinkling stars. Shlomo rejects the German's offer to let him live. Instead of repairing the clock, he tears out its springs and gears, smashing them to pieces. As his strength ebbs, he "stops all the clocks," destroying what he had once "brought back to life." The story ends with the note that Shlomo liked to have the clocks in perfect order in honor of the October Revolution, so that they would measure time "second by second with the revolution" (*sekunde in sekunde mit der revolutsye*).[7] His last strength utterly exhausted, he dies his own death, a small but significant triumph over the German captain.

Bergelson had used the image of the clock many times before. In "Among Refugees" clocks mark the anniversaries of death. In *Judgment* the cheap alarm clock seems to beat out the last minutes of Filipov's life. The clock in the Berlin apartment in "Old Age" continues to measure time as if the "great wind" of destruction had not swept through Ukraine during the civil war. The clock of the future hovers over Moscow in 1926, making everyone younger. In contrast, the engraved clock in Bergelson's unpublished story from the 1940s points beyond human time. The world is threatened by complete destruction; "floodwaters pour out over the earth" (*der mabul gist*); elsewhere Bergelson had written about the Germans drenching the earth in blood. The October Revolution is pitted against the new world order of the Third Reich. Biblical time and cosmological order unfold in a realm beyond human conflict. Adam and Eve and Noah and his ark indicate the pattern of creation, sin, punishment and redemption. Unlike his World War I–era story "At Night," in the clockmaker's story, the narrator does not remark on Noah's finding favor with God. Redemption hangs in the balance as a question not yet answered. The major themes of this unpublished miniature—resistance, creation, destruction, and redemption—also animate Bergelson's literary and journalistic work on World War II and the Nazi genocide, the subject of this chapter. Although Soviet patriotism and loyalty to the Jewish people are not mutually exclusive, I argue that Bergelson was less the former and more the latter—a patriot of the Jewish people. In a radio address of August 1943, Bergelson said the patriotism of Soviet Jews "did not diminish their loyalty to their Jewish people, for whom they were ready to die in the sanctification of God's name."[8]

Approximately 1.5 to 2 million Jews were killed on Soviet territory. Since the term "Holocaust" was not used at the time and not in circulation in the former Soviet Union almost until its dissolution, I generally avoid it. In his writing for *Eynikayt* generally, Bergelson documents the murder of Jews, registers Jewish heroism, calls for revenge, proclaims the continued existence of the Jewish people, and celebrates ongoing Jewish cultural productivity despite the war and occupation. In his articles "A Heroic People" ("*A folk-a giber,*" 1943), "Our Holiday" ("*Undzer yontev,*" 1945), "Praise and

Punishment" (*"Loyn un shtraf,"* 1945), his play *I Will Live*, and his review of the Moscow State Yiddish Theater production of *Joy* (*Freylekhs*, 1945), among other work, he emphasizes creativity and the future, thereby expanding his affirmation of "I will not die, but live." In "Our Holiday," Bergelson writes that the "way is open for blessing and creativity."

In his review of *Joy*, published in *Eynikayt* in 1945, Bergelson explicitly states, "The people will live on" (*dos folk lebt vayter*). The play was a theatrical adaptation of a Jewish wedding. The particular artistic accomplishment of the production, Bergelson notes, is the dance, which is no mere "pantomime" but "whole dialogues and monologues" and "ecstasy in plastic form." The dance is thus a form of communication that builds a bond among its participants and spectators. The philosopher Jonathan Lear remarks, in another context but still pertinent to Bergelson's 1945 review, "It is one thing to dance as if nothing has happened; it is another to acknowledge that something singularly awful has happened—the collapse of happenings—and then decide to dance."[9] Uncharacteristically, Bergelson inserts an autobiographical note: he remembers his own excitement and joy as a child in heder when he would hear, "They are leading the couple to the wedding canopy" (*me firt tsu der khupe*). Bergelson uses the wedding as a point of departure to argue for the coherence of the Jewish community prior to and beyond the Soviet Union. In the absence of their own territory, the wedding ceremony and customs associated with it united individuals and the entire Jewish people together.[10]

I have argued elsewhere against the assumption that there was no Soviet Jewish response to the murder of Jews. In the former Soviet Union, the scholarly and artistic response to the destruction of the Jews took on its own distinct outline in which the perspectives of Jewish victims, Jewish avengers, and Jewish victors overlapped.[11] Bergelson's insistence on the continued life and creativity of the Jewish people expresses his faith in the future—difficult to imagine in the aftermath of genocide. This is not mere conformity to Soviet propaganda or the result of ignorance about Jewish loss. His review of "Joy" comes after the liberation of Kiev, Majdanek, and other killing sites, by which time the mass murder of Jews had been exposed—and which Bergelson himself had described in other articles for *Eynikayt*.[12] Even though Bergelson praises Stalin and the Soviet Army, unlike some of his Yiddish and Russian-language contemporaries (Itsik Fefer and Il'ia Ehrenburg, for example), Bergelson does not create images of soldier superheroes, glorify violence, or gloss over suffering in order to arrive more quickly at the next phase of the bright future. His characters remain injured and burdened by their wartime losses, which are nothing less than catastrophic.

Bergelson's response to the Nazi genocide is something akin to faith, something approaching radical hope. I take this concept from Lear, whose essay on the Crow Indian nation examines how the Crow continued to imagine their lives as Crow even when they felt that their way of life was utterly destroyed. Radical hope is hope in the absence of a conception of the future, in the face of a loss of the framework in which experience can be legible. It is the decision to act even after the point when nothing can happen.

More than thirty years earlier, Bergelson had written *The End of Everything*, a novel exploring the aftereffect of the collapse of an entire way of life. Mirl Hurvits could not live the lives of her mother and father, even though she was bound to the world of the past by invisible threads, as Bergelson noted in a letter. For Mirl there was nothing to do and no place to do it; nothing mattered anymore. In a world of people bustling about, pursuing this or that goal, she was aimless. She alone faced this collapse of meaning, and she alone protested that the world kept silent despite it; "Do you hear how the world keeps silent?" she asks. The original Yiddish title of Elie Wiesel's *Night* was *And the World Kept Silent*. My point is not that Bergelson anticipated the Nazi genocide when he wrote *The End of Everything* in 1913. It is rather that before the world wars, Bergelson had already begun working out a poetics of the aftermath. The way he expresses emotion, describes the appearance of his characters, and accounts for their actions, along with his choice of words and syntax, creates a particular rhythm, a literary effect of afterwardsness and belatedness. The difference in 1946 is that the whole world of people bustling about and negotiating their relation to the past and future is gone. The problem is to reimagine another world for the remnant.

An absolute end has been reached, and there is nothing to do but be a witness to destruction, and yet at this very moment an utterly new future is coming into existence. History has not merely left the Jews behind; history has very nearly destroyed the entirety of the Jewish people. The impossible future is contemplated in the aftermath of overwhelming destruction and horror. The two visions are linked and inseparable from each other. The first part of this chapter is about aftermaths, focusing on Bergelson's 1946 story *"An eydes"* ("A Witness") and the problem of memory and testimony. Bergelson's incomplete 1946 novel *Aleksander Barash* serves as a transition to the second part, because it is a story of return to life after the unmaking of the world. Memory plays a key role in recovery.

The second part of the chapter turns to futurity by focusing on Bergelson's play, *Prince Reuveni* (*Prints Ruveni*), which, like the 1941 essay, uses the Inquisition as its point of departure. Confronted in the aftermath of the Russian civil war with mass Jewish death on an unprecedented scale, Bergelson imagined the justice of judgment delayed. Putting off the execution of judgment and allowing for more time could lead to some recalibration of the relation between victims and perpetrators of the mass violence of the revolutionary period. Immediate retribution would not allow for change, which takes time. In *Prince Reuveni*, however, Bergelson imagines redemption on an altogether different scale. Time unfolds beyond clocks and calendars. *Prince Reuveni* both relies on history and imagines a new history along with an uncertain, redemptive future. The temporality of the play is distinct from everything Bergelson had previously written. *Reuveni* offers radical hope in the face of utter hopelessness. Rehearsing the play with the actors of the Moscow State Yiddish Theater, Solomon Mikhoels said the figure of Reuveni meant "hope, resistance, and struggle."[13]

Afterimages/Aftermaths

Bergelson was among the first writers in any language to engage the problem of witnessing in relation to the mass murder of Jews during World War II. His 1943 novella *Geven iz nakht un gevorn iz tog* (*Night Became Day*), set in the mountains of the Caucasus, tells the story of three Germans and their prisoner, a young Jewish student named Godashvili. Lost in the "labyrinth" of the mountains, the Germans kill Godashvili's parents and attempt to force him to lead them out, but hunger, exhaustion, and lack of discipline lead to their undoing. Bergelson uses the framework of this unlikely plot to literalize the metaphor of the "eye-witness." One of the German soldiers was an avid participant in the killing of Jews. His fellow soldier teases him about the consequences:

> In the eyes of each [victim], you should know, is a negative, as in a camera—everything is reflected there. Experienced murderers take the trouble to close the eyes of their victims so that afterwards their photographs cannot be retrieved. This is no small matter for you . . . when the Russians win, they will extract your red image from the eyes of all the people whom you murdered.[14]

The eyes of the dead no longer see but nonetheless contain physical evidence of their own murder. The retinal afterimage of mass murder emerges out of the concern that the evidence against the Nazi perpetrators is lacking.

Bergelson imagines that the materialization of what the victims saw—the image left on their retinas as a deposit—could be preserved and harvested after their deaths. In so doing he contemplates the fantasy of impossibly perfect forensic evidence from beyond the grave.

The afterimage also appears in another story dedicated to the war and the Nazi genocide, "The Sculptor" ("*Der skulptor*"). The title character, a Jewish soldier and artist, returns from the front to his destroyed city and learns about the fate of his father, a hearing-impaired barber. The plot is unlikely: the barber took weapons and grenades to partisans in the woods and died resisting the Germans. The father has left behind his huge, heavy barber's mirror, elaborately carved with images of human faces. Carrying the mirror back home from the place where it was hidden, the son feels that he is bearing on his shoulders the body of the dead man. The son concludes that since his father stood at the mirror as he worked, it still contains his reflection (*opshpiglung*) even after his death.[15] The image of his murdered father haunts the sculptor.

Afterimages—retinal, ghostly, and photographic—can be found throughout Bergelson's work, beginning with his first published novella, "At the Depot."[16] In the 1926 story "Blindness," Otto, a veteran of World War I, is tormented by the terribly bright day: the last thing he saw and the only thing he remembers after a battlefield injury left him blind. The fantasy of the retinal afterimage of the victims of the Nazi genocide arises out of concern that their history will be suppressed and lost. Bergelson's rendering of the victims' retinal afterimage as photography resonates with earlier scientific and technological discoveries and innovations having to do with the afterimage, discussed in chapter 5. The difference between the earlier work and the wartime fiction is the uncanny legal framework. Bergelson imagines the availability of the record beyond the limits of the victims' agency and capacity for speech—beyond death—as a posthumous indictment of the perpetrator. He transforms the material deposit of the murder into a deposition against the murderer.[17]

In Bergelson's earlier modernist experimentation with extended metonymy, parts of bodies and disparate features of the human face act independently. The same experimentation appears in his work from the 1940s. In "The Sculptor," the son imagines that every feature of his father's face and even the hair on his head became organs of sight to compensate for the loss of hearing. The modernist disaggregation of any form of wholeness, as Bergelson wrote in 1919, especially including the human body, reflected both new scientific knowledge of the late nineteenth century and the decentering of the individual subject more generally. The protagonist of "The Hole Through Which Life Slips" limps behind his body, which takes the side of the Bolsheviks in advance of his psyche: the body is ahead, politically.

In his earlier fiction, Bergelson imagines a playful exchange of qualities between the human and animate world on the one side and the material and inanimate world of objects and things on the other. Humans leave marks and traces on the surrounding world, and the surrounding world responds to human experience, often in the absence of an expected human response. The boundary between the inanimate and the animate is blurred. The photograph in his 1909 "At the Depot" is an example. When Beynish Rubinstein marries for the second time, he tears up the photograph of his first wife, who died, and scatters the pieces. On one scrap, only one eye of the dead wife is visible, and it "looks gently and without reproof" at him. This eye forgives, in contrast to the dead eyes in "Night Became Day," whose evidence condemns the murderers. Eyes are opened not to see again but to make visible the moment of death. The realignment of the relations between individuals, bodies, and things celebrated by avant-garde aesthetics in the first quarter of the twentieth century takes a horrific turn in the confrontation with technologically enhanced genocide.

Testimony

"Who today is not a witness?[18] This searing question appears in the opening pages of Bergelson's 1946 story "A Witness" ("*An eydes*").[19] In an era of genocide, there is nothing else to do or be other than a witness. Everyone alive is in some sense a "sole survivor" and a "witness." The title character of the story is the sole survivor of a death camp outside Lvov where a million people died.

The closest figuration of the witness to disaster in the Jewish textual canon is found in Lamentations: "I am the man who has seen affliction by the rod of him who chastises in his anger" (3:1). Bergelson includes the first part of the sentence in the original Hebrew in another story of the same period, "Memorial Candles," which I will discuss later. Bergelson's familiarity with this text, read aloud in the synagogue every year on the ninth of Av, is undeniable. During his trial in 1952, the author spoke at length about the profound impact that the commemoration of the destruction of the Temple had on him as a little boy. Recounting his impressions from fifty years earlier, Bergelson said, "I was so immersed in the atmosphere of that temple being burned . . . that when I was six or seven years old it seemed to me that I could smell the fumes and the fire."[20]

The "atmosphere of that temple being burned" pervades Bergelson's portrait of the witness in his 1946 story. The witness's "blackened face was reminiscent of a stick of wood that had been rescued from the flames and fires."[21] He gives off the smell of burnt bones. In Lamentations, the witness to Israel's affliction has been "humbled in ashes"; the captive Jews have a "visage . . . blacker than soot, / they are not recognized in the streets;/ their skin has shriveled upon their bones, / it has become as dry as wood" (Lam. 4:8). It is difficult to imagine that Bergelson was not thinking of Lamentations when he wrote "A Witness." But in contrast to *"An eydes,"* Lamentations interweaves its picture of catastrophe with a message of comfort and hope. The framework of consolation is missing from Bergelson.

In 1926, soliciting colleagues for his new journal *In Harness,* Bergelson had called upon his fellow writers as "obligated to the time"—as the bearers of an extra burden of responsibility for their people. In 1945 everyone, not only literary authors, bore the burden. An unnamed "Jew" (*a yid*) stands in the dilapidated entranceway of an apartment building, and a passerby, Dora Aronski, feels as if the Jew is addressing her, even though he does not speak. She responds to this unspoken call with the question, "Me?— she asks the Jew—do you need me?" (*Mikh?—fregt zi bam yidn—mikh darf ir?*).[22] Even before he speaks, the witness creates a sense of obligation in the other. The witness needs an addressee in order to state his testimony; the addressee feels the witness's demand for a listener.

The Jew, who remains unnamed in the story, identifies himself as a "witness" (*ikh bin an eydes*), but Dora does not grasp his meaning: "The woman wanted to comprehend what the Jew meant."[23] Dora's incomprehension focalizes the reader's confusion. Indeed, this is the central problem of the story: What does witnessing mean? What is testimony? The ordinary meaning of the term "witness" in Yiddish and English arises from the legal context: witnesses speak to the matter at hand on the basis of what they saw, heard, or otherwise directly experienced. The term *eydes* in Yiddish can refer both to what the witness says (*eydes zogn*), in the sense of testimony or evidence, and to the person doing the witnessing (*zayn an eydes*).[24] The witness in Bergelson's story is less a person and more a reanimated fragment of testimony; he is thus an *eydes* in both senses of the Hebrew term. Like the retinal afterimage of the murdered victims in "Night Became Day," the witness resembles a material deposit of destruction; like the afterimage, he transformed into a deposition against those responsible for destruction. The word "witness" in Hebrew also has a temporal dimension: *mo'ed* (time) "implies and proceeds from meeting or appointment," including the encounter with God, the "tent of meeting," *ohel mo'ed*.[25] In Bergelson's fictionbefore the Nazi genocide and even before World War I, human beings unfailingly missed their opportunity to meet with God. After the destruction of the Jews, the terms change and the situation is reversed: mass death takes the place of God, not because it is sacralized, but because bearing witness to it is couched in terms of an impossible encounter—the experience of the death camp that cannot be known except belatedly.

As "A Witness" unfolds, the only activity that the characters perform is to add more and more written testimony to the sheets of paper containing the title character's account of the death camp. Attempting to explain his silence during the World War I, Bergelson had said that he could not write while blood was gushing everywhere. Linking writing to witnessing mitigates the problem. Earlier versions of "A Witness" (from 1945) are titled *"Farshraybendik"* ("Writings"), emphasizing the inscription of testimony as its major theme.[26] The act of writing already figures loss; the act of writing testimony in the aftermath of the Nazi genocide multiplies the loss to an impossible degree. The difference is between the intractable condition of ordinary ongoing time (which constantly changes, meaning that each written sign is belated, after the fact) and the ironclad afterwardsness of post-1945. In 1913 only Mirl Hurvits experienced afterwardsness"; in 1946, the experience is general for the entire Jewish people.

Bergelson uses actual testimony as a key part of "A Witness." In an article for *Eynikayt* about the German occupation of Minsk, Bergelson describes the fate of a Jewish professor of medicine (whom he names), renowned throughout the city for saving countless lives with his expert knowledge. The Germans harnessed the professor to a barrel of water on wheels and forced him, with whips and blows, to drag it across the city all day, providing water for their soldiers. A Belorussian offered to be harnessed to the barrel in place of the Jew and was shot on the spot.[27] Bergelson uses this episode in his work of fiction, titled in the drafts and in *Eynikayt* as "Writings." In the fiction, the professor's field is chemistry, not medicine, and he becomes Dora's father. The professor's wife, Dora's mother, and not a Belorussian worker, tries to help her husband shoulder the burden. The Germans beat and rape her, and even though she is drenched in blood, she gets up to help her husband again. Dora concludes her account of her parents' death with the moral that the Germans were fought not only with bullets but also with "beauty, ordinary human beauty." The nonfiction account ends dismally with the death of the worker who tried to sacrifice himself and was shot. The work of fiction that appeared in *Eynikayt* ends with the attempt at moral uplift. The final version, titled "A Witness," includes Dora's story about her parents but ends with the figure of the moribund witness.

Testimony as a Problem

Holocaust scholars have written extensively about the difficulty, dilemma, and paradox of Holocaust testimony. Giorgio Agamben writes about the "essential lacuna" in survivor testimony and the need to interrogate and "attempt to listen to it."[28] Bergelson's approach in "A Witness" is an "attempt to listen" to the gap in testimony.In contrast to the 1943 *It Was Night and Became Day*, which focuses on the visual record of the victims' death, "A Witness" centers on the problem of transcription and translation. The narrative weight of the story is not so much on the drama of what the witness says but rather on the writing of experience and memory across numerous boundaries, including that between life and death. The witness serves as a mediator between the dead and the living, both by addressing the living and by attempting to answer the demand from the dead. There is no mention of Stalin or the heroic Red Army in this story; neither is there any obligation to serve them; the obligation is to the dead.

It is worth dwelling on the opening in detail. "A Jew" (*a yid*) stands in the entranceway of a dilapidated building in a newly liberated city. Just above him is "a sign that had been blotted out, on which only the word *'mash'* could be read."[29] The witness testifies to the loss of an entire people and does so in the face of the obliteration of their memory. Bergelson confronts the danger that the remembrance of the Jewish people would be "blotted out," like the sign in the entranceway.

Bergelson compares the immobility of the Jew's figure to the immobility of the word on the sign. The description continues,

> from the side it seemed for a minute that he was not alive, that he was only an image painted in the dark emptiness of the missing door, and something seemed to be missing from his face, exactly in the same way as something was missing from the word *"mash"* on the sign over his head.[30]

In emphasizing his likeness to a word painted on a sign, Bergelson emphasizes the lacuna of testimony, which always includes a lack, the "something" that is missing from the Jew's face. The survivor is a piece of a materialized text that can never be complete. He too is an afterimage of monumental destruction.

In an exchange I discussed earlier, a passerby, Dora Aronski, asks the Jew in the doorway whether he needs help. The Jew answers that he is the sole survivor of over a million who perished in a death camp outside Lvov and that "everything he saw must be written down."[31] The use of the third-person form of reported speech heightens the distance between the words that were spoken and their reporting in this statement. The structure maximally removes the listener/reader from the utterance. Near the Jew is a wall on which "a useless and senseless inscription can be read: 'Khane was taken from the ghetto very early in the morning of the 27th.'"[32] Did Khane write the inscription or did someone else? Who is, or was, Khane? Is the inscription useless because no one who knew Khane is left to read it? The story continues without answering these questions. When the Jew makes his request to Dora, it seems to her that "from all the remaining walls here in the city countless other useless and senseless inscriptions scream at her."[33] The screaming inscriptions, transformed from graffiti to a form of address, produce more inscriptions: Dora agrees to serve as the witness's scribe.

The survivor speaks in Yiddish, but Dora first translates his words into Russian before writing them down, and Bergelson gives a Yiddish-language account of the process. In *The End of Everything* and *Descent*, he translates conversations that would have been held in Russian into Yiddish. In "Blindness" the narrator translates the heroine's Russian-language diary into Yiddish. Here, in contrast to the earlier work, the difference that Yiddish makes is emphasized: "Dora wrote faithfully and without hurrying, especially careful that in her translation into Russian of what the Jew said in Yiddish there would be no mistakes and no distortions from the Russian language."[34] Russian would change the nature of the testimony. Dora then reads her Russian translation aloud to the Jew and asks whether she has properly understood his words. He answers, "You are asking for my expertise? What can I tell you? The suffering was in Yiddish."[35]

The statement "The suffering was in Yiddish" is another way of saying that the suffering the witness saw and experienced was unique to Jews. Tellingly, the phrase was omitted from the 1957 Russian translation of the work.[36] There is another important dimension of this statement: only Yiddish can adequately express and describe what the suffering was, not only because the suffering uniquely belonged to Jews, but also because Yiddish is the best language of testimony. Bergelson thus anticipated what Elie Wiesel would say about Yiddish by more than forty years. Yiddish possesses unique capacities to describe the "dark times," according to Wiesel.[37] In the September 29, 1945, version published in *Eynikayt* and in the manuscript version of Bergelson's "Witness," the emphasis on the singularity of Yiddish as a language of witnessing is even greater. In these versions but nowhere else, the line "The suffering was in Yiddish" is followed by "Just try to explain today what the pain was like in another language" (*Haynt gey veys, vos far a tam zey hobn in an ander loshn*).[38]

The question about language raises another set of problems. Suffering is not in any language; rather, it is the deprivation of language, the reduction of the human being to a mere body without speech. Suffering radically isolates the sufferer from the interlocutor. The suffering of a victim makes no sense to another. Testimony about suffering, even if the original language of the speaker is preserved, is always a translation across a boundary. Describing witnessing/testimony/evidence as a problem of translation underscores the exteriority and belatedness of testimony. The very thing that extends the memory into the world as a material object and thus preserves it necessarily remains always outside it, something that comes later. The witness's oral testimony comes after the events that took place in the death camp. Transcribing his testimony takes the place of speaking it; translating takes the place of the original language in which it was spoken; and describing in Yiddish the process of translating and transcribing Yiddish testimony into Russian situates the reader at yet another remove from the original events and words.

To be sure, "A Witness" ("*An eydes*") recounts specific episodes of Nazi brutality (for example, the shooting of a woman who had just given birth), but these episodes are few and far between. Indeed, Bergelson explicitly deflates readers' expectations about the horrific and extraordinary nature of the content of his story. Another character, Kiril, reads what Dora translated and transcribed, expecting to find "something very searing, something that no one until now had ever uttered before." Instead what he reads is "ordinary, simple, and dry."[39]

Structuring the problem of testimony as a problem of translation emphasizes that the testimony is about loss and death. In "The Task of the Translator," Benjamin writes, "A translation proceeds from the original. Not indeed so much from its life as from its 'afterlife' or 'survival' [*Überleben*]."[40] Death is the originating experience from which the testimony as translation "survives." Bergelson frames the problem of testimony as translation between life and death, between oral and written speech, between memory and materialization, and between languages: between Yiddish and Russian.

The witness is a living corpse and a living document. He has no name but is referred to only as "*a yid*" or "*der yid*" (a Jew; the Jew). We know only that he was a tinsmith from Western Ukraine and that he is about sixty years old. He has no desires, preferences, habits, or dislikes, no memories of his own, and no emotions—except grief. He has no personality but is only a witness. Another way to say this is that he has no life. He is so weak that he cannot sit up straight, and Dora attaches a plank of wood to the table where they work, so that the witness can half recline as he speaks. At the end of the story, Dora fears that the Jew is dead, but he cries out, "How can I die? . . . I am still a witness!"[41] And it is not his mouth that speaks but rather his cheeks that seem to "throw out" these words, as if apart from his will and intention—as if, in other words, he no longer possesses his own will but is animated purely by the countless dead whose testimony he transmits. The ending is particularly important in light of the *Eynikayt* version of the story, which concludes with the uplifting story of Dora's mother sacrificing herself for her father. By giving testimony, the witness puts off his own death, or as Hannah Arendt says, he acts "beyond" his death.[42] The act of testimony resembles the task of Benjamin's translator. Both testifying and translating take place beyond the death of the original.

Bergelson's "A Witness" rethinks the problem of testimony. It is not the first-person oral account of injury, violence, or atrocity but instead a particular form of writing, a materialization of memory. To speak even of the authorship of testimony in the context Bergelson creates is misleading, because authorship suggests individual creativity and expression, but the story emphasizes the collective, mediated, material, and even mechanical production of the text. For example, after an evening of transcribing the witness's testimony, Dora suddenly senses from somewhere in her brain the words inscribed on the wall: "Khane was taken from the ghetto very early in the morning of the 27th." Then "her hand mechanically writes on the left, clean side of the last page she had written on" the same words about Khane. An overriding sense of compulsion pervades the witness's testimony, evidenced, for example, in the line "everything he saw must be written down" and in the senseless graffiti that "screams" at Dora, who transcribes and translates the testimony and this graffiti.

I am not saying that the Nazi genocide of the Jews cannot be represented because it constitutes some sort of sublime or limit. I am saying that Bergelson's approach to the problem of witnessing never lets readers get off the hook by allowing them to become spectators and consumers of horror and death. In structuring the time frame of "A Witness" as "after" and beyond the death of the victims (or to use Benjamin's idea of translation, as the afterlife of an original), the story asks that readers acknowledge their own position in relation to the events. The representation of testimony as action beyond death, the image of the witness as the embodiment of the camp's collective memory, and the trope of translation work together to make a maximal demand on readers. Testimony, according to Bergelson, should not say, "I have unheard-of horrors to tell you"; what it should do, rather, is make its readers feel a sense of obligation, as if they have been enjoined to do something, the same way that Dora feels when she asks the witness, "Do you need me?"

Inhabiting a position between life and death, the title character of "A Witness" embodies the testimony of the dead. In "Memorial Candles" ("*Yortsayt likht*"), written immediately after the war, Bergelson continues to grapple with the obligation of the living toward the dead. As in *Night Became Day* and "The Sculptor," the motifs of vision, seeing, blindness, and light are central to the metaphorical structure of the work. A survivor, a Jewish ophthalmologist named Dr. Soyfer, restores the sight of a Russian soldier blinded while serving in the Red Army. In the manuscript version, Bergelson underscores Jewish history and memory. From Vilnius, Dr. Soyfer experienced "the history of the Jews in the years 1939–1945" and is "truly the 'I have seen affliction.'"[43] The Yiddish text quotes the Hebrew lines of Lamentations without inserting the explanatory phrase "the man who," which would render the line "he is truly the man who has 'seen affliction.'" Embodying the Hebrew text, Dr. Soyfer is a walking fragment of Lamentations. The citation does not appear in the published version. Another small but important detail is that the "Great Patriotic War" began in 1941 with Operation Barbarossa. The killing of Jews began earlier, in 1939. Bergelson chose the Jewish date. The version appearing in *Eynikayt* omits the phrase, to avoid the emphasis on the Jewish experience of the war.

The Germans murdered Dr. Soyfer's mother, but he doesn't know how or when, and thus he cannot light a "memorial candle" (*yortsayt likht*) on the anniversary of her death. He struggles to honor her memory, coming to the conclusion that the successful operation he performed also kindles a light "in memory of his mother." "Memorial Candles" differs significantly from earlier work on similar themes. The Berlin-era story "Blindness" ends without restorative surgery for the World War I veteran and with the suicide of the heroine. It would be mistaken, however, to conclude that the happier ending of "Memorial Candles" represents mere conformity to the doctrine of the "friendship of nations" or an externally imposed optimism, a return to the "bright future" rhetoric of the 1930s, although there is an element of these tendencies and there are other stories that highlight the positive relations between Jews and other nationalities.[44] Regardless of these elements, what changes the dynamic is the context of utter catastrophe. Bergelson writes,

> There are groups of people who lose individuals. Yes, this is a loss that everyone acknowledges. But here is Dr. Soyfer with his loss: he was someone who lost his people.
> "What? What did he lose?"
> No, no one's ever experienced such a loss.[45]

It is not only the immensity of the loss that is significant. The larger framework of meaning has been destroyed; Dr. Soyfer can't see the sense of going to the synagogue (let alone the question as to whether synagogues survived the war). In the face of unprecedented catastrophe, Dr. Soyfer rewrites Jewish custom by framing the surgery in its light.

The story was originally part of a longer work, a novel titled *Aleksander Barash*, published serially but incompletely in *Eynikayt* in 1946. Bergelson never finished the novel. It has not been previously examined in the critical literature. My discussion uses both the published and the manuscript versions, in order to give the fullest possible account.[46] The title character is Dr. Soyfer's cousin. Severely wounded while fighting with the Red Army, Aleksander Barash is a young Jewish engineer trying to repair a damaged hydroelectric station in an unnamed and ruined city—in all likelihood, Kiev.[47] One of Barash's legs is amputated below the knee, and he walks with the aid of crutches.[48] He has a sister who was a promising actress until an automobile accident left her with a deformed back. While Bergelson's Birobidzhan fiction features healthy, muscled Jews, Bergelson's stories about the war and the Nazi genocide return to motifs from twenty years earlier, in which characters are injured and maimed both before and during the great historical conflicts of the time. In "Among Refugees" the left side of the "Jewish terrorist's" face has a horrifying wound that echoes images of the "broken men" of World War I, yet the hero's injury was not caused by the war; instead, the young man was born maimed. The overwhelming preponderance of wounded and maimed figures in Bergelson's fiction and journalism of the 1940s suggests an overarching wound in Jewish history itself, something fundamental that demands restoration.

Aleksander Barash is married but separated from Tatiana, his non-Jewish wife. They have a child, who is living with Tatiana's parents; Barash refuses to resume contact with his son. For reasons that are unclear, but in part stemming from her marriage to a Jew, Tatiana was sent to a ghetto and then to a concentration camp. Unlike Pushkin's Tatiana, explicitly mentioned in the text, who is faithful to her husband, Bergelson's Tatiana betrayed Barash with another man, by whom she became pregnant. The war has shattered the hero, his family, and the city. The city is in ruins, and the "ruins demand repair": Bergelson uses the religious term *tikkun* for the word I have translated as "repair," which implies cosmic and divine restoration. More than thirty-five years earlier, Bergelson began his career with a ruined train station in need of restoration; he returns to the same motif in the postwar years, in *Barash* and finally in *Prince Reuveni*, discussed later in this chapter.

At first, Aleksander and his sister feel alienated from their cousin. To them, Dr. Soyfer's gestures "replicate an old, decrepit world." Dobrish (the sister) nonetheless pursues the relation with the old doctor because he is her only link to her past and her dead father. Dr. Soyfer thinks about the generational difference between himself and his cousins in terms of two conceptions of Jewish identity. For the older generation, which would include the author, the term "Jew" is "a religious-cultural concept, or an expression of a difficult life in exile [*goles*]."[49] His younger cousins, however, belong to "another culture" with which he is unfamiliar. Later, Dr. Soyfer comes to another understanding of his Soviet Jewish relatives. Aleksander Barash's failure to speak openly about his suffering and his single-minded devotion to his work do not mean that he lacks emotion. Borrowing a motif from Chekhov, Bergelson compares his hero Aleksander to a clock in a steel case, whose inner workings are hidden from view.[50] Bergelson is making Soviet Jews and Soviet Jewish culture unfamiliar and difficult, something that is hidden and hard to understand. The war, Aleksander tells Dr. Soyfer, deprived him of both his leg and his past. He won't return to his house in the city center, because his wife's photograph is hanging on the wall. Photographs in Bergelson's fiction bear an auratic power to address their viewers from the past.

Regardless of the differences that divide them, Aleksander and his cousin face a similar problem: how to reattach themselves to life. Jewish memory and history play a vital role in the solution to the problem. The entire novel resembles an extended commentary, a *midrash* on a single line of Hebrew, "*tsrurah b'tsror ha'chaim*" ("bound up in the bond of life"). This phrase appears on Jewish headstones and in the prayer used for commemorating the dead. In the published version of "Memorial Candles" as well as the *Eynikayt* excerpts from the unfinished longer novel, Bergelson quotes the Hebrew and translates it into Yiddish as "*anknipn in lebn*." His question is not how the souls of the dead can be bound in the world to come; it is how the Jews remaining after the war can be bound up in life in this world. One episode gives a hint. Dobrish has told Dr. Soyfer that her brother can't bear to see her, because she is the living memory of the past that was destroyed. Dr. Soyfer says that there is no life without memory, and by memory, the narrator says, Dr. Soyfer means "Jewish historical memory"—memory that belongs to both the young engineer and Dr. Soyfer. This passage appears in the published version of the novel.[51] After an awkward meeting between the two male cousins, the younger man rushes after the older one, trying to remember his cousin's first name, and realizes that they are both named after the same grandfather: He calls out, "Aleksander, Asher." They share a namesake and thus both have the same name, only one is in Russian and the other, Yiddish. The young Soviet Jew Aleksander begins to recognize his connection to his own past, to Asher. The generational difference, the name, and the reflection on two types of culture suggest that Bergelson imagined himself in the role of a Dr. Soyfer, whose task as a Yiddish writer in the postwar period was to preserve Jewish memory. *Soyfer* means "scribe."

As in the stand-alone "Memorial Candles," the larger novel contemplates recovery in the context of utter loss and devastation. In the manuscript, Dr. Soyfer befriends a young girl who survived the occupation in her shtetl because the Germans didn't notice her hiding in an attic. Her clothes matched the color of the attic crossbeam, and in her mind it was the crossbeam that saved her, "not a human being, not an angel, but a crossbeam."[52] She has lasting nightmares about the crossbeam, which she regards as a living being, almost a god. This is part of her illness, Dr. Soyfer concludes. Bergelson had long been interested in the intensified human qualities of objects, but here the intensity borders on pathology. Everyone the girl knew in the shtetl, including her parents, had been killed. The narrator explains the effect that loss had on her:

> Human conceptions of the world come from established norms and laws, which provide human beings in any given moment the certainty that they will continue to exist in the next moment. But this "next moment" together with all established norms and laws was removed. Without this next moment

a girl wandered away from her shtetl, where everyone was murdered and all the houses ransacked, the doors and windows knocked out. There was a kind of distance around the girl, which did not permit her to feel any norms or laws. Didn't this mean that for her the world was destroyed?[53]

There is more than one kind of loss. There is the loss that Dr. Soyfer feels: the loss of a lifeworld with its specific traditions and customs, including the custom of lighting memorial candles. Mirl Hurvits was condemned to live a life without holidays, without festive time; for her, time was just one thing after another. The loss of time in this passage is more fundamental and more terrible. It is the radical shattering of the continuity of one's life. In the regime of terror inflicted by the Nazis, time is reduced to a series of starts and stops, without past or future, without the possibility of anything happening except sudden death. This condition, which is a form of death before biological death, is the opposite of Bergson's duration, in which one state flows into another like the notes of a melody. Repairing the destroyed city and its ruined inhabitants means more than getting the electricity to work again and more even than restoring sight to a man blinded in battle. It means restoring faith in the continuity of time and with it a sense of possibility and futurity. It requires radical hope. This is Bergelson's goal in *Prince Reuveni*. In *Reuveni* the future emerges out of a new past.

Time Has Been Mistaken

In the same period as his work on *Reuveni*, Bergelson published *Two Worlds* (*Tsvey veltn*), another work on Birobidzhan. The 1947 novel is permeated by Cold War competition between the Soviet Union and the United States. In the Soviet Union, every act, no matter how trivial, is carried out to "strengthen justice," in contrast to the United States, where everything is done for the sake of money.[54] The hero, an agricultural specialist from Chicago, travels to Birobidzhan to see what he can accomplish in the new Soviet reality. His journey has another motive as well: to rekindle a romance from his youth. Neither undertaking is successful. In *Prince Reuveni*, in contrast, Bergelson sets back the clock to the sixteenth century, to the time when the Inquisition still flourished. In so doing he brackets the Soviet project altogether, making Lenin, Stalin, the heroic Red Army, and socialism disappear. The Moscow State Yiddish Theater, directed by Solomon Mikhoels, paid Bergelson 20,000 rubles for *Prince Reuveni* in September 1944.[55] Bergelson had worked together with Mikhoels and the Moscow State Yiddish Theater earlier, in the 1933 staging of *Judgment* and "The Deaf

Man." *Prince Reuveni* was in rehearsal in 1944–45 and was given the official green light but never was performed. Multiple versions of a Russian translation of the play in the GOSET archive indicate that it was likely under consideration for publication in Russian, although this never came to fruition; the play was not published in the Soviet Union either in Yiddish or in Russian, although it was slated for publication with the *Der emes* Yiddish press in Moscow. *Prince Reuveni* was the last thing Mikhoels worked on before he was killed in 1948. Notwithstanding its ultimate suppression, the Yiddish-speaking world was aware of Bergelson's play. An article published in *Eynikayt* in 1946, describing an event in honor of Bergelson held in Moscow, characterizes *Aleksander Barash* and *Prince Reuveni* as important contributions the author had given Yiddish literature during the war years.

The story of the play's production and publication is a story of what could have been and what almost was; the theme of the play, similarly, is what could be: the imagination of an alternative or virtual reality. Bergelson's *Reuveni* coalesces multiple disparate times: the twentieth, sixteenth, eleventh, and second centuries. The Spanish refugees are compared to the victims of the Nazis; the sixteenth-century historical figure of David Reuveni appears on stage together with the eleventh-century martyr R. Amnon; Pope Clement compares Reuveni to Bar Kokhba, the leader of the Jewish revolt against the Roman Empire. The coalescence of disparate time periods is typical of traditional Jewish historiography, which typically relates one period of suffering to another; thus the Holocaust is referred to as the "third destruction," the first two being the destruction of the Temples. The multiple temporalities of *Prince Reuveni*, however, like the changing nature of personal identity that it dramatizes, have less to do with the biblical pattern of sin, suffering, and redemption and more to do with the animation of possibilities not yet realized from the past. Bergelson renders the sixteenth century as a new past from which an alternative future can arise.

The story of the real-life David Reuveni (1490?–1538) is also a tale of what could have been but was not—what was credible and thus possible but turned out not to be true. Reuveni was an impostor. Described as "a small dark man" in sixteenth-century accounts, he appeared in Venice in 1524, claiming that his brother Joseph was the king of the Jewish country of Habor, located along the river Sambation and populated by Jews from three of the ten lost tribes.[56] Where he came from is the subject of speculation; some scholars see evidence of a European origin. The so-called

Jewish prince promised Pope Clement VII that his brother's Jewish army of 300,000 men would help Christians drive the Turks out of Constantinople. With a letter of recommendation from the pope, Reuveni went to Portugal seeking financial and military support from King John III. Diego Pires, a *converso* and a high official in the Portuguese court, converted back to Judaism, taking the name Shlomo Molkho. He became a close associate of Reuveni and prophesied the coming of the messianic era in 1540, although whether Reuveni believed himself to be the messiah is unclear. Whether the two succeeded in approaching Charles V, the Holy Roman Emperor, is also unclear, but the attempt brought catastrophe. Shlomo Molkho was burned at the stake as a heretic in 1532, and Reuveni was executed in Spain in 1538. Regardless of the fantastical elements of his story, Reuveni was a credible figure to the elite of his own time, including Jews and non-Jews.[57]

Bergelson was not the only Yiddish author to have been fascinated by the history of Reuveni and Shlomo Molkho. In the interwar period, the Yiddish authors David Pinski and Joseph Opatoshu also created literary works about Reuveni, and Max Brod published a German novel, *Reubeni, Fürst der Juden* in 1925.[58] The novel was soon translated into Russian, with a preface by the noted Soviet critic Isaac Nusinov. According to Nusinov, Brod's version of the Reuveni story is an expression of bourgeois nationalism or Zionism. Reuveni fights against the oppression of the Jews with violence, sin, and the deceit of his own imposture; he rejects pure spirituality and claims that God is to be served with the body as well as the soul. In emphasizing the paradoxically salvific force of sin and violence, Nusinov attributes some of the characteristics of Sabbatai Sevi to Reuveni, especially the notion of redemption through sin. Some of these motifs can be found in Bergelson's text as well. Bergelson's Reuveni is tired of spirituality without the body, for example.

The most obvious difference between Bergelson's *Reuveni* and other literary treatments is timing. Bergelson uses the play to respond to the Nazi genocide; his *Reuveni* draws on the parallel between the Inquisition and the specific fate of the Jews during World War II. The earliest manuscript versions of the play opens with a scene at the home of a Jewish banker in Portugal. In later manuscripts and in the text published in New York in 1946 (the text I use), the play opens at sea with a ship carrying Jewish refugees from Spain to Portugal. The captain betrays them and announces that he will select who is to be killed and who sold into slavery. The first spoken line of the play unmistakably links the Inquisition with the Holocaust: "You ask why? Because you are Jews" (*Farvos, fregt ir, farvos? Vayl ir zayt yidn!*").[59] All Jews have to die because they are Jews, and nothing can save them, not assimilation or conversion. The later version, which opens with this scene, was the text in rehearsal at GOSET. In his remarks to the actors, Mikhoels emphasized the significance of the captain's lines: "With these very words he reveals the entire tragedy. Then comes the selection."[60] The term "selection" is also linked to Nazi practice.

After the opening scene in the middle of the ocean, the first act moves to the palatial mansion of a Jewish banker in Venice, where the major characters meet. Dina, formerly one of the Jewish passengers on the doomed ship, resists being sold into slavery and works as a servant in the house. Shabsay, Reuveni's servant, speaks with Dina. Shabsay is Bergelson's invention; he does not appear in other literary treatments of the Reuveni story.[61] Shabsay is a "buffoon" (*lets*) working in the Portuguese circus; the role was to be performed by Veniamin Zuskin. Mikhoels as Reuveni and Zuskin as Shabsay thus were to reprieve their partnership from *King Lear*, in which Zuskin played the Fool to Mikhoels' Lear. Shlomo Molkho makes his first appearance in the play as Diego Pires, the Christian secretary to King John of Portugal. In Act II, he reappears as the Jew Shlomo Molkho, who proclaims Reuveni to be the messiah and names himself Reuveni's prophet. The second act takes place in the court of Pope Clement; Reuveni persuades the pope that he is the ambassador from the Jewish kingdom and proposes that the pope arm the Jewish refugees waiting in the Portuguese harbor; the pope gives Reuveni letters of safe passage. Reuveni quotes the Bible in Hebrew throughout his conversation with the pope and others at the pope's court. From offstage, singing can be heard. These are the voices of Jews who have fled Spain and Portugal and come to Rome. With them, lying on a stretcher, is the eleventh-century Jewish martyr R. Amnon, who converted to Christianity and then recanted; although all his limbs were severed, he stayed alive to compose one of the most famous prayers in all Jewish liturgy, recited on the New Year, the *Unsane Tokef*. God marshals all creatures before him, opens the Book of Remembrances, and judges each and every living being; even the angels tremble.

In the course of the play, Reuveni is put on trial at the Vatican; he escapes and returns to the Portuguese harbor where the Jewish refugees are waiting. Reuveni and Shabsay lead them in a last, desperate battle. The final lines are Reuveni's "testament": "You fight, my people; that is, you live, my people."[62] While other literary adaptations of the Reuveni story end with waiting (for example, Pinski's play), Bergelson's text repeats the call to fight. *Prince Reuveni* thus also marks a departure from Bergelson's previous work in which waiting, dreaming, belatedness, and failure to act play a central and even a positive role.

Jeffrey Veidlinger argues that Bergelson's concept of time in *Reuveni* comes from "traditional rabbinic literature as noted by Yosef Hayim Yerushalmi." According to Yerushalmi, the rabbis saw the Bible as containing the "revealed pattern of the whole of human history."[63] The rabbis "play with time as though it were an accordion, expanding and collapsing it at will," because all of time fits into the patterns laid out in the Bible. Veidlinger goes on to say that the ending of the play, in which Reuveni dies "sacrificing himself *al kidesh hashem*" (in the sanctification of God's name), conforms to the fundamentally Jewish traditional temporal pattern of sin, punishment, and redemption. Hitler, and by implication Stalin, could be added to the long list of other Jewish persecutors explicitly mentioned in the play. Quotations from the *Unsane Tokef* prayer and other Jewish liturgy indicate the central importance of repentance and suggest that Bergelson and Mikhoels were repenting for the promises they could not deliver to Soviet Jews.

This interpretation highlights key issues of the play, but there is much more to be said about each one. Jewish time is not confined to the rabbinic use of the biblical template. Yerushalmi distinguishes various types of historical sensibility in the Jewish tradition. The sixteenth century, he argues, marked a new era in Jewish historiography. The catastrophe of the Spanish expulsion changed the way Jews constructed the narrative of their past. They widened the geographical and chronological scope of their historiography.[64] As Sylvie Anne Goldberg makes clear, there is a "plurality of time in Judaism." Holidays unfold in an annual cyclical pattern, but redemption is teleological, although the form it takes could disrupt time's stable patterning in a violent apocalypse—or time's stable patterning could absorb redemption into itself. More importantly, Bergelson was not limited by Jewish time, no matter how complex. By the time that he was working on *Reuveni*, Bergelson had engaged with multiple other temporal patterns in addition to those he had received from Judaism, including those offered by Bergson and Marxism–Leninism. For the French philosopher Bergson, looking to the past does not mean the repetition of a cycle but the realization of something new. It is true that Bergelson used the fundamental feature of Jewish memory culture that constructs analogies between ongoing time and prior events. He did so in his autobiographical novel *At the Dnieper*, as I showed in chapter 8, and he did so in the war years. His 1941 article and *Prince Reuveni* are built on comparisons between the Inquisition and the Nazi genocide. *Reuveni*, however, also breaks the pattern.

Employing analogies and comparisons between distinct time periods does not mean that Bergelson accepted the religious pattern of sin, suffering, and redemption associated with the rabbinic paradigm. In the play, as in the historical reality it reflects, Diego Pires recants Christianity, circumcises himself, and creates a new Jewish identity for himself: Shlomo Molkho. He offers his services to Reuveni, who rejects him. Reuveni's project is to make the Jews an "earthly force," not a spiritual one, and therefore penance does not fit his aims: "My dream is fast encircled, protected against/ All Jewish penitents" (*beli-tshuve-yidn*).[65] To argue that Bergelson himself is the penitent, that he sought "atonement for leading young Soviet Jews away from their faith," flies in the face of this explicit evidence against repentance.[66] Bergelson rejected Jewish belief decades before he became a Soviet Yiddish writer. His project, mission, and goal were not about faith; they were about Yiddish and the Jewish people. His faith, to put it another way, was not Judaism but Yiddish. Abandoning Yiddish for English, as American Jews had done, was tantamount to baptism; this statement was no less true in the 1940s than when he made it in 1926. Bergelson did not see himself as a penitent or as a crypto-Jew, because he had never converted—according to his own definition of conversion. He continued to write and speak in Yiddish, and he had said in "A Witness" that the suffering of the Jewish people during World War II was "in Yiddish."

In the play, Reuveni rejects the notion that belief alone, without territory, can make a people out of the Jews. In the play Reuveni says he wants to make the Jews a people, not only spiritually but also physically and materially, with "a foothold somewhere on earth" (*an onshpar ergets-vu af erd*).[67] He wants them to be a people like other people; that is, contesting over and securing a new world for themselves, just as other nations are doing:

Rescue, see, that's what Jews always seek
In their past, not their present—
Why not? Our epoch is a great one [*Es iz atsind a tsayt a groyse*]
For now is the time of Columbus and for new land
There is strife, and in this struggle
I will thrust my people.[68]

In act II, Reuveni reiterates this theme: "So many new worlds have been discovered / And still not the least little world / For this people."[69] The colonization and settlement of "new land" was no less a factor in the immediate postwar period than in the early modern one. It is not only land but also sea power that Reuveni emphasizes, noting that it was not for nothing that Jews historically were denied both. The "nationalist" features of the play were the object of attention by the Soviet authorities in 1946: "The salvation of the Jewish people lies in organized strength, supported by their own state."[70] While the rabbis jumble together distinct time frames because ongoing history matters little to them, ongoing history is of prime importance to Bergelson.

An unpublished article in Bergelson's arrest dossier from 1952—which has not been discussed in previous scholarship—contains the author's reflections on the new state of Israel. Bergelson expresses the gratitude of the Jewish people to the Soviet government for having been the first to recognize Israel. The establishment of a Jewish state in Palestine is nothing less than the "redemption" (*oyslezung*) of the people. "The Jewish people have survived"—this is how the article begins. For their entire history, they have been driven from place to place "through so many countries and peoples," carrying with them their desire to have "an address on Planet Earth" (*zayn baderfenish tsu hobn an adres af der planete erd*).[71] "*An adres af der planete erd*" is very nearly the same phrase that Bergelson uses in *Prints Ruveni*, "a foothold somewhere on earth" (*an onshpar ergets-vu af erd*). The similarity of the two lines suggests that in the play *Reuveni* just as in the article, Bergelson emphasizes the importance of a Jewish state. In earlier work, Bergelson typically portrayed Zionists as *luftmenshn* and misfits, hopeless dreamers dependent on the support of wealthy patrons. *Prince Reuveni* and other writing from the late 1940s indicate a significant change.

The catastrophe of the Spanish expulsion and the Holocaust shook Jewry and Judaism to their foundations. Both time periods saw unprecedented disaster on a massive scale. The fifteenth-century Ottoman victories and expulsions raised messianic expectations to a fever pitch, and according to Yerushalmi, the Reuveni/Molkho episode, aimed at provoking a new conflict between Christians and Muslims, was a way of hastening the end.[72] In contrast, Bergelson's play and Mikhoels's statements about it do not emphasize mass death and the end; rather, they emphasize a new beginning. Key passages refer to "new time" and "new space" ("*naye tsayt*," "*naye land*"). Reuveni says, "I seek refuge for my people in this new / Great time—a ray of light, a crack even." In act III, he addresses time directly:

> In the spirit of this time of renewal—
> Columbus's time . . . what's happened?
> Dazed, I ask of this great time:
> Will you bring gifts for everyone
> Except my Jewish people?
> Perhaps we alone remain guilty,
> Because we have not succeeded in taking from time
> That which it could have given us. . . . But my play is not yet over [ellipsis in original].[73]

Time excluded the Jews from its plenitude, but time was mistaken, regardless of what Shklovsky said in 1926. ("Time cannot be mistaken.") Time is not rigid, a fixed and immobile idol to whom obeisance is owed. Bergelson sets aside socialist realist time, with its demands, in favor of an open, malleable time that can be transformed. Time is not like God, who in the *Unsane Tokef* prayer opens the Book of Remembrances and judges all living things. It is not God but Bergelson who opens the book and rewrites what is written in it, changing the past. Time's openness appears only fleetingly in Bergelson's earlier fiction. The momentary coalescence of disparate events occurs in contingent moments of individual experience. It is all the more extraordinary that Bergelson should choose to expand time in a work devoted to Jewish national disaster. His depiction of the open, malleable qualities of time shares much in common with Bergson's notion of temporal dynamism and heterogeneity.

The most important elaboration of this dimension of Bergsonian time comes from Gilles Deleuze. In *Cinema 2: The Time-Image*, Deleuze writes about a "web of time which approaches, forks, is cut off or unacknowledged for centuries, embracing every possibility."[74] Time forks, and the path yet to be taken reveals another possibility. The past can be new. The recovery of a past that has not yet been depends on "images of a past in general" in which distinct time frames meet.[75] *Reuveni* unites the Babylonian and Roman time periods with the eleventh, sixteenth, and twentieth centuries. The suspension of routinized perception and reaction makes the emergence of virtuality possible, and one of the pathways toward these alternative versions of the past is through memory mistakes. In Bergelson's previous fiction, especially "The Deaf Man" and *Descent*, disturbances of memory are linked with new events both tragic and joyous. The deaf man experiences déjà vu when he sees his daughter's dead body, and Khanke has a similar experience when she realizes she is in love with Khaym-Moyshe in *Descent*. The deaf man and Khanke are under the mistaken impression that they have already lived the moment they are currently experiencing. Near the end of *Judgment*, Bergelson suggests a collective experience of déjà vu: several prisoners, including Jews and non-Jews, are sent to a concentration camp for various economic misdeeds. The timeframe is the late 1920s, when Lenin had already established a concentration camp on the White Sea island of Solovki. In Bergelson's novel, the prisoners think they are reexperiencing the past: "They went with the feeling that all this happened—a long, long time ago—they had once traveled like this, and moreover, they had to, and nothing could prevent it."[76]

In contrast, the collective déjà vu that Bergelson creates for his postwar audience in *Prince Reuveni* is not tragic, no matter how strange this may seem. It is not only that a specific catastrophic moment has happened again (the Nazis have replayed the Inquisition); in addition to this, a new past is revealed. The play brings together multiple time periods not to dramatize the eternal return of Jewish historical tragedy but rather to bring out of the past possibilities not yet realized. The rabbis disregarded historical time because it was irrelevant to the temporal pattern established once and for all in the Bible. The mixture of time periods in Bergelson's play, far from disregarding historical time, makes it supremely important. By placing the present in a past that could have been, *Reuveni* makes the present new with fresh possibilities, among which the new Jewish state is key.

The permeability of past and present reverberate throughout the play, particularly when it comes to its central trope, the fluidity of identity. Bergelson emphasizes Reuveni's awareness of his role-playing; Reuveni says, "I inspired the prince in myself / And bear the role with difficulty / As if I've been possessed by a *dybbuk*."[77] Even though Shlomo Molkho, Shabsay, and Reuveni create their own roles beyond the givens of their birth, Mikhoels singles out Shabsay and Reuveni as the two characters who conduct a play within the play; each is playing a role within his role: Shabsay plays the fool and Reuveni the prince.[78] Role-playing allows for the possibility of renewal. When Reuveni tells one of the cardinals at the Vatican that the Christians took their God from the Jews, the cardinal dismisses him by saying, "This is a very old story" (*Dos alts iz alt shoyn zeyer*). Reuveni takes the opportunity to distance himself from this narrative by saying, "If that is old, I am entirely new."[79] The condition of being "new" is not typical for Bergelson characters. Yoysef Shur is not "new" in this sense; Mirl Hurvits is "a transition point"; and Khaym-Moyshe's attachment to the dead Meylekh is an impediment to his own renewal. Reuveni is new in the sense that he has created himself anew more than once. His final "new" identity is defender of the Jews.

Shabsay emphasizes his limitless capacity to remake himself over and over again:

> I'm dead?
> From under the dirt
> A new skin grows on me
> I look with surprise
> At how my limbs
> Live again.[80]

He claims that this capacity for change and rebirth is also characteristic of the Jews as a people. The Jews have played the role of buffoon for the entire world and for the world's entire history. The malleability of time, space, and identity emphasized in the play thus ought not to be seen as punishment for sin—departure from the one true way—but rather as providing an opening into what is new and unpredictable in the present. This focus directly contradicts socialist temporality, especially in the Stalin period, which elides the present and, according to some scholars, replaces historical time altogether with the new eternity of socialist achievement.

Throughout his career, Bergelson explored the complex relation between the past and the present. It is difficult to find a work in which there is not some reflection on this issue. The abstract concept of the past in the present takes the concrete artistic form of the reanimation of the dead, from the forgiveness offered by the hero's dead wife in "At the Depot," to Khaym-Moyshe's conversations with the dead Meylekh in *Descent*, to the reanimated fragment of the testimony of the dead in "A Witness." Khaym-Moyshe's own reanimation comes, however, when he stops talking to the dead and (even if only in the briefest of moments) starts talking to the living, by addressing Khanke's need to be heard by him. Remembering the dead is not enough. Being alive to the present is also required.

The past cannot be reanimated in its original form; something new must be added in order for change to take place. In his remarks to the actors of GOSET preparing the play, Mikhoels reflects on the malleability of various social roles: "Human thought can be clothed in various guises. In the clothing of a king, a philosopher, a buffoon." The reality of the past does not necessarily limit the present but helps to create a new present. When new connections are formed across boundaries of space and time, new identities can be created. Mikhoels had something like this in mind when he encouraged his actors to find the connections, intersection, resonance, or "echo" (*pereklichka*) between their roles as defined by Bergelson's text and other figures from literature and history. Mikhoels went on to say that for Reuveni, the gallery of historical figures includes the golem, Ivan the Terrible, Shakespeare's Shylock, and an unnamed "pretender" (*samozvanets*), presumably the False Dmitrii immortalized by Pushkin, since he goes on to cite not quite accurately from memory a line from Pushkin's *Boris Godunov*: "Tsarevich ia, ten' Groznogo menia usynovila" ("I am the tsarevich, Ivan the Terrible's ghost adopted me"). Russia's dynastic crisis occurred in the late sixteenth and early seventeenth centuries, with the murder of Ivan the Terrible's youngest son, Dmitrii of Uglich, giving rise to a string of royal pretenders (False Dmitriis), and ultimately leading to the ascendance of the Romanov line. Mikhoels's use of the word *pereklichka* (resonance) echoes Bergelson's new radical vision of the permeability of past and present, including, most importantly, the possibility of new worlds. It is striking that Mikhoels describes the impression that Reuveni makes on the other characters in the play by giving an account of his own meeting with Albert Einstein during his trip to the United States. This was the most extraordinary encounter of his life, Mikhoels says. He had the opportunity to see for himself the person who was the definition of "eternity."[81] Einstein was the twentieth-century figure responsible for the most radical rethinking of the unitary nature of time, and it is striking that Mikhoels should mention him in the context of *Prince Reuveni*.

The fluidity of time emphasized by Bergelson in the text of the play resonates with the fluidity of identity emphasized by Mikhoels. For both, open time and malleable identity are positive. The Russian literary response to the history of royal imposture, however, differs significantly from Bergelson and Mikhoels's treatment of the same theme. Pushkin's pretender uses a wide panoply of linguistic styles to match whatever is required of him at a given moment, revealing a fascination with the notion of changeable identity. In contrast, in Dostoevsky's *Demons*, as the title suggests, imposture and theatricality have no positive role. Nikolai Stavrogin, the black hole at the center of the novel, is denounced by his half-mad wife as a "pretender" (*samozvanets*); she explicitly names him as "Grisha Otrep'ev, who was cursed in seven churches."[82] Grisha Otrep'ev is the true name of the False Dmitrii. Whereas imposture is demonic and destructive in Dostoevsky, in Bergelson it is rich with possibility. The figure of the impostor David Reuveni opens up a new form of Jewish historical action (namely resistance and struggle) that could bring secular redemption to the Jews.

For Bergelson and Mikhoels, the play *Prince Reuveni* was a form of struggle, not capitulation and penance. If Bergelson imagined himself reflected in it, he was David Reuveni; Shlomo Mikhoels was Shlomo Molkho. The two sixteenth-century figures, like those of the twentieth, performed their roles not to deceive and injure their people but rather to help them. In his remarks to the actors of the Moscow State Yiddish Theater, Mikhoels said that Reuveni embodied the secret of Jewish survival. The secret consisted of "resistance, struggle, and hope." In 1944, Bergelson sent the play to Zishe Weinper of the Yiddish Cultural Alliance (*Yiddisher Kultur Farband*), urging him to have it performed either in Yiddish or in English. "We are on the verge of victory," Bergelson writes. "We must also live to see comfort, to the point where our wounds will be healed." Soviet victory and Jewish restoration are separate and distinct, and Bergelson goes on to say that the latter is something Jews must do for themselves.

Prince Reuveni is a gesture of comfort and healing built from Jewish historical memory, the very thing that Asher Soyfer, the old doctor in *Aleksander Barash*, believes his young cousin lacks. Comfort does not come easily. There is almost nothing left of the Jewish people. Bergelson underscores this point again and again in his journalistic work. In his article on the Nuremberg trials, Bergelson accuses the Nazis in the voice of the remnant of the Jewish people. The voice of the Jewish people who remain says, "We, from whom the guilty ones cut off an arm or a leg, and we, from whom they took a child or several children, and we, whose mother and father were killed."[83] The Nazis deprived the Jews of life, limb, and family and reduced a "considerable portion of their people" to ashes. The title character of "A Witness" speaks from out of the ashes. The voice of the witness, like the voice of the remnant in Bergelson's Nuremberg article, only survives to bear witness to the death of his people.

The Jews are a fragment of what they once were; their collective body thus resembles the mutilated body of R. Ammon, carried on a stretcher. In the historical context of the play's composition, his significance is not only to invoke judgment and repentance. R. Ammon has no arms or legs but nonetheless urges Reuveni to fight. The radical hope of the play emerges out of the radical destruction that it confronts. Hope is easy and empty if there are abundant reasons to be hopeful. *Prince Reuveni* is Bergelson's form of radical hope, the revival of a framework of meaningfulness in Jewish terms. The clocks have been stopped, as Auden would have wished it, to mourn the dead, but they will be started again so that the living can live.

Notes

1. See Joseph Sherman, "David Bergelson (1884–1952): A Biography," in *David Bergelson: From Modernism to Socialist Realism*, ed. Joseph Sherman and Gennady Estraikh (London: Legenda, 2007), 57. For a translation of the speech, see Shimon Redlich, *War, Holocaust and Stalinism: A Documented Study of the Jewish Anti-Fascist Committee in the USSR*, New History of Russia (Oxford: Harwood Academic Publishers, 1995), 180–81.

2. Letter to Shakhne Epshteyn, March 9, 1942, in GARF, f. R-8114, opis 1, delo 982; David Bergel'son.

3. For more on the film project, see Olga Gershenson, *The Phantom Holocaust: Soviet Cinema and Jewish Catastrophe* (New Brunswick, NJ: Rutgers University Press, 2013), 31. The censorship committee permitted the play to be staged but demanded that references to Moses and Bergelson's "polemic against antisemitism" be removed. RGALI. Fond 656, opis' 5, ed. khr. 678. "D. Bergel'son, 'Budu zhit', p'esa v 3x. deistviiakh. Prilozhen protokol GURK, March 13, 1942.

4. For a discussion that focuses on this aspect of Bergelson's wartime journalism, see David Shneer, "From Mourning to Vengeance: Bergelson's Holocaust Journalism (1941–1945)," in *David Bergelson: From Modernism to Socialist Realism*, ed. Joseph Sherman and Gennady Estraikh (Oxford: Legenda, 2007), 248–68.

5. Richard Gottheil and Meyer Kayserling, "USQUE - JewishEncyclopedia.com," accessed July 9, 2016, http://www.jewishencyclopedia.com/articles/14614-usque. Bergelson could have read a discussion of, and detailed quotations from Usque in Heinrich Graetz, *Popular History of the Jews* (Hebrew Publishing Company, 1919), 243, 252, 361–362, 393–394. In *At the Dnieper*, Bergelson's child hero Penek reads Graetz's work.

6. W. H. Auden's poem "Funeral Blues," published in the late 1930s, opens with the lines: "Stop all the clocks, cut off the telephone, / Prevent the dog from barking with a juicy bone, / Silence the pianos and with muffled drum / Bring out the coffin, let the mourners come."

7. The title of the story is "Di velt muz vern in kaas." GARF, f. R-8114, opis 1, delo 982; David Bergel'son. Courtesy of Yad Vashem. I am indebted to Arkadi Zeltser, director of the Moshe Mirilashvili Center for Research on the Holocaust in the Soviet Union at Yad Vashem for sharing this material with me.

8. Transcript of radio address of August 22, 1943.

9. See Jonathan Lear, *Radical Hope: Ethics in the Face of Cultural Devastation* (Cambridge, MA: Harvard University Press, 2006), 153.

10. David Bergelson, "Freylekhs," *Eynikayt*, August 30, 1945.

11. Harriet Murav, *Music from a Speeding Train: Jewish Literature in Post-Revolutionary Russia* (Stanford, CA: Stanford University Press, 2011), 150–209.

12. I cannot agree with Jeffrey Veidlinger, who argues, "Since the mass graves, the crematories, and the annihilation of six million Jews was not yet common knowledge, the

strength of life and dignity could still be celebrated." See Jeffrey Veidlinger, *The Moscow State Yiddish Theater: Jewish Culture on the Soviet Stage* (Bloomington: Indiana University Press, 2000), 246.

13. Solomon Mikhoels, "Prints Reubeni: Rezhisserskie zametki k p'ese Davida Bergelsona na russkom i evreiskom iazykakh" (Moscow, 1945), RGALI, F 2693-1-14.

14. This is my translation. The Yiddish reads: "Ba yedn in di oygn, zolst du visn, iz faran a negativ, vi in a knipser—alts vert dort opgeshpilgt. Genite merder bamien zikh deriber, az bam obyekt, ven zey harigen im, zoln di oygn zayn tsugemakht, un me zol nokhdem nit konen aroyskrign fun dort zeyer fotografye. Es iz dir nit keyn kleynikayt . . . tomer zign di rusn krign zey aroys dayn royte tsure in di oygn ba ale mentshn, vos du host do avekge-harget." David Bergelson, *Geven iz nakht un gevorn iz tog* (Moscow: Der emes, 1943), 21.

15. David Bergelson, *Naye dertseylungen* (Buenos Aires: ICUF, 1949), 93. For a discussion of this and other postwar works, see Joseph Sherman, "'Jewish Nationalism' in Bergelson's Last Book (1947)," in *David Bergelson: From Modernism to Socialist Realism*, ed. Joseph Sherman and Gennady Estraikh (Oxford: Legenda, 2007), 285–305.

16. For a broad-ranging discussion of the afterimage, see Joan Ramon Resina and Dieter Ingenschay, eds., *After-Images of the City* (Ithaca, NY: Cornell University Press, 2003).

17. I am using language from Eric L. Santner, *On Creaturely Life: Rilke, Benjamin, Sebald* (Chicago, IL: University of Chicago Press, 2006), 75.

18. "Ver iz den haynt nit keyn eydes?" Unless otherwise noted, all translations from *"An eydes"* ("Witness") are mine and all come from Bergelson, *Naye dertseylungen*, 52.

19. For another discussion of this story, see Sherman, "Jewish Nationalism," 288–94.

20. Joshua Rubenstein and Vladimir Naumov, *Stalin's Secret Pogrom: The Postwar Inquisition of the Jewish Anti-Fascist Committee*, Annals of Communism (New Haven, CT: Yale University Press, 2001), 151.

21. Bergelson, *Naye dertseylungen*, 56.

22. Bergelson, *Naye dertseylungen*, 50.

23. The Yiddish reads: "Dos meydl vil toyfes zayn, vos meynt mit dem der yid." Ibid., 51.

24. Nahum Stuchkoff, *Der oytser fun der yidisher shprakh* (New York: YIVO Institute for Jewish Research, 1991), 282.

25. Sylvie Anne Goldberg, *Clepsydra: Essay on the Plurality of Time in Judaism*, trans. Benjamin Ivry (Stanford, CA: Stanford University Press, 2016), 78–79.

26. The story was first published in *Eynikayt* in 1945.

27. "Minsker hoypt-talyen General Von Kube" in GARF, f. R-8114, opis 1, delo 982. I have not been able to find this article in published form.

28. Giorgio Agamben, *Remnants of Auschwitz: The Witness and the Archive*, trans. Daniel Heller-Roazan (New York: Zone Books, 2002), 13.

29. The Yiddish: "An opgemekte shild, af velkher me kon iberleyenen nit mer, vi dos vort 'mash.'" Bergelson, *Naye dertseylungen*, 49.

30. The original: "Un fun der zayt dakht zikh minutnvayz, az er iz nit keyn lebediker—az er iz bloyz oysgemolt in der tunkeler pustikayt fun der felindiker tir un tsu zayn gezikht felt zikh epes, punkt vi s'felt epes tsum vort 'mash' af der shild, vos iber zayn kop." Bergelson, *Naye dertseylungen*, 49.

31. "Me darf, meynt er, farshraybn alts, vos er hot gezen." Bergelson, *Naye dertseylungen*, 52.

32. "Khanen hot men avekgefirt fun geto dem 27tn gantsfri." Bergelson, *Naye dertseylungen*, 52.

33. "Fun ale gantse geblibene vent do in shtot shrayen itst ir arop on a shir azelkhe umnutslekhe un umzinike oyfshriftn." Bergelson, *Naye dertseylungen*, 52.

34. "Dore farshraybt getray un nit gekhapt bamiendik zikh, deriker, az inem ibergebn af rusish dos, vos der yid dertseylt af yidish zol nit arayn keyn grayzn un keyn farvildungen fun der rusisher shprakh." Bergelson, *Naye dertseylungen*, 55–56.

35. "Mikh fregt ir do mevines? . . . Vos ken ikh aykh deruf zogn? . . . Di tsores zaynen geven af yidish." Bergelson, *Naye dertseylungen*, 56.

36. David Bergelson, *Izbrannoe* (Moskva: Sovetskii pisatel', 1957), 374.

37. "As long as we're talking about those dark times [*nakhttsaytn*] it is perhaps the right moment to stress that there isn't another language in the world that can describe them like Yiddish." Elie Wiesel, "Rand-makhshoves vegn yidish," *Di goldene keyt* 123 (1987): 28. By invoking "night" Wiesel suggests that the French version and subsequent English translation of his Yiddish memoir—titled *Night*—should be understood as Yiddish-language works, as if the French or English were only an afterthought. For a discussion of this passage that offers a different translation of this line, see Annette Wieviorka, *The Era of the Witness*, trans. Jared Stark (Ithaca, NY: Cornell University Press, 2006), 31–40.

38. David Bergelson, "Farshraybendik," *Eynikayt*, September 29, 1945.

39. Bergelson, *Naye dertseylungen*, 64.

40. Steven Rendall, "The Translator's Task: Walter Benjamin," *Traduction, Terminologie, Redaction* X, no. 2 (1997): 153.

41. "Vi ken ikh shtarbn? . . . Ikh bin dokh an eydes!" Bergelson, *Naye dertseylungen*, 65.

42. Hannah Arendt, *The Origins of Totalitarianism* (New York: Harcourt Brace Jovanovich, 1973), 451.

43. David Bergelson, "Aleksander Barash" (Moscow, April 1952), GARF, f. R-8114, opis 1, delo 982.

44. "Friendship" ("*Frayntshaft*"), the story of the friendship of an orphaned Jewish girl and a Russian army commander, published in 1947 in Moscow in a collection of stories, *Naye dertseylungen*.

45. Bergelson, *Naye dertseylungen*, 104. For another discussion of this passage, see Wieviorka, *The Era of the Witness*, 4–5.

46. I will indicate which is which. For the serially published novel, see David Bergelson, "Alexandr Barash," *Eynikayt*, January 1, 3, 5, 8, 10, 12, 17, 19, 22, 24, 26, 29, 31, February 2, 5, 1946.

47. Bergelson wrote several articles for *Eynikayt* about the occupation and liberation of Kiev. Some were collected in David Bergelson, *In der sho fun oyspruv* (Moscow: Sovetskii pisatel', 1985), 19, 21, 41.

48. Boris Polevoi's *Povest' o nastoiashchem cheloveke* (*Story of a Real Man*), about a double amputee who resumes his bomber missions for the Soviet army, was published in the same year, 1946.

49. Manuscript version of Bergelson, "*Aleksander Barash*."

50. Chekhov's story "The Man in a Case" ("*Chelovek v futliare*") describes the unsuccessful attempt of an isolated man to connect to the external world.

51. Bergelson, "Aleksander Barash," Jan 8, 1946.

52. Manuscript version of Bergelson, "Aleksander Barash."

53. Manuscript version of ibid.

54. Shmuel Niger, "David Bergelson's tsvey veltn," *Der tog*, December 5, 1948.

55. "Dogovor" (Moscow, September 1, 1944), RGALI, f. 2307 [GOSET],Opis 1, delo 7. For a history of the Moscow State Yiddish Theater, see Veidlinger, *The Moscow State Yiddish Theater: Jewish Culture on the Soviet Stage*.

56. For the history of Reuveni, see Miriam Eliav-Feldin, "Invented Identities: Credulity in the Age of Prophecy and Exploration," *Journal of Early Modern History* 3 (1999): 203–32; Miriam Eliav-Feldin, *Renaissance Imposters and Proofs of Identity* (New York: Palgrave Macmillan, 2012); and Natalie Zemon Davis, *Trickster Travels: A Sixteenth Century Muslim Between Worlds* (New York: Hill and Wang, 2006), 88–90. Excerpts from Reuveni's travel diary, translated into English, can be found in David Reubeni, "The Travel Diary of David Reubeni," in *Masterpieces of Jewish Literature: A Treasury of 2000 Years of Jewish Creativity*, ed. Curt Leviant (New York: Ktav Publishing House, 1969), 503–20.

57. As Eliav-Feldin points out.

58. David Pinski, "Shlomo Molkho un David HaRubeni," in *Meshikhim: Dramen* (Warsaw: David Pinski Inkorporirt, n.d., 135–239. Mikhoels's daughter writes in her memoir of her father, "He found the theme of the person seeking truth and falling into error in David Bergelson's marvelous dramatic adaptation of Max Brod's *Prince Reuveni*" (my translation). Natal 'ia Vovsi-Mikhoels, *Moi otets Solomon Mikhoels: Vospominanie o zhizni i gibeli* (Moscow: Vozvrashchenie, 1997), 184. When Bergelson read Brod is difficult to say; it is possible that he had encountered the novel earlier. In the Brod work, the future Prince Reuveni has a deaf-mute servant, Tuvya. In Bergelson's 1929 novel *Judgment*, Dr. Babitsky has a deaf-mute ward who functions as housekeeper, cook, and errand boy.

59. David Bergelson, *Prints Ruveni* (New York: Yidisher kultur farband, 1946), 11. There is no English translation; all translations are mine.

60. RGALI, Fond. 2693, opis' 1, ed. khr. 15. Mikhoels. Prints Rubeini, Besedy akteram na repetitsiiakh p'esy Bergel'sona. Stenograma. 1945.

61. The name may suggest the seventeenth-century pretender Sabbatai Sevi, who ultimately converted to Islam, but in Bergelson's play, the point is not to convert and not to give up.

62. Bergelson, *Prints Ruveni*, 126.

63. Yosef Hayim Yerushalmi, *Zakhor: Jewish History and Jewish Memory* (New York: Schocken Books, 1989).

64. Yerushalmi, *Zakhor*, 58–59.

65. Bergelson, *Prints Ruveni*, 43.

66. See Jeffrey Veidlinger, "'Du Lebst, Mayn Folk': Bergelson's Play Prints Ruveni in Historical Context (1944–1947)," in *David Bergelson: From Modernism to Socialist Realism*, ed. Joseph Sherman and Gennady Estraikh (Oxford: Legenda, 2007), 283.

67. Bergelson, *Prints Ruveni*, 81.

68. Bergelson, *Prints Ruveni*, 36.

69. Bergelson, *Prints Ruveni*, 83.

70. Report by M. Shcherbakov to A. A. Kuznetsov, October 7, 1946, cited by Redlich, *War, Holocaust and Stalinism: A Documented Study of the Jewish Anti-Fascist Committee in the USSR*, 419.

71. GARF, f. R-8114, opis 1, delo 982; David Bergel'son,, "Bez nazvaniia."

72. Yosef Hayim Yerushalmi, "Messianic Impulses in Joseph Ha-Kohen," in *Jewish Thought in the Sixteenth Century*, ed. Bernard Dov Cooperman (Cambridge, MA: Harvard University Press, 1983), 460–484.

73. Bergelson, *Prints Ruveni*, 103.

74. The language is from Borges's "The Garden of Forking Paths." See Gilles Deleuze, *Cinema 2: The Time Image* (Minneapolis: University of Minnesota Press, 1989), 49.

75. Deleuze, *Cinema 2*, 55.

76. David Bergelson, *Mides-hadin*, vol. 7, *Geklibene verk* (Vilnius: B. Kletskin, 1929), 235.

77. "Dem prints hob ikh aleyn / Arayngehoykht in mir and trog im shver / In zikh, vi kh'volt bazetst in zikh a dibuk." Bergelson, *Prints Ruveni*, 35.

78. For a discussion of self-fashioning in this period, see Stephen Greenblatt, *Renaissance Self-Fashioning* (Chicago, IL: University of Chicago Press, 1980).

79. Bergelson, *Prints Ruveni*, 57.

80. Bergelson, *Prints Ruveni*, 69.

81. Mikhoels, "Prints Reubeni: Rezhisserskie zametki k p'ese Davida Bergelsona na russkom i evreiskom iazykakh."

82. For a discussion of imposture in Dostoevsky, see Harriet Murav, *Holy Foolishness: Dostoevsky's Novels and the Poetics of Cultural Critique* (Stanford, CA: Stanford University Press, 1992).

83. The archive contains versions in Yiddish and a Russian translation, and although the article was to be sent abroad to New York, Tel Aviv, and Toronto, I cannot find evidence that it was ever published. The Russian translation is dated December 21, 1945. I am translating from the Yiddish.

CONCLUSION

D AVID BERGELSON, TOGETHER WITH THE POETS DAVID HOFSHTEYN, Perets Markish, Isaak Fefer, and Leyb Kvitko, the GOSET actor Benjamin Zuskin, Solomon Lozovskii, Leon Tal'mi, and Emilia Teumin from Sovinform Bureau, and others, was shot on August 12, 1952. Most of the victims, but not all, had been members of the Jewish Anti-Fascist Committee. Bergelson was arrested in January 1949; the secret trial began in May 1952 and ended in July of the same year. No adequate reason for the long interval between the arrest and the trial has been found. Delay and postponement, the defining characteristics of Bergelson's fiction, found their way into Bergelson's real-life tragedy. Lina Shtern was exiled, but Bergelson and the others were convicted under article 58, counterrevolutionary activity and propaganda aimed at undermining the workers' and peasants' state, which carried the death penalty. The counterrevolutionary activity was passing secrets to the Americans, which Bergelson and others denied; the propaganda was Jewish nationalism. "Defendant Bergelson . . . spread the idea that the Jews are a people set apart . . . and he extolled biblical images" (ellipsis added).[1] When Bergelson said that he was guilty "in part," he was referring to so-called Jewish nationalism; that is, the latter two charges, promoting the separateness of the Jewish people and promoting the power of biblical language. For the Stalinist government, the separate existence of the Jewish people and patriotism for the Soviet Union were incompatible concepts, but for Bergelson they were not. He had gone so far as to express this view by calling upon the religious language of martyrdom. In a radio address in August 1943, Bergelson had said that the patriotism of Soviet Jews "did not diminish their loyalty to their Jewish people, for whom they were ready to die in the sanctification of God's name."[2]

Twenty years before his arrest, Bergelson had published *Mides-hadin* (*Judgment*), his novel about the new form of socialist justice inaugurated by the Bolshevik revolution. Since Bergelson used his earlier fiction in his own defense during the 1952 secret trial, it is worth recalling some of its details. Set during the civil war in a Bolshevik outpost on the border between Ukraine and Poland, the novel describes the struggle to establish

Soviet power and the constant battles against counterrevolutionaries, Jewish smugglers, recalcitrant Red Army soldiers, and indifferent peasants. Filipov, the "boss" and head of the Cheka (All-Russian Extraordinary Commission for Struggle with Counter-Revolution and Sabotage), not Jewish, is a giant of a man who terrifies everyone. He hands out severe sentences to all who oppose him. Although it was not published until 1929, he began writing and publishing *Judgment* in part in 1926, in his own journal, *In Harness* (*In shpan*), after having publicly announced his support for the Soviet Union. He was living in Berlin at the time. Bergelson had composed other works about the theme of justice, courts, and judgments not having to do with the Cheka, but rather in response to the overwhelming anti-Jewish violence of the Russian civil war and the near-complete failure of any juridical system to bring the perpetrators to trial. In addition to *Judgment*, these include "Two Murderers," "Old Age," "Among Refugees," "Birth," "Gusts of Wind," and "Civil War," discussed in part 3.

Significantly, in the civil war fiction as a whole, harsh judgments are not executed. In "Among Refugees" the would-be Jewish terrorist kills himself and not the Petliura figure he believes responsible for the pogroms in Ukraine; Dr. Steinberg, the protagonist of the 1928 story "Birth," sets out to assassinate the man who refused to give the doctor's pregnant wife shelter during a pogrom but changes his mind and does not pull the trigger. The date is significant. Even after the fanfare about his public shift toward the Soviet Union, Bergelson is still writing about the failure of state justice, the impunity of perpetrators and bystanders of civil war pogroms, and the helplessness of the survivors. There is a striking continuity between these civil war–era protagonists and the heroes and heroines of Bergelson's earlier fiction set in the shtetl. Bergelson had transformed the delay and hesitation characteristic of the shtetl timescape and its characters into much broader philosophical terms characteristic of interwar thought. Gershom Scholem wrote about the significance of the Jonah story for the meaning of history and the problem of justice on a cosmic scale. Putting off divine judgment and retarding the onward rush of time allows humans, including the perpetrators and the survivors of massive violence, to act differently, making the emergence of some new future possible. The swift execution of judgment, whether human or divine, would foreclose this possibility. The delay in the execution of human judgment allows for divine justice, tantamount simply to the extension of time. Bergelson also used the Jonah story in a similar way. Substantial excerpts from the text of Jonah appear in Bergelson's 1926 story "Old Age." Delay in the case that the Soviets prosecuted against him in 1952, of course, did not further the cause of justice.

Twenty years later, in the aftermath of World War II and the Nazi genocide, Bergelson's mood is still not apocalyptic. He still hopes for the possibility of joy and recalls the excitement and joy he felt as a young child when there was a wedding in the shtetl. In 1919, he had characterized the revolution as a "wedding for all humanity," but in the late forties, he describes weddings in the shtetl as a bond uniting Jews. There is a significant shift toward identification with Jews. The celebration of marriages in daily life and the performance of the play *Joy*, about weddings, both serve to recreate the Jewish community; after the war, this public performance of both is particularly important and meaningful.

The would-be avengers of Jewish deaths in Bergelson's stories hesitate; their action and the action of the plot slow down. In contrast, *Judgment* allows for no delay: penal sentences are executed immediately. Sofia Pokrovskaya, the leader of the local Socialist Revolutionaries, is shot, as is Aaron Lemberger, the tannery owner who retains profits for himself, and the White courier, the femme fatale with eyes "as kosher as two crucifixes." When Filipov, the head of the Cheka, hesitates, it is so unusual that one of the characters explicitly remarks that it is the first time he has heard him say the word "maybe." Bergelson's critics in the West dismissed the novel as Bergelson's literary pledge of allegiance to the new Soviet Union, in contrast to his critics in the new Soviet Union, who saw it as insufficiently doctrinaire. The preeminent literary critic Isaac Nusinov took an alternative position. His article about Bergelson in the most important Russian-language literary encyclopedia of the time said the novel "proclaimed the justice of the fact that the revolution had to judge not by mercy, but according to the cruel deeds of the past, for only then could it fulfill its great historic tasks."[3] Nusinov's description of the novel is a gloss on its title term *Mides-hadin*, which suggests "harsh justice"; that is, judgment without the mitigating quality of mercy. The supposed message of *Judgment*—the endorsement of cruel judgment and thus the Cheka —did not make any impression on Bergelson's judges in 1952, however.

For the presiding official at Bergelson's secret trial in 1952, Bergelson's novel *Judgment* was immaterial and did not carry any weight in the determination of his guilt or innocence. What counted a great deal more heavily was the fact that Bergelson had written the novel in Berlin. Bergelson had left Moscow in 1921 with a Lithuanian passport, traveling through Kaunas to Berlin. Bergelson's accusers characterized this departure as his "illegal flight across the Soviet–Polish border." Bergelson offers an explanation for his "illegal flight" based on *Judgment,* although its relevance to the question is hard to see. I quote at length from Bergelson's statement in the trial transcript:

> Living in Berlin, when there were terrible attacks against the Cheka, I wrote a book called *Mera strogosti* [*Judgment*], where I showed (this was the end of 1924 and the beginning of 1925) that the Soviet authorities morally had the right to the most severe punishments and the right to examine each crime committed against it through a magnifying glass. And so when I was arrested, the first day was terrifying, and I had to orient myself somehow, and I told myself: "You wrote then that that the Soviet authorities had the right to examine each crime committed against it through a magnifying glass, and now you too must look at your things [*veshchi*] through a magnifying glass."[4]

Although he does not specify what the attacks against the Cheka were, it is likely that he is referring to the reorganization that took place in 1922. Bergelson went on to say that when he crossed the border in 1921, he did not consider it a crime, but he did so at the present, in 1952. In the novel published in 1929, crossing the Soviet–Polish border without the proper papers is a crime for which the penalty is death—in cases in which the smuggled goods are anti-Bolshevik propaganda or stolen documents (the "blonde" is a White courier).

It goes without saying that Bergelson's imagined prison of 1929 is nothing like the real prison in which he found himself in 1949. In the fictitious prison, there are no beatings or conveyor belt interrogations. The food seems decent: women prisoners bake bread, which smells good to Dr. Babitsky. As far as Bergelson's characterization of his own novel is concerned, there is no "magnifying glass" in *Judgment.* The phrase does not occur; no one says that the Soviet government has the right to examine crimes committed against it through a magnifying glass. The process by which Yuzi Spivak changes his mind does not take place by means of the "magnifying glass" of interrogation, probing, requests for information, and demands for specific dates, times, places, or conversations. The Jewish Anti-Fascist Committee members arrested in 1948–49 and tried in 1952 were subject to interrogations that lasted for weeks; sleep deprivation was a form of torture. Bergelson's fictitious Yuzi Spivak, in contrast, grows more and more frustrated as the days pass without interrogation. He concludes that the failure to grant him any kind of attention is a deliberate strategy designed to make him more malleable.

If the content of *Judgment* (the novel) has nothing to do with the right of the Soviet government to examine putative acts of criminality against it, Bergelson's citation of it during his actual judgment must serve another purpose—aside from the rather craven but understandable goal of showing himself always to have been a supporter of the secret police. The novel itself provides a hint. One of the prisoners, Aaron Lemberger, underreported the quantity of goods his tannery produced, shipping the hidden products abroad and receiving foreign currency as payment. The penalty for this crime is death. The night before his execution, he tells Yuzi Spivak about judgment in the Talmud: "In the tractate called Sanhedrin . . . [i]n the section known as 'the execution of judgment'—that's where it's all written down." Lemberger goes on to name the four punishments (fire, stoning, decapitation, and strangulation) and concludes by drawing a connection between the Bolsheviks and the Talmud: "And 'they'—the Bolsheviks—here, on earth, 'they' are no more than messengers." God, and not the Bolsheviks, determines human fates, meting out punishments accordingly.

It is important to clarify what I am not saying. I am not saying that Bergelson in the mid-twenties or in 1952 believed that the Soviet government was the agent of God or secular justice, even though his fictitious character Aaron Lemberger seems to think so. There is no evidence that Bergelson "repented" of his alleged crime of nationalism; on the contrary, during the trial he affirmed who and what he was—a Yiddish writer. I am saying that Bergelson imitates the behavior of his own fictitious character. The citation of the Talmud by the fictitious character Aaron Lemberger in the novel *Judgment* provides a parallel for the citation of the novel *Judgment* by its author during his judgment. *Judgment* the novel fulfills a similar function for Bergelson the accused in 1952 as the Talmud did for Aaron Lemberger in the novel *Judgment*. The literary fiction serves as the authoritative text framing the judgment of the author. The literary fiction *Judgment* provides the framework that should have been given by Soviet law and the Soviet constitution (in the late 1930s, he had, like many other writers and prominent cultural figures, written a short article praising the Stalin constitution). Of course, the authoritative source for the 1952 secret trial was not Soviet law, the Soviet constitution, or any text; the authority was Stalin, who both created and destroyed the Jewish Anti-Fascist Committee and its members. Bergelson is not attacking Stalin either but rather sidestepping him.

In citing his own literary fiction, Bergelson pushes against the strictures of his own fate, rewriting his situation in a language that he knows intimately. His own work of fiction from 1929 provided the terms by which Bergelson could understand what was happening to him in 1952. He had many years earlier created an imaginary universe, a "strange new world" where nothing was what it seemed and in which judgments were not postponed but executed, and in 1952 he was living in the Lubyanka prison, his "strange new world," and would die in it.

In the novel *Judgment*, it is not the agents of the Cheka whose interrogations prompt Yuzi Spivak to recant his own prior activity on behalf of the Socialist Revolutionaries. There is no depiction of an externally imposed process—as in aggressive, lengthy interrogations or an interior process of psychological self-examination—that reveals how Yuzi changed his mind. The only question that penetrates his consciousness is Filipov's rhetorical one: "*A ty kto, rabochii?* Do you take yourself for a worker?" Russian is used in the Yiddish text for this line. When he returns to his cell, he enters a strange dreamy state and finds himself back in his childhood during the New Year's holiday:

> Suddenly his thoughts shifted to his early years. He remembered his grandfather's voice and his father who died young, who used to read Torah, and his mother's Hebrew verses, and his grandfather's unresolved lawsuit against the landowner. His grandfather was gray, big, and strong, and had piety to match. He used to wear a long white *kittel* under his talis on Yom Kippur and both days of Rosh Hashanah, and would chant the morning prayers for the congregation with great intensity. Once on Rosh Hashanah his grandfather gave a great cry while exalting God—with such a quiver and in such a loud voice, that outside, where Yuzi was playing with the other children, his little brother Muli got so frightened that he fell down the steps of the synagogue . . .
>
> Yuzi remembered all this so clearly that the border of the white holiday tablecloth actually sparkled in his eyes and the fragrance of a piece of watermelon from that distant Rosh Hashanah morning tickled his nose. At the same time he tried to recall the question that he had to answer, and remembered Filipov's sleepy appearance—and his angry voice: "*A ty kto, rabochii?* Do you take yourself for a worker?"[5]

Remembering your experience of Rosh Hashanah, the Day of Remembrance, doubles the importance of memory. It is significant that in Bergelson's earliest works, Jewish holidays hold no particular meaning for his heroes and heroines; in *Judgment*, which Bergelson's Western-leaning critics attacked for being too pro-Bolshevik, the Jewish holiday is emotionally important for the hero. Yuzi has almost a Proustian experience of memory; all his senses are awakened—smell, hearing, sight; he seems to remember not only his own memories but also those of the generations before him, their knowledge, and their accomplishments—only there is no cup of tea and no madeleine that provokes these memories, but instead the harsh, grating voice of the "boss." There is no immediate connection between Filipov's question and Yuzi's memory of Rosh Hashanah. There is no linear chain of cause and effect. The absence of an immediate precipitating cause for the Rosh Hashanah memory is important. Yuzi has placed himself in the past rather than merely responding to a stimulus in the present. In the time leading to his first interrogation, Yuzi had engaged in a process of disconnecting himself from ongoing life—even the ongoing life of the prison had ceased to interest him. He taught himself to enter a dreamy, moribund state in preparation for his death, which he was certain would come. In the conditions of normal, active life, according to the French philosopher Henri Bergson, we remember only that which is necessary to negotiate the requirements of everyday life. If we have the will to dream, to value the useless, we may enter regions of the past that we are unaware we possess in our memory. Not faced with the demand of the next moment, we open ourselves up to vaster regions of memory. This is Yuzi's state of mind when he remembers the Rosh Hashanah of his childhood. Yuzi is like other Bergelson characters, including the protagonist of the 1909 novella "At the Depot," whose distraction and memories of the past prevent him from becoming a successful grain trader. The difference is that Yuzi's situation is a matter of life and death.

The memory of childhood also played a significant role in Bergelson's own judgment in 1952. Bergelson attempted to justify his so-called nationalism by describing his childhood experience of the observance of the ninth of Av, the commemoration of the destruction of the two Temples. Unlike his fictitious Yuzi Spivak, Bergelson did not remember the festive holiday table of the New Year. Instead, he spoke at length about the profound impact that the mournful commemoration of the destruction of the Temple of Solomon had on him as a little boy:

> There is a day that falls in August when the Temple of Solomon was burned. On this day all Jews fast for twenty-four hours, even the children. They go the cemetery for an entire day and pray there "together with the dead." I was so immersed in the atmosphere of that temple being burned—people talked about it a great deal in the community—that when I was six or seven years old it seemed to me that I could smell the fumes and the fire. I tell you this to indicate the extent to which this nationalism was engraved in my mind.[6]

Bergelson is recounting his impressions from sixty years earlier, including the smell that he imagined. Even if Bergelson is fictionalizing in order to provide an explanation for his so-called nationalism and not remembering, the image he conjures of the atmosphere of the ninth of Av and the impression it would leave on a little boy is nonetheless vivid and compelling. Bergelson had previously used the motifs of praying with the dead and the burning of the temple in Jerusalem. The child hero of his two-volume autobiographical novel *At the Dnieper* (*Baym Dnyepr*) goes to the cemetery to watch how his family members "pray with the dead." The first volume of the novel was published in 1932; the second followed in 1940. Bergelson had used Lamentations, the text chanted on the ninth of Av, as the basis for the title character of his 1946 story "A Witness." The Holocaust witness in Bergelson's story has features that echo the protagonist of Lamentations, the "man who has seen affliction." Both give off the smell of burning.

Moreover, the ninth of Av plays an important role in Bergelson's fiction from before World War I. It occurs, for example, in *The End of Everything*, first published in 1913. When Bergelson returned to the Soviet Union in 1934, *Literaturnaia gazeta* featured a front-page article heralding the event and citing this novel as among the author's outstanding achievements. Mirl Hurvits feels cut off from Jewish holidays; she is out of sync with all calendars and clocks, and she laments that her whole life will be *vokhedik*, "workaday." The ninth of Av, ironically, is one of the few days on which Mirl's mood and the tragedy of her personal life coincide with the commemoration of the Jewish national tragedy, the destruction of the two Temples. Bergelson's statement at his trial about the impression that the observance of the ninth of Av had on him as a little boy, understood in the broader context of his fiction as a whole, suggests a linkage between personal and national disaster—only in 1952 it is not a fictitious character who undergoes tragedy but the author himself.

In admitting to "nationalism" by confessing his memory of his childhood, Bergelson reveals his emotional attachment to the Jewish people through his attachment to Jewish memory culture. He had written scenes of public Jewish remembrance in *At the Dnieper* and *Prince Reuveni,* and in *Aleksander Barash* he had explicitly stressed the importance of Jewish memory for recovery after the Nazi genocide. His recitation of his childhood memory is no mere rationalization for his so-called nationalism, however. His autobiographical statement also contains a subtle hint that his own imminent death (and those of his fellow writers) would be something to be remembered by the Jewish people, something resembling a Jewish national disaster and linked to the ninth of Av, the day that the temples were destroyed and the day of collective Jewish mourning. Bergelson gave his last statement on July 11, 1952, a day after the Fast of Tammuz, which commemorates, among other events, the breach of the walls of Jerusalem. He knew that he would not be allowed to live, and he said in his final statement to the judges, "I know that I do not have long to live."[7] Whether he thought the secret trial would be revealed and the transcript would someday be published is difficult to say, although it seems unlikely. The statement he made thus resembles a message placed in a bottle and thrown into an ocean, not as a penitential act for having been mistaken about the Soviet Union, and thereby seeking to undo his past, but rather as a creative act by which he enters Jewish memory culture in the future, after his death. Remembering himself as a little boy on the ninth of Av, Bergelson "re-members" himself to the Jewish people. August 12, the day of Bergelson's execution, and also the date of his birthday, has indeed entered Jewish memory.[8] Bergelson and the other writers who were also members of the Jewish Anti-Fascist Committee are remembered more for the way they died than for the extraordinary body of literature they produced while alive.

In his final statement to the panel of judges at the secret trial, Bergelson asked that even though he had not "attained the level of a real Soviet man," the court should take into account that his pathway to that goal had begun "somewhere back in the Middle Ages."[9] Boris Polevoi's *Story of a Real Man* (*Povest' o nastoiashchem cheloveke*), published in 1946, told the heroic tale of a Soviet bomber pilot whose severe injuries—both legs were amputated—did not prevent him from flying again. Polevoi also reported on the Nuremberg trials for the mainstream Russian news media. Bergelson's last words suggest a sly irony. He had been in prison since January 1949, and while he had not lost his limbs, he had been subject to beatings, nighttime interrogations, sleeplessness, threats, and other conditions of confinement in the notorious Lubyanka prison. If being a "real man" in the Soviet Union meant being less than a fully intact human being, Bergelson and all the other members of JAC who had been arrested with him had certainly attained that elevated status.

Bergelson's words highlight belatedness, the central theme of his entire oeuvre. He attempts to use the backwardness and obsolescence of his birth culture as a mitigating circumstance. He was on the way toward real Soviet manhood, but since his starting point was farther back in the past than that of others, he had longer to go and thus had not reached the goal. He was indeed older than most of his co-defendants, but not all. He was younger than Lina Shtern the biochemist and Solomon Lozovskii, the former head of the Sovietinformburo. Ilya Vatenberg, the former senior editor at the State Publishing House of Foreign Languages, another co-defendant, only three years younger than Bergelson, said that he was free of the burden of "ancient Jewish culture" that the Yiddish writer bore.[10] Of course, Bergelson was not referring to chronology alone. He was born in 1884, but the world of his childhood lagged behind its own era and belonged more to the thirteenth or fourteenth century than to the nineteenth, or so Bergelson claimed. He was still traveling gray, dusty roads of remote, small shtetls, like the would-be Jewish terrorist of "Among Refugees." He was more like Dr. Soyfer, the scribe, the writer chronicling Jewish history, and less like Aleksander Barash, brought up in the Soviet time. In his unfinished novel *Aleksander Barash*, the older Dr. Soyfer, who belongs, like Bergelson himself, to the generation that had attended heder and studied the Talmud, realizes that his understanding of what it meant to be a Jew is distinguished from that of his younger cousin. In the unfinished novel, the Jewish historical memory that Dr. Soyfer embodies, from the beard he wears on his face to the gestures and movements he makes, is a necessary part of life in the present and the possibility of life in the future. There is no recovery from the wound of the war without it. In 1926 Bergelson said that Moscow made everyone younger, but all his writing affirmed, to the contrary, what the French philosopher Bergson called "time's bite": the traces that the ever-expanding past leaves on the present. Time had bitten into the Yiddish author Bergelson, and he could not remake himself any more quickly into a real Soviet person. Lagging behind Soviet progress was nonetheless preferable to the loss of Yiddish. During his trial, Bergelson said that the process of assimilation was nothing less than "prolonged agony."[11]

The shtetl may have been obsolete, but the Yiddish language and Jewish culture, even including some of its religious customs, were not. Especially important is the fundamental distinction between holiday and weekday time, which is a leitmotif in Bergelson's work as a whole. Transformed into the features of Penek's father's face, which was half weekday and half holiday, and reinterpreted as the empty or full artistic imagination, the Jewish temporal pattern was engraved in the structure of Bergelson's artistic creativity.

In his final statement, Bergelson said that his "nationalism" boiled down to his love of Yiddish:

> I have worked in the language for twenty-eight years, and I love it, although it has many shortcomings. I know that I do not have long to live, but I love it like a son who loves his mother. I genuinely envy Russian authors because the Russian language is much richer.[12]

For Bergelson, Yiddish was not merely the language of the suffering of the Jews; it was a language of joy. It could transcend rational sense, slow time, and express the passion of both hatred and love. Bergelson spoke these words of love for Yiddish in Russian, straddling the border between the two. His literary Yiddish was a language of translation, an estranged, difficult language condensed nearly to the point of illegibility, wonderfully evocative. He used it to tell the plotless story of afterwardsness and aftermaths in *The End of Everything*, "Blindness," and "A Witness," both before and after the catastrophic events of the twentieth century. His Yiddish also tells the story of new, modernist displacements and beginnings, in which things, people, parts of bodies, and technologies exchange places and functions and address each other, demanding and not receiving answers and falling in love at last sight.

Bergelson's declaration of love for the Yiddish language to his judges at his secret trial may be compared to other, similar expressions also made after World War II. In his 1961 "The Joy of the Yiddish Word" ("*Di freyd fun yidishn vort*"), the American Yiddish poet Yankev Glatshteyn, for example, wrote:

> O let me through to the joy of the Yiddish word.
> Give me whole, full days.
> Tie me to it, weave me in,
> Strip me of all vanities.
> Send crows to feed me, bestow crumbs on me.
> A leaking roof, a hard bed.
> But give me whole, full days.
> Let me not forget for a single moment
> The Yiddish word.[13]

Glatshteyn embraces the poverty and hardship of being a Yiddish poet, proclaiming his loyalty to it in the face of the loss of Yiddish speakers and the decline of Yiddish generally.[14] Glatshteyn suggests a comparison between Yiddish and a burial shroud; the poet asks to be bound and woven into Yiddish, losing himself in its fabric. In other contexts he spoke about the tremendous burden of responsibility facing Yiddish poets after the Holocaust.[15] Bergelson similarly suggests the difficulty and impediments facing the Yiddish writer by emphasizing the distinction between the richness of Russian and the poverty of Yiddish as languages. Yiddish is a younger literary language than Russian, and its vocabulary is more limited. Indeed, in remarks published in 1934, Bergelson had complained of the lack of Yiddish vocabulary for nature and for feminine beauty, noting the repetitiveness of Sholem Aleichem's diction with regard to these topics.[16] Bergelson did not explicitly mention the catastrophic loss of Yiddish speakers in his declaration of love for Yiddish, but poised at the brink of his own personal catastrophe, the catastrophe for Yiddish in the Soviet Union, and fully aware of the catastrophe suffered by Jews, Bergelson names himself a son of Yiddish and not Russian, declaring his allegiance and filiation to the Yiddish language and implicitly the Jewish people.

In Bergelson's major fiction the end of the action, the end of a character's life—and the end of an epoch—are not really endings. Something lingers beyond the ending, possibly, the seed of something new. Meylekh is dead, but he and Khaym-Moyshe keep up their conversation. The end of *Descent* suggests the beginning of a new conversation between Khaym-Moyshe and Khanke. In *Judgment*, the monastery is in ruins, "and yet everything seemed to be infinite, it seemed that this was no end, but instead, a beginning."[17] The moribund title character of the postwar story "A Witness" stops breathing, or so it appears, but he comes back to life by claiming a kind of eternity for himself: "How can I die? I am a witness!"

Bergelson was best known during his lifetime for his 1913 novel *The End of Everything*. The sense of an ending echoes throughout this work, from the end of the engagement at its opening to Mirl's letter at its conclusion. The title words reappear when Mirl returns to her parents' home only to find that everything had ended there. An entire way of life was gone. Mirl's problem, as Bergelson explained in a letter to his friend Shmuel Niger, was that she was still tied to the past with invisible threads. So was Bergelson.

At the end of the novel, Mirl departs, but Bergelson does not say whether she has moved to another city or to the next world. Whether she committed suicide or not, she lived on in Bergelson's imagination. In the same letter to Niger, Bergelson says that Mirl is wandering about somewhere; Bergelson does not know where. If Niger should happen to catch sight of her, he should pass along Bergelson's greetings, but quietly, and from a distance. Bergelson warns Niger not to get too close, because Mirl is easily frightened. Let me reiterate that the object of Bergelson's concern is a fictitious character. Bergelson's desire to stay in touch with Mirl as if she were real points to an inner world of imagination where there are no endings, only departures. Departures, leave-takings, and postscripts imply future meetings. The impossibility of determining in advance what form the future will take is the best guarantee that the future will be something new, and not merely a rearrangement of what has already taken place. The unpredictable past continues into the future.

Notes

1. Joshua Rubenstein and Vladimir Naumov, *Stalin's Secret Pogrom: The Postwar Inquisition of the Jewish Anti-Fascist Committee,* Annals of Communism (New Haven, CT: Yale University Press, 2001), 488. Although this is the most complete English-language source for the trial, but it (and the earlier Russian version) does not include the autobiographical statements of the defendants.

2. Transcript of radio address of August 22, 1943.

3. For a discussion that sees Bergelson's *Judgment* in a similar light, see Susan Slotnick, "The Novel Form in the Works of David Bergelson" (PhD diss., Columbia University, 1978), 233, 330.

4. Vladimir Naumov, ed., *Nepravednyi sud: Poslednii Stalinskii rasstrel (Stenogramma sudebnogo protsessa nad chlenami Evreiskogo antifashistskogo komiteta)* (Moscow: Nauka, 1994), 80.

5. Bergelson, *Mides-hadin,* 7: 137.

6. Rubenstein and Naumov, *Stalin's Secret Pogrom: The Postwar Inquisition of the Jewish Anti-Fascist Committee,* 151.

7. Rubenstein and Naumov, *Stalin's Secret Pogrom,* 452.

8. For example, during the Soviet time, and in the manner of writing between the lines, the Russian-Yiddish dictionary lists under the entry for the ordinal number 12, "the twelfth of August." See Shapiro, Spivak, and Shulman, eds., *Russko-evreiskii slovar'* (Moscow: Russkii iazyk, 1984), 121.

9. Rubenstein and Naumov, *Stalin's Secret Pogrom,* 478. For the Russian, see Vladimir Naumov, ed., *Nepravednyi sud: Poslednii Stalinskii rasstrel (Stenogramma sudebnogo protsessa nad chlenami Evreiskogo antifashistskogo komiteta)* (Moscow: Nauka, 1994), 370.

10. Rubenstein and Naumov, *Stalin's Secret Pogrom,* 459.

11. Rubenstein and Naumov, *Stalin's Secret Pogrom,* 152.

12. Rubenstein and Naumov, *Stalin's Secret Pogrom,* 452.

13. Benjamin Harshav and Barbara Harshav, *American Yiddish Poetry* (Berkeley: University of California Press, 1986), 365.

14. For a discussion of Glatshteyn's latter period in the context of his work as a whole, see Michael Galchinsky, "One Jew Talking: Jacob Glatstein's Diminished Imperative Voice," *Prooftexts* 11, no. 3 (1991): 241–57.

15. Yiddish Book Center, *Jacob Glatstein on Yiddish Poetry after the Holocaust,* 2012, https://www.youtube.com/watch?v=jYEkAvnXvBc.

16. David Bergelson, "Materyaln tsu D. Bergelsons bio-bibliografye," *Visnshaft un revolutsye* 1–2 (1934): 67–73.

17. Bergelson, *Judgment,* 62.

BIBLIOGRAPHY

Agamben, Giorgio. *Remnants of Auschwitz: The Witness and the Archive.* Translated by Daniel Heller-Roazan. New York: Zone Books, 2002.

———. *What Is an Apparatus?* Stanford, CA: Stanford University Press, 2009.

Alexopoulos, Golfo. *Stalin's Outcasts: Aliens, Citizens, and the Soviet State, 1926–1936.* Ithaca, NY: Cornell University Press, 2003.

———. "Soviet Citizenship, More or Less: Rights, Emotions, and States of Civic Belonging." *Kritika* 7, no. 3 (2006): 487–528.

———. "Stalin and the Politics of Kinship: Practices of Collective Punishment, 1920s–1940s." *Comparative Studies in Society and History* 50, no. 1 (2008): 91–117.

Almi, A. "Letste teg fun teater un opere." *Literarishe bleter.* April 4, 1930: 1–2.

Antliff, Mark. "Bergson and Cubism: A Reassessment." *Art Journal* 47, no. 4 (1988): 341–49.

———. *Inventing Bergson: Cultural Politics and the Parisian Avant-Garde.* Princeton, NJ: Princeton University Press, 1993.

———. "The Jew as Anti-Artist: Georges Sorel, Anti-Semitism, and the Aesthetics of Class Consciousness." *Oxford Art Journal* 20, no. 1 (January 1, 1997): 50–67.

———. "Cubism, Futurism, Anarchism: The Aestheticism of the 'Action D'art' Group, 1906–1920." *Oxford Art Journal* 21, no. 2 (1998): 101–20.

Apel, Dora. "'Heroes' and 'Whores': The Politics of Gender in Weimar Antiwar Imagery." *Art Bulletin* 79, no. 3 (1997): 366–84.

Ardoin, Paul, S. E. Gontarski, and Laci Mattison, eds. *Understanding Bergson, Understanding Modernism.* New York: Bloomsbury Academic, 2013.

Arendt, Hannah. *The Origins of Totalitarianism.* New York: Harcourt Brace Jovanovich, 1973.

Auerbach, A. "Imagine No Metaphors: The Dialectical Image of Walter Benjamin." *Image [&] Narrative* 18 (2007).

Babel, Isaac. *Complete Works.* Translated by Peter Constantine. New York: Norton, 2002.

Baehr, Stephen. "The Locomotive and the Giant: Power in Chekhov's 'Anna on the Neck.'" *Slavic and East European Journal* 39, no. 1 (1995): 29–37.

———. "The Machine in Chekhov's Garden: Progress and Pastoral in the Cherry Orchard." *Slavic and East European Journal* 43, no. 1 (1999): 99–121.

Bahun, Sanja. *Modernism and Melancholia: Writing as Countermourning.* Oxford: Oxford University Press, 2013.

Bakhtin, Mikhail. *Rabelais and His World.* Translated by Hélène Iswolsky. Cambridge, MA: MIT Press, 1965

———. *Speech Genres and Other Late Essays.* Translated by Vern McGee. Austin: University of Texas Press, 1986.

Banfield, Ann. "Narrative Style and the Grammar of Direct and Indirect Speech." *Foundations of Language* 10, no. 1 (May 1973): 1–39.

Baron, Wendy. "Art and the First World War." *Burlington Magazine* 136, no. 1099 (1994): 715–16.

Bartlett, Rosamund, and Sarah Dadswell, eds. *Victory Over the Sun: The World's First Futurist Opera*. Exeter, UK: University of Exeter Press, 2012.

Benjamin, Walter. *Illuminations*. New York: Schocken Books, 1969.

———. *The Arcades Project*. Cambridge, MA: Harvard University Press, 2002.

Bergelson, David, and Solomon Mikhoels. *Mera strogosti: Midas hadin, libretto*. Moscow: Der emes, 1933.

Bergelson, Lev. "Memories of My Father: The Early Years (1918–1934)." In *David Bergelson: From Modernism to Socialist Realism*, edited by Joseph Sherman and Gennady Estraikh, 79–88. Oxford: Legenda, 2007.

Bergson, Henri. *Laughter: An Essay on the Meaning of the Comic*. New York: Macmillan, 1911.

———. "Dos geheymnis fun shafn." *Di literarishe velt* 1, no. 12 (1913): 3–4.

———. *The Meaning of the War: Life & Matter in Conflict*. London: T. F. Unwin, 1915.

———. "Araynfir tsu metafizik." *Shriftn*. Summer 1919.

———. *Mind-Energy: Lectures and Essays*. New York: H. Holt, 1920.

———. *Araynfir in der metafizik*. Chicago, IL: Naye gezelshaft, 1923.

———. "Yekhid un gezelshaft." *Globus* 2, no. 6 (1932): 49–60.

———. *The Two Sources of Morality and Religion*. Garden City, NY: Doubleday, 1954.

———. *An Introduction to Metaphysics: The Creative Mind*. Totowa, NJ: Littlefield, Adams, 1965.

———. *Creative Evolution*. Lanham, MD: University Press of America, 1984.

———. *Matter and Memory*. New York: Zone Books, 1991.

Biale, David. *Gershom Scholem: Kabbalah and Counter-History*. Cambridge, MA: Harvard University Press, 1982.

Bialik, Hayyim Nahman, and H. Ravnitzky, eds. *Sefer Ha'agadah*. Translated by S. Epstein. London: Soncino, 1948.

Bishop, Ryan, and John Philips. "The Slow and the Blind." *Culture and Organization* 10, no. 1 (March 2004): 61–75.

Bloom, Harold. *The Anxiety of Influence: A Theory of Poetry*. 2nd ed. New York: Oxford University Press, 1997.

Blumental, Nakhmen. "Anri Bergson's Gelekhter in yidish." *Literarishe bleter* 247, no. 4 (1929): 78.

Blümlinger, Christa. "Lumière, the Train and the Avant-Garde." In *The Cinema of Attractions Reloaded*, edited by Wanda Strauven, 245–64. Amsterdam: Amsterdam University Press, 2006.

Blumshteyn, Y. *Darvinizm un zayn teorye*. New York: Folksbildung, 1915.

Bowlt, John E. *Russian Art of the Avant-Garde: Theory and Criticism, 1902–1934*. New York: Viking Press, 1976.

Brenner, Naomi. "Milgroym, Rimon and Interwar Jewish Bilingualism." *Journal of Jewish Identities*, 7, no. 1 (January 2014): 23–48.

———. *Lingering Bilingualism: Modern Hebrew and Yiddish Literatures in Contact*. Syracuse, NY: Syracuse University Press, 2015, 63–71.

Buber, Martin. "Di yehudes un di menshhayt." *Di yidishe velt* 2 (1913): 91–101.

———. *On Judaism*. New York: Schocken Books, 1967.

Buck-Morss, Susan. *The Dialectics of Seeing: Walter Benjamin and the Arcades Project*. Cambridge, MA: MIT Press, 1989.

———. "Walter Benjamin: Between Academic Fashion and the Avant-Garde." *Pandaemonium Germanicaum* 5 (May 2001): 73–88.

Budnitskii, Oleg. "Shots in the Back: On the Origin of the Anti-Jewish Pogroms of 1918–1921." In *Jews in the East European Borderlands: Essays in Honor of John D. Klier*, edited by Eugune M. Avrutin and Harriet Murav, 187–201. Boston, MA: Academic Studies Press, 2012.

Budnitskii, Oleg, and Aleksandra Polian, eds. *Russko-evreiskii Berlin, 1920–1941*. Moscow: NLO, 2013.

Buldakov, Vladimir. *Krasnaia smuta: Priroda i posledstviia revoliutsionnogo nasilia*. Moscow: Rosspen, 1997.

Bulgakova, Oksana. *Fabrika zhestov*. Moscow: NLO, 2005.

Caplan, Marc. *How Strange the Change: Language, Temporality, and Narrative Fiction in Peripheral Modernisms*. Stanford, CA: Stanford University Press, 2011.

Caruth, Cathy. *Unclaimed Experience : Trauma, Narrative, and History*. Baltimore, MD: Johns Hopkins University Press, 1996.

Castree, N. "The Spatio-Temporality of Capitalism." *Time and Society* 18, no. 1 (2009): 26–61.

Chaplin, Charlie. "In vos bashteyt der sod fun mayn derfolg." *Literarishe bleter*, no. 56 (1925): 3.

Charney, Daniel. "A briv fun Moskve." *Tealit* 5 (1924): 22–23.

———. "Vi David Bergelson iz farnart gevorn keyn rusland." *Der tog*, August 5, 1956, sec. 2.

Chekhov, A. P. *Dramy i komedii*. Berlin: I. P. Ladyzhnikov, 1920.

———. *Five Plays*. Translated by Ronald Hingley. New York: Oxford University Press, 1977.

Clark, Katerina. *The Soviet Novel: History as Ritual*. Chicago, IL: University of Chicago Press, 1985.

Clifford, Dafna. "Dovid Bergelson's Bam Dnieper: A Passport to Moscow." In *Politics of Yiddish: Studies in Language, Literature, and Society*, edited by Dov-Ber Kerler, 4: 157–70. Winter Studies in Yiddish. Thousand Oaks, CA: Sage, 1998.

———. "From Exile to Exile: Bergelson's Berlin Years." In *Yiddish and the Left*, edited by Mikhail Krutikov and Gennady Estraikh, 242–58. Oxford: Legenda, 2001.

Colebrook, Claire. "The Joys of Atavism." In *Understanding Bergson, Understanding Modernism*, edited by Paul Ardoin, S. E. Gontarski, and Laci Mattison, 281–96. New York: Bloomsbury, 2013.

Crary, Jonathan. "Techniques of the Observer." *October* 45 (Summer 1988): 3–35.

———. "Unbinding Vision." *October* 68, 1 (Spring 1994): 21–44.

———. *Suspensions of Perception: Attention, Spectacle, and Modern Culture*. Cambridge, MA: MIT Press, 1999.

Curtis, James. "Bergson and Russian Formalism." *Comparative Literature* 28, no. 2 (1976): 109–21.

Darwin, Charles. *The Descent of Man and Selection in Relation to Sex*. New York: D. Appleton, 1897.

———. *On the Origin of Species*. Cambridge, MA: Harvard University Press, 1964.

de Lauretis, Teresa. *Alice Doesn't: Feminism, Semiotics, Cinema*. Bloomington: Indiana University Press, 1984.

Dekel-Chen, Jonathan. *Farming the Red Land: Jewish Agricultural Colonization and Local Soviet Power, 1924–1941*. New Haven, CT: Yale University Press, 2005.

Deleuze, Gilles. *Cinema 2: The Time Image*. Minneapolis: University of Minnesota Press, 1989.

———. *Bergsonism*. New York: Zone Books, 1991.

Der Nister. "A briv tsu Dovid Bergelsonen." *Forpost* 2–3 (1940): 34–38.

———. *Di mishpokhe Mashber*. Vol. 1. 2 vols. New York: Ikuf, 1948.

Derrida, Jacques. *Writing and Difference*. Chicago, IL: University of Chicago Press, 1978.

Doane, Mary Ann. *The Emergence of Cinematic Time: Modernity, Contingency, the Archive*. Cambridge, MA: Harvard University Press, 2002.

Dobrenko, Evgeny. *Metafora vlasti: Literatura Stalinskoi epokhi v istoricheskom osveshchenii*. Munich: Verlag Otto Sagner, 1993.

———. *The Making of the State Writer: Social and Aesthetic Origins of Soviet Literary Culture*. Stanford, CA: Stanford University Press, 2001.

———. "Socialism as Will and Representation, or What Legacy Are We Rejecting?" *Kritika: Explorations in Russian and Eurasian History* 5, no. 4 (2004): 675–709.

Dobrushin, Yekhezkel. *Farnakhtn*. Kiev: Y. Shenfeld, 1917.

———. *Dovid Bergelson*. Moscow: Der emes, 1947.

"Dogovor." Moscow, September 1, 1944. Rossiiskii gosudarstvennyi arkhiv literatury i iskusstva (RGALI), Fond 2307 GOSET, Opis 1, delo 7.

Douglas, Charlotte. "The New Russian Art and Italian Futurism." *Art Journal* 3 (1975): 229–39.

———. "Suprematism: The Sensible Dimension." *Russian Review* 34, no. 3 (1975): 266–81.

Duve, Thierry de. "Time Exposure and Snapshot: The Photograph as Paradox." *October* 5 (Summer 1978): 113–25.

Eikhenbaum, Boris. *Anna Akhmatova: Opyt analiza*. N.p.: St. Petersburg, 1923.

Eisenstein, Sergei. *Eisenstein: Writings 1922–1934*. Edited by Richard Taylor. Bloomington: Indiana University Press, 1988.

Eliav-Feldin, Miriam. "Invented Identities: Credulity in the Age of Prophecy and Exploration." *Journal of Early Modern History* 3 (1999): 203–32.

———. *Renaissance Imposters and Proofs of Identity*. New York: Palgrave Macmillan, 2012.

Engel, David. *The Assassination of Symon Petliura and the Trial of Scholem Schwartzbard 1926–1927: A Selection of Documents*. Gottingen: Vandenhoeck & Ruprecht, 2016.

Erenburg, Il'ia. *A vse-taki ona vertitsia*. Berlin: Gelikan, 1922.

Erik, Max. *Konstruktsiye-Shtudyen*. Warsaw: Farlag arbeter-kheym, 1924.

———. "David Bergelson." *Literarishe bleter* 53 (May 8, 1925): 2–3.

Erlich, Victor. *Modernism and Revolution: Russian Literature in Transition*. Cambridge, MA: Harvard University Press, 1994.

Estraikh, Gennady. "From Yehupets Jargonists to Kiev Modernists: The Rise of a Yiddish Literary Centre, 1880s–1914." *East European Jewish Affairs* 30, no. 1 (2000): 17–38.

———. "David Bergelson: From Fellow Traveller to Soviet Classic." *Slavic Almanach* 7, no. 10 (2001): 191–222.

———. *In Harness: Yiddish Writers' Romance with Communism*. Judaic Traditions in Literature, Music, and Art. Syracuse, NY: Syracuse University Press, 2005.

———. "Bergelson in and on America (1929–1949)." In *David Bergelson: From Modernism to Socialist Realism*, edited by Joseph Sherman and Gennady Estraikh, 205–21. Oxford: Legenda, 2007.

——— "Kushnirov, Arn." *The YIVO Encyclopedia of Jews in Eastern Europe*. Accessed June 17, 2018. http://www.yivoencyclopedia.org/article.aspx/Kushnirov_Arn.

———. "The Yiddish Kultur-Lige." In *Modernism in Kyiv: Jubilant Experimentation*, edited by Irene R. Makaryk and Virlana Tkacz, 197–217. Toronto: University of Toronto Press, 2010.

———. *Evreiskaia literaturnaia zhizn' Moskvy 1917–1991*. St. Petersburg: Evropeiskii universitet v Sankt-Peterburge, 2015.

Estraikh, Gennady, David Bergelson, and Balmakhshoves. "Gefunene manuskriptn: A kolkoyre tsu Amerikaner kolegn." *Forverts*, March 17, 2006, 18.

Estraikh, Gennady, and Mikhail Krutikov, eds. *Yiddish in Weimar Berlin : At the Crossroads of Diaspora Politics and Culture*. Studies in Yiddish. London: Modern Humanities Research Association, 2010.

Fine, Lawrence. *Physician of the Soul, Healer of the Cosmos: Isaac Luria and His Kabbalistic Fellowship*. Stanford, CA: Stanford University Press, 2003.

Fineman, Mia. "Ecce Homo Prostheticus." *New German Critique* 76 (Winter 1999): 85–114.

"Far der premyere fun David Bergelsons 'Der toyber.'" *Literarishe bleter*. April 11, 1930, 294.

Fink, Hilary L. *Bergson and Russian Modernism, 1900–1930*. Studies in Russian Literature and Theory. Evanston, IL: Northwestern University Press, 1999.

Finkenthal, Michael. *Lev Shestov: Existential Philosopher and Religious Thinker*. New York: Peter Lang, 2010.

Finkin, Jordan. "Constellating Hebrew and Yiddish Avant-Gardes." *Journal of Modern Jewish Studies* 8, no. 1 (2009): 1–22.

Foster, Hal, ed. *Vision and Visuality*. Seattle, WA: Bay Press, 1988.

Freud, Sigmund. *Beyond the Pleasure Principle*. New York: W. W. Norton, 1961.

———. *Civilization and Its Discontents*. New York: W. W. Norton, 1961.

———. *The Interpretation of Dreams*. New York: Avon Books, 1965.

Frieden, Ken. *Classic Yiddish Fiction: Abramovitsh, Sholem Aleichem, & Peretz*. Albany: State University of New York Press, 1995.

Gardiner, Michael. "Alterity and Ethics: A Dialogical Perspective." *Theory, Culture & Society* 13, no. 2 (1996): 121–43.

Garner, Stanton B. "The Gas Heart: Disfigurement and the Dada Body." *Modern Drama* 50, no. 4 (2007): 500–516.

Garrett, Leah. *Journeys Beyond the Pale: Yiddish Travel Writing in the Modern World*. Madison: University of Wisconsin Press, 2003.

Gershenson, Olga. *The Phantom Holocaust: Soviet Cinema and Jewish Catastrophe*. New Brunswick, NJ: Rutgers University Press, 2013.

Gitelman, Zvi. *Jewish Nationality and Soviet Politics: The Jewish Sections of the CPSU, 1917–1930*. Princeton, NJ: Princeton University Press, 1972.

Glatshteyn, Yankev, A. Leyeles, and N. Minkov. "In zikh." In *In zikh: A zamlung introspektive lider*, edited by M. Apranel, 5–27. New York: M. N. Mayzel, 1920.

Gliksman, Avraham. "V. Natanson, Shpinoza un Bergson." *Bikher-velt* 3, no. 1–2 (1924): 38–40.

Gogarten, Friedrich. "Between the Times." In *The Beginnings of Dialectic Theology*, edited by James Robinson, 277–82. Richmond, VA: John Knox, 1968.

Goldberg, Sylvie Anne. *Clepsydra: Essay on the Plurality of Time in Judaism*. Translated by Benjamin Ivry. Stanford, CA: Stanford University Press, 2016.

Gollerbakh, Sergei. "David Burliuk i futurizm glazami nashego vremeni." *Novyi zhurnal* 256 (2009): 194–201.

Golub, Spencer. "Clockwise-Counterclockwise (The Vowelless Revolution)." *Theatre Journal* 56, no. 2 (2004): 183–203.

Gordon, Rae Beth. *Ornament, Fantasy, and Desire in Nineteenth-Century French Literature*. Princeton, NJ: Princeton University Press, 2014.

Gottheil, Richard, and Meyer Kayserling. "Usque." Jewish Encyclopedia. Accessed July 9, 2016. http://www.jewishencyclopedia.com/articles/14614-usque.

Graetz, Heinrich. *Popular History of the Jews*. New York: Hebrew Publishing, 1919.

Greenblatt, Stephen. *Renaissance Self-Fashioning*. Chicago, IL: University of Chicago Press, 1980.

Grossman, I. "Bakunin i Bergson." *Zavety* 5 (1914): 47–62.

Grossman, Jeffrey. "The Yiddish-German Connection: New Directions." *Poetics Today* 1–2 (2015): 61–110.

———. "Yiddish Writers/German Models in the Early Twentieth Century." In *Three Way Street: Jews, Germans, and the Transnational*, edited by Jay Howard Geller and Leslie Morris, 66–90. Ann Arbor: University of Michigan Press, 2016.

Groys, Boris. *The Total Art of Stalinism: Avant-Garde, Aesthetic Dictatorship, and Beyond*. Translated by Charles Rougle. Princeton, NJ: Princeton University Press, 1992.

———. *Introduction to Antiphilosophy*. New York: Verso, 2012.

Gubser, Michael. "Time and History in Alois Riegl's Theory of Perception." *Journal of the History of Ideas* 66, no. 3 (July 2005): 451–74.

Guerlac, Suzanne. *Thinking in Time: An Introduction to Henri Bergson*. Ithaca, NY: Cornell University Press, 2006.

Gumbrecht, Hans Ulrich. *In 1926: Living at the Edge of Time*. Cambridge, MA: Harvard University Press, 1997.

———. "Reading for the Stimmung? About the Ontology of Literature Today." *Boundary 2* 35, no. 3 (2008): 213–21.

———. *Atmosphere, Mood, Stimmung: On a Hidden Potential of Literature*. Stanford, CA: Stanford University Press, 2012.

Häglund, Martin. "Chronolibidinal Reading: Deconstruction and Psychoanalysis." *New Centennial Review* 9, no. 1 (2009): 1–43.

Hansen, Miriam. "Benjamin, Cinema and Experience." *New German Critique* 40 (1987): 179–224.

———. "Benjamin's Aura." *Critical Inquiry*, Winter 2008: 336–75.

Harshav, Benjamin. "The Role of Language in Modern Art: On Texts and Subtexts in Chagall's Paintings." *Modernism/Modernity* 1, no. 2 (1994): 51–87.

———. *Marc Chagall and His Times: A Documentary Narrative*. Stanford, CA: Stanford University Press, 2004.

Harshav, Benjamin, and Barbara Harshav. *American Yiddish Poetry*. Berkeley: University of California Press, 1986.

Harte, Tim. *Fast Forward: The Aesthetics and Ideology of Speed in Russian Avant-Garde Culture, 1910–1930*. Madison: University of Wisconsin Press, 2009.

Harvey, David. *The Condition of Postmodernity: An Enquiry into the Origins of Cultural Change*. Cambridge, MA: Blackwell, 1989.

Haynes, Stephen R. "'BETWEEN THE TIMES': German Theology and the Weimar 'Zeitgeist.'" *Soundings* 74, no. 1/2 (1991): 9–44.

Hazan-Brunet, Nathalie, and Ada Ackerman, eds. *Futur antérieur : l'avant-garde et le livre yiddish, 1914–1939*. Paris: Skira Flammarion, 2009.

Heidegger, Martin. *Being and Time*. New York: Harper and Row, 1962.

Hofshteyn, David. "Grief." In *From Revolution to Repression: Soviet Yiddish Writing 1917–1952*, edited by Joseph Sherman, 66–90. Nottingham, UK: Five Leaves, 2012.

Holquist, Peter. *Making War, Forging Revolution : Russia's Continuum of Crisis, 1914–1921*. Cambridge, MA: Harvard University Press, 2002.

Howe, Irving, and Eliezer Greenberg. *Ashes Out of Hope: Fiction by Soviet-Yiddish Writers*. New York: Schocken Books, 1977.

Hutchings, Stephen. *Russian Modernism: The Transfiguration of the Everyday.* Cambridge, UK: Cambridge University Press, 1997.

Huyssen, Andreas. *Present Pasts: Urban Palimpsests and the Politics of Memory.* Stanford, CA: Stanford University Press, 2003.

Jacobson, Eric. *Metaphysics of the Profane: The Political Theology of Walter Benjamin and Gershom Scholem.* New York: Columbia University Press, 2003.

Jakobson, Roman. *Language in Literature.* Cambridge, MA: Harvard University Press, 1987.

Jameson, Frederic. *A Singular Modernity: Essay on the Ontology of the Present.* London: Verso, 2012.

Janecek, Gerald. *Zaum: The Transrational Poetry of Russian Futurism.* San Diego, CA: San Diego State University Press, 1996.

Jankélévitch, Vladimir. "Bergson and Judaism." In *Bergson, Politics, and Religion,* edited by Alexandre Lefebvre and Melanie White, 217–45. Durham, NC: Duke University Press, 2012.

Jay, Martin. *Downcast Eyes: The Denigration of Vision in Twentieth-Century French Thought.* Berkeley: University of California Press, 1993.

Jones, Donna. "The Eleatic Bergson: Review of *Thinking in Time: An Introduction to Henri Bergson* by Suzanne Guerlac." *Diacritics* 37, no. 1 (Spring 2007): 21–31.

Kaganovsky, Lilya. *How the Soviet Man Was Unmade: Cultural Fantasy and Male Subjectivity under Stalin.* Pittsburgh, PA: University of Pittsburgh Press, 2008.

Kahan, Itsik. "Melody in Dovid Bergelson's Yiddish Prose Style." *Zukunft* 74 (1969): 430–34.

Katsman, Roman. "Matvei Kagan: Judaism and the European Cultural Crisis." *Journal of Jewish Thought and Philosophy* 21 (2013): 73–103.

Kazovksy, Hillel. *The Artists of the Kultur-Lige.* Jerusalem: Gesharim, 2003.

Kellman, Ellen. "Uneasy Patronage: Bergelson's Years at Forverts (1922–1926)." In *David Bergelson: From Modernism to Socialist Realism,* edited by Joseph Sherman and Gennady Estraikh, 183–204. Oxford: Legenda, 2007.

Kern, Stephen. *The Culture of Time and Space 1880–1918.* Cambridge, MA: Harvard University Press, 1983.

Kittler, Friedrich A. *Discourse Networks 1800/1900.* Translated by Michael Metteer. Stanford, CA: Stanford University Press, 1990.

Klinov, Yeshaye. "Tsi hot Bergson, 'der zun funem Varshever soykher,' fardint dem Nobel-Prayz?" *Haynt* 272, no. 21 (November 21, 1928): 4.

Koch, Gertrud. "Ex-Changing the Gaze: Re-Visioning Feminist Film Theory." *New German Critique* 34 (1985): 139–53.

Kohn, Hans. "The Essence of Judaism." *American Scholar* 3, no. 2 (Spring 1934): 161–70.

Koralnik, Avram. "R. Nakhmen's mayses." *Dos yidishe folk* 1, no. 30 (1906): 1–4.

Kotlerman, Boris. "'Why I Am in Favour of Birobidzahn': Bergelson's Fateful Decision (1932)." In *David Bergelson: From Modernism to Socialist Realism,* edited by Joseph Sherman and Gennady Estraikh, 222–35. Oxford: Legenda, 2007.

Kracauer, Siegfried. *The Mass Ornament: Weimar Essays.* Cambridge, MA: Harvard University Press, 1995.

Kronfeld, Chana. *On the Margins of Modernism: Decentering Literary Dynamics.* Contraversions. Berkeley: University of California Press, 1996.

Kruchenykh, Aleksei. "Declaration of Transrational Language." In *Russian Futurism through Its Manifestoes, 1912–1928,* edited by Anna Lawton and Hebert Eagle, 182–83. Ithaca, NY: Cornell University Press, 1988.

Krutikov, Mikhail. *Yiddish Fiction and the Crisis of Modernity, 1905–1914*. Stanford, CA: Stanford University Press, 2001.

———. "Narrating the Revolution." In *David Bergelson: From Modernism to Socialist Realism*, edited by Joseph Sherman and Gennady Estraikh. Oxford: Legenda, 2007, 167–182.

———. "Rediscovering the Shtetl as a New Reality." In *The Shtetl: New Evaluations*, edited by Steven T. Katz, 211–32. New York: New York University Press, 2007.

———. *From Kabbalah to Class Struggle: Expressionism, Marxism, and Yiddish Literature in the Life and Work of Meir Wiener*. Stanford, CA: Stanford University Press, 2011.

Kukulin, Il 'ia. *Mashiny zashumevshego vremeni*. Moscow: Novoe literaturnoe obozrenie, 2015.

Kumar, Shiv K. *Bergson and the Stream of Consciousness Novel*. New York: New York University Press, 1963.

Kushnirov, Arn. *Vent*. Kiev: Kultur-Lige, 1921.

Kwinter, Sanford. *Architectures of Time: Toward a Theory of the Event in Modernist Culture*. Cambridge, MA: MIT Press, 2001.

Laplanche, Jean. *Essays on Otherness*. Florence, KY: Routledge, 1999.

Large, David Clay. "Out with the Ostjuden: The Scheunenviertel Riots in Berlin, November 1923." In *Exclusionary Violence: Antisemitic Riots in Modern German History*, 123–41. Ann Arbor: University of Michigan Press, 2002.

Lawton, Anna. *Russian Futurism through Its Manifestoes, 1912–1928*. Translated by Anna Lawton and Hebert Eagle. Ithaca, NY: Cornell University Press, 1988.

Lear, Jonathan. *Radical Hope: Ethics in the Face of Cultural Devastation*. Cambridge, MA: Harvard University Press, 2006.

Lenin, V. I. *Collected Works*. Vol. 26. 45 vols. Moscow: Progress Press, 1977. Accessed June 17, 2018. https://www.marxists.org/archive/lenin/works/cw/pdf/lenin-cw-vol-26.pdf.

Livshits, Benedikt. *The One and a Half-Eyed Archer*. Newtonville, MA: Oriental Research Partners, 1977.

———. *Polutoraglazyi strelets*. Leningrad: Sovetskii pisatel', 1989.

Losskii, N. "Nedostatki gnoseologii Bergsona i vlianie ikh na ego metafiziku." *Voprosy filosofii* 3, no. 118 (1913): 224–35.

Lovell, Stephen. "Politekonomiia sotsrealizma, Der Gorki-Park: Freizeitkultur im Stalinismus 1928–1941, and: Sovetskaia prazdnichnaia kul'tura v provintsii: Prostranstvo, simvoly, istoricheskie mify (1917–1927)." *Kritika* 10, no. 1 (Winter 2009): 205–15.

Lubin, David M. "Masks, Mutilation, and Modernity: Anna Coleman Ladd and the First World War." *Archives of American Art Journal* 47, no. 3/4 (2008): 4–15.

Luppol, I. K., and M. M. Rozental, eds. *Pervyi vsesoiuznyi s"ezd sovetskikh pisatelei: stenograficheskii otchet*. Moscow: Sovetskii pisatel', 1934.

Makaryk, Irena R. "Dissecting Time/Space: The Scottish Play and the New Technology of Film." In *Modernism in Kyiv: Jubilant Experimentation*, edited by Irena R. Makaryk and Virlana Tkacz, 443–77. Toronto: University of Toronto Press, 2010.

Mandelshtam, Osip. *The Complete Critical Prose and Letters*. Ann Arbor, MI: Ardis, 1979.

Mantovan, Daniella. "Language and Style in *Nokh alemen* (1913): Bergelson's Debt to Flaubert." In *David Bergelson: From Modernism to Socialist Realism*, edited by Joseph Sherman and Gennady Estraikh, 89–112. Oxford: Legenda, 2007.

Markish, Peretz. "Milgroym." *Bikher velt* 4–5 (1922): 396–401.

Marx, Karl. *Karl Marx: Selected Writings*. Edited by David McLellan. Oxford: Oxford University Press, 1977.

Massey, Heath. "Bergson on Memory." In *Understanding Bergson, Understanding Modernism*, edited by Paul Ardoin, S. E. Gontarski, and Laci Mattison, 325–26. New York: Bloomsbury, 2013.

Mathy, Jean-Phillipe. *Melancholy Politics: Loss, Mourning, and Memory in Late Modern France*. University Park, PA: Penn State Press, 2011.

Mayne, Judith. "Eisenstein, Vertov, and the Montage Principle." *Minnesota Review* 5 (Fall 1975): 116–24.

Mayzel, Nakhmen. "David Bergelson: Tsum ershaynem fun ale zayne verk in Berlin." *Bikhervelt* 1 (1922): 239–44.

———. *Noente un vayter*. Warsaw: Kultur-Lige, 1924.

———. "Yontevdikayt." *Literarishe bleter* 37 (1929): 217–20.

———. "Dovid Bergelson tsugast in Varshe." *Literarishe bleter* 22 (1930): 401–2.

———. *Forgeyer un mittsaytler*. New York: YKUF, 1946.

———. *Onhoybn: David Bergelson*. Kibuts Alonim: Bet Nahman Maizel, 1977.

Meir, Natan M. *Kiev, Jewish Metropolis: A History, 1859–1914*. Bloomington: Indiana University Press, 2010.

Mendes-Flohr, Paul. *From Mysticism to Dialogue: Martin Buber's Transformation of German Social Thought*. Detroit, MI: Wayne State University Press, 1989.

Mikhoels, Solomon. "Prints Reubeni: Rezhisserskie zametki k p'ese Davida Bergelsona na russkom i evreiskom iazykakh." Moscow, 1945. RGALI. Fond 2693, opis'1, ed. khr.14.

Prints Rubeini, Besedy akteram na repetitsiiakh p'esy Bergel'sona. Stenograma. 1945. RGALI, Fond. 2693, opis' 1, ed. khr. 15.

Mintz, Alan L. *Ḥurban: Responses to Catastrophe in Hebrew Literature*. New York : Columbia University Press, 1984.

———. "Kishinev and the Twentieth Century: Introduction." *Prooftexts* 25, no. 1 & 2 (2005): 1–7.

Miron, Dan. "The Literary Image of the Shtetl." *Jewish Social Studies* 1, no. 3 (1995): 1–43.

———. *From Continuity to Contiguity: Toward a New Jewish Literary Thinking*. Stanford, CA: Stanford University Press, 2010.

Mirskii, D. "U Dnepra." *Izvestiia*. 1936.

Mulvey, Laura. "Visual Pleasure and Narrative Cinema." *Screen* 16, no. 3 (1975): 6–18.

Murav, Harriet. *Music from a Speeding Train: Jewish Literature in Post-Revolutionary Russia*. Stanford, CA: Stanford University Press, 2011.

Naiman, Eric. "Shklovsky's Dog and Mulvey's Pleasure: The Secret Life of Defamiliarization." *Comparative Literature* 50, no. 4 (1998): 333–52.

Naumov, Vladimir, ed. *Nepravednyi sud: Poslednii Stalinskii rasstrel (Stenogramma sudebnogo protsessa nad chlenami Evreiskogo antifashistskogo komiteta)*. Moscow: Nauka, 1994.

Nethercott, Frances. *Filosofsksaia vstrecha: Bergson v Rossii (1907–1917)*. Moscow: Modest Kolerov, 2008.

Niger, Shmuel. "Briv vegn der nayer yidisher literatur." *Di yidishe velt* 9 (1913): 50–71.

———. "David Bergelson's tsvey veltn." *Der tog*. December 5, 1948.

———. "Briv fun Dovid Bergelson." *Zamlbikher* 8 (1952): 85–119.

Niger, Shmuel, and Jacob Shatzsky. *Leksikon fun der nayer yidisher literatur*. Vol. 1. New York: Congress for Jewish Culture, 1956.

Nordau, Max. *Degeneration*. New York: Appleton, 1895.

Novershtern, Avraham. "Aspektim mivniyim ba-prozah shel David Bergelson me-reshitah 'ad 'Mides ha-din.'" PhD diss., Hebrew University, 1981.

———. "Hundert yor Dovid Bergelson: Materialn tsu zayn lebn un shafn." *Di goldene keyt* 115 (1985): 44–58.

———. "Bergelson, Dovid." Translated by Marc Caplan. YIVO Encyclopedia of Jews in Eastern Europe. Accessed July 25, 2017. http://yivoencyclopedia.org/article.aspx /Bergelson_Dovid.

Nusinov, Yitskhak. "David Bergel'son." In *Literaturnaia Entsiklopediia*, 1: 455–56. Moscow: Izdatel'stvo kommunisticheskoi akademii, 1930. Accessed June 17, 2018. http://feb-web .ru/feb/litenc/encyclop.

Olin, Margaret. "Forms of Respect: Alois Riegl's Concept of Attentiveness." *Art Bulletin* 71, no. 2 (1989): 285–99.

———. *Forms of Representation in Alois Riegl's Theory of Art.* University Park: Pennsylvania State University Press, 1992.

Ort, Thomas. *Art and Life in Modernist Prague: Karel Capek and His Generation, 1911–1938.* New York: Palgrave Macmillan, 2013.

Papernyi, Vladimir. *Kul'tura dva.* Moscow: Novoe literaturnoe obozrenie, 2006.

Parker, Luke. "The Shop Window Quality of Things: 1920s Weimar Surface Culture in Nabokov's *Korol', dama, valet.*" *Slavic Review* 77, no. 2 (Summer 2018): 390–416.

Pearson, Keith Ansell. "Introduction." In *Mind Energy*, edited by Keith Ansell Pearson and Michael Kolkman Pearson, xi–xli. New York: Palgrave, 2007.

Pensky, Max. "Method and Time: Benjamin's Dialectical Images." In *The Cambridge Companion to Walter Benjamin*, edited by David S. Ferris, 177–98. Cambridge, UK: Cambridge University Press, 2004.

Perlina, Nina. "Mikhail Bakhtin and Martin Buber: Problems of Dialogical Imagination." *Studies in Twentieth-Century Literature* 9, no. 1 (1984): 13–28.

Petrov, Petre. *Automatic for the Masses: The Death of the Author and the Birth of Socialist Realism.* Toronto: University of Toronto Press, 2015.

Pinsker, Shachar. "Deciphering the Hieroglyphics of the Metropolis: Literary Topographies of Berlin in Hebrew and Yiddish Modernism." In *Yiddish in Weimar Berlin*, edited by Gennady Estraikh and Mikhail Krutikov, 28–53. Oxford: Legenda, 2010.

———. "The Literary Cafes of Berlin as Urban Spaces of Jewish Modernism." Frankel Institute for Advanced Judaic Studies, 2008. Accessed June 17, 2018. http://hdl.handle .net/2027/spo.11879367.2008.011.

———. *Literary Passports: The Making of Modernist Hebrew Fiction in Europe.* Stanford, CA: Stanford University Press, 2011.

Pinski, David. "Shlomo Molkho un David HaRubeni." In *Meshikhim: Dramen*, 135–239. Warsaw: David Pinski Inkorporirt, n.d.

Pomerants, Aleksandr. "Dovid Bergelson: Tsum 30'yorign yubiley zint s'iz dershinen zayn ershte bukh 'Arum vokzal.'" *Morgn-frayheyt*, December 31, 1939.

Rabinbach, Anson. "Between Enlightenment and Apocalypse: Benjamin, Bloch and Modern German Jewish Messianism." *New German Critique* 34 (Winter 1985): 78–124.

———. *The Human Motor: Energy, Fatigue, and the Origins of Modernity.* New York: Basic Books, 1990.

Rancière, Jacques. "Rethinking Modernity." *Diacritics* 42, no. 3 (2014): 6–20.

Ravitsh, Meylekh. "Di filosofye fun lakhn: Anri Bergson: Der gelekhter." *Naye folkstsaytung* 3, no. 261 (1928): 6.

Redlich, Shimon. *War, Holocaust and Stalinism: A Documented Study of the Jewish Anti-Fascist Committee in the USSR.* New History of Russia. Oxford: Harwood Academic Publishers, 1995.

Rendall, Steven. "The Translator's Task: Walter Benjamin." *Traduction, Terminologie, Redaction* 2 (1997): 151–205.

Rendle, Matthew. "Revolutionary Tribunals and the Origins of Terror in Early Soviet Russia." *Historical Research* 84, no. 226 (2011). 693–721.

Resina, Joan Ramon, and Dieter Ingenschay, eds. *After-Images of the City.* Ithaca, NY: Cornell University Press, 2003.

Reubeni, David. "The Travel Diary of David Reubeni." In *Masterpieces of Jewish Literature: A Treasury of 2000 Years of Jewish Creativity,* edited by Curt Leviant, 503–20. New York: Ktav Publishing House, 1969.

Ricoeur, Paul. *Memory, History, Forgetting.* Chicago, IL: University of Chicago Press, 2004.

Riegl, Alois, and Benjamin Binstock. "Excerpts from 'The Dutch Group Portrait.'" *October* 74 (1995): 3–35.

Riegl, Alois, and Christopher Heuer. "Jacob van Ruisdael." *Art in Translation* 4, no. 2 (2012): 149–62.

Robin, Régine. *Socialist Realism: An Impossible Aesthetic.* Stanford: Stanford University Press, 1992.

Rosenstock, Bruce. *Philosophy and the Jewish Question: Mendelssohn, Rosenzweig, and Beyond.* New York: Fordham University Press, 2009.

———. "*Palintropos Harmoniê*: Jacob Taubes and Carl Schmitt 'Im Liebenden Streit'," *New German Critique* 41, no. 1 (2014): 55–92.

Roskies, David. *Against the Apocalypse: Responses to Catastrophe in Modern Jewish Culture.* Cambridge, MA: Harvard University Press, 1984.

———. "Sholem Aleichem: Mythologist of the Mundane." *Association for Jewish Studies Review* 13, no. 2 (1988): 27–46.

Rozental', Nisn. *Yidish lebn in ratnfarband.* Tel Aviv: I. L. Peretz, 1971.

Rubenstein, Joshua, and Vladimir Naumov. *Stalin's Secret Pogrom: The Postwar Inquisition of the Jewish Anti-Fascist Committee.* Annals of Communism. New Haven, CT: Yale University Press, 2001.

Rubin, Yisroel. "Bay di tishlekh fun Romanishn kafe: Dovid Bergelson." *Literarishe bleter* 3 (January 17, 1930): 53–54.

Rudnyanski, Sh. "Anri Bergson vegn estetik." *Di yidishe velt* 8 (1913): 82–88.

Ryan, James. "The Sacralization of Violence: Bolshevik Justifications for Violence and Terror during the Civil War." *Slavic Review* 74, no. 4 (2015): 808–31.

Sadan, Dov. "Three Foundations: Sholem Aleichem and the Yiddish Literary Tradition." *Prooftexts* 6, no. 1 (1986): 55–63.

Safran, Gabriella. *Wandering Soul: The Dybbuk's Creator, S. An-sky.* Cambridge, MA: Harvard University Press, 2010.

Sandomirskaia, Irina. *Blokada v slove: ocherki kriticheskoi teorii i biopolitiki iazyka.* Moscow: Novoe literaturnoe obozrenie, 2013.

Schachter, Allison. "Modernist Indexicality: The Language of Gender, Race, and Domesticity in Hebrew and Yiddish Modernism." *Modern Language Quarterly: A Journal of Literary History* 72, no. 4 (2011): 493–520.

————. *Diasporic Modernisms: Hebrew and Yiddish Literature in the Twentieth Century.* New York: Oxford University Press, 2012.

Schivelbusch, Wolfgang. *The Railway Journey: Trains and Travel in the 19th Century.* New York: Urizen Books, 1979.

Schmitt, Carl. *Political Theology: Four Chapters on the Concept of Sovereignty.* Translated by George Schwab. Cambridge, MA: MIT Press, 1985.

Schneersohn, Fischel. *Studies in Psycho-Expedition.* Translated by Herman Frank. New York: Science of Man Press, 1929.

Scholem, Gershom. *Major Trends in Jewish Mysticism.* New York: Schocken Books, 1971.

————. *Sabbatai Sevi, The Mystical Messiah.* Princeton, NJ: Princeton University Press, 1973.

————. *The Origin and Meaning of Hasidism.* Atlantic Highlands, NJ: Humanities Press International, 1988.

————. *The Messianic Idea in Judaism and Other Essays on Jewish Spirituality.* New York: Schocken Books, 1995.

————. "*Devekut*, Or Communion with God." In *Essential Papers on Hasidism: Origins to Present,* edited by Gershon David Hundert. New York: New York University Press, 1991, 275–298.

————. "On Jonah and the Concept of Justice." Translated by Eric J. Schwab. *Critical Inquiry* 25, no. 2 (1999): 353–61.

Schur, Anna. "Shades of Justice: The Trial of Sholom Schwartzbard and Dovid Bergelson's 'Among Refugees.'" *Law and Literature* 19, no. 15 (2007): 15–43.

Seelig, Ravhel. "A Yiddish Bard in Berlin: Moyshe Kulbak and the Flourishing of Yiddish Poetry in Exile." *Jewish Quarterly Review* 102, no. 1 (2012): 19–49.

Senderovich, Sasha. "In Search of Readership: Bergelson Among the Refugees." In *David Bergelson: From Modernism to Socialist Realism,* edited by Joseph Sherman and Gennady Estraikh, 150–166. Oxford: Legenda, 2007.

Sherman, Joseph. "Bergelson and Chekhov: Convergences and Departures." In *The Yiddish Presence in European Literature: Inspiration and Interaction,* edited by Joseph Sherman and Ritchie Robertson, 117–33. Oxford: Legenda, 2005.

————. "'Jewish Nationalism' in Bergelson's Last Book (1947)." In *David Bergelson: From Modernism to Socialist Realism,* edited by Joseph Sherman and Gennady Estraikh, 285–305. Oxford: Legenda, 2007.

————. "David Bergelson (1884–1952): A Biography." In *David Bergelson: From Modernism to Socialist Realism,* edited by Joseph Sherman and Gennady Estraikh, 7–78. Oxford: Legenda, 2007.

Shestov, Lev. "Tvorchestvo iz nichego." Biblioteka "VEKHI." Accessed June 17, 2018. http://www.vehi.net/shestov/chehov.html.

Shkandrij, Myroslav. "National Modernism in Post-Revolutionary Society: The Ukrainian Renaissance and Jewish Revival, 1917–1930." In *Shatterzone of Empires,* edited by Omer Bartov and Eric D. Weitz, 438–48. Bloomington: Indiana University Press, 2013.

Shklovsky, Victor. "O poezii i zaumnom iazyke." In *Poetika,* edited by Osip Brik, 13–26. Petrograd, 1919.

————. *Theory of Prose.* Normal, IL: Dalkey Archive Press, 1990.

————. *Zoo, or Letters Not about Love.* Normal, IL: Dalkey Archive Press, 2001.

————. *Eshshe nichego ne konchilos'.* Moscow: Vagrius, 2002.

————. *Third Factory.* Normal, IL: Dalkey Archive Press, 2002.

————. *Knight's Move.* Normal, IL: Dalkey Archive Press, 2005.

————. *Energy of Delusion: A Book on Plot.* Champaign, IL: Dalkey Archive Press, 2007.

Shmeruk, Khone, ed. *A shpigl af a shteyn*. Jerusalem: Magnes Press, 1964.

Shneer, David. *Yiddish and the Creation of Soviet Jewish Culture*. Cambridge, UK: Cambridge University Press, 2004.

———. "From Mourning to Vengeance: Bergelson's Holocaust Journalism (1941–1945)." In *David Bergelson: From Modernism to Socialist Realism*, edited by Joseph Sherman and Gennady Estraikh, 248–68. Oxford: Legenda, 2007.

Shore, Marci. "On Cosmopolitanism, the Avant-Garde, and a Lost Innocence of Central Europe." In *Utopia/Dystopia*, edited by Michael D. Gordin, Helen Tilley, and Gyan Prakash, 176–202. Princeton, NJ: Princeton University Press, 2010.

Shtakser, Inna. *The Making of Jewish Revolutionaries in the Pale of Settlement*. Hampshire, UK: Palgrave Macmillan, 2014.

Singer, Isaac Bashevis. "Vegn Dovid Bergelsons Baym Dnyepr (ershter teyl: Penek)." *Globus* 5 (1932): 56–65.

Slezkine, Yuri. *Arctic Mirrors: Russia and the Small Peoples of the North*. Ithaca, NY: Cornell University Press, 1994.

Slotnick, Susan. "The Novel Form in the Works of David Bergelson." PhD diss., Columbia University, 1978.

Smith, Scott. *Captives of the Revolution: The Socialist Revolutionaries and the Bolshevik Dictatorship, 1918–1923*. Pittsburgh, PA: University of Pittsburgh Press, 2011.

Soulez, Philippe. "Bergson as Philosopher of War and Theorist of the Political." In *Bergson, Politics, and Religion*, edited by Alexandre Lefebvre and Melanie White, 99–125. Durham, NC: Duke University Press, 2012.

Spitzer, Leo. "Classical and Christian Ideas of World Harmony: Prolegomena to an Interpretation of the Word 'Stimmung' (Part II)." *Traditio* 3 (1945): 307–64.

Steinberg, Mark. *Petersburg Fin de Siècle*. New Haven, CT: Yale University Press, 2011.

Stern, Michael. "Tevye's Art of Quotation." *Prooftexts* 6, no. 1 (1986): 79–96.

Stuchkoff, Nahum. *Der oytser fun der yidisher shprakh*. New York: YIVO Institute for Jewish Research, 1991.

Sulloway, Frank J. *Freud, Biologist of the Mind: Beyond the Psychoanalytic Legend*. New York: Basic Books, 1983.

Tabachnikova, Olga, ed. *Anton Chekhov Through the Eyes of Russian Thinkers: Vasilii Rozanov, Dmitrii Merezhkovskii and Lev Shestov*. Cambridge, UK: Cambridge University Press, 2012.

Tanner, Tony. *Adultery in the Novel: Contract and Transgression*. Baltimore, MD: Johns Hopkins Press, 1979.

Taubes, Jacob. "Martin Buber and the Philosophy of History." In *From Cult to Culture: Fragments Toward a Critique of Historical Reason*, edited by Charlotte Elisheva Fonrobert and Amir Engel, 11–27. Stanford, CA: Stanford University Press, 2010.

Taylor, Jennie Bourne. "Psychology at the Fin de Siècle." In *The Cambridge Companion to the Fin de Siècle*, edited by Gail Marshall, 13–30. Cambridge Companions Online, 2008.

Tihanov, Galin. "The Politics of Estrangement: The Case of the Early Shklovsky." *Poetics Today* 26, no. 4 (2005): 666–96.

Tihanov, Galin, and Katerina Clark. "Literary Criticism and the Transformations of the Literary Field during the Cultural Revolution, 1928–1932." In *A History of Russian Literary Theory and Criticism*, edited by Galin Tihanov and Evgeny Dobrenko, 43–63. Pittsburgh, PA: University of Pittsburgh Press, 2011.

Tillberg, Margareta. "'Be a Spectator with a Large Ear': Victory over the Sun as a Public Laboratory Experiment for Mikhail Matiushin's Theories of Colour Vision." In *Victory*

Over the Sun: The World's First Futurist Opera, edited by Rosamund Bartlett and Sarah Dadswell, 208–23. Exeter, UK: University of Exeter Press, 2012.

Todorova, Maria. "The Trap of Backwardness: Modernity, Temporality, and the Study of Eastern European Nationalism." *Slavic Review* 64, no. 1 (2005): 140–64.

———. "Modernism." In *Modernism: The Creation of Nation-States*, edited by A. Ersoy and M. Gorny, 4–22. Budapest: Central European Press, 2010.

Tshubinski, B. "Dovid Bergelson." In *Leksikon fun der nayer yidisher literatur*, edited by Shmuel Niger and Yekev Shatski, 1: 379–83. New York: Congress for Jewish Culture, 1956.

Tsivian, Yurii. "O Chapline v russkom avangarde i o zakonakh sluchainogo v iskusstve." *Novoe literaturnoe obozrenie* 5 (2006): 99–142.

Vaingurt, Julia. *Wonderlands of the Avant-Garde*. Evanston, IL: Northwestern University Press, 2013.

Vayter, A. [Ayzik-Mayer Devenishki]. *Ksovim*. Vilnius: B. Kletskin, 1923.

———. "David Bergelsons 'Arum vokzal.'" In *Oysgeklibene shriftn*, edited by Shmuel Razshanski, 292–93. Buenos Aires: Literatur-gezelshaft baym Yivo in Argentine, 1971.

"Vecher D. Bergel'sona." *Literaturnaia gazeta*. November 14, 1934.

Veidlinger, Jeffrey. *The Moscow State Yiddish Theater: Jewish Culture on the Soviet Stage*. Bloomington: Indiana University Press, 2000.

———. "'Du Lebst, Mayn Folk': Bergelson's Play *Prints Ruveni* in Historical Context (1944–1947)." In *David Bergelson: From Modernism to Socialist Realism*, edited by Joseph Sherman and Gennady Estraikh, 269–84. Oxford: Legenda, 2007.

Vishnitser-Bernshtayn, Rokhl. "Di naye kunst un mir." *Milgroym* 1 (1922): 2–7.

Vovsi-Mikhoels, Natal'ia. *Moi otets Solomon Mikhoels: Vospominanie o zhizni i gibeli*. Moscow: Vozvrashchenie, 1997.

Wanner, Adrian. *Russian Minimalism: From the Prose Poem to the Anti-Story*. Evanston, IL: Northwestern University Press, 2003.

Ward, Janet. *Weimar Surfaces: Urban Visual Culture in 1920s Germany*. Berkeley: University of California Press, 2001.

Wehr, Gerhard. *Martin Buber: Leben-Werk-Wirkung*. Munich: Random House, 2010.

Weinberg, Robert. *Stalin's Forgotten Zion: Birobidzhan and the Making of a Soviet Jewish Homeland*. Berkeley: University of California Press, 1998.

Weinreich, Max. "Fun der eyropeisher literatur: Futurizm." *Di yidishe velt* 4 (1914): 145–47.

Weld, Sara Pankenier. *Voiceless Vanguard: The Infantilist Aesthetic of the Russian Avant-Garde*. Evanston, IL: Northwestern University Press, 2014.

Wiener, Meir. "David Bergel'son." *Literaturnaia gazeta*, April 26, 1940.

Wiesel, Elie. "Rand-makhshoves vegn yidish." *Di goldene keyt* 123 (1987): 26–29.

Wieviorka, Annette. *The Era of the Witness*. Translated by Jared Stark. Ithaca, NY: Cornell University Press, 2006.

Williams, Raymond. *Politics of Modernism*. New York: Verso, 2007.

Wisse, Ruth. "At the Depot." In *A Shtetl and Other Yiddish Novellas*, 81–139. New York: Behrman House, 1973.

Wolfson, Elliot R. "Light Through Darkness: The Ideal of Human Perfection in the Zohar." *Harvard Theological Review* 81, no. 1 (1988): 73–95.

Wolitz, Seth. "Bergelson's Yordim and I. B. Singer's." *Prooftexts* 2, no. 3 (1982): 313–21.

———. "Chagall's Last Soviet Performance: The Graphics for Troyer, 1922." *Jewish Art* 21–22 (1995–96): 95–115.

———. *Yiddish Modernism: Studies in Twentieth Century Eastern European Jewish Culture.* Bloomington, IN: Slavica, 2014.

Worrall, Nick. "Meyerhold's Production of 'The Magnificent Cuckold.'" *Drama Review* 17, no. 1 (1973): 14–34.

Yalen, Deborah. "Red Kasrilevke: Ethnographies of Economic Transformation in the Soviet Shtetl 1917–1939." PhD diss., University of California, Berkeley, 2007.

Yampolsky, Mikhail. "In the Shadow of Monuments: Notes on Iconoclasm and Time." In *Soviet Hieroglyphics: Visual Culture in Late Twentieth-Century Russia*, edited by Nancy Condee, 93–112. Bloomington: Indiana University Press, 1995.

Yerushalmi, Yosef Hayim. "Messianic Impulses in Joseph Ha-Kohen." In *Jewish Thought in the Sixteenth Century*, edited by Bernard Dov Cooperman, 460–484. Cambridge, MA: Harvard University Press, 1983.

———. *Zakhor: Jewish History and Jewish Memory.* New York: Schocken Books, 1989.

Zarrit, Saul. "The World Awaits Your Yiddish Word: Jacob Glatstein and the Problem of World Literature." *Studies in American Jewish Literature* 34, no. 2 (2015): 175–203.

Zavadivker, Polly. "Blood and Ink: Russian and Soviet Jewish Chroniclers of Catastrophe from World War I to World War II." PhD diss., University of California at Santa Cruz, 2013.

Zemon Davis, Natalie. *Trickster Travels: A Sixteenth Century Muslim Between Worlds.* New York: Hill and Wang, 2006.

Zhitlovsky, Khaim. "Anri Bergson: Araynfir in der metafizik." *Bikher velt* 3, no. 1–2 (1924): 14–17.

Zipperstein, Steven J. *Pogrom: Kishiniev and the Tilt of History.* New York: Liveright Publishing Corporation, 2018.

Zylbercweig, Zalmen, ed. *Leksikon fun yidishn teater.* Vol. 1. 6 vols. New York: Elisheva, 1931.

*Note: Bergelson's output is listed here
in chronological order.*

Bergelson, David. "Letters to Shmuel Niger." n.d. YIVO, RG 360, Shmuel Niger, Box 7, Folder 9e.

———. "Opgang." *Eygns* 2 (1920): 1–115.

———. "A gesheener oyfbrokh." *Milgroym* 1 (1922): 41–43.

———. Letter, March 20, 1922. YIVO, RG 1139, Abraham Cahan.

———. "Onheyb Kislev TaRAT." *Milgroym* 1, no. 1 (1922): 25–26.

———. "Tsvey vegn." In *Verk: Naye farbeserte oysgabe*, 3: 97–100. Berlin: Vostok, 1922.

———. "Yordim." In *Verk*, 2: 151–65. Berlin: Vostok, 1922.

———. *Kogda vse konchilos'.* Berlin: Grani, 1923.

———. "Der letster Rosheshone." In *Verk: Naye farbeserte oysgabe*, 4: 21–38. Berlin: Vostok, 1923.

———. "Yidishe komunistn in Rusland bashlisn, az es iz shoyn mer nito keyn yidn af der velt." *Forverts.* March 4, 1923.

———. "A briv fun Dovid Bergelson." *Der emes.* March 3, 1926.

———. "Dray tsentren." *In sphan* 1 (April 1926): 84–96.

———. "Moskve." *Frayheyt*, September 5, 1926, 5.

———. "Sholem-Aleichem un di folks-sphrakh." *Frayheyt.* August 29, 1926, 5.

———. "Vi azoy vet oysen dos yidishn lebn in Rusland shpeter mit etlekhe yor." *Frayheyt.* May 29, 1926.

———. "Arum vokzal." *Geklibene verk*, 1: 7–91. Vilnius: B. Kletskin, 1929.

———. "Blindkeyt." *Geklibene verk*, 6: 57–75. Vilinius: B. Kletskin, 1929.

———. "Di dinamishe rege." *Geklibene verk*, 6: 115–24. Vilinius: B. Kletskin, 1929.

———. "In a fargrebter shtot." *Geklibene verk*, 3: 7–59. Vilnius: B. Kletskin, 1929.

———. "Der letster Rosheshone." *Geklibene verk*, 1: 155–67. Vilnius: B. Kletskin, 1929.

———. *Mides-hadin. Geklibene verk*, 7. Vilnius: B. Kletskin, 1929.

———. *Nokh alemen. Geklibene verk*, 2. Vilnius: B. Kletskin, 1929.

———. "Skhar-tirkhe." *Geklibene verk*, 6: 249–263. Vilnius: B. Kletskin, 1929.

———. "Der toyber." *Geklibene verk*, 1: 95–122. Vilnius: B. Kletskin, 1929.

———. "Yoysef Shur." *Geklibene verk*, 3: 61–126. Vilnius: B. Kletskin, 1929.

———. "Birgerkrig." *Geklibene verk*, 5: 9–64. Vilnius: B. Kletskin, 1930.

———. "Geburt." *Geklibene verk: Tsugvintn*, 8: 97–119. Vilnius: B. Kletskin, 1930.

———. "Der lokh, durkh velkhn eyner hot farloyrn." *Geklibene verk*, 8: 79–95. Vilnius: B. Kletskin, 1930.

———. "Problemen fun der yidisher literatur." *Literarishe bleter* 24 (1930): 437–39.

———. "Tsugvintn." *Geklibene verk*, 8: 7–43. Vilnius: B. Kletskin, 1930.

———. "Tsvishn emigrantn." *Geklibene verk*, 5: 175–99. Vilnius: B. Kletskin, 1930.

———. *Geklibene verk.* 8 vols. Vilnius: B. Kletskin, 1929–30.

———. *Birebidzhaner: Dertseylung.* Moscow: Emes, 1934.

———. "Materyaln tsu D. Bergelsons bio-bibliografye." *Visnshaft un revolutsye* 1–2 (1934): 67–73.

———. *Baym Dnyepr: Penek.* Vol. 1..Moscow: Der emes, 1932.

———. "Karaiushchii mech naroda." *Literaturnaia gazeta.* February 1, 1937.

———. *Baym Dnyepr: Yunge yorn.* Vol. 2. Moscow: Der emes, 1940.

———. Budu zhit', p'esa v 3x. deistviiakh. Prilozhen protocol GURK, March 13, 1942. RGALI. Fond 656, opis' 5, ed. khr. 678

———Letter to Shakhne Epshteyn, March 9, 1942, in GARF, f. R-8114, opis 1, delo 982; David Bergel'son.

———. *Geven iz nakht un gevorn iz tog.* Moscow: Der emes, 1943.

———. "Farshraybendik." *Eynikayt.* September 29, 1945,3.

———. "Freylekhs." *Eynikayt.* August 30, 1945, 4.

———. "Aleksander Barash." *Eynikayt.* January 1-15, 1946.

———. *Prints Ruveni.* New York: Yidisher kultur farband, 1946.

———. *Naye dertseylungen.* Buenos Aires: ICUF, 1949.

———. "Aleksander Barash." Moscow, April 1952. GARF, Fond. R-8114, opis' 1, delo 982.

———."Bez nazvaniia." GARF, Fond R-8114, opis' 1, delo 982.

———. *Izbrannoe.* Moskva: Sovetskii pisatel', 1957.

———. "Civil War." In *Ashes out of Hope: Fiction by Soviet-Yiddish Writers*, edited by Irving Howe and Eliezer Greenberg, translated by Seth Wolitz, 84–123. New York: Schocken Books, 1977.

———. *In der sho fun oyspruv.* Moscow: Sovetskii pisatel', 1985.

———. "In a Backwoods Town." In *A Treasury of Yiddish Stories*, edited by Irving Howe and Eliezer Greenberg, translated by Bernard Guerney, 471–504. New York: Penguin Books, 1989.

———. *The Stories of David Bergelson.* Translated by Golda Werman. Syracuse, NY: Syracuse University Press, 1996.

———. *Descent*. Translated by Joseph Sherman. New York: Modern Language Association of America, 1999.

———. *Opgang*. Edited by Joseph Sherman and David Goldberg. Texts and Translations. New York: Modern Language Association of America, 1999.

———. "The Deaf Man." In *No Star Too Beautiful: Yiddish Stories from 1382 to the Present*, edited and translated by Joachim Neugroschel, 424–43. New York: W. W. Norton, 2002.

———. "Two Roads." In *No Star Too Beautiful: An Anthology of Yiddish Stories from 1382 to the Present*, edited and translated by Joachim Neugroschel, 417–18. New York: W. W. Norton, 2002

———. *The Shadows of Berlin: The Berlin Stories of Dovid Bergelson*. San Francisco, CA: City Lights, 2005.

———. "Belles-Lettres and the Social Order." In *David Bergelson: From Modernism to Socialist Realism*, edited by Joseph Sherman and Gennady Estraikh, 338–45. Oxford: Legenda, 2007.

———. "Three Centres: Characteristics." In *David Bergelson: From Modernism to Socialist Realism*, edited by Joseph Sherman and Gennady Estraikh, 347–54. Oxford: Legenda, 2007.

———. *The End of Everything*. Translated by Joseph Sherman. New Yiddish Library. New Haven, CT: Yale University Press, 2009.

———. "The Beginning of December 1919." In *From Revolution to Repression: Soviet Yiddish Writing 1917–1952*, edited by Joseph Sherman, 61–65. Nottingham, UK: Five Leaves, 2012.

———. *Judgment*. Translated by Harriet Murav and Sasha Senderovich. Northwestern World Classics. Evanston, IL: Northwestern University Press, 2017.

INDEX

HARRIET MURAV is Professor of Slavic Languages and Literatures and Comparative and World Literature at the University of Illinois at Urbana-Champaign and the editor of *Slavic Review*. She is author of *Holy Foolishness: Dostoevsky's Novels and the Poetics of Cultural Critique*; *Russia's Legal Fictions*; *Identity Theft: The Jew in Imperial Russia and the Case of Avraam Uri Kovner*; and *Music from a Speeding Train: Jewish Literature in Post-Revolution Russia* and translator (with Sasha Senderovich) of David Bergelson's 1929 novel *Judgment*.

CPSIA information can be obtained
at www.ICGtesting.com
Printed in the USA
LVHW091038140419
614124LV00002B/830/P